TEN BOYS WHO CHANGED THE WORLD

LIGHT KEEPERS

Irene Howat

CF4·K

Copyright © 2001 Christian Focus Publications
Reprinted 2002, 2003, 2004, 2005 twice, 2007, 2008, 2010,
2011, 2012, 2015, 2016, 2017 (twice), 2019, 2020
Paperback ISBN: 978-1-85792-579-1
epub ISBN: 978-1-84550-838-3
mobi ISBN: 978-1-84550-839-5

Published by Christian Focus Publications,
Geanies House, Fearn, Tain, Ross-shire
IV20 1TW, Scotland, Great Britain

www.christianfocus.com
email:info@christianfocus.com
Cover design by Alister MacInnes
Cover illustration by Elena Temporin,
Milan Illustrations Agency.
Printed and bound in Turkey

All incidents retold in these stories are based on true situations. Where specific information about childhood incidents has been unobtainable the author has written these paragraphs using other information concerning family life, hobbies, home life, relationships freely available in other biographies as well as appropriate historical source material.

Front cover: Brought up in Scotland, Eric Liddell practised running for the Olympics in the glens and valleys of his native land. This picture depicts Eric's unique running style where he would wave his arms enthusiastically.

For Helen and Elsie

Contents

Brother Andrew

Andrew crept along the dark side of the hedge, stopping only long enough to look behind him into the night to listen for any sounds that would warn him he was being followed. All he heard was the hooting of an owl in the wood near the village. He crept on.

A shaft of light fell across the footpath where there was a break in the hedge. The boy edged towards the gap, pulling his balaclava down over his face so that anyone looking out of the window wouldn't see him. Slowly, so slowly, Andrew leant forward, glanced at the window and sighed with relief. Although the light was on, there didn't seem to be anyone in the room, at least not at the window end. He darted round the hedge and out of the shaft of light. Only a few more steps and he'd know if it was there. As he edged his way along the side of the house, Andrew kept his ears open for any sound from inside, and his hands out in front of him to feel for it. Suddenly it was there! First one hand then another came in touch with the cold metal of bicycle handlebars.

The boy knelt down, every bit of him as tense as a cat about to spring, and felt over the bike. Was it tied to a drainpipe? Was there a chain that would stop it moving? There didn't seem to be. Taking a long piece of string from his pocket – it had been put there specially for the purpose – Andrew passed it from side to side along the back of the bike until he was absolutely sure that it was not attached to anything. Then he sat down and leant against the wall. He knew what he had to do. But he was scared ... scared half out of his mind.

Anger suddenly filled every part of him. And the anger of a twelve-year-old can be terrifically powerful. 'What right has he to work for the Germans?!' he demanded of himself. 'How can a Dutchman work for the enemy?! He's a traitor! All of his family are traitors! Well, he'll find it harder to do his dirty work without his bike!' Stuffing his hankie into the bell so that it would be absolutely silent, and taking off the chain to prevent it click-clicking as it moved, Andrew retraced his steps, this time with the bike beside him. Through the shaft of light he went, knowing that if he was caught he might not see his family again, round the hedge into the blissful darkness, then down the road to safety. Only when he was in the wood did Andrew replace the chain, take the hankie from the bell to wipe the sweat from his face, and mount the bicycle. There was not a sweeter moment in his life till then, when he braked at the school, ringing the bell for all he was worth. A member of the Dutch resistance opened the door to see what the noise was.

'Well done!' the man said, slapping the boy on the back. 'You're doing a man's job, Andrew. The war will be won by the likes of you.'

And that's what Andrew was in the middle of, a war, the Second World War.

Suddenly Andrew was surrounded by men, and they were all talking.

'That traitor will be useless without his bike!' one said.

'And we can put it to good use for the cause,' added another.

But it was what the third man said that thrilled the boy. 'You're a natural for the underground, son, a natural!'

The kind of cleverness that Andrew used for the resistance he also used to get out of attending church. Because his father was deaf, the family sat in the short front seat. Sunday by Sunday he would lag behind so that he was the one for whom there was no room. 'I'll have to sit at the back again !'

he'd moan, moving quickly to the rear of the church before anyone offered to swap with him. Then during the first hymn he was off, coming back only when he knew the service was about to end.

It probably didn't come as a surprise to anyone when Andrew decided to be a soldier, although it made his mother very sad. The Second World War was by then over, and he was posted not to the German border, but to Indonesia. As a boy, he had been really scared when he was working for the resistance, but as a soldier he thought he was invincible. He came to believe that whoever was hit by a bullet, it certainly wouldn't be him. But Andrew was wrong. And the bullet that went right through his ankle, left him crippled for a time. He was just twenty years old.

'Do you want this?' the nurse in the army hospital asked, when he had begun to recover from surgery. She had a Bible in her hand. 'It was in your kit.'

Andrew looked at the Bible his mother had given him when he joined the army. He hadn't opened it once, and he didn't want to look at it now. He was angry with God, if there was a God. But hospitals can be boring places, and eventually he was bored into reading his mother's Bible.

'I think you should sleep for a while,' a young doctor said, finding his patient still reading hours later.

'I'm not tired,' Andrew replied. 'Have you ever read this?' he asked. 'I'd no idea it was interesting. It's like an adventure.'

'I suppose it depends which bit you read,' suggested the doctor.

Andrew looked puzzled. 'I started at the beginning. That's where books usually start.'

Between reading his Bible and writing to his seventy-two Dutch penpals, Andrew's time in hospital passed quite quickly. One of his penpals, a Christian girl called Thile, answered as best she could all his questions about the Bible.

In November 1949, Andrew left the army and was sent home. With part of his pay he bought a bicycle. 'I'd better buy one than steal one,' he thought, remembering back to his childhood.

'Is he all right?' his father asked over and over again after he returned home. 'He's either stuck in the Bible or he's cycling off to church services all over the place.'

Andrew's sister shook her head. 'I'm worried about him too. It's just not natural! Maybe the war has bent his mind.'

'I don't know about that,' Father said. 'I think it's his way of coping with being crippled. But I hope he grows out of it. Nobody likes people who are too religious.'

Andrew didn't grow out of it. Not very long after coming back home from Indonesia, he discovered for himself that the Bible was true. The former underground boy and soldier found new life in Jesus. And as he wondered about his future, Andrew's prayer was, 'Lord, show me what you want me to do with my life.'

God did show Andrew what he wanted him to do, and he also showed him that his childhood experience of the Dutch resistance, during wartime, was good training for Christian service.

Brother Andrew (that's what he became known as) found himself working as a smuggler for God. After the Second World War, many communist countries banned the Bible. It was as though a line - it was known as the Iron Curtain - was drawn across Europe. On the western side, people were free to come and go, to be Christians or Muslims or nothing at all. On the eastern side, behind the Iron Curtain, men and women were not free to travel, not free to have Bibles, not even free to teach their own children about the Lord. It was for those people that Brother

Andrew became a smuggler, taking Bibles and other Christian books and Christian leaflets to people who could be put in prison if they were found in possession of them.

'I can hardly take in all that the Lord has done in the ten years since I became a Christian,' Brother Andrew said to his companion. 'Take this car, for example. Do you want to know how I got it?'

His friend nodded then listened to the story.

'A couple I knew heard about the work I was doing, smuggling Bibles and tracts behind the Iron Curtain. They realised that I could take much larger quantities if I had a car. And they know I don't walk well and thought it would make my job a whole lot easier. I was in West Berlin when I phoned to tell them my plans. "You'd better come right back here for the keys," my old friend told me. "What keys?" I asked. I remember him chuckling at the end of the phone. "We've got you a car," my friend said. "If you come for the keys, you can drive it all the way to Moscow if you dare." I went right back, collected the car and tucked as many boxes of Bibles in it as I could!'

'Is that why you call it the miracle car?' the young man asked.

Brother Andrew laughed. 'That's one reason. Another is that it keeps on going!'

It was that same car that Brother Andrew was driving when he reached the Yugoslavian border one day. Drawing up at the checkpoint he prayed, 'Lord, I have Bibles in the car. When you were on earth, you made blind eyes see. Please make seeing eyes blind now, so that the guards don't see the Bibles.'

'Anything to declare?' the guard asked.

'My watch, money, camera ... only small things.'

He was telling the truth because the Bibles were small.

'We don't need to bother about them,' the guard said, handing Brother Andrew's passport back.

'Thank you for making them blind to the boxes!' he prayed, as he drove into Yugoslavia with his precious load. For the next seven weeks he was there and he held eighty meetings and gave out hundreds of Bibles and tracts.

Marta, a young Christian girl, was delighted to have a Bible of her own.

'Tell me about yourself,' Brother Andrew invited.

'I was brought up in a Christian home,' she said, 'and I became a Christian myself. At school I always said grace before my lunch. Because of that, I was expelled from school by the Communists. I was told I couldn't go back because I was filling the other pupils' heads with nonsense. But I'm a Christian, and I can't pretend I'm not. That would be denying Jesus.'

Brother Andrew prayed with Marta, asking God to give her strength and courage for the future.

The road was dusty as he left Marta's town. 'It's amazing this car doesn't seize up,' Brother Andrew said to Nikola, a Yugoslav believer, as the dust blew all around. 'You'd think the dust would get into the engine. I'm sure God stops that happening because we pray about it each morning.'

Nikola smiled. 'I'd never heard anyone praying over a car before I met you!'

As they drove along, a small lorry approached them from the opposite direction. It also had foreign number plates. When the drivers saw each other, they stopped to discuss the state of the road.

'You're Brother Andrew,' the other driver said. 'And this is the miracle car.'

Nikola grinned. 'All the Christians know him,' he thought. 'It's amazing the Communists haven't found out about him!'

'May I have a look at your car?' the lorry driver said. 'I'm a mechanic, and it wouldn't do any harm to give it a going over. You do so many miles.'

Having spent some time under the bonnet, the lorry driver scratched his head and looked puzzled.

'Is there anything wrong?' Brother Andrew asked.

'No,' the man answered, 'the car's going well. But I can't work out how it can go at all. The carburettor is clogged, so are the spark plugs. And the air filter is totally clogged up. This car should have ground to a standstill thousands of miles ago!'

Setting to, the mechanic unclogged the carburettor and spark plugs and did what he could about the air filter. Then he tuned the engine and changed the oil.

'Look after it,' he told the two men. 'It's a miracle car so don't abuse it.'

And it was just as big a miracle meeting a Christian mechanic on a lonely road in Yugoslavia, and one who knew Brother Andrew! God provided a mechanic for the car, he provided the car for Brother

Andrew, and through that Dutch Christian, the Lord provided Bibles and Christian leaflets to many thousands of people who would otherwise not have been able to read God's Word for themselves.

FACT FILE

Communism: Communism was the form of government which existed on the eastern side of the Iron Curtain.

State control extended to all parts of society, and individual freedom was restricted. Newspapers and books had to follow the communist line, and religious beliefs were discouraged.

Communism in eastern Europe lasted until 1989, when it finally fell and brought the Berlin wall down with it. Movement across borders was no longer restricted, and freedom of worship was restored.

Keynote: God miraculously provided Brother Andrew with a car, a mechanic who could fix it and thousands of Bibles and Christian leaflets. These were smuggled behind the Iron Curtain and given to people who would otherwise never have been able to read about Jesus.

Learn from how God amazingly provided for Brother Andrew. See God's hand in everything. Believe that he can bring about miracles in your life too.

Think: Have you ever thought about how wonderful it is to be free to read the Bible in your own language?

Pray for missionaries involved in translating the Bible and bringing it to people who have never been able to read it before.

 Prayer: Lord Jesus, thank you for how wonderfully you have provided for me. Thank you for my Bible. Help me to treasure it more than I do.

Bless those who are trying to bring your Word to people who have never been able to have their own Bibles. Amen.

John Newton

The ship's boy ran to the rail to see Liverpool disappear into the distance. He waved to the shore and wondered if anyone was waving back. Then he got to work, tidying the coils of rope on the deck. The rope was heavy with sea water, and his arms struggled with the weight of it. But the weight that was bothering John was not the wet rope, it was the feeling he had of carrying a heavy stone where his heart should have been.

'What's your name, lad?' a deckhand asked, as he helped the boy with the rope.

'John Newton, sir.'

The deckhand smiled. Not many people called him 'sir'! 'And what age are you?'

'I'm nine, sir.'

The man thought about his own son, who was almost the same age. 'Did your mother not think you were too young to be at sea?' he asked.

'My mother's dead, sir. And my stepmother doesn't seem to think I'm too young. I'm strong for my age,' John said defiantly.

The deckhand looked the lad up and down. 'I can see that,' he said. 'You certainly are a strong young man. What about your father? Doesn't he mind you being at sea?'

'My father's a sea captain, sir.'

And there was no arguing with that.

That night, as John curled up in the corner where the ship's boys slept, he thought about his mother. She had loved her little son, and his heart was broken when she died. Now all he had to remember her by were her stories, most of them about Jesus.

The boy tried to tell himself one of her stories, but, before he got to the end of it, he was sound asleep. Sea air and hard work had exhausted him.

If that first night at sea was bad, there was a very much worse one to follow five years later, in 1739.

'I'm going for a drink,' John, told his friends. He thought he was very grown up. 'Anyone else coming?'

Nobody was.

'Why's that man watching me?' the teenager wondered, as he drank his rum. 'I'm sure I've never seen him before.'

Because the man's gaze made him feel uncomfortable, John left as soon as he had finished his drink.

'Stop!' a voice said, from just beside him.

Fear ran through his veins, and John sprinted away as fast as he could. Several footsteps followed his. The boy's mind raced as fast as his feet. 'It's a press gang ... I've got to get out of here!'

But the footsteps were getting closer and louder. John dodged up an alley and raced for all he was worth. His lungs felt as though they were bursting.

'Gotcha!' spat a voice, as he was grabbed by the coat.

The boy struggled, but two sets of strong arms held him and swung him round. He was face to face with the staring man from the public house.

'That was a fair try,' the man gasped, for he too was winded. 'But the King wants you on board.'

John didn't need to be told any more. He knew he had been press-ganged into the King's navy. He'd be lucky if he stood on dry land again for months.

Although John Newton knew he couldn't do a thing about it, he didn't go willingly. He was half dragged, half carried to the man-of-war where he was held tightly while the hatch to the hold was opened. Then he was thrown into the darkness below. John didn't have long, and he knew it.

'Psst!' he said, holding some pennies through a fine grill in the roof of the hold each time he heard feet passing overhead.

The other men and boys who had been press-ganged jeered. 'You'll not buy yourself out with two pence!' one said, amid ugly laughter.

'What are you wanting?' a voice asked through the grill eventually.

'Take this,' John Newton said, 'and tell the Lieutenant I want to speak to him. My name's Newton.'

'That was a right waste of money!' a prisoner laughed in the darkness.

But John fared better than the others. The Lieutenant did come, and when he discovered that the boy's father was a captain, John was taken out of the hold and given a job as a midshipman. But his promotion didn't last long. John tried to jump ship and was caught. When HMS *Harwich* set sail, he was an ordinary seaman. And when he got the chance to change ships,

John was off, this time not to a naval boat, but to a merchant ship, *Pegasus*, and the cargo it normally carried was slaves.

With its hold full of drink and silks and other goods, the ship set sail for West Africa, for the Gulf of Guinea. And when they docked there, the hold was emptied of its cargo which was used to barter for slaves.

'That's a fine one,' the captain said looking at a tall young African. Then he saw another. 'I'll take him too.' A shorter, thinner man was pushed forward. 'He's not worth having.' The man was shoved back and a strong-looking young woman thrust forward. 'I'll take her,' shouted the captain. 'Put her on.'

John Newton watched as their cargo was loaded. Men were thrown into one hold, women and children into another. They were manacled together, and any who struggled had iron collars locked around their necks and were fixed to the wooden side of the ship. The Africans were packed together so that they had no room to move, and their chains held them fast. Even the children were chained.

'We should get a good price for that lot,' John said, looking at the terrified cargo.

'Let's just hope they survive to be sold,' answered the captain. 'It's a long way across the Atlantic to America.

'How many went overboard today?' a sailor asked, as John added up the figures.

'Four,' he answered. 'One man, two women and a baby.'

'All dead of the fever?' inquired the sailor.

'Not the baby. Its screaming got on the captain's nerves.'

And the ship ploughed on through a stormy sea. The foul air in the hold was choking, and the movement of the ship turned the Africans in each hold into one lump of terrified and miserable humanity.

Those who survived were sold as slaves in America, and their lives there were no better than on board the ship. The longest a slave lived in the lime fields, even a young, strong man, was nine years.

The captain of *Pegasus* and John Newton became good friends, and they spent a lot of time together. But that didn't please the captain's island wife. And when John took ill with fever, she left him starving and without water. The captain, thinking his wife was looking after his friend, went inland.

Too weak to move, John lay nearly dying. There was a rustle at his side, and a hand reached out with a little food for him.

'Thank you,' Newton whispered weakly to the African slave.

A short time later another slave came, this time with water which he poured down Newton's throat. The Africans John had brought into slavery were the only ones who helped him.

For several days he lay there dreadfully ill, getting only the food and drink the slaves brought out of their pitiful rations. When the Captain came back, he believed the lies his wife told, and John was put out in the fields and set to work with the slaves.

It was only by smuggling a scrap of a note back to his father, that help came in the shape of Captain Manesty of the *Greyhound*, a ship on its way to Ireland.

And it was on that voyage, when a furious storm threatened to wreck the boat with the loss of all hands, that John Newton started thinking about the God of whom his mother had told him when he was a boy.

Slave trading was seen as a good career, and on John's next voyages, which he eventually made as captain, he tried to be less harsh on the people he carried to slavery, only putting them in iron neck collars if there was no other way of controlling them. He did have them all in wrist rings and chains though. His crew wouldn't have taken the ship out of port otherwise. But, while he didn't see it as a cruel trade, John's wife, Mary, did. They had married when he was on shore leave, and what he did for a living saddened her terribly.

On his final voyage, the horror of it all dawned on John Newton. Suddenly he saw the slaves as people. He saw the men as brothers and husbands and fathers. Looking at the women, he saw sisters and wives and mothers. And when he turned his eyes on the young slaves, he saw them for what they were: boys and girls, children.

Jesus kept coming into John Newton's mind. Things were happening to him that he wanted to understand but didn't. And he longed for the day he'd be home and able to talk them over with his wife.

'It's so good to be back,' he told Mary, hugging her tightly some months later. 'I can't tell you how good it is to be home.'

His wife smiled. 'I just wish I could keep you here. I've looked forward so much to the end of your voyage.'

John looked into her eyes. 'So have I,' he said. 'So have I.'

John had been a working man for twenty one years. He started as a ship's boy at nine, and he was now thirty, a captain and very happily married. His home leave was coming near its end when strong, fit, John Newton, suffered a stroke. It was a minor stroke, and he recovered well, but it marked the end of his life at sea.

While she was concerned about her husband's health, Mary was delighted to see the back of his involvement in the slave trade. And so was John, especially as he became a Christian a very short time after his illness. John was turned around from a life of unbelief to a life of following and trusting in God. John knew that from now on God would guide him, instruct him and teach him to become more like his Saviour, Jesus Christ. It was the year 1755.

'Mary, I really think the Lord is calling me to be a minister,' John told his wife, not long afterwards.

A thrill surged through her as she took in what he was saying.

'Do you think that's possible?' he asked. 'Could a slave trader become a minister?'

Mary could hardly trust herself to speak. But her shining eyes and her smile answered his question. And that's what John Newton did. He became a minister of the Church of England.

'Tell me more about the slave trade,' a young politician asked John Newton some years later. His name was William Wilberforce.

John smiled. 'When you first came to see me,' he said, 'you were more worried about your own sins than about the conditions of slaves.'

The young man's eyes lit up at the memory. 'That's true,' Wilberforce agreed. 'But you showed me that Jesus could take away my sins and throw them into the depths of the sea.'

The two men talked for hours, of being saved from their sins, and of the terrible sins of slavery.

Wilberforce was determined to use his political influence to change things. And he did. In 1807, an Act of Parliament abolished the slave trade. Having just heard that the Act had been given its Royal Assent, John Newton slipped into a coma and never regained consciousness. The last thing he heard on earth was that wonderful news. The next thing he heard was God's voice welcoming him home to heaven.

FACT FILE

Press-ganging: Press gangs were groups of tough navy petty officers and seamen who scoured English seaports for men to take to sea. Since there were never enough volunteers for the navy, these men were 'pressed' into service by force, as John Newton was.

Sometimes mayors of harbour towns supplied the press gangs with the men they needed by clearing out the prisons. Press-ganging ended in the early 1800s.

Keynote: God opened John's eyes to see his need of Jesus and the awfulness of the slave trade. It didn't stop there though. John's influence on his friend William Wilberforce ended the slave trade for good.

Learn from how God used John Newton to influence a politician and bring about a positive change in the world. Don't underestimate how God can use you and never be afraid to speak out for him.

Think: There are a lot of issues on which the Christian viewpoint needs to be heard in parliament, for example, abortion and religious education in schools. Why not write your local politician explaining how you feel about these issues?

Pray that Christians in the world of politics will be able to present the Christian view when decisions are made.

 Prayer: Lord Jesus, thank you for Christians who are able to influence decision-making in this country. Give them the courage to speak up for you and help me to do the same. Amen.

Billy Graham

The horse easily made it over the jump, but the rider didn't. His descent started off as a wobble, went on to be a gentle slide, and finished as a splash into a muddy puddle. Billy picked himself up, shook the worst of the mud out of his hair and grinned at his horse which had stopped and made its way back to him. He remounted. 'I guess you and I have to keep Suzie in work,' he told the horse. 'We can't have her sitting around doing nothing all day!'

'Billy Graham!' Suzie, the maid, gasped. Her smiley eyes sparkled, and her strong weather-beaten arms, were placed firmly on her hips. 'What have you been doing? Did you think the laundry basket needed filling?'

The boy grinned. 'It wasn't my fault,' he explained, clapping his mount. 'This fellow just wanted to keep you busy, so he found the biggest puddle in the ranch and dumped me into it.'

'Well, come you down here and strip off.'

Suzie was a big woman, but even though he was just fifteen, Billy Graham was bigger. 'Six feet two in his socks,' his mother often said. Having peeled off his muddy clothes, he dumped them on the floor and headed to his room.

'I guess you'll be back with some sweaty baseball gear later,' Suzie said to his back as he closed the door.

'At least I'm predictable!' Billy laughed.

Suzie sang as she worked. The Grahams were good to work for. She liked the ranch and she liked the children, especially Jean, the little cutie who came along years after the other three. But Suzie was what people called 'The help'. As an African American she knew she would always be working for others. 'But I'm not complaining. There's a lot worse off than me. And maybe one day the Lord will make things different.'

'Still at it?' Billy asked, as he passed through the kitchen on his way out.

The maid laughed and lifted a still muddy shirt from even more muddy water. 'You did it good and proper,' said Suzie, 'so I've got to do it good and proper too. Are you riding to school?'

'Yeh! I sure am!'

'Well, you mind that puddle, Billy Graham, you just mind that puddle.'

The gangly youth sang as he rode. It was baseball night, and he wanted to be a pro. The fact that he wasn't a great player didn't seem to matter to him. He enjoyed the game and that was enough for Billy. In fact, he just enjoyed life.

'Your dad's had an accident, and your mom's gone with him to the hospital,' Suzie told Billy, when he came home that evening.

The boy sank on to a chair. 'What happened?'

'He was using the mechanical saw in the barn when a piece of wood flew out of the saw and smashed his head open.'

His eyes searched hers for the truth. 'Is it serious?'

He saw the answer in Suzie's eyes.

'Is he ... going to die?' Suddenly the six-foot-two teenager looked and sounded like a little boy. What he most wanted to do was cry and have Suzie's big arms round him. But he was too old for that now; he was trying to be a man.

'He's hurt real bad,' she said, 'and I've not stopped praying since it happened.'

'Keep praying,' Billy said urgently. At the same time he knew that he wouldn't be praying. What good would that do?

It looked as though Mr Graham was going to die. His doctors certainly expected him to. But Mrs Graham, who had just started to attend a Bible class three weeks before the accident, called all her friends and asked them to pray. She was utterly convinced that the Lord would hear their prayers and heal her husband. And that's what happened. From then on Billy's father and mother took their faith seriously, which was more than he did. He reckoned it was rubbish.

'Time to get up, Billy!' Mrs Graham shouted. 'It's half past five!'

The boy rolled over, stretched, and hoisted himself out of bed. He was hardly awake when he reached the kitchen, where a steaming mug of coffee and brown bread with maple syrup were laid out for him.

'Why can't we fix cows' body clocks so that they can be milked when it's light instead of at quarter to six in the morning.'

His mother laughed. 'Dad's working on that,' she said. 'But it's not coming quickly!'

A short sprint down to the cowshed and Billy slipped into the milking routine. He enjoyed this time of day. After the cold air, he loved the warm smell of the cows, the playful flick of their tails, and their deep pools of brown eyes. And there was no drink sweeter to him than the frothy milk that drained through the corrugated cooler. The mug he had when he finished milking, left him with a white moustache. He was usually wiping it off with his sleeve when he went back into the kitchen to Suzie, and his post-milking breakfast.

'There are Christian meetings on these evenings,' Mr Graham said. 'Want to come?'

Billy shook his head firmly. 'No way!'

But he changed his mind when one of his friends assured him that the preacher was no cissy; he was a real man's man.

Billy did go, and he went back again. One night something happened that changed his life. There were no cissy stories, just hard-hitting facts about man's sin - about Billy's sin - and about his need for a Saviour.

'Would anyone who wants to become a Christian move to the front,' the preacher said.

And Billy Graham, who thought Christianity wasn't for him, got to his feet and went to the front. That night he trusted himself to the Lord Jesus Christ.

Two years later, in 1937, when Billy was nineteen years old, he went to Bible School. It was there that he first spoke at a meeting. All he did was tell what the Lord had done for him. There was nothing special about how he spoke. He wasn't dramatic, wasn't memorable. There was nothing whatever that night to show that, before the end of his life, he would preach to over forty million people, in hundreds of different countries. His first congregation had no way of knowing that hundreds of thousands of people would become Christians as a result of Billy Graham crusades. And if they'd been told that would happen, they would probably not have believed it.

It was in the 1940s that Billy became known as a conference speaker, and, before long, invitations were coming thick and fast.

'Will you come to Los Angeles?'

'Would you consider a crusade in England?'

'Here's an invitation to go to Australia.'

The crusade team which Billy formed had its work cut out.

In the fifties, radio broadcasts and television appearances took his voice and his face into homes all over America and beyond.

'Have you heard Billy Graham?' people asked, not 'Have you heard of Billy Graham?' Everyone had.

During the 1960s, America was torn apart on the subject of race. African American children were taken miles by bus to 'black schools', where there would not be one single white pupil. There were separate churches, separate shopping areas, separate housing estates. Americans of different races and skin colours did not mix. And when efforts were made to break down the race barrier, fighting broke out at school gates, bombs were placed in churches, and people were maimed and killed. It was an ugly time in American history.

Billy Graham had grown up with Suzie, the African American maid. He was brought up in a culture of white masters and black servants. And it wasn't until after he was converted that he realised the wrongness of it all. Billy's crusade team was one of the first major American organisations to have black and white members working together as equals.

'Would you consider speaking in Birmingham, Alabama?' Billy Graham was asked. 'Terrible things have been happening there. Worst of all, four children were killed in the bombing of a black church. Only the love of God can cut through that kind of hatred.'

Graham agreed to go, insisting that there be much prayer in the run-up to his visit.

'Look at that!' said the man who had issued the invitation. 'See what God's doing.'

It was Easter Sunday 1964, and the two men were standing in front of a crowd in a vast stadium.

'There are 30,000 people here,' he went on. 'They're about half-and-half black and white.' The man's eyes shone with joy and tears.

And they're sitting together side by side,' Billy smiled, 'just as they'll do in heaven.'

Billy preached his heart out that night in Alabama. And when he invited people to come forward, black and white came together, actually touching each other as they walked out to the front and stood together before the Lord. God's love broke through man's hatred in Birmingham, Alabama.

When Billy Graham was a boy, his world was southern America, and he wasn't much interested in anywhere else. Years later, his vision stretched right round the globe as he travelled from country to country, continent to continent, telling anyone who would come to listen, that God loved sinners enough to die for them. He told ordinary men and women from backgrounds like his own. He could talk in a way that cowhands understood. He had been a cowhand himself. But he could also talk to presidents and to kings and queens, telling them that they, too, were sinners, that there was a King of Kings they would meet one day, who would judge them.

FACT FILE
The First World War: The First World War ended in 1918, the year Billy was born. There had been a terrible loss of life. Millions of young men died, many of them in the trenches, which were ditches dug deep into the ground.

The trenches were meant to shelter soldiers from enemy gunfire, but they offered little protection from the shells which exploded overhead. Soon they filled up with mud, water, rats and dead bodies. Many soldiers drowned in them or died from disease.

Keynote: At first Billy didn't see the point of praying and going to hear about Jesus at a Christian meeting. It was the last thing he wanted to do. But God changed all that!

Billy came to love Jesus, became convinced about the power of prayer and went on to share Jesus with millions.

Learn from how God turned Billy's life around and believe that

God can reach and use even those who have no time for him.

Think: God lifted Billy's eyes beyond his homeland, giving him a vision for the world. He wanted to take the message of Jesus around the globe.

Pick seven different countries across the world (one for every day of the week) and find out more about them. Pray for these countries each week - for the people, the Christians and the missionaries.

Prayer: Lord Jesus, thank you for showing me that prayer is powerful.

Help me to believe that, as I pray for countries across the world, my prayers can make a difference. Amen.

Eric Liddell

Robbie and Eric raced round the table, but the stray kitten could run faster than they could. She dodged under the table and came out the other side, but the boys had to stop and move the chairs. Their mother, Mrs Liddell, came in to see what the noise was, though it wasn't unusual for the boys to run helter-skelter round the table. Eric always seemed to be running somewhere.

'Kitten likes our home!' three-year-old Eric wailed, as the end of a tail disappeared round the door.

Robbie, who was a year-and-a-half older, decided this was the time to bring up the subject of pets ... yet again.

'Why can't we have a kitten like this one?' he asked.

Eric stopped crying. 'Me want a dog.'

Mrs Liddell sat down to talk to the boys, explaining to them for the hundredth time that in China there was a disease called rabies, and that animals who caught rabies could pass it on to people.

'But the people would get better,' Robbie said.

'No,' his mother told him. 'Often they die. That's why we can't have a cat or dog.'

The boys didn't give up, and neither did their little sister when she was old enough to know what was going on. Eventually, Mr and Mrs Liddell decided that they would adopt a family of goats who lived near them.

'The billy goat's mine,' Robbie said proudly.

'My goat's the nanny,' announced Eric.

And Jenny, their little sister, helped look after the kid.

'Run for it!' Eric yelled in Chinese, as the billy goat raced after them.

Robbie's pet was turning out to be quite an aggressive creature. All three ran as fast as they could, though it wasn't easy for them to get up much speed as they were dressed in traditional thickly-padded Chinese clothes. But at least the padding meant that if they were butted by Billy, it wasn't as sore as it might have been!

'You're getting faster and faster every time he chases you,' Mr Liddell told Eric one day. 'But you run in the funniest way. Your arms seem to go in every direction apart from the right one!'

But Eric wasn't always able to run.

'He's lost so much weight,' Mrs Liddell said, looking at him, pale and thin in bed. 'He's never been as poorly as this before.'

Mr Liddell shook his head. 'I'm so glad you're a nurse,' he added. 'We might have lost him otherwise. And he seemed to be recovering as well as the other two at first.'

'It's strange,' his wife thought aloud. 'He's such an active boy, but when he's ill, he goes down like a ton of bricks.'

Eric's eyes opened. 'Would you like a drink?' Mrs Liddell asked.

The boy nodded, and she held a cup of meat juice to his lips. That was all he was able to take.

'That boy will never be able to run again,' a pessimistic and insensitive visitor said, when she saw Eric two weeks later.

Mrs Liddell winked at her son so the visitor couldn't see. 'I'm quite sure he will,' she said, continuing to massage his stiff legs. 'He'll learn to walk again very soon, and before long he'll be out playing football with his friends.'

Eric looked down at his spindly legs. 'Would he walk again?' he wondered, especially as his knees didn't want to bend at all. Then he thought about his mother. 'Sure I will,' he decided. 'Mum's a nurse so she knows best.'

It took time, but Eric did walk again, and he did run, and he did play football.

'Will you come and play at my house on Sunday?' one of Eric's Chinese friends asked.

Eric shook his head. 'May I come on Saturday instead?'

'Why?'

'Christians believe that Sunday is God's special day, and we do different things on Sundays than on other days.'

The Chinese boy looked puzzled. 'Like what?'

'Well, we go to church, and we read Christian books, and we play Bible games, and we have a special dinner ... lots of things like that. It's a really good day.'

'Is that just because your dad's a missionary?'

'No,' explained Eric. 'It's because God's law tells us to keep Sunday special.'

His friend shrugged his shoulders. 'I suppose you'd better come on Saturday then.'

And that Saturday, the two boys organised a sports day for their friends.

Like many missionary children at that time (Eric was born in 1902) the boys came back to Britain for their education. After school in London, both Robbie and Eric went to Edinburgh University. Eric studied science, but his two great passions were his faith in the Lord Jesus and his running, even if his arms still went in every direction but the right one! And in 1924, he was making such good speeds that he was chosen to race in the Olympic Games!

'Liddell! Liddell! Liddell!' the university team screamed, as he reached the tape in a practice race.

The team manager looked at his stopwatch. 'Great!' he shouted. 'Your speed's getting better and better.'

Eric got his breath back. 'It's coming on for the 100 metres,' he said. 'But I only seem able to cope with that and the 200 metres. Any more than that and I just slow down.'

His coach smiled. 'We're pinning our hopes on you for the 100 metres,' he said. 'Anything else is a bonus.'

'The 100 metres heat is on Sunday ....' Eric was told.

'I'm not running on a Sunday,' he said quietly, but very firmly.

The Bible says that Sunday is special.

Those who knew Eric understood, even if they didn't agree with him. Others thought he was a traitor, letting his country down. Even some newspaper headlines were cruel. Instead of preparing for the 100 metres race, Eric trained for the 400 metres instead, even though he wasn't a distance runner.

Despite all the upset, the Games were exciting. Eric's British team-mate, Harold Abrahams, won the gold in the 100 metres, and Eric was right there at the tape to cheer him. His was the first British 100 metre gold ever. Then came the 200 metres. Harold, Eric and four Americans were running in the final. The two friends started well, but they couldn't keep up the speed. Harold fell behind. Eric just couldn't catch the top two Americans. The Scotsman's legs pounded on, reaching the tape in third place. He had won the bronze medal, equal to the best done by a British runner in the 200 metres at the Olympics. Things were going really well for the British team.

The 400 metres wasn't Eric's distance and his times over 400 metres were nothing special at all, certainly not Olympic special. But, despite all that, he would run. Eric got through the first heat, and the second. He qualified for the semi-final, and got into the final. But what chance had he? In one of the heats, a Swiss runner ran the distance in 48 seconds, which was listed as the world record at the time. In one semi-final an American had clocked just under 48 seconds.

As the runners lined up for the final, a pipe band burst into the skirl of a Scottish tune, and, when the band finished, the runners crouched for the off. The starting pistol cracked, and Eric shot away in first position, running as though he was going for the 100 metres.

'He's away far too quickly!'

'He'll never keep that up!' his friends shouted to each other above the noise of the crowd.

Arms and legs going everywhere, Eric pounded on, past the 100 metres, still in the lead. The 200 metres mark came up and he hadn't slackened off. His head was back, he was racing blind, but on and on he went. At the 300 metres mark, an American was gaining speed and closing on Eric.

'He's slowing,' one of his team-mates moaned.

'He's tiring,' said another.

As the 300 metres mark was passed, Eric heaved air into his lungs, willed his legs to move even more quickly, and pounded on and on, gaining speed! The American, whose burst had failed to succeed, saw only his rival's back as Eric Liddell swept through the tape 5 metres ahead of him, and smashed what was listed as the world record at the time!

Hundreds of Union Jacks and Scottish flags waved from side to side, and a cheer raised the roof of the stadium.

'Thank you! Thank you!' Eric breathed, to his heavenly Father.

Suddenly, a remarkably fresh athlete was surrounded.

'Congratulations!' Harold Abrahams laughed. 'That was amazing!'

'Great race!' 'Well done!' 'Amazing!' rang all around.

Newspaper reporters slapped him on the back, telling him what a wonderful guy he was. Some of them had torn him to shreds over the previous months. But that didn't matter to Eric. Nothing mattered to him except that he had kept God's law; he had kept Sunday special, and God had blessed him in a way he had never thought possible. The cheer that swept through the stadium when Eric received his gold medal rang on and on and on and on. And in the Flying Scotsman's brain, the prayer, 'Thank you! thank you! thank you!' nearly drowned it out.

It seemed as though Eric Liddell had a glittering career in athletics to look forward to. But none of his close friends were surprised when he told them that he was going to be a missionary, that he was going back to China where he had been born, and where he had the descendants of a certain billy goat to thank for his ability to run!

Eric Liddell married and became a father. His children had the same upbringing as he had, and in the same part of China. But by that time it was no longer a happy place, for China and Japan were fighting each other, and troops seemed to be everywhere. Li-Mu-Shi – that was Eric's Chinese name – tried his best to care for the Christians and to tell others about the Lord Jesus. He was a ray of light in a dark and fearful place.

The situation became so dangerous that Eric's wife and children were evacuated to Canada. Although he missed them hugely, Liddell must have thanked God that they were at last out of the war zone and safe.

'All British and American enemies report to Weihsien internment camp,' the Japanese soldier spat out.

Over the next three days they were taken, Eric among them, hundreds of miles to Weihsien and locked behind the high walls and electric fence of the camp.

'You can teach the children maths,' Liddell was told, when the prisoners tried to sort themselves into some sort of order.

'Uncle Eric' became one of the most popular men in the camp. And we can be sure that the children he taught learned more than maths from their Christian teacher.

Eric Liddell must have longed to see his own children again, but he never did. Desperately thin, dressed in rags and suffering from a brain tumour, the Flying Scotsman, who at the end could only stagger, died as a prisoner of war.

FACT FILE

The Olympics: The ancient Greeks held a series of Olympic Games at Olympia in Greece from 776 B.C. until the abolition of the Games in A.D. 393.

A French sportsman, Baron Pierre de Coubertin, had the idea of reviving the Games, and the first modern Olympics took place in 1896.

The Games have been held every four years since then, apart from 1916, 1940 and 1944 when they were cancelled because of the two world wars.

Keynote: Eric gave up the chance of an Olympic medal in the 100 metres because he knew that Sunday, God's day, should be kept special. Then he gave up a promising career in athletics to go to China and work for God.

Learn from how Eric always put Jesus first in everything, and remember that God said, 'Those that honour me, I will honour.'

Think: Do you have a favourite sport? Remember always to put Jesus first when you play any sport.

Look out for organisations that support Christians in sport. They can show you how to witness for Jesus by what you do and how you do it. They will also encourage you by telling you about other Christians who enjoy competitive sport.

Prayer: Lord Jesus, thank you for the sports I enjoy. Thank you for giving me the health and strength to enjoy them.

Make me a good witness for you as I play with my friends. Help me to put you first in everything. Amen.

William Carey

The boy shielded his candle with his hand and silently went into his bedroom. Several pairs of eyes reflected the light of the candle's flame. Two mice looked up at it from their box on the floor. Several birds stared, unblinking, from their cage made of willow withes. And there were tiny eyes too, so tiny that they couldn't be seen. There were crickets, woodlice, a number of spiders and a brown hairy caterpillar. William Carey had a bedroom to himself, but he shared it with as many animals and birds and insects as he could catch.

'I wonder what tigers are like,' the nine-year-old thought, as he pulled his rough blanket over his head. 'And zebras, they must look odd with all their stripes. But why do they have stripes? I'll have to think about that.' But he didn't, because he fell sound asleep and didn't waken up until the noise of mice, scratching in their box, broke through his dreams of faraway places, of jungles and wild animals.

Even after William had grown up, he was interested in faraway things. But, when he finished school aged fourteen, he only moved to a village a few miles from his home in Paulerspury, near Northampton, to learn to be a shoemaker.

Another teenager was also learning from the same master craftsman, and the two boys got on well although William, who had been brought up to know about the Lord Jesus, argued with the other boy because he was a Christian. William didn't think he needed a saviour, but what happened one Christmas made him really think about that.

'Would you like a sixpence or a shilling?' the ironmonger asked William, when he went into his shop.

William wondered what the catch was. A shilling was worth two sixpences – a lot of money to be offering a shoemaker's boy.

'A shilling, please,' he answered, not able to refuse the larger coin. And he had a great time spending some money on his way back to work. But the money he spent belonged to the shoemaker, and, when he went to replace it with his own shilling, he discovered it was a fake! The ironmonger had tricked him! He tried to lie his way out of trouble, but his boss found out. That experience made William Carey think. It was not too long afterwards that he became a Christian.

Over the following few years, there were many changes in Carey's life. He married Dorothy, and to support her and their children, as well as working as a shoemaker, he opened a little school. And at weekends he was a preacher.

'What are you doing?' Dorothy asked him one day. 'Whoever you're making that shoe for, has very funny feet.'

William smiled. 'Wait and see,' he teased.

Dorothy watched as he sewed strange shapes of leather together. And she was even more puzzled when her husband took out his ink pot, drew on the leather and then wrote words all over it! Only when it was finished, did William tell her what it was.

'It's a globe,' he announced, showing her the stuffed leather ball. 'And I've drawn on the countries and written in their names. This will help my pupils to learn what the world is like.'

'It's wonderful,' Dorothy said. 'There's India ... and Africa ... and Australia is right underneath.'

Perhaps William's pupils thought of other things they could have done with a leather ball, the size of a football!

William's interest in the world wasn't restricted to learning about animals and mountains, flowers and forests. He was most of all interested in people, and in telling them about the Lord Jesus Christ. That's why he was so eager to hear John Thomas speaking.

'Tell us about your work as a doctor in Bengal,' he urged Mr Thomas.

John Thomas was one of those people who couldn't stop speaking after he started.

William listened and listened, and, when the speaker eventually did stop, all William wanted to do was go home, pack up his clothes, and go to Bengal in India.

'No, no, no,' Dorothy insisted, when he made the suggestion later that evening. 'How can you even suggest we go to the other side of the world? We've got three little boys.

The eldest is only eight, and there's another baby on the way!'

The months that followed were difficult for many reasons, but after the baby arrived, Dorothy agreed that the whole family could go to Bengal if her sister went with them to help. And that's what happened in 1793. John Thomas was on the same boat.

'Look at Father!' Carey's eldest son shouted, when he saw William on the deck of the boat one day. 'He's not got his wig on!'

'Did it blow away?' one of the other boys asked. 'Your head will get the shivers!'

All three boys went into such a fit of giggles that their mother, who was feeding the new baby, came to see what the noise was about. Her mouth fell open when she saw her husband!

William took a deep breath. 'I know I've worn my wig since my hair fell out years ago, but it's so hot and sticky and uncomfortable I decided to stop wearing it.'

'It was ugly too,' one of the boys said.

His father nodded. 'So it was.'

'Can we have it to play with?' two of his sons asked at once.

William shook his nearly bald head. 'I'm afraid not. I threw it into the sea.'

All three boys ran to the edge of the deck to look for it, but it had sunk without trace.

It took weeks to get to India, but the great day came when they saw that country for the very first time.

'Look!' William pointed to the far distance. 'That's our new home. That's India.'

The boys stayed on deck with their father as they drew closer and closer to land.

'Where do we go ashore?' one of William's sons asked.

'The boat goes to Calcutta,' Carey explained. 'But we are going to get off before that. A little boat will take us to Calcutta.'

'Why can't we go on this one?' he was asked.

'Because missionaries are not very welcome in India just now. If we were seen getting off, we might be sent all the way back home!'

That's how they came to be clambering down the side of the boat where the Hooghli river went into the sea.

After some months in India, the Careys moved inland to Mudnabatty where William was to work, and again they travelled by small boat.

'What's that?' 'What are they?' 'Look at that!' 'Wow!' 'This river smells!' 'There's a village!' 'It's SO hot!'

The boys hardly stopped talking as they travelled, even though two of them had been really quite ill.

'Why's the river getting narrower?' one asked, a long time into the journey.

William pulled the child on to his knee. 'That's because we're in the jungle now.'

'Are there tigers here?'

'Yes,' William admitted. 'There are tigers.'

Dorothy looked at her husband. Her eyes seemed to be asking what on earth he was doing, taking them all to such a dangerous place. And she was positively cross when they arrived and discovered the house, they were to stay in, was already occupied! Thankfully, the Englishman who was living there, invited them to stay. In fact, he and Dorothy's sister fell in love and were eventually married.

'Hasn't God been good?' William said, after they had been in Mudnabatty a short time. 'I've a steady job working on the indigo estate, and that feeds and clothes us. I also have time to learn the language, so much so that I'll soon be able to preach to the people.'

Dorothy smiled. 'And to think that I didn't even know what indigo was before we left England. Now I know that its dye is what makes clothes a beautiful purply blue - indigo, in fact!'

'I'd never heard the word till we came here,' agreed Carey.

William was so good at languages that within a few months he had learned Bengali, written Bengali grammar, and translated parts of the Bible into the language too! And every Sunday he went preaching in the villages near where they lived.

Several things happened over the next while. Other missionaries came out from England to help with the work, and they were especially welcome as poor Dorothy Carey developed an illness that made her withdraw into herself.

In 1800, they all moved to Serampore where missionaries were welcome. A printing press was set up there to print the Bible and other Christian material in Bengali.

The missionaries all lived in one big house, though they did all have their own rooms.

'We need some house rules,' Carey said, when they had all settled down. 'Does anyone have any suggestions?'

'I think we should allow each other privacy,' someone said.

'Yes,' they agreed.

'After all,' one of the wives pointed out, 'We may be missionaries, but we are still human!'

'I have a suggestion,' a new member of the group said. 'I think we should meet every Saturday and settle any differences we've had that week.'

'What a good idea,' Carey enthused. 'Then we'll go into Sunday without any grudges or arguments.'

And that's what they did.

'Look at this!' was the excited cry, just three months after they had all moved to Serampore.

Everyone looked up.

'It's the first ever printed page of the New Testament in Bengali!'

'Praise the Lord!' Carey said.

That was a joyful day, and a very historic one too. But there were two problems: how were they to pay for printing materials? And how were they to distribute what they printed?

'Let's put an advertisement in the Calcutta newspaper,' Carey suggested, 'asking people who want parts of the Bible in Bengali to pay for them in advance.'

So many people answered the advertisement that there was enough money to keep on printing.

'Ow! Argh! Ouch!'

The screams came from outside the Serampore mission house. Carey and Thomas ran outside and found Krishna Pal, a Bengali carpenter, yelling with pain.

'His shoulder is dislocated,' Thomas said. 'We'll have to put it back in for him.'

As there was no anaesthetic, Krishna Pal was tied to a tree, and his shoulder was jerked back in.

The Bengali's screams changed. 'I'm a great sinner!' he cried. 'Krishna Pal is a great sinner.'

Thomas and William didn't think he understood what he was saying. But Krishna Pal did understand, and he was the first Bengali to become a Christian at Serampore. When Krishna Pal was baptised, so was William Carey's eldest son. A white English boy and a Bengali man were baptised together in the river.

In England, William Carey had been a schoolteacher, and he found himself doing the same thing in Serampore. Some of the missionaries there died, but those who were left, started a school. Nobody knows what Carey used as a globe, when he was teaching Bengali children about the world, but it may even have been another leather football!

FACT FILE

India: In 1498, Portuguese ships captained by Vasco da Gama, reached southern India, and European influence in India had its beginning.

British merchants knew that Indian goods – especially cotton cloth, drugs and dyestuffs (such as indigo) – fetched high prices in Europe.

In 1600, they set up the East India Company to organise trade. By 1757, it controlled the richest parts of India and almost all Indian trade.

Keynote: William answered God's call even when it took him and his family to the other side of the world to a country full of danger, where Christians weren't made welcome.

Learn from William's wholehearted commitment to Jesus even when it made life difficult. Ask God to give you the same commitment whatever happens in your life.

Think: Remember that there are still countries where Christian missionaries are not welcome.

Pray for Christian medical staff and aid workers in these countries. Pray that God would give them opportunities to share Jesus with the people they meet, without fear of injury or imprisonment.

Prayer: Lord Jesus, thank you for sending missionaries across the world. Keep them safe as they work for you.

Help me to be 100 per cent committed to you, even if it makes things difficult. Thank you for always being with me, no matter what. Amen.

David Livingstone

The foreman pushed David through the rows of clanking machinery, guiding him to John Purdie, cotton mill worker. When they reached him, the boy stood between the two men watching their faces as they spoke to each other. He couldn't hear a word over the noise of the machines, and he wondered how they could. Then it dawned on him, they weren't hearing at all, they were lip-reading. Nodding to David, the foreman left, checking each worker as he went down the long row. John Purdie crouched down to the boy's height, he wasn't tall for ten years old, and shouted into his ear.

'You copy what I do, and be quick about it. And watch your hands and your hair don't get caught in the machines!' he shouted.

David Livingstone nodded. He'd seen enough people in the village of Blantyre, where he lived, who had fingers missing, and bald patches on their heads where hair had been pulled out by the roots.

'Dad told me about that!' he shouted.

John Purdie looked puzzled.

'Dad told me!' the lad screamed, but his light voice was lost in the noise of the mill.

Purdie shrugged his shoulders and set to work.

David's first job was picking up the cotton dust from under the machine. Crawling on the floor with his head down, he grabbed handful after handful of the stuff, shoving it into a sack that seemed bottomless. It didn't matter how much he pressed in, it always seemed to be able to take more.

'Atchoo! Atchoo!' The dust caught in his nose, and when sneezing made him open his mouth, the stuff got into his throat, and he started to cough. Coughing made his eyes water, but, when he rubbed them, the fine fibres of dust on his hands found their way into his eyes. At last, his sack was full, and he crawled out from under the machine, guided by Purdie's pale-grey boots. Puzzled by their colour, David looked at himself and found that he was the same grey colour from head to toe.

John Purdie looked down and frowned, but not in an angry way. He had children himself, and he knew what the boy at his feet was going through. Taking a hankie from his pocket, he folded it into a triangle and tied it round David's face to stop him choking on the dust. 'He'll get used to it, poor boy,' Purdie thought. 'They all do.'

Taking David by the shoulder, Purdie pointed to the cotton threads on the loom, showing him how it held the threads in tight, straight lines, lifting alternate threads up and down with the action of the machine. Then he pointed to the shuttle that zipped forwards when one set of threads were up and backwards when the alternate threads rose. David watched, mesmerised by the up and down, backwards and forwards action of the vast machine.

Purdie suddenly jumped, and David saw immediately what had happened. One of the threads had snapped. In a flash, Purdie was under the machine to catch the loose thread then, grabbing the other loose end, he tied the two together and worked on. A nod of Purdie's head told David that was what he had to do. All week David worked hard with John Purdie, and by the end of the week he had learned to see broken threads, not so much by staring at the machine all the time, but by watching for the sudden jerk of a broken end.

'You've done well,' Mr Livingstone said, patting his son on the back that Saturday night. 'I'm proud of you.'

David smiled.

'And so am I,' his mum added. 'I'm just sorry you've got to work to help feed your wee brothers and sisters. But there will always be something for yourself,' she added, pressing some coins out of his first pay into the boy's hand.

David looked at the money. 'I know what I want to buy,' he said.

And what he bought with his very first pay was a book of Latin grammar! That book became well known in the mill, for the boy kept it propped up against his loom so that he could glance down at it and learn Latin grammar as he worked!

But the book David liked best of all was the Bible. His father read it with his family every evening, and much of Sunday was spent at church or reading God's Word. That suited the boy fine, because he believed in the Lord Jesus and wanted to find out more and more about him.

It was through his church that he heard about China, and how hard it was for the people there. Not only was there a terrible shortage of doctors in China, but most of the people there didn't know about the Lord. David decided to go to China as a missionary doctor - not easy for a poor mill boy.

David studied by day at his loom, and at night school too. Then he went to university for two years to learn some medicine. But, when he applied to go to China, there was a war going on there, and he found himself being sent to Africa instead.

In 1840, David sailed from London to South Africa via South America, a voyage which took many weeks. God had a surprise waiting for David. When he arrived, he went to work with another missionary, Robert Moffat. And Moffat's daughter, Mary, and David Livingstone fell in love and were eventually married.

'Why's that boy running so fast?' Mary asked one day.

David, who was treating a patient, looked up and saw a child racing for all he was worth toward the mission. Even from that distance, he could see his frightened expression. 'There's someone chasing him!'

'You finish this,' he said urgently, nodding towards his patient.

Livingstone ran, aiming to get between the child and the man who was chasing. The lad ran on, reaching Mary safely. The man slowed down, took in the situation, and slunk into the bush. But David wasn't going to let it finish there. 'What's wrong?' he demanded, when he cornered him.

'The boy, he ran away,' blurted out the breathless African.

David was pretty sure something fishy was going on.

'He's my son,' the man said. 'He tried to run away.'

But Livingstone recognised a lie when he heard one. In any case, the boy didn't look anything like the man who was chasing them – David was certain they were not related. 'Wait there!' he ordered. The African, frightened by the stern Scot, sat down and waited.

'This lad's been sold as a slave!' Mary announced when he reached her. 'His parents are poor, and that rogue you've just caught bought him for next to nothing, and he's going to sell him for as much as he can get. The child will have no life at all if that happens. He'll just be worked to death!'

'Is this true?' Livingstone asked the terrified child.

And the whole story poured out, just as it had done to Mary. Suddenly, David's mind was not in Africa; it was back in Scotland, in the mill at Blantyre. He remembered how he had felt as a child labourer; he remembered the choking dust, his dry, cracked throat, and his red, running eyes. And he vowed to do whatever was in his power for Africa's child slaves. He, at least, had had loving parents; the poor boy at his feet had been sold to a rogue.

Suddenly, Livingstone remembered the man in the bush. He swung round ... but there was nobody there.

With terrific energy Livingstone threw himself into an amazing variety of work. He became a friend of the African people he met and did his best to understand them. His passion for preaching the good news of Jesus meant that he was always a student of the Bible and used every opportunity to preach to other people. But he didn't only care for their souls, he used his medical training to care for their sick and injured bodies too. And, as if that wasn't enough, he set out to explore Africa without the help of planes and helicopters, powered riverboats and quad bikes.

David and Mary loved young people, and God kindly gave them children of their own. How very sad he must have been, therefore, when his little family went home to Britain away from the diseases and troubles of Africa.

'I shall not see you again for a long time,' he wrote to his daughter Agnes, whom he often called Nannie, 'and I am very sorry. I have no Nannie now. I have given you back to Jesus, your friend, your Papa who is in heaven. He is above you, but he is always near you when we ask things from him - that is, praying to him – and if you do or say a naughty thing, ask him to pardon you, and bless you, and make you one of his children. Love Jesus much, for he loves you, and he came and died for you.'

Compared to Scotland, Africa is enormous, but David Livingstone set out to explore it, from top to bottom and from side to side.

'Apart from around the coast, Africa is all desert,' friends told him.

'It can't be,' he insisted. 'Look at the rivers that run into the sea. You don't get vast rivers in deserts!'

His friends shook their heads. 'But why do you want to go anyway?'

'There are people there who've never heard of Jesus,' David told them. 'There are tribes that haven't yet been discovered. There's a continent to explore.'

'There's no stopping him,' they decided, for his friends knew that exploring was one of his passions.

His journeys took ages because he travelled by ox-drawn cart or walked. And for very long periods of time, nobody knew where he was. There were no mobile phones in those days!

In 1867, David set off once again through Africa, exploring, map-making, and being a doctor and missionary all at once. His aim was to reach a place called Ujiji.

'What's that?' he asked the Africans who travelled with him to carry the luggage. They were known as bearers.

They turned their eyes away. They didn't want to see. Livingstone went over to look, only to find two bodies. And he knew from the marks on their wrists that they were slaves who had died as they were dragged to the slave ships.

'I must open up Africa,' he said to himself. 'I must. I must! It's the only way to stop this cruel trade in people.'

Through blistering sun and torrential rain they travelled, on and on and on. It took a year for them to reach central Africa.

'I want to divert a bit,' David Livingstone told his men, after looking at his compass for direction.

They shook their heads furiously. 'No!' some of his bearers said. 'We will never be home if you don't go straight to Ujiji. If you divert, we go home.'

The missionary explorer was torn. What should he do?

'How many of you will stay with me?' he asked.

Only five men agreed to go on with him, on a journey that saw them covered with leeches as they walked waist deep through rivers, torn by vicious thorns, bitten to distraction by mosquitoes, dodging crocodiles, and often putting their lives at risk. But still they went on, for a time carrying Livingstone who was ill for weeks. And their problems didn't end when they reached Ujiji. The supplies they had hoped to find there had been stolen.

The explorations of David Livingstone were by then very well known, and people in Britain, Canada, America and beyond had begun to think he had died in the middle of Africa. It was two years since news of him had reached home.

'I think we should run a story on Livingstone,' the editor of the New York Herald suggested to his staff.

'He's probably dead by now,' one man commented.

The editor nodded agreement. 'Dead or alive, that's not important. What's important is that we find out and publish the story. Would you be prepared to research this?' he asked a man called Stanley.

And that's how an American came to be in the interior of Africa looking for a Scotsman. And when he found him, Stanley held out his hand in greeting, saying, 'Dr Livingstone, I presume.' It could hardly have been anyone else!

FACT FILE

Cotton: A field of cotton ready for picking is covered with cotton balls. These balls are made up of soft, white fibres that are really pieces of very fine hair growing from the skin of many small seeds. The fibres have to be removed from the seeds before they can be spun into long pieces of thread or yarn. This separation process was done by hand.

Then, in 1793, Eli Whitney invented the cotton gin, which could be worked by one person and separate as much cotton as fifty to sixty people working by hand.

Keynote: David Livingstone saw Africa as a land full of people needing Jesus and vast areas waiting to be explored. He wasn't afraid to take on the challenge!

Learn from David's courage and his adventurous spirit. Remember that God is with you, too, so don't be afraid to take on a challenging task for him.

Think: Look up an atlas and compare the size of David's homeland, Scotland, with the vastness of Africa.

Isn't it amazing that God used a boy from a small town in Scotland to explore a continent the size of Africa? David's expeditions also brought a message of hope to people who had never heard about Jesus before.

Ask God to use you too, no matter where he takes you!

Prayer: Lord Jesus, thank you for men and women who have taken on big challenges for you.

Help me to look to you for strength and courage to deal with the challenges I face in my life today. Amen.

Nicky Cruz

Nicky hid under the back stairs of his home in Puerto Rico. No way did he want to see the people who were arriving. They were the snake people!

'Will your dad make them dance with snakes today?' his friend asked. 'I wanna see the snakes dance.'

Shuddering as he answered, Nicky said, 'You go watch. I'm heading off when the door shuts behind them. Papa'll beat me if he catches me watching in the window.'

'He wouldn't dare beat me,' the other boy boasted. 'My dad's the law here.'

Nicky chuckled. 'And what's the law compared to the witch doctor! I tell you, I'd rather be you than me. Do you think it's fun, everyone calling your home the witch's house?'

The door had closed. He started to run, stopped once and called out, 'You try it! You try living there! See how you like it!'

He was only ten years old, but Nicky Cruz thought he knew some terrible things. He was sure his mother hated him. Why else would she call him the devil's child. He knew he hated his father. And he hated anyone who bossed him around.

'Bully Cruz,' children shouted at him from a safe distance, and they were right.

'You'll either be murdered or be a murderer,' he was told more than once.

And when Nicky got a gun for killing birds, nobody came close. Nobody felt safe when he was around. Angry with everyone, he couldn't wait to get out of Puerto Rico; he couldn't wait to get to New York, the big city. Six of his older brothers were already there, and he was desperate for it to be his turn.

Eventually, at long last, the great day came. He turned his back on his family, aged fifteen, climbed on to a plane for the U.S.A., and hoped he'd never be back.

'Papa said to phone Frank when I arrive,' he said to himself. 'No way! I've had enough family to do me. I'll make my own way. Nobody will get the better of me!'

'It's freezing here,' Nicky decided, as he walked the city streets that night. 'But that looks hopeful.' He pulled a rag out of a dustbin. It was an ancient, buttonless, coat, but it felt like a blanket to the cold boy. 'One up to me!' he laughed.

But he wasn't laughing a day or two later as he sat huddled in a doorway.

'Wazzat!' He jumped, wiping hot tears away.

A mangy dog snuggled up beside him and licked his hand. The boy put his arms round the dog and wept ... until he noticed police boots in front of him.

In less than an hour, he was in Frank's flat and listening to a lecture. But Nicky knew in his heart that his brother's suggestion of school was not for him. He'd had enough of that in Puerto Rico. And before two months were out, the New York school Frank sent him to had had enough of him ... and his switchblade.

'Gimme that!' Nicky demanded.

The boy hesitated.

'Now!' The voice was menacing.

There was a click, his switchblade was open, open in front of the boy's face.

Dropping his money and the food he was carrying, the boy stumbled then half-ran, half-crawled, from the teenage madman with the blade.

Nicky picked up the wallet, grabbed an apple and sprinted away.

'No problem,' he said aloud, 'I can steal what I want, and, if anyone says "no" – he stroked his knife – I can persuade him.'

What Nicky Cruz didn't know was that he was being watched, but not by the police. The Mau Maus, one of New York's most vicious gangs, had their eye on him. He was just the kind of guy they were looking for.

Nicky was sixteen when he held his first revolver, and it felt good in his hands.

'You're our kind,' the gang leader told him. 'We can sure use you. You're a Mau Mau now, and there's no getting out. You're one of us – for good.'

Guns are just cold metal until they are fired. The first time Nicky fired his gun – and he fired it over and over and over again – was at a small boy in another gang. He was the most popular of all the Mau Maus after that fight, and he felt great.

It only took six months until Nicky Cruz was the Mau Mau president; that's how vicious he was. By then the police knew him well.

'I didn't do it, and I don't know anything about it!' he lied, about robberies, gang fights, assaults, drug raids, even murders.

The police knew he was guilty. Nicky knew he was guilty. But they could never pin anything on him. Although Nicky was popular with the gang, he wasn't always happy, especially at night when he had nightmares. For the next two years he was afraid to go to sleep. Nicky Cruz, the thug everyone feared, was scared of going to sleep.

It was summer 1958, and it was hot. Nicky and some other gang members sat at the edge of the street as young folk ran past.

'Coming to the circus?' one yelled.

Nicky looked up. 'What's going on?'

'There's a circus at the school,' the voice said, from the distance.

'We're going,' Nicky announced, and when Nicky announced something, everyone jumped to do it.

Outside the school a trumpeter played the same tune over and over and over again. Next to him was a skinny, weedy-looking man. Nicky could hardly believe his eyes. The trumpeter stopped, and the skinny guy climbed on to a stool and opened a book.

'Shout!' Nicky commanded. And the Mau Maus shouted, long and loud.

The man looked scared. He stood with his head bowed.

This was not Nicky's scene. Suddenly, the man wasn't the only one who was scared; Nicky Cruz was too.

When the crowd sensed the atmosphere, there was a tense silence. The man opened his book and read aloud, 'For God so loved the world that he gave his only son, that whoever believes in him, should not perish, but have everlasting life.' Then he went on talking to the quiet crowd of gang members. 'If you're so big and tough, you wouldn't be afraid of coming up here and shaking hands with a skinny preacher, would you?' he finished.

Some of the audience went up, shook hands, and got down on their knees right there in the street!

'They're showing you up, Nicky!' someone shouted.

His street cred was under threat. Nicky and his best friend marched to the front of the crowd, but when he reached the preacher, the young Puerto Rican didn't shake hands - he threatened to kill him.

'Jesus loves you,' the preacher said. 'Jesus loves you.'

The next day Dave Wilkerson, the preacher, found Nicky. 'I've just come to tell you that Jesus loves you. He really does.'

Nicky Cruz could have flattened him with one punch, and both knew it.

'One day, you'll stop running,' Wilkerson said, 'and you'll come running to Jesus.'

And that's how it was. Nicky did stop running, and he did come to Jesus. But what is much more amazing than that, is that Jesus wanted him to come. Jesus loved Nicky Cruz even though he had done unspeakable things. Jesus wanted to forgive him.

'I won't need this again,' thought Nicky, as he shoved his Mau Mau jacket in a bag. 'Things are going to be different.'

The gang was waiting for him, waiting to see what was going to happen. They had all been there when Nicky Cruz said in public that he was going to follow Jesus.

'Right, you lot,' their president told the Mau Maus, 'get your guns, blades and bullets and meet me in Washington Park.'

The gang relaxed. Everything was just as usual.

'We're gonna march to the police station and hand them over.'

They looked at each other, then at Nicky. But his look was like cold steel. They did exactly as they were told, much to the amazement of the police who thought it was some kind of trick!

'I want you to go to Bible School,' Dave Wilkerson told the new Christian before much time had passed. 'That gets you out of New York, and God's got plans for you at Bible School.'

'School.' Nicky was even allergic to the word! But he went, only to discover he was like a fish out of water. His English was poor; as a Puerto Rican he was a native Spanish speaker. He didn't know how to behave. And when he was told to do something, his instinct was to do the opposite. He tried to fit in. Nicky really, really tried, but it was such hard work. God helped him though, and he especially helped him by allowing him to fall in love. Gloria was also at Bible School, and they set out together to see what God wanted them to do with their lives.

'Hey Dave,' Nicky Cruz said into the phone. 'I've got news for you.'

Dave Wilkerson groaned. It was evening where Nicky was, but the middle of the night with Dave! 'Can't it wait till morning?'

'No! I'm calling to tell you I'm coming to work with you in New York for the summer.'

That wakened Dave. 'That's great! That's really great!'

And it was. Some of Nicky's old friends from the Mau Maus recognised him, even though he was clean and wearing different clothes. They listened to what he had to tell them about Jesus, and some became Christians.

At the beginning of that summer, Nicky had news for Dave; at the end, Dave had news for him.

'Someone has given me money to send you on a trip home to Puerto Rico to see your folks.'

Nicky swallowed hard. Since he'd become a Christian, he'd really wanted to see them again. He'd no hate in his heart for them any more. The trip was arranged, and he set off. While he was in Puerto Rico, Nicky was asked to preach. And at the end of the service, when he asked anyone who wanted to become a Christian to come to the front, his own mother moved forward, knelt down and asked Jesus to be her Saviour.

'I'm enjoying school so much better this year,' Nicky told Gloria, after returning from New York and his visit home. 'Now that I know God can use me, I can see the point of studying.'

Because of that, the year passed quickly. It didn't seem like several months later when a letter arrived from Dave Wilkerson.

'Gloria!' Nicky yelled, when he read it. 'Dave wants me to go back to New York when I finish, to Teen Challenge Centre, to work with gangs and addicts and drunks, people just like I used to be. But I'll be carrying a Bible instead of a revolver or a switchblade.'

The girl watched his excitement. 'Yes,' she thought, 'that's just what Nicky's cut out for. That's just the work God has spent all these years preparing him to do.'

Nicky Cruz moved back to New York, and he and Gloria were married. The work they did through Teen Challenge was tough. They were working with the hardest of all young folk. They had great sorrows when gang fights led to murders, when kids died of drug overdoses, when some took their own lives. And they had tremendous joys when others kicked their drug habit, quit their fighting, left gang life behind them and followed Jesus.

FACT FILE
New York:
New York lies on the Atlantic coast of America, at the mouth of the Hudson River.

Every traveller, entering or leaving New York harbour, sees the great Statue of Liberty on Liberty Island. The statue, made by F. A. Bartholdi, was given to the United States by France in 1886.

Another feature of New York is the great collection of skyscrapers which tower over Manhattan, in the heart of the city.

Keynote: Nicky's family life taught him to hate, and his time in a New York gang encouraged this anger into violence. Love was something that Nicky had never experienced.

Learn from how the love of Jesus broke through the hatred in Nicky's heart and completely changed his life. Believe that the love of Jesus can do the same today too!

Think: Maybe there's a bully in your school - someone who is rebellious and angry and doesn't care about hurting others. Think of the impact there would be if the bully's heart was full of love for God, instead of hatred towards others!

Focus on praying for that person. Pray that God will change bullies, and believe that he can do it.

 Prayer: Lord Jesus, thank you for loving us so much that you died for us.

Help me to show your love, not just to my friends, but also to those whom I feel are my enemies. Use me to bring the message of your love and forgiveness to them too. Amen.

Adoniram Judson

Two pigs snuffled around the boy's feet, as he emptied the scraps from his little bucket into their trough. Then the maid poured in a much larger pail of food.

'Listen to them!' she laughed, as she picked the child up out of reach of the mess. 'I'm glad you don't make a noise like that when you're eating!'

Three-year-old Adoniram laughed. 'Piggies speak with their mouths full,' he said. 'They say "shlurp, shlurp".'

'What does the cockerel say then?'

The child grinned. He loved the cockerel. 'Cockadoodledoo!' he crowed.

'You are a clever little boy,' the maid said, as they picked their way through the mud at the back of the house and up the path to the kitchen door.

'Master Adoniram knows all the animal sounds now,' the maid told Mrs Judson, the child's mother.

Mrs Judson smiled. 'And he says them all with your Boston accent.'

'It's the best accent in all of America!' the girl said. 'And it's the one all his little friends will have when he goes to school.'

'On the subject of school, Adoniram,' his mother said, 'let's you and me go through to the parlour. There's something I'd like us to do.'

Mrs Judson sat down on her rocking chair, pulled her son on to her knee, and opened her big Bible.

The child looked confused. 'Is it bedtime?' he asked, knowing that his mother or father always read him a Bible story before he went to bed.

Smiling at the thought, Mrs Judson explained that she read the Bible a number of times each day as well as at bedtime.

'That's good,' said Adoniram, 'cos I'm not sleepy.'

Then a thought crossed his mind. 'Mama, why does Papa have to go away so often?'

'He has to go away to preach,' she explained, 'to tell people about the Lord Jesus.'

Adoniram knew about preaching, because his father was a minister.

'Would you like to give Papa a surprise when he comes home next week?' Mrs Judson asked the little boy.

'What surprise?'

His mother opened the Bible. 'Let's see if we can teach you to read for Papa.'

She pointed to a word. 'That says God, and the three letters are G - o - d. Can you see anywhere else on the page that says God?'

Adoniram searched over the page of print. 'There!' he said triumphantly, 'and there! and there!'

'Well done!' laughed his mother. 'You can read a word already, and such an important word. Now let's find another one.'

She pointed to the page. 'That word says Jesus, and the five letters are J - e - s - u - s. Can you see anywhere else it says Jesus?'

It took him a minute, but the lad found the word Jesus.

'I like this game,' he said.

A week later, a very excited little boy watched at the window for his father.

'Papa! Papa!' he shouted, when he saw him coming. 'Come and see the surprise.'

Rev Adoniram Judson, tired after a long journey, took off his coat, sat down on his chair and pulled his son on to his knee.

'You have a weary papa,' he said, 'but you make up for me. You're so full of energy.'

'May I show you my surprise?' the child begged. 'It's in the parlour.'

Adoniram told his papa to sit by the fire. The boy sat down in his own little chair, and his mother handed him the Bible open at the place. Then Adoniram Judson read a whole chapter to his amazed papa! The words were read quite slowly, but correctly. Only when he had finished reading did the child look up.

'Why are you crying, Papa?' he asked, shocked at his father's response.

Rev Adoniram Judson hoisted his son on to his knee and hugged him close. 'These are not sad tears,' he explained. 'These are happy tears, very happy tears. Who taught you to read the Bible?'

Mrs Judson was grinning.

'Mama did,' the child explained. 'She said I could learn to read a chapter when you were away for a week, and I did.'

'And you've made me the happiest father in Boston. And the most amazed. What a clever boy you are. And what better book to read than the Bible.'

'It's my favouritest book,' the child said, stroking its leather cover.

By the time he went to Master Dodge's School, some time around 1786, he had read much of the Bible for himself.

'Let's play churches,' Adoniram suggested to his little brother and sister some years later, when they were old enough to play with him. Their mother smiled from her seat by the fire.

The two younger children sat down. They liked this game because it meant a lot of noisy singing.

Adoniram opened his Bible in the middle, and read, 'I have hidden your word in my heart.'

'Mama,' he said. 'Why would anyone want to hide God's Word, even in their heart?'

Mrs Judson thought for a moment. 'It doesn't mean it's all hidden away and forgotten about; it means that you love it so much that you learn it by heart and remember it. Do you understand?'

The boy nodded, but it still seemed to him a strange idea to hide a Bible.

Years later, the little boy, who had liked playing at preachers, was a real preacher, and not in America, but on the other side of the world, in the Buddhist country of Burma.

He and his wife, Ann, were missionaries. But there were problems, big problems in Burma's Golden City, because the Burmese were fighting the English.

'The situation is getting desperate,' Adoniram said. 'Rangoon has fallen to the British, and we're being suspected as spies.'

'But we're not British!' insisted Ann.

'But we're white, we speak English, and we're not Buddhists. That's more than enough to make us suspects.'

There was loud banging at the door of the mission house. Adoniram rose to answer, but it was shoved open in his face.

Ann turned deadly white. It was the spotted faces![1]

'You're under arrest!' they told Judson, tying his elbows together behind his back.

Ann struggled to reach her husband but was held back by the Burmese Christian who lived with them.

After Judson was hauled out the door, the little group in the mission house stood in stunned silence. Then all the questions came at once.

'Where will they take him?'

---

1. The spotted faces were criminals whose crimes were tattoed on their faces, hence the name. Groups of them were used by the authorities as hit squads.

'Will they torture him?'

'The spotted faces ... they're the most feared of the guards.'

'They're all former criminals.'

'They're all still criminals.'

The Burmese Christian, Judson's first convert, led the little group in prayer. That evening, Ann, with the help of her friends, burned any papers in English. But one big pile of papers was not burned; it was buried in the space under the mission house.

'Death Prison!' Ann Judson gasped. 'They've taken Adoniram to Death Prison.' She shuddered, thinking of all the terrible things that went on there. Straightening her back, she looked at her friends. 'We have to be brave,' she said. 'And we have to take food every day to Death Prison. The guards don't feed the prisoners, so we must.'

Each day, rice, wrapped in leaves, was taken to the prison, but often whoever took it, didn't tell Ann all that they had seen and heard. Sometimes, the prisoners were strung upside down, with only their shoulders on the floor, all night. They were beaten and tortured in dreadful ways.

'Take this to Adoniram,' Ann told her Burmese friend one day. 'He needs a pillow.'

She handed him a brown, cloth pillow. It wasn't soft and fluffy; it was hard and lumpy. And Adoniram's heart rejoiced, even in Death Prison, when he got the uncomfortable pillow.

Many months after Adoniram was imprisoned, there was frightening news.

'They're not in Death Prison!' the Burmese Christian said, as he came in the door. 'They've been moved away.'

A shudder ran round the room. Had they been moved away, or had they ...?

Ann, who had only recently had a baby and was still very weak, went to visit an important lady in the city who would be able to tell her if it was good news or bad. The news was not good, but it was better than it might have been.

'All the white prisoners have been moved to Amarapura,' she told her friends, when she came back. 'We'll need to go there to feed Adoniram and the others.'

The little group, including baby Maria, were bundled up and taken by boat to Amarapura, near where they found the prisoners in a derelict jail.

'My pillow,' Adoniram said sadly to his wife; 'I wasn't able to bring my pillow with me. All my work is lost, all my years of work.'

Only Ann Judson understood what his pillow meant to him.

That night, Adoniram Judson prayed and prayed. His pillow was lost. And he and his fellow prisoners, whose feet had been locked in stocks, were again hanging upside down with only their shoulders on the ground. His heart wept in prayer for the people of Burma.

Shortly afterwards, a new prisoner arrived, a huge and hungry lioness in a cage!

'What's she here for?' the chief guard demanded.

'Maybe the prisoners have to be fed to her!' another guard suggested.

And that's what all the prisoners thought too.

Things seemed to be at their very worst when two things happened. The lioness died, and soldiers came with news that the prisoners had to be released and taken back to the Golden City. The King of Burma needed them because they spoke English. The war with England was over, and he needed English speakers to negotiate the peace treaty.

What a welcome the pathetic little group got when they arrived back in the mission house in Golden City.

'How did you come to be here?' Mr Judson asked a teenage boy who seemed to be living there. His father, though not a missionary, had been in prison with Judson.

The boy told his story, and he ended it by saying that he'd gone to Death Prison to see his father the day the prisoners were taken away. In his distress, he had looked for something to remind him of his father and had found Mr Judson's pillow. And he had discovered its secret!

Adoniram Judson had translated the New Testament into Burmese, and when it looked as though it might be destroyed, Ann buried it. Then she dug it up, sewed it into a pillow, and sent it to her husband in prison.

'Praise the Lord!' Adoniram, weak and exhausted, was nearly dancing his thanks to God. 'Praise the Lord!'

The boy had more to tell. 'When I discovered it was a book,' he said, 'I read it. I read all about Jesus, and I became a Christian.'

Adoniram Judson had preached the gospel in Burma for years with only one or two people coming to faith. But God used his terrible time in Death Prison to turn a teenager from a Buddhist into a believer in the Lord Jesus Christ.

FACT FILE

Memory: How good is your memory? Some people find it easier to remember things by picturing them in their mind's eye, as if they were taking a mental photograph. Others have good memories for sounds and tunes. Some try to remember things by repeating them quietly to themselves.

However weak your memory might be, you can make up for it by listening carefully to what you want to remember and repeating it over and over again.

Keynote: Years later, in a Burmese prison, Adoniram would thank God that as a little boy he had memorised so many Bible verses. He knew that these verses were stored in his memory forever and would help him through his ordeal.

Learn from how Adoniram drew comfort from God's Word and try memorising some key Bible verses yourself. You never know when you might need them!

Think: Did you know that, even today, many Christians are imprisoned because of their faith? Thank God for how freely we can worship him and live as Christians.

Don't forget to pray for those whose freedom has been lost and whose lives are at risk because of their love for Jesus.

Prayer: Lord Jesus, thank you for your Word and for everything it tells me. Help me to treasure it more.

Be with Christians around the world who are in prison because of their love for you. Bless them with your presence and care in a special way. Amen.

George Müller

George stomped about the room, only just resisting the thought of kicking the table leg as he went past. He was in a rotten mood, and he didn't care who knew it.

'I want to go out to play football,' the boy moaned.

George's father looked stern. 'You can go out after you've done your accounts.'

His son stamped his feet. 'It's not fair!' he said. 'None of my friends have to write down how they spend their pocket money.'

Herr Müller was cross. 'You'll sit down and do what I tell you. And I'm telling you that you've to keep a note of how you spend every single penny you get. I'll be back in five minutes to see what you've done.'

Herr Müller shut the door behind him.

George took out his notebook and screwed his face into a scowl. Then he wrote down that he had spent that week's pocket money on a pencil, rubber and a notebook. The boy sat back and grinned. 'He'll never find out that I really lost it on a bet.'

The door handle rattled, and Herr Müller came back in. George handed his father the notebook.

'That's good,' he told his son. 'I'm glad you don't waste your money. You know,' he went on, 'because I'm a taxman for the Prussian government, I know a lot about what people do with their money, and so many just spend it on rubbish. They think I don't know, but I do.'

'May I go out to play now?' the boy asked. He didn't want to hear any more about his father's work, and he didn't want to hear any more about money either.

'I wish I had some sweets,' George thought the next day. 'But I haven't any money to buy them. I lost all this week's pocket money on that bet!'

Then he noticed the money his father had gathered in taxes. It was in a box with a lock, but the key was in the lock. Looking round to make sure nobody was coming, he opened the box and took out some money.

'Where can I put it?' he asked himself.

Then he had an idea. Taking off his shoe, he slipped the coins into it and put it back on again. He was only just in time because his father came into the room.

Herr Müller sat down at his desk, opened the money box and started to count what was in it. George walked quietly towards the door.

'Come here!' barked his father.

The nine-year-old boy did what he was told.

'Have you taken anything out of this box?'

George tried to look shocked. 'Me!' he said. 'I didn't go anywhere near it!'

'Take off your jacket,' Herr Müller told his son firmly.

George took it off.

His father checked the pockets, but there was no money there. Then he searched George, but found nothing.

'Now take off your shoes,' he told the boy.

George took them off very, very carefully.

'What was that?' the man demanded, when he heard the chink of coins.

The lad ducked to avoid his father's slap. But he wasn't quick enough.

'I left the key in that box deliberately,' Herr Müller said, 'because I was quite sure you were stealing from me, and I wanted to double-check. Don't you ever, ever do anything like that again. It's a terrible thing when a father can't trust his son with money.'

Instead of getting better, George went from bad to worse. He left home as soon as he possibly could, got into bad company, and by the time he was sixteen, in 1821, he was in prison for dishonesty. Several times he tried to be good, but it always went wrong, and he ended up worse than ever. Then a friend of George's became a Christian. In desperation, George asked his friend if he could go with him to a Christian meeting at the home of Herr Wagner.

'Come in,' Herr Wagner said, opening the door wide. 'Welcome to my home and my heart.'

The other boy went first because he knew the way.

'That's a nice welcome,' thought George, as he took off his coat. He began to relax in the roomful of people.

'What on earth's he doing?' Müller asked himself.

They had just sung a hymn, and now one of the men was kneeling down and praying.

George had never seen such a thing before! In Prussia, at that time, people used prayers out of books. Nobody made up their own prayer in public. It was unheard of.

Müller looked at the kneeling man and listened.

'It's as though he's speaking to a king,' he thought.

After praying, the man read the Bible and preached a sermon. George was amazed! The man was breaking the law! Only men ordained by the church were allowed to preach. So shocked was the youth that he listened to every word that was said.

Something happened in George's heart during that meeting. He not only met men and women who were friends of Jesus, he met the Lord Jesus himself. He didn't see him with his eyes or hear him speak, but his heart knew that God was present in that room. By the time George left Herr Wagner's meeting, he had asked God to forgive his sin.

'I challenge you to a drinking match,' one of his student friends said a few days later.

George looked at the group of young men. They were all drinkers and gamblers as he had been.

'No,' he said, 'I'm not coming. I'm a Christian now.'

The group all stopped speaking. Then one grinned.

'A Christian! We'll see about that. I bet you're back in the pub tomorrow.'

They turned and swaggered away, leaving George looking at their backs. He didn't go with them that day, and he never went with them again.

'We need missionaries,' a preacher said one day, when Müller was back at Herr Wagner's house. 'We need people who will tell others about the Lord Jesus.'

George stared at the man. 'A missionary?' he thought to himself. 'I wonder ....'

God did call George Müller to be a missionary, which is why he moved to London where he worked for a time with Jewish people. And it was in England that he met the young woman he married. Eventually, the Müllers and George's friend, Henry Craik, moved to Bristol to be joint ministers of a church there. But soon after they arrived, cholera struck the city, and many people died, leaving hundreds of children hungry and homeless. George and

Henry opened a small orphan home, then another, then a third.

Some years later, God led them to build a huge new home just outside the city, at Ashley Down. Amazingly, a second home was built there, and a third one too! Over the years Müller and Craik worked together; they provided a home, food, clothes and education for over two thousand children. Never once did they ask anyone for a penny. They took all their needs to God in prayer, and they had some spectacular answers.

The matron of the infants' home went to Müller one day.

'I don't have money for the milk we need,' she explained.

George took the money box out of his desk and counted what was in it. They were two pence short of what was needed.

'Let's pray about it,' he said.

They prayed that the Lord would provide money for milk for the infants. When George opened the door to let the matron out, a poor woman stood there.

'I don't have much money,' she told him, 'but the Lord led me to bring this to you.'

She handed over two pence, exactly what was needed for the milk.

Some time later, the children thought it was just an ordinary day. But it wasn't. They did their schoolwork and finished their chores, not knowing that there wasn't enough food for their dinner. The staff in the home knew, and they also knew that there was no money to buy what was needed. Suppertime came nearer. The children were ready for their meal, and the staff prayed with all their hearts. God answered their prayers. Just as they all sat down to say grace, the baker arrived at the door to ask if they could use some bread! He had made more than he needed and had plenty to spare! The children gave thanks and ate their meal, never thinking that God had provided it that very minute. In all the years the homes ran, no child ever went hungry.

'The heating boiler isn't working,' an assistant at the home told George one winter day. 'There's a serious leak.'

'But it's so cold, and we can't have the children chilled,' Müller said to the man. 'How long would it take to get a new boiler?'

'A month,' was the reply.

George and his wife prayed about it and felt that they should get someone else to come and investigate the problem. But that would mean putting the boiler out and letting the children get cold.

'We'll pray that God will change this freezing north wind to a warm south wind the day the boiler's off,' they agreed. And that was their prayer.

On the day the workmen came, the cold north wind turned to the south and blew mild and warm! The following day, it was freezing again!

'Where does the money come from to run these huge housefuls of children?' a visitor to Ashley Down once asked.

'It comes from the Lord,' George Müller answered.

His visitor looked puzzled. 'Tell me what you mean.'

George stood up, went to the window, and looked out. The children were playing, hundreds of them. Each was dressed in neat, good quality clothes and shoes. The girls had nice haircuts. And they had balls to play football with and dolls to cuddle.

'I mean that the Lord miraculously provides every single penny. We receive no grants and accept no loans. We don't send begging letters, and we don't make appeals for funds. We don't tell people what we need, and we don't tell them we have bills to pay.'

The visitor watched Müller's face as he talked. Although he was eighty years old, he looked as excited as a child.

'What we do is this. We get down on our knees, and we tell the Lord all about it, and he has never, ever failed to answer our prayers. We receive gifts of food and material for clothes. Some people arrive at the door and give us pennies, others come with hundreds of pounds. Over the years we've run the homes, we've been given in money or kind over a million pounds. And remember, we've never asked for a penny.'

'Mr Müller,' the visitor said, 'that's an amazing story. But may I ask you one last question?'

The old man smiled and nodded. 'What's that?'

'What was your training before you were a minister? Were you an accountant? You certainly seem gifted in handling money.'

George Müller wondered how much he should say to this man, and decided to tell him all.

'My training in accountancy was carried out by my father before I was ten years old. And as for being gifted with money, before I became a Christian, I was a gifted young thief.'

FACT FILE

Napoleon: Napoleon was a Corsican soldier (originally known as Napoleon Bonaparte) who became Emperor of France in 1804, the year before George was born.

Napoleon set out to conquer Europe, but, after victories at Austerlitz and Jena, he made the fatal mistake of invading Russia in 1812. He reached Moscow, but lost many men in the severe winter cold.

In 1813, Napoleon was defeated, and he abdicated the following year. After returning to rule France for 100 days in 1815, Napoleon was finally completely defeated in the Battle of Waterloo. He spent the rest of his life in exile.

Keynote: George depended on God for everything. He knew that if he shared his needs with God, he could be sure that everything would be taken care of. He had absolute trust in God, and the Lord never let him down.

Learn from how George handed over all his needs to God in prayer and trust him to take care of you too.

Think: When you pray, remember to:

- thank God for everything he's given you.
- tell him about what you need, not what you want. There's a difference!
- give God the glory when your needs are met.

Prayer: Lord Jesus, thank you for how you have answered my prayers in the past.

Help me to trust in you more and always to bring my needs to you first. Make me more and more dependent on you every day. Amen.

Luis Palau

Luis and his sister Matil crouched under the canvas sheet that was covering their father's bags of cement.

'What's that?!' Luis jumped.

'Shhhhh...' Matil whispered. 'It's Dad's belt. We've had it now!'

The pair huddled together. It had seemed a good game to pretend to run away from home. But it had turned sour on them. Both knew what the jingle of their dad's belt meant.

'Come out of there the pair of you!' Mr Palau's voice said, right above their heads.

First Luis crept out, dusty and shamefaced. Then came Matil who was already in tears.

'Bend over,' their father ordered. And both did.

Tea that night was not comfortable for two reasons. Mr Palau's long prayer before they ate, seemed to have more to do with asking forgiveness for sin than for thanking God for their tea, and two bottoms were not very comfortable for sitting on.

Although Mr Palau was strict, he loved his children very much, and they knew it. One of the things that young Luis really liked doing, was creeping into his father's study first thing in the morning. He knew that he would find his father there, wrapped up in a poncho to keep himself warm in the chill of the Argentinian morning, and praying. Luis loved hearing his father praying for him and for the rest of the family. Somehow, he felt that as long as his father was wrapped in his poncho and praying each morning, everything would be all right. He might get rows, he might even be beaten with his father's belt, if he was especially naughty, but everything would end up all right.

'Now that you're seven,' Mr Palau said to his son, 'you're old enough to go to boarding school. What do you think of that?'

Luis didn't know what to think. He would have to stay in a dormitory with other boys. He would miss his family.

'Will there be midnight feasts?' he asked.

His father laughed. 'There might be sometimes.'

'It'll be brilliant!' the boy enthused, trying to sound keen. 'But I'll miss you.'

'And we'll miss you, big boy,' Mr Palau said, hugging him. 'But we'll be praying for you, and you'll be praying for us. God will keep us close.'

'Dear Mum and Dad,' Luis wrote, after a few days at boarding school. 'I miss you. I cried under the covers last night. Please let me come home.' Then he tore the page out of his pad and started again. 'Dear Mum and Dad, I'm sharing a dormitory with other boys. Some of them are nice, and I'll be friends with them. Please write and please send me a parcel.'

But he soon became used to boarding school and began to enjoy it. Every month he went home for a weekend. And that's how his life was for nearly three years.

'There's a message for you, Luis,' a teacher told the ten-year-old. 'Come to the phone, please.'

'Luis!' the voice said. 'It's your grandmother here. I've news for you. Your father is very ill, and we have to pray for him.'

The boy's head spun, and he felt suddenly sick. What if this was serious? What if his dad was really bad? What if he died?

'I'll get a train ticket for you,' his grandmother went on. 'And you'll go home tomorrow. Your mom wants you home.'

Luis didn't sleep much. He tossed and turned all night, thinking about his father.

The train journey home lasted three hours, but for Luis it lasted forever. 'Go faster ... go faster ...' he told the train. 'Get me home. I need to be home.'

The train eventually stopped at the station, and the boy jumped off and bolted home. Fear made him race to get there, and fear made him want not to be there at all.

'Why does God allow this?' he heard his aunt say, as he reached the door.

Then another voice. 'So many little children left without a father.'

Suddenly, it was as though Luis's heart wasn't there. There was just a cold space inside him. Racing past relatives who tried to grab him, the boy only stopped when he came to his father lying in bed, dead.

It was 1944. Luis was ten, but suddenly he was a man, a little man with a broken heart.

It was a very sad Luis Palau who went off some months later to start his secondary education at another boarding school. And his first year there wasn't very happy.

'I know Dad's gone to heaven,' he would say to comfort himself. 'But I don't know if that's where I'll go.' He was in a muddle, not knowing what to believe. In bed at night, he sometimes tried to put into words what was happening in his heart.

'I want to be a Christian, but I like things Christians shouldn't like. I want to go to heaven to be with Dad, but I'm not sure if I want to be different from my friends.' And from time to time he would fall asleep saying over and over to himself, 'I don't know what I want. I just don't know.'

At the end of his first year in secondary school, Luis went to a Christian camp, and there he discovered that Jesus was who he needed and who he wanted. When he went home from camp, it was with good news for his mother. He was a Christian.

'Luis!' she said, cuddling him close enough to take his breath away. 'Luis, I've not been as happy since your dad died.' Tears rolled down her cheeks, tears of pure joy. 'You've made me the happiest mum in Argentina!'

There were many ups and downs in Luis Palau's life after that, but God had a plan for him. And when God has a plan, he works it out exactly.

When Luis Palau was in his twenties, he was a preacher, but he realised how few people went to church compared to the vast numbers who didn't.

'Why can't we hire a sports stadium and fill it with people?' he asked his Christian friends.

'Because they would come for baseball, but not for a sermon,' one said.

Luis insisted. 'They go to hear Billy Graham ... hundreds of thousands of them. The more I think about it, the more I'm convinced that's how to reach people. They won't come to church, but they might come to a stadium.'

'That's all you talk about, Luis,' a friend complained. 'You're setting your sights too high.'

Luis Palau looked him in the eye. 'Are you telling me God's not able to do it?'

There was no answer to that.

'Give me a hug, son,' sighed Mrs Palau, as she and Luis said goodbye.

'I'm only going to America to Bible School,' he said, holding her close. 'It's not exactly outer space.'

And when he was in America, he married Pat, and they set out to serve God together for the rest of their lives.

In the years that followed, Luis's dream of huge crowds gathering to hear the gospel, began to come true. And since he started preaching, it's estimated that over six hundred thousand people have said, at Luis Palau crusades, that they would like to become Christians.

Palau didn't only speak to people at huge meetings, he also gave regular live broadcasts on television and radio. And it was on the morning, after one television broadcast, that three people arrived at the door.

'Will you come in?' Luis said to the woman and two burly men.

The woman entered. 'One of them will stand outside the door, the other at the gate,' she announced.

Before she sat down, she looked into all the corners of the room and checked behind a picture! Suddenly, she let fly with twenty minutes of abuse about Christianity.

Luis looked at her as she spoke, but he was praying rather than listening to the terrible things she was saying.

'How can I help you?' he asked eventually, when she stopped for breath.

The woman sank into her chair, suddenly sobbing fit to burst.

'You're the first person ever to offer to help me,' she wept.

Luis smiled gently. 'What's your name?'

'Why do you want my name?' barked the woman.

'Just because I don't know what to call you.'

She relaxed a little and gave her name. Immediately, Palau realised she was from a hugely wealthy family.

'I'm a Communist,' she said. 'I don't believe in God. But I'm going to tell you my story. I ran away from a religious family, then married and divorced three times. After I became a Communist leader, I organised student rebellions, demonstrations and uprisings.'

Nearly three hours later, she was still going strong, then, as suddenly as she started, she stopped.

'Supposing there's a God – and I'm not saying there is – would he have anything to do with a woman like me?' she asked, after a pause.

Luis opened his Bible.

'I don't believe the Bible,' she snapped.

'You're supposing there's a God,' Palau said quickly. 'Then let's suppose this is his Word. It says here that God doesn't remember the sins of those who trust in him.'

'But I've committed adultery. I've been married three times.'

Quietly, Luis repeated what he'd said. 'God doesn't remember their sins.'

'I've stabbed a comrade who later committed suicide.'

'God doesn't remember their sins.'

'I've led riots where people have been killed.'

'God doesn't remember their sins.'

Seventeen times, the woman told of terrible things she'd done. Seventeen times, Luis reminded her that God would not remember her sins if she trusted in him.

Finally, she sighed. 'Well,' she said. 'It would be a miracle if he could forgive me.'

And with that she left with her bodyguards.

Two months later, Luis was back in that woman's city in Ecuador and went to see her. When she opened the door, he was shocked at what he saw. She stood there, covered in bruises and with several teeth missing.

'What's happened?' he gasped.

The woman explained. 'I'm no longer an atheist,' she said. 'I believe in Jesus. But when I told my comrades and resigned from the Party, they tried to run me down with a jeep, then they attacked me and smashed my face until I was unconscious.'

There was a Communist revolution planned for some months after that woman's attack. On the morning the revolution was to start, the Party leader came to talk to her, just a few hours before it was planned that he would take over as ruler of Ecuador.

'Why did you become a Christian?' he asked.

She explained how Jesus had changed her life.

'I've been listening to that programme on the radio,' he said. 'And it almost has me believing in God.'

'Why don't you?' the woman urged. 'Why don't you think about it?'

And he did.

Later than morning, what was supposed to be a revolution, fizzled into chaos, and Ecuador was saved from a bloodbath.

Becoming a Christian means change. All who have become Christians, through Luis Palau's crusades, have had their hearts changed. Some have changed their lifestyles, others their aims and ambitions. And a few, like that woman, have changed the future of a country.

FACT FILE
Ecuador: Ecuador is a country of huge volcanoes, deep valleys, swampy coastlands and exotic wildlife.

There are humming-birds, brilliantly coloured finches, parrots, antbirds and flycatchers. Mountain animals include alpacas and llamas. Monkeys, tapirs, jaguars, pumas, caymans and boa constrictors live in the rainforests. Strange fish, like the plated catfish and the volcano fish, swim in the mountain rivers.

Keynote: Luis's heart was broken when his father died. His father was in heaven, and Luis wanted to be sure that he would get there too. Luis was worried about what his friends would think, but he knew that he needed Jesus in his life.

Learn from how Luis didn't just follow the crowd. Being a Christian would make him different from his friends, but he would have Jesus as his best friend - forever!

Think: God doesn't remember the sins of those who trust him.

We're not as forgiving when someone lets us down, are we? Sometimes we even enjoy reminding that person about where they went wrong. It makes us feel better about ourselves!

Ask God to change your heart, so that you bear no grudges and are willing to forgive.

 Prayer: Lord Jesus, thank you for reminding me that you don't remember the sins of those who trust in you.

Take away any bitterness in my heart towards people who have hurt me. Make me willing to forgive them instead. Amen.

QUIZ

How much can you remember
about the ten boys who
changed the world?

Try answering these questions
to find out ...

BROTHER ANDREW

1. What injury left Brother Andrew crippled?

2. What did Brother Andrew smuggle behind the Iron Curtain?

3. What wall came down when Communism ended in eastern Europe?

JOHN NEWTON

4. How did the mayors of harbour towns sometimes supply the press gangs with the men they needed?

5. John Newton left the navy and joined a merchant ship, *Pegasus*. What was that ship's cargo?

6. What job did John take on when he ended his life at sea?

BILLY GRAHAM

7. Billy Graham was born in the same year as the end of which war?

8. Where did Billy go when he was nineteen years old?

9. What subject divided America in the 1960s?

ERIC LIDDELL

10. Eric Liddell ran in the 1924 Olympics. Where were they held?

11. Eric's father had been a missionary in which country?

12. Eric won his gold medal in which race?

WILLIAM CAREY

13. What did William Carey do when he left school?

14. What did William Carey use as a globe?

15. William worked on an estate that produced a purple dye. What was the name of that dye?

DAVID LIVINGSTONE

16. Where did David Livingstone work as a boy?

17. David went as a missionary to Africa, but where had he originally applied to go?

18. Which newspaper sent Mr Stanley out to Africa to find Livingstone?

NICKY CRUZ

19. Where was Nicky Cruz from?

20. What was the name of the New York gang that Nicky joined?

21. Which member of Nicky's family became a Christian after Nicky preached in Puerto Rico for the first time?

ADONIRAM JUDSON

22. Where did Adoniram Judson go as a missionary?

23. What was hidden in Adoniram's pillow?

24. What was the name of the prison that Adoniram was taken to?

GEORGE MÜLLER

25. Where did George Müller hide the money he had stolen from his father?

26. George opened children's homes in which English city?

27. What was the name of the large, new children's home that was opened on the outskirts of the city?

LUIS PALAU

28. Where was Luis Palau from?

29. How old was Luis when his father died?

30. Through the woman who trusted in Jesus, after speaking to Luis, a Communist revolution was prevented in which country?

How well did you do?

Turn over to find out ...

ANSWERS

1. A bullet went through his ankle.
2. Bibles, Christian books and tracts.
3. The Berlin Wall.

4. They emptied the prisons.
5. Slaves.
6. A minister.

7. The First World War.
8. To Bible School.
9. The subject of race.

10. Paris.
11. China.
12. The 400 metres.

13. A shoemaker.
14. A stuffed leather ball.
15. Indigo.

16. A cotton mill.
17. China.
18. The New York Herald.

19. Puerto Rico.
20. The Mau Maus.
21. His mother.
22. Burma.
23. The New Testament in Burmese.
24. Death Prison.

25. In his shoe.
26. Bristol.
27. Ashley Down.

28. Argentina.
29. Ten years old.
30. Ecuador.

Start collecting this series now!

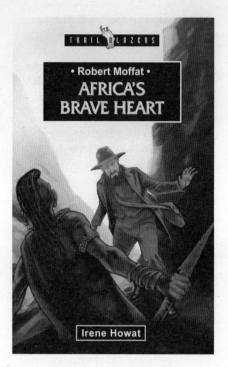

Robert Moffat, Africa's Brave Heart
by Irene Howat
ISBN 978-1-84550-715-2

The story of a Scottish minister and his wife in Africa – the precursors to David Livingstone. With a sword, a shovel, a Bible, and great courage, Robert used the skills he had learned growing up in a Scottish village to translate the Bible into Tswana and to share God's love with Africa.

OTHER BOOKS IN THE
TRAILBLAZERS SERIES

The Adventures Series

Have you ever wanted to visit the rainforest? Have you ever longed to sail down the Amazon river? Would you just love to go on Safari in Africa? Well these books can help you imagine that you are actually there.

Pioneer missionaries retell their amazing adventures and encounters with animals and nature. In the Amazon you will discover Tree Frogs, Piranha Fish and electric eels. In the Rainforest you will be amazed at the Armadillo and the Toucan. In the blistering heat of the African Savannah you will come across Lions and elephants and hyenas. And you will discover how God is at work in these amazing environments.

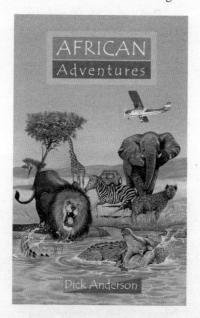

AFRICAN
Adventures

Dick Anderson

ISBN: 978-1-85792-807-5

African Adventures by Dick Anderson
ISBN 978-1-85792-807-5
Amazon Adventures by Horace Banner
ISBN 978-1-85792-440-4
Antarctic Adventures by Bartha Hill
ISBN 978-1-78191-135-8
Cambodian Adventures by Donna Vann
ISBN 978-1-84550-474-8
Emerald Isle Adventures by Robert Plant
ISBN 978-1-78191-136-5
Great Barrier Reef Adventures by Jim Cromarty
ISBN 978-1-84550-068-9
Himalayan Adventures by Penny Reeve
ISBN 978-1-84550-080-1
Kiwi Adventures by Bartha Hill
ISBN 978-1-84550-282-9
New York City Adventures by Donna Vann
ISBN 978-1-84550-546-2
Outback Adventures by Jim Cromarty
ISBN 978-1-85792-974-4
Pacific Adventures by Jim Cromarty
ISBN 978-1-84550-475-5
Rainforest Adventures by Horace Banner
ISBN 978-1-85792-627-9
Rocky Mountain Adventures by Betty Swinford
ISBN 978-1-85792-962-1
Scottish Highland Adventures by
Catherine Mackenzie
ISBN 978-1-84550-281-2
Wild West Adventures by Donna Vann
ISBN 978-1-84550-065-8

The Ivan Series

Ivan and the Informer

Ivan is at a secret Bible study but when he leaves the Secret Police are waiting outside. Find out how Ivan tackles the police and some false accusations.

ISBN 978-1-84550-134-1

Ivan and the Hidden Bible

Ivan and Katya are at the Lenin Collective Farm to help with the harvest. There is a hidden Bible on the farm. Can they find it?

ISBN 978-1-84550-133-4

Ivan and the Secret in the Suitcase

Ivan has been asked to take part in a dangerous mission. While on holiday Ivan has to have a secret meeting and pick up a suitcase. But what is in the suitcase? And will the Secret Police find out?

ISBN 978-1-84550-136-5

Ivan and the Daring Escape

Ivan's friend Pyotr has been kidnapped. How will Ivan help his friend to get back home? Find out how Ivan outwits the Secret Police once again!

ISBN 978-1-84550-132-7

Ivan and the Moscow Circus

Ivan and Katya meet Volodia, a trapeze artist with the Moscow Circus. Volodia's uncle is in prison for criticizing the communist government. Can anything be done to help him?

ISBN 978-1-84550-135-8

Ivan and the American Journey

Ivan has won a trip to America. But what will he do when he discovers there is a defector in their group? Should he help or should he just walk away?

ISBN 978-1-84550-131-0

CHRISTIAN FOCUS PUBLICATIONS

Christian Focus | Christian Heritage | CF4K | Mentor

Christian Focus Publications publishes books for adults and children under its four main imprints: Christian Focus, CF4K, Mentor and Christian Heritage. Our books reflect our conviction that God's Word is reliable and Jesus is the way to know him, and live for ever with him.

Our children's publication list includes a Sunday School curriculum that covers pre-school to early teens, and puzzle and activity books. We also publish personal and family devotional titles, biographies and inspirational stories that children will love.

If you are looking for quality Bible teaching for children then we have an excellent range of Bible stories and age-specific theological books.

From pre-school board books to teenage apologetics, we have it covered!

Find us at our web page: www.christianfocus.com

CF4•K
Because you're never too young to know Jesus

TEN BOYS WHO DIDN'T GIVE IN

LIGHT KEEPERS

Irene Howat

CF4·K

TEN BOYS WHO
DIDN'T GIVE IN

LIGHT KEEPERS

Irene Howat

CF4·K

For John, Samuel and Joseph

Copyright © 2004 Christian Focus Publications
Reprinted 2005, 2006, 2007, 2009, 2011, 2013, 2015,
twice in 2017, 2019, 2020
Paperback ISBN: 978-1-84550-035-1
epub ISBN: 978-1-84550-840-1
mobi ISBN: 978-1-84550-841-8

Published by Christian Focus Publications,
Geanies House, Fearn, Tain, Ross-shire,
IV20 1TW, Scotland, Great Britain.
www.christianfocus.com; email:info@christianfocus.com
Cover design by Alister MacInnes
Cover illustration by Elena Temporin,
Milan Illustrations Agency
Printed and bound in Turkey

All incidents retold in these stories are based on true situations.
Where specific information about childhood incidents has been
unobtainable the author has written these paragraphs using
other information concerning family life, hobbies, home life,
relationships freely available in other biographies.

*The front cover depicts Nate Saint as a young boy, in 1928, fishing with his
dog. It would be two years later before he took his first flight in an aeroplane,
but he would eventually work as a pilot for Mission Aviation Fellowship. Nate
Saint became one of the Auca Five - Missionaries who were murdered by the
very tribes people they had tried to help.*

Contents

Polycarp

The child had never felt so frightened in all of his life. And it wasn't helped one little bit that his mother was crying so hard, that it looked as though she would never stop.

'I don't want to go away and leave you,' said Polycarp. 'I want to stay here at home with you for ever.'

His mother tried to pull herself together. Wrapping her son in her arms, she whispered into his ear.

'I wish you could stay here with me too, my son. But slaves don't make decisions; they are told what to do. And we've been told that the time has now come for you to be sold to another master. It may be that he will be a kind man and not work you too hard.'

Recognising the effort his mother was making, young Polycarp did the same. He wiped the tears from his cheeks, undid himself from his mother's arms, and stood as tall and straight as he could.

'I'll work hard,' he said. 'And even if my new master is not a kind man, I'll work so hard that he'll come to respect me. When I'm grown up, he'll maybe put me in charge of all his slaves, and I promise I'll be good to them if he does.'

Smiling through her tears, the woman nodded.

'I know you will, my son. I know you will.'

For the last time, she sat by his mat in the darkness of their poor home and told the boy a story before he went to sleep.

'This is the story of a slave family,' she began, 'a family just like our own. They had a son about your age whom their master didn't want to keep. So, he was taken to the slave market where he stood with all the other child slaves waiting to be bought by new masters. Strange men came and looked at them, felt their arm and leg muscles and looked to see if their eyes were clear and if they were free from obvious diseases. Eventually, a man approached the boy. He looked him up and down, turned him round, asked his age and what he was good at. Then the man walked away. The boy was just beginning to breathe normally again when the man reappeared with the market official.

"I'll take that one," the man said.

The official cut the rope that bound the boy to his neighbours on either side, though he left his hands tied together. Not knowing what lay before him, and whether he would ever see his parents again, the boy slave went with his new master into his new life, determined to make the very best of it.'

Polycarp knew his mother was preparing him for what was to come.

'Did the boy ever see his parents again?' he asked quietly.

His mother smiled sadly. 'I don't know the end of the story, my son,' she said. 'I only know that when the boy went to his new master, he went bravely.'

Kissing him goodnight for the very last time, the woman wrapped herself in her sadness and curled up tight on her mat on the floor.

Polycarp had no sleep at all that night, not a single wink. 'Is that how I'll be sold?' he wondered. Then a shudder ran right through his thin body. 'Will I be tied up in the slave market, or has the master already arranged where I'll be going? Will I ever see Dad and Mum again?' The whole night was full of questions and shudders that seemed to shake his whole world, then more and yet more questions. In the first light of dawn, he looked across the room at his mother, and his heart gave such a lurch he thought he was going to be sick. Then, just as he thought he could be no more miserable, his mother stirred. It was time she was up and at work. Pretending to be asleep, Polycarp put a hand over his eyes so that he could watch what she was doing between his fingers. Before she left to begin her day's work, the poor soul knelt beside her son, laid her hand on his shoulder, and whispered near his ear, 'Be brave, my son. And I will be brave for you.'

Later that morning, Polycarp discovered that he had a mistress rather than a master, a mistress named Calisto. New things seemed to come at him from all sides, so much so that by evening he felt as though he'd got up in a rush in the morning and put his head on backwards! And when bedtime came, it seemed like he'd closed the door of one world and opened the door of another, and somehow it didn't seem quite as scary as he thought it would be. The boy hoped his mother knew where he was and what kind of home he'd gone into.

'She won't worry so much if she knows,' thought Polycarp.

And that was certainly true, though we don't know whether his family knew or not.

The years that followed were very different from the ones that had gone before. As a little boy, when Polycarp's master clapped his hands, everyone jumped to attention and did exactly what they were ordered. Nobody ever asked a slave to do things; they gave orders that had to be obeyed. He had had enough food, but only just. And the cloth of his tunic was the cheapest in town, and it was covered in darns and patches. His bed had been a mat on the floor, and the nearest he ever got to a book was when he had to carry one to his master. As he settled down in Calisto's home, the boy thought back to his 'old days'.

One night, he lay in bed thinking over all the changes that had come about in his life.

'There's the bed to start with,' Polycarp smiled. 'I don't sleep on the floor now because I've got my own straw mattress. There are no patches on my tunics. Then he grinned. It was tunics, not tunic. He had three, one to wear and two to change with. No wonder they didn't wear through and need patching! 'And what would Mum say if she knew I was learning to read and write?' The truth of it was that Calisto was bringing Polycarp up as her son, not as a slave in her household. Eventually the day came when the boy realised that servants were looking after his needs rather than him being a servant. He remembered his promise to his mother and was good to them.

We don't know how it happened, but we do know that by the time Polycarp was a man he had come to faith in the Lord Jesus Christ. That was the biggest blessing in his life, but there was another blessing too. When Calisto died, she left Polycarp everything she owned! The little slave boy had become a wealthy and educated man in the ancient town of Smyrna. (Smyrna is now known as Izmir, and it is on the west coast of Turkey.)

Polycarp's money didn't make him self-centred; instead he used it to help spread the good news about Jesus Christ.

'Sometimes I wish I'd been born a hundred years ago,' he thought to himself, 'for then I might have seen Jesus for myself. But old John knew him well, and I can trust all he has told me about the Master.'

As he thought about the word 'Master', an idea flashed through Polycarp's mind.

'The night before I was sold, I promised Mum that I'd be a good slave to my new master. Little did I know that, one day, the best of all masters would call me into his service, and that I'd become a willing slave of the Lord God Almighty. He has called me to minister to his people here in Smyrna, and I'll do it to the very best of my ability.'

Many years later, the persecution of Christians became the sport of the day. Those who trusted in Jesus had been persecuted to a greater or lesser degree, ever since the Lord had risen from the dead, but it developed into a fine art. Polycarp watched as member after member of the church was targeted, and he knew that his day would probably come before long.

'I'm an old man anyway,' he thought. 'I'd rather they took me and left young energetic men to continue the Lord's work.'

Then one night, Polycarp had a dream, a dream he felt sure would come true. And in his dream he was burnt at the stake for being a Christian. He had just told his friends about his dream, when news spread that Roman soldiers were on the hunt for old Polycarp.

'Come away with us,' some church members insisted, as they hustled him off to a village near the town. 'We'll keep you safe.'

But they had no sooner arrived, than their bishop told them that he wasn't going to run away and hide, that he would face up to whatever was to happen to him.

Just three days after his dream, soldiers appeared in the village to which he'd been taken. Far from hiding away from them, the old man strode out to meet them and invited them in for a meal! Taken by surprise – and hungry as soldiers always are – they accepted the invitation and went in.

'May I pray while you eat?' Polycarp asked his captors.

They saw no harm in that, and for the next two hours the bishop prayed aloud to his Father in heaven. Some of the soldiers were so impressed by what he said in his prayer that they were uncomfortable about arresting him after all ... not that their feelings made any difference to their orders. But they did try to make things easier for him.

'Just do what they say,' the kinder soldiers told him, when they arrived back in the city and put Polycarp into a chariot. 'Just agree that Caesar is god and offer a sacrifice to him. There's no harm in that, and if you do it, they'll release you and that will be an end of it.'

'I will not do what you want me to do,' the old man said firmly, much to the annoyance of his captors.

'I thought this one would be a walkover,' one soldier said to another.

His colleague shook his head. 'The old ones can be obstinate,' he muttered.

Some time later, in a fit of mass fury, the crowd that had gathered to watch the spectacle threw Polycarp from the chariot. He landed on his side and badly injured his thigh. Seeing him lying there seemed to set the bloodthirsty crowd alight, and they screamed for his execution.

'You're an old man,' one of the judges said, in an effort to help. 'Just say you're sorry and deny that you believe in Jesus.'

'Eighty and six years have I now served Christ, and he has never done me the least wrong,' Polycarp told him. 'How then can I blaspheme my King and my Saviour?'

Again the judges tried to make him change his mind, but the old man's mind was not for changing.

That was it. Three times the judge called out to the crowd what Polycarp's crime was.

'He is a Christian, the leader of the Christians here, and he's an enemy of our gods. He has taught many people that they should not sacrifice to our gods or worship them.'

Sentence was passed.

'Take him to the stake and burn him alive.'

Polycarp nodded.

'So my dream is to come true after all,' he thought.

The old man was led away to be burned. But when the soldiers prepared to secure him to the stake before lighting the fire, he told them not to bother. 'Let me alone as I am,' he said. 'God will give me courage to stay in the fire. I won't move away.'

It was then that Polycarp stopped speaking to men and began speaking to God. Looking up to the heavens, he prayed aloud, thanking his heavenly Father for the privilege of being a martyr for Jesus Christ. And when he had finished praying, the executioner lit the fire.

When the Apostle John wrote the book of Revelation, God gave him these words: 'Be faithful to death, and I will give you a crown of life.' Seventy years after John wrote these words, Polycarp, who as a young man is said to have met the Apostle John, was faithful to death. And when he died and went to heaven, God kept his promise and gave him a crown of life.

Polycarp died not much more that 100 years after Jesus' death, which is a very long time ago. But papers from that time still exist, including some letters written by Polycarp himself, one written to him by another famous Christian martyr, and a brief account of his life written shortly after he died.

Fact File

Slavery: At the time that Polycarp lived in Smyrna, Turkey was known as the Province of Asia and was part of the Roman Empire. Slavery was a big part of the Roman economy, and the Romans viewed their slaves very differently from the way that we view people today. In the eyes of the law, slaves were not really people. They did not own anything themselves. All that they had was really owned by their master. In earlier times, the owner had the power of life and death over his slaves, although public authorities did more to control this by the time that Polycarp died.

Keynote: Polycarp was very scared about being sold to a new owner and moving away from his mum and dad. It meant moving to a new place and leaving everyone he had ever known. However, God used it to place him with a much kinder master and to give him the chance to hear about Jesus. God is still the same. He can use situations that seem very scary, to work for our good and to give us more opportunity to serve him.

Think: Polycarp did not fight with the Roman soldiers when they came to arrest him. He followed Jesus' instruction to turn the other cheek instead (Matthew 5:39). This did not mean that Polycarp was a coward or ready to back down. He showed courage and loyalty, but not by fighting. Can you think of any situation where you can turn the other cheek and follow Jesus' and Polycarp's examples?

 Prayer: Lord Jesus, thank you for caring for us and being with us wherever we are. Please help me to trust you in every situation and to be brave enough not to use violence. Amen.

Alban

Two boys climbed the earth bank that surrounded their town, then lowered themselves into the ditch beyond it.

'If I was leading an invasion, I'd bring my troops up the twenty miles from Londinium and then have them hide overnight, just a few miles south-west of Verulamium,' said Alban. 'Hiding them would give them time to regain their strength.'

'What would you do then?' asked his friend.

'I'd use diversionary tactics,' Alban explained. 'Like this.'

With a short stick the ten-year-old drew his plans on the summer-dry earth.

'See, here's the town with its earth bank surrounding it, and the deep ditch all round the outside of that. Away down there is Londinium.' (A long time later, Londinium changed its name to London).

The younger boy watched with interest as Alban worked it all out on the ground.

'Here is the river north-east of Verulamium. A small detachment of soldiers would leave the others resting, go due west till they reached the river where they would commandeer boats, making sure they tied up the people they'd taken them from, so that no one could raise the alarm. Then they'd row up river, silently in the darkness, until they were north-east of the town.'

'Why would you want most of your troops south-west of Verulamium and a detachment right at the opposite side of the town?'

Alban sat back on his heels.

'That's the trick,' he grinned. 'Before dawn broke, the detachment would act as though they were invading from the north-east, making as much noise and causing as much chaos as possible. The townsmen would rush to defend the town. And while they were all away on that wild goose chase, the main body of men would storm Verulamium from the south-west. They'd be down the ditch, up over the earth bank and in the town, before anyone knew what had happened.'

'That's a great plan!' the other boy laughed.

Alban looked serious. 'It could happen,' he said. 'If I were in charge of the Romans, I'd build a stone wall on top of the earth bank all the way round the city. It would be much safer then.'

'Maybe they'll think of that one day,' laughed his friend. 'And if they don't, you could study town planning and draw up the design for them.'

'I don't know if I'll be in Verulamium when I grow up,' Alban told his pal, as they walked. 'Father says that he's going to take me on his travels ... and I might not come back.'

'Where are you going?' the other boy asked.

'We're going to the most exciting place in the world,' Alban laughed. 'In fact we're going right to the centre of the world!'

Alban's friend still couldn't guess.

'Father and I are going to reverse the Roman invasion. Instead of going from Rome to Verulamium, we're going to go from Verulamium to Rome.'

'Rome!' whispered the other lad. 'Will you go to see fights in the Colosseum, and chariots racing in the Circus Maximus? I heard one of the Roman soldiers say that, when it was built, the Circus Maximus could hold a quarter of a million people!' The boy looked at Alban and laughed. 'I suspect that if you go with your father, he's more likely to take you to the Roman Forum.'

'I think we'll do both,' said Alban. 'And if Dad spends too much time at the Roman Forum on business or listening to the politicians or worshipping in the temples, I'll remind him about the chariot races and suggest we head for the Circus Maximus.'

Alban did go to Rome. We don't know what he did there, but he most likely saw all the places he and his friend had talked about, and many more besides. Imagine him standing under the Trajan Column, and straining his head back as far as it would go to see the top. And think of him walking along the Via Sacra (the Sacred Way) to the temples where he and his father would worship the Roman gods. Perhaps he made an offering to the god Saturn in one of the most ancient temples in the whole of Rome for, like most people at the time of the Roman Empire, Alban and his family worshipped the Roman gods.

He was no sooner home from his travels when Alban met his old friend in Verulamium.

'I heard you were back,' the other lad said, 'and I was hoping to meet you. I'm really looking forward to hearing about your time in Rome.'

More than willing to talk on every aspect of the subject, Alban described fights in the Colosseum and chariot races in the Circus Maximus, and even the business and politics of the Roman Forum.

But his young friend could hardly wait for the story to finish.

'What do you think of Christians being thrown to the lions in the Colosseum?' he asked, hoping for some gory stories told in great detail.

Alban shook his head. 'I've met Christians,' he said, 'and they believe some very strange things. But I've never met one who seemed to do anything that deserved the death sentence.' The teenager shuddered. 'And certainly not to be killed by wild animals just to entertain Emperor Septimus Severus and the thousands of others who pay to get in.'

'So why are they thrown to the lions?' asked his friend.

'That's a great puzzle to me,' Alban replied. 'Because it's a terrible way to die.'

Alban grew up to be a fine young man. Because his family was wealthy, he was well known in Verulamium. But he was also respected for his own sake because he was kind and helpful. People who were in trouble felt able to go to Alban for help, even Christians. And there came a time in Verulamium when Christians certainly did need help, because Septimus Severus decided that Christians in Britain, as well as in Rome, should die if they would not give up their faith in the Lord Jesus Christ.

'Master,' Alban's servant said urgently, 'a man has arrived asking for your help. He says he's about to be arrested and killed.'

'Bring him to me immediately,' said Alban.

The servant was back within minutes, bringing with him an elderly man called Amphibalus.

'How can I help you?' Alban asked.

'My lord,' said Amphibalus, 'the Emperor's soldiers are searching for me.'

'Why?' asked the puzzled Alban, trying to imagine what terrible crime the old man could have committed.

'They are just following their orders,' Amphibalus explained. 'The Emperor Septimus Severus says that Christians should die.'

'Have you done wrong?' the young man asked, wanting to be quite sure.

'I have not broken the law of Rome,' said Amphibalus. 'My crime is that I am a Christian.'

'And how can I help you?'

'Hide me,' pleaded the old man. He looked round himself before saying, 'There is plenty of room here to hide me.'

'Fear nothing,' said Alban. 'I have heard a great deal about Christians, but nothing that is bad. You will be safe here.' And for a time he was, because the Roman soldiers didn't think to search a heathen's home to find a runaway Christian!

Every day that Amphibalus hid in Alban's house was a day of discovery for the young man. His fugitive told him the story of Jesus. Alban listened with interest. He knew about the Druid religion, and he knew about the Roman gods, but none were at all like Jesus.

'Tell me more,' Alban asked each day.

And Amphibalus told him more. He spoke of Jesus' birth in Bethlehem, of his teaching and stories. The young man was amazed at Jesus' miracles, and terribly saddened at the thought of his crucifixion.

'Three days after Jesus was crucified,' Amphibalus said one day, 'Jesus rose from the dead. His body was not in the tomb when his friends went to look for it.'

'You can imagine the search the Romans mounted for Jesus,' said the old man. 'It makes their search for me look like a children's game.'

'And did they find his body?' asked Alban.

'No, of course they didn't,' Amphibalus insisted. 'There was no body because Jesus Christ had risen from the dead; his spirit had returned to his body. He was not dead. He was gloriously alive ... and he still is.'

Alban was amazed and thrilled at what the old man was saying.

'Master!' said Alban's servant. 'They're here! The Roman soldiers have discovered about Amphibalus, and they've come to take him away.'

'My son,' said the old man. 'I must go now for I am about to die.'

'No,' Alban whispered, 'I think I can still save you.'

Amphibalus looked puzzled.

'Quickly, give me your robe,' urged Alban, as he took off his fine robe.

The two men exchanged robes, and stood looking at each other. Alban was wearing a simple, rough robe that was a little short for him, and Amphibalus had on a grand robe that was just a little too long for him.

'Take this,' whispered Alban.

Amphibalus looked down and saw that his young friend had pressed a purse of money into his hand.

'My servant will take you to safety by back roads, and I'll not give you away to the soldiers. Make the most of the time. Hurry now! And God go with you. But before you go,' said Alban, 'ask God to bless me.'

Kneeling down, Alban prayed with Amphibalus as the old man asked God to bless him.

'May God reward you for your kindness,' the Christian prayed. 'And may he lead you in the true way of Christ.'

Alban wrapped Amphibalus's robe around him, hitched the hood up over his head, and waited. The soldiers rushed into the room, saw a man dressed in the old Christian's clothes, and it never occurred to them to look under the hood to check who was there.

'Take him to the Governor!' the officer said, when the prisoner's wrists were tied together.

As he was marched along the roads of Verulamium, Alban might have detected an air of excitement in the soldiers who had captured him. The Emperor Septimus Severus had commanded that Christians in Britain should be killed, and now at last they had caught one and would carry out his command. That couldn't do their chances of promotion any harm!

Still with his hood round his head, the prisoner was led to the Roman Governor of Verulamium who was offering a sacrifice to one of his gods. Alban's wrists were loosened, and he raised his hand and pulled the hood off his head.

'What!' exclaimed the officer. 'That's not the Christian!'

'Get these soldiers out of here and punish them severely!' ordered the Governor, before turning his rage on Alban.

'How dare you help a Christian to escape!' he stormed. 'You know the Emperor's orders as well as I do. The Christian rebels have to be hunted out and killed if they won't give up their new beliefs!'

Alban stood with his head held high.

'Tell me where Amphibalus is hiding,' demanded the Governor. 'Then sacrifice to the gods to show them how sorry you are for what you've done.'

There was a minute of silence before Alban answered.

'I can do neither of these things,' he said quietly, but very firmly.

'Who do you think you are to defy me? What is your name?'

'My name is Alban.'

'Then, Alban,' said the Governor, trying to control himself, 'if you want the gods to forgive you, I suggest that you repent and make your sacrifices to them right away.'

'I cannot do that,' Alban told the official. 'I no longer believe in these gods. They teach people to be cruel and wicked. Amphibalus is the opposite. He is good and gentle, yet these gods tell the Emperor that he should be tortured and killed. I would rather believe in the God of Amphibalus. His teaching is that we love one another.'

In a fury, the Governor had Alban taken away, a condemned man.

Very soon afterwards, Alban, who had only been a Christian since his discussions with Amphibalus, was led out to a hillside to be executed. The news about what was to happen spread throughout Verulamium, and a great crowd gathered. Most were there because they were sorry that such a popular young man should be put to death for being such a fool. Although Alban was given every opportunity to deny his faith in Jesus, he did nothing of the sort. Just before he died, a remarkable thing happened. The soldier, whose job it was to behead him, wouldn't do it because he said that Alban was a good man.

'I would rather die than kill him,' the soldier bravely told his captain.

And he did. The captain first beheaded Alban, then he beheaded the soldier too.

Alban, who had been a Christian for just a few days, was not only the first martyr in Verulamium, he was the first Christian to die in Britain because he would not deny his faith in the Lord Jesus. Alban died for Jesus around 200 years after Jesus died on the cross for Alban, and for everyone else whose faith is in the Saviour.

Many years after Alban lived and died, his home town of Verulamium changed its name to St Albans. And that's what it's known as today.

Fact File

Rome and Christianity: Roman emperors tended to be suspicious of Christians, but some were a lot fiercer than others. Perhaps the most notable was the Emperor Nero, who blamed Christians for a huge fire which nearly destroyed Rome and which some people believe he was responsible for himself. However, the persecution did not stop lots of people becoming Christians. By AD 313 the Roman Empire had split in two, and that year the two emperors, Constantine and Licinius agreed to stop persecuting the Christians.

Keynote: Amphibalus escaped because Alban took his place. We have all sinned, and this means that we deserve to be punished by God. However, Jesus has come to take our place so that we do not have to bear that punishment, if we put our trust in him.

Think: Alban wanted Amphibalus to pray for him because he could see that praying to God was not like praying to the Roman or Druid gods. Prayer to God really makes a difference because he has promised to hear us when we pray in Jesus' name. Think about who you could help by praying for them.

 Prayer: Lord Jesus, thank you for loving us so much that you came to take the punishment that we deserve. Help me to trust in you, so that I can have a special relationship with you and so that I can pray for those in need. Amen.

Sir John Oldcastle

'Left! Right! Left! Right!' said John, as he and his friend marched through Almeley in Herefordshire.

'Stop before the crossroads!' ordered his friend Walter. 'And dive for cover in case enemy forces are marching in from Leominster.'

The boys marched nearly to the crossroads that marked the centre of the village. Then they threw themselves down behind a hedge, before squirming right up to the junction, to check that the road in both directions was free of enemy action.

'All clear! Stand to attention!' barked John.

Walter scrambled to his feet.

'Quick march!'

The boys continued in step – at least they were in step after John double-hopped on his left foot to get into step with Walter.

'Now troops, straight to the castle!' yelled John. 'And duck under cover before you come to the ditch.'

The boys were as serious as though they were real soldiers. As soon as they neared the ditch that surrounded the castle mound, they were both on the ground squirming forward under cover of gorse bushes.

'We're nearly there,' Walter whispered. 'Another twenty feet and we'll be safe.'

Keeping as low to the ground as possible, and making no sound at all, other than the rustling of branches and the popping of gorse seedpods they disturbed along the way, they eventually reached their den, slid down the grassy slope into it and lay silently for a minute till they could be sure they'd not been followed.

'So what's the big secret?' Walter asked.

John had come for him earlier and had refused to explain the need for secrecy until they were in their den and absolutely sure they were alone.

'I heard my father talking to soldiers last night,' the boy whispered. 'He said that there was trouble in the Black Mountains, and that we'd to watch out for it spreading down in our direction.'

'What kind of trouble?' his friend wanted to know.

'Big trouble,' John explained. 'I don't know any more than that. But if it's from that direction, it could be more raids across the Welsh border. I got the impression that it was more serious than that. I think we should make plans to do undercover surveillance, and, if we see anything unusual, I can tell Dad.'

'What's surveillance?' asked Walter.

John put on an intelligent expression, much like his tutor did when he was asked a question to which he knew the answer.

'It's what soldiers do when they go spying on the enemy. From their hiding-places they spy out the enemy and take the information they gather to their commanding officer, who decides what to do about it.'

But as there didn't seem to be any urgent surveillance to be done, the two boys discussed soldiering in general, and John's future plans in particular.

'Are you really going to be a full-time soldier?' Walter asked. 'I thought your father might want you to do something else, and that's why he was having you educated.'

'Soldiers need an education too,' insisted John. 'And that's what I'm going to be. I've never wanted to do anything else. What about you?'

Walter grinned. 'I'll be a soldier if the king asks your father to raise an army from around these parts, but in between wars I'll be a miller like Dad.'

'The world needs millers as well as soldiers,' John laughed. 'When I come back from the wars, I'll enjoy bread made from flour you've milled.'

John did become a professional soldier, and a good one too. He fought in France and made such an impression on his officers that he was given a knighthood. Enter SIR John Oldcastle! And in 1406 he was awarded a pension of £40 a year – a fortune in those days. Back from the army, John had time for other interests. One thing especially interested him, and he discussed this with his friend Walter, as they walked from his home to the mill one day.

Taking a small sheet of paper from his pocket, John held it out to Walter.

'Look at that,' he said, with almost a sense of reverence in his voice.

'What is it?' asked Walter.

John explained that it was paper, paper with writing on it.

'I've never seen paper before,' his friend said. 'Dad says that by the beginning of next century, most homes will have paper in them. But I've never seen any before.'

'We have books at home, but this paper's rather special.'

'You've only got books because your dad's Sir Richard Oldcastle of Almeley. My dad's just a miller. In any case, why's this bit special?'

'Do you want to know what the writing says?' John asked, exasperated that Walter hadn't asked. 'I'll read it to you.'

Walter held the scrap of paper in his hand as carefully as he might have held a bird's egg. John leant over his shoulder, cleared his throat, and read.

'And Jhesus, seynge the puple, wente vp in to an hil; and whanne he was set, hise disciplis camen to hym.

And he openyde his mouth, and tauyte hem, and seide,

Blessed ben pore men in spirit, for the kyngdom of heuenes is herne.

Blessid ben mylde men, for thei schulen welde the erthe.

Blessid ben thei that mornen, for thei schulen be coumfortid.

Blessid ben thei that hungren and thristen riytwisnesse, for thei schulen be fulfillid.

Blessid ben merciful men, for thei schulen gete merci.

Blessid ben thei that ben of clene herte, for thei schulen se God.

Blessid ben pesible men, for thei schulen be clepid Goddis children.

Blessid ben thei that suffren persecusioun for riytfulnesse, for the kingdam of heuenes is herne.'

(Matthew 5:1-10)

'That's from the Bible,' explained John.

'You can read Latin and say the words in English at the same time!' Walter gasped. He'd no idea his friend was so well educated.

'No,' John said. 'That's not written in Latin. The words Jesus said are written in English. They're from Mr Wycliffe's translation of the Bible into English.'

Walter's face drained of its colour.

'Where did you get that?' he whispered, though there wasn't anyone within a quarter of a mile.

John shrugged. 'It's best you don't know. What you don't know, you can't tell, even if you're tortured.'

Handing the paper back to his friend, Walter announced he'd have to go.

'I'm not sure when I'll be able to see you again. And you be careful who you show that to.'

John watched his friend disappearing. He bit his lip in thought.

'Maybe I shouldn't have shown him it,' he thought. 'Maybe that was a stupid thing to do.'

Mr John Wycliffe and his friends translated the whole Bible verse by verse into English. Printing presses had not been invented, and the whole thing was done by hand. As each section was translated, it was copied, again by hand, then the copies were copied, then the copies of the copies were copied, then the copies of the copies of the copies were copied! You get the idea? The next time Walter had the courage to meet his friend, this was their topic of conversation.

'Did you tell anyone what I showed you?' John asked.

Walter shook his head. 'But I asked my dad about that Mr Wycliffe. He said the man is a menace!'

'What else did he say?' his friend asked quietly.

'He said that the priests are angry that Mr Wycliffe translated the Bible into English, because they don't want ordinary people to read it. Dad says that if ordinary people read the Bible, we won't need priests, and they'd all be out of a job!'

John smiled at the thought. 'Did your dad tell you that what the priests teach is often not in the Bible at all? And the priests are scared that people will read the Bible for themselves and discover that.'

'No,' Walter said. 'Is that true?'

Nodding his head, John gave an example.

'The priests say that, when we die, we go to Purgatory, don't they?'

His friend shivered at the thought. 'And we will only get out of there if those who are still alive pray for our souls and give money to the priests.'

'Well,' John said triumphantly. 'That's not in the Bible. Mr Wycliffe says that the Bible teaches that everyone who believes in the Lord Jesus Christ and asks him to forgive their sins, goes to heaven. There's no such place as Purgatory!'

For a minute, Walter's face lit up, then he looked really scared.

'I wish that was true,' he said, 'for I'm scared stiff of Purgatory. What if there's nobody left to pray for me after I die? I'll end up being there forever.'

'But there's no such place,' John insisted. 'Mr Wycliffe and his friends finished their translation work twenty years ago. Now we can all read the Bible and discover for ourselves if what the Church teaches is true or not.'

Walter shook his head. 'No way,' he said. 'If the priests found out, there'd be trouble. In any case, I can't read.'

John Oldcastle studied Mr Wycliffe's Bible and knew in his heart it was true. He became a Christian and was baptised in a stream near his home. He married Joan in 1408, and, through her, he inherited the title Lord Cobham. It wasn't long before his name changed again, but not everyone agreed with the new one. John was known among Christians as Good Lord Cobham, though there were many who thought he was far from good, mostly priests and followers of the Roman Church. Those who called him Good Lord Cobham were Lollards, men like John Wycliffe, who read the Bible for themselves and knew the church of their day was in error.

'What a busy house we have,' Joan laughed, 'if there's not someone coming, someone has just left.'

John looked at his wife and smiled. 'You're very patient with all our visitors. And it's part of a wonderful work.'

'Tell me exactly what we're involved in,' she said. 'I'm sure there are things going on that I don't really understand.'

It was evening, the fire was blazing in the huge fireplace, and the candles were dancing in their holders. John Oldcastle was relaxed and happy, especially as his wife had recently had a little boy whom they'd called Henry.

'We're so privileged,' he said. 'We have a big house and no money worries. And we have the glorious gospel of Jesus Christ to give us hope, for time and for eternity.'

Joan looked at her little boy and hoped that, one day, he too would be a Christian.

'There are many in England and Wales who are still being misled by Romanist priests. They are imprisoned by the fact they don't have access to the Bible, in which they can find the truth that would set them free. That's why I'm happy that our home is used for travelling preachers of the truth, and for those who want to come to study the Bible here.'

'How safe is what we're doing?' Joan asked.

'We're safe as long as Henry IV is on the throne, as we've been friends since he was Prince of Wales. How safe we'll be if he dies, I really don't know.'

In 1413 that's just what happened. Henry IV died, and his son, Henry V, became king. The Roman Church leaders, who knew perfectly well what John was doing, decided that the time had come to act, even if they had to lie to have him arrested.

'I'm charged with what?' Sir John asked the soldiers who came to arrest him.

'You're charged with being involved in an illegal uprising,' he was told.

Before his friends could get organised to help him, John was locked up in the Tower of London. As he looked out of the window to the river Thames and thought of the Welsh hills, he made plans to get back there. Even when they were boys, Walter was impressed by his friend's ability to make military plans; he was even more impressed by his escape from the Tower of London when he heard about it. All John's training stood him in good stead for travelling in secret, and he was soon reunited with his wife and baby son. The authorities were furious at what had happened, and a warrant was put out for his arrest.

It was three years before the authorities caught up with John again, and when they did, they made sure he could not escape from the Tower a second time. In December 1417, Good Lord Cobham was taken before Parliament where he was found guilty of heresy and treason.

'What will happen to him now?' his friends asked each other.

And they watched as he was put on to a wooden hurdle and drawn through the streets of London to St Giles Fields. What happened to him there was unspeakable; sufficient is it to say that he was horribly tortured before being burned to death.

'He thought his money would save him,' the priests said to one another. 'But we got him in the end.'

John was a wealthy man, but his greatest treasure of all was not on earth but in heaven. When he died and went there, Jesus welcomed him home.

The verses John read from the Bible are exactly as they were written in Mr Wycliffe's translation. And as Mr Wycliffe wanted people to be able to read the Bible in the language they normally used, we must assume that's how Sir John Oldcastle spoke.

FACT FILE

Translations of the Bible: The translation that John showed his friend was not a translation from the original languages. Instead, it was translated from a Latin version of the Bible called the Vulgate. This translation was originally meant for ordinary people. It was called the 'Vulgate' because it was written in the common language. (At that time the word vulgar meant common rather than rude). By the 1400s, however, very few people could read Latin so the Vulgate was not doing its job, and a translation into English was needed. In later years, translations made directly from the original languages appeared.

Keynote: Walter was afraid of Purgatory because the priests had told him about it. He was too scared to read the Bible for himself to find that it said nothing about Purgatory. If we do not look at the Bible for ourselves, we can be very easily misled because we can't check if things are right or not. Now we all have an opportunity to read the Bible without fear of persecution. But if we don't take it, we will be just the same as Walter was.

Think: When John spoke to his wife, he was very thankful for all the good things that God had given him. The thing that he was most grateful for was having heard the gospel so that he could believe in Jesus. Because he wanted to make sure that others could do the same, he helped preachers even when it put him in danger. Think of all of the good things that you have been given and how you can use them to serve God and to help others.

 Prayer: Lord Jesus, thank you for letting me hear about all that you have done. Please help me to listen carefully when I am taught about you, and to read the Bible for myself. Please bless those people who are still translating the Bible into many languages around the world. Amen.

Thomas Cranmer

Thomas was the middle of the three boys standing on the bridge over the river, that ran through the small village of Aslacton. Each was holding a beech leaf as far over the side of the bridge as he could, and all were waiting for their mother to give the word.

'Go!' she said, and laughed as the boys dropped their leaves into the river then dashed to the other side of the bridge to see which one came through first.

'Mine doesn't have a stalk!' said Thomas.

But as the first leaf floated through – minus its stalk – his brothers said in unison, 'Neither does mine!'

Mrs Cranmer laughed. 'In that case, a very funny thing happened midstream, as the two leaves that are floating through now both have stalks on them. It seems that there's mischief going on under the bridge, because someone is sitting under there sticking stalks on to leaves that have lost theirs, just to confuse the game.'

Thomas's brothers looked a little shamefaced.

'Let's play again,' said one.

'Only if you work out which is which beforehand,' Mrs Cranmer suggested.

'Mine doesn't have a stalk,' Thomas pointed out.

'One side of mine is yellow,' one brother said.

'And mine has a nick out of it,' announced the other.

The game was played once again, and Thomas's stalkless leaf won fair and square.

'The three of you are so competitive,' complained Mrs Cranmer, as they walked the short distance from the bridge to their home. 'If you're out with your bows and arrows, you've always got to be better than each other, and it's the same when you're riding the horses. Sometimes I wake up in the night dreaming that you're all shouting at each other, "I won! I won!"'

'But I did win this time,' laughed Thomas.

Mrs Cranmer shook her head. 'I don't know what I'll do with you all, if it's not knocking your heads together to put some sense into them!'

The boys realised that they'd wound their mother up quite enough for one day, and that if they went much further they might find themselves doing some horrible chores when they got home.

'Is Squire Cranmer at home?' a man asked, as they reached their house door.

'I don't rightly know,' said Mrs Cranmer, 'I'm just coming home myself. Wait for a minute and I'll see.'

Bustling into the house, she left the boys to chat to the man.

'Have you come far?' asked Thomas. 'You don't sound as though you come from Nottinghamshire.'

'No, young sir,' the man replied. 'I've come from over the English Channel. My master sent me to Nottingham and said that I'd to visit Squire Cranmer before my return.'

Thomas' father came rushing out of the door to see who the stranger was. One look from their father and the boys knew that they'd best be off and leave the men in peace. That was no hardship as they went round the back of the house to their shooting range, set up a target and had a competition with their longbows. But the visitor was no sooner away than all three boys tumbled into the house to find out all they could about him.

'Who was that?' they asked their father, all at once.

Mr Cranmer was smiling. 'He works for a distant relation of ours.'

'But I thought he was French,' said the oldest boy. 'He said he'd come from over the English Channel.'

'So did your many-times-great-grandfather,' Mr Cranmer reminded his sons. 'Don't you forget your heritage. One of your forebears came over the English Channel with William the Conqueror and landed in Hastings before heading north for the great battle, that shaped English history from that day to this.'

'But that was hundreds of years ago,' said Thomas.

'This is the year 1499, so it was 433 years ago, and landed families have long memories.'

The next day, Thomas discovered the ideal way of distracting his teacher from Latin.

'Please Mr Morice,' he said. 'Father says our family came to England with William the Conqueror in 1066, and I wondered if you could tell us more about that conquest.'

'Yes, please,' said his brothers, one after the other.

Ralph Morice smiled at his pupils' sudden interest in history and was more than happy to oblige. For three boys who had just realised their roots, it took on a whole new meaning. Thomas thought long and hard about his family history and decided that 1066 was a long time ago, and that he was a true Englishman, and the English king was his king.

Just a short time later, the three boys were glad that they'd listened to their father tell the family story, because Mr Cranmer died, and it might have gone to the grave with him.

In 1503, when Thomas was fourteen years old, he left Aslacton (now spelt Aslockton) and went to Cambridge University to study. Mr Morice must have been proud of his former pupil because he did very well indeed. Seven years later, he became a Fellow of Jesus College, and it looked as though he had settled down to a quiet academic life. It was there that he discovered that his many-times-great-grandfather was not the only good thing that came over the Channel from Europe, because, in the first half of the 15th Century, new thinking was finding its way into Cambridge from various parts of Europe, and Thomas was not slow to find out what it was.

'I must think,' Thomas said to himself, as he walked along the River Cam. 'I need peace to think.'

Mallards paddled their way along the river, stopping from time to time to do a bottoms-up, all the better to catch their dinner. Sometimes the sight of them amused Dr Cranmer, but not today. His mind was on weightier things.

'If what the European Reformers say is right, then the Roman Church is wrong. And if the Roman Church is wrong, then ... then what?'

And as his thinking ground to a halt, he noticed the mallards. 'It's all right for them,' he thought. 'They know what they're looking for, and they puddle about till they find it.'

Leaving the mallards behind him, he walked on. A few strides further along the way, he turned back to look at the ducks. 'You're right,' he told them. 'And I'm going to follow your example. I know what I'm looking for; I'm looking for the truth. And I'm going to puddle about till I find it.'

Cranmer studied three things: his Bible, the Roman Church and the teaching of the European Reformers. It took time, but eventually he came to the conclusion that what the Reformers taught was the same as the Bible, and much of what the Roman Church taught at that time was not. Thomas was not the only one who was thinking along these lines; the King of England was coming to the same conclusion, though he travelled along a different route to arrive there. Both men were leaving their Roman faith behind them and becoming Protestant in their thinking.

For Thomas the issues were theological. That's a big word, but here's a 100-word outline of the issues that helped him make up his mind. The Roman Church said that the Communion bread and wine were really the body and blood of Jesus; the Reformers (and the Bible) said they were symbols. The Roman Church thought people could buy their way into heaven by giving money to the Church;

the Reformers (and the Bible) said that we are saved by faith in Jesus. The Roman Church believed that people had to approach God through priests or dead saints; the Reformers (and the Bible) said that everyone could come to God through Jesus. And the Roman Church didn't like people reading the Bible, whereas the Reformers did. Oops! That's 101 words! King Henry VIII came to the problem from quite a different angle. He wanted to divorce his wife; and the Pope, who was head of the Roman Church, would not agree to it.

'I think that I'll move from Cambridge for the summer,' Thomas told a friend in 1529. 'There's such a lot of illness here just now that getting away seems a good idea.'

His friend agreed, and Cranmer made plans to spend some months in Waltham, Essex. While he was there he met two men, Edward Fox and Stephen Gardiner. That meeting was to change the course of Cranmer's life. Fox and Gardiner were advisors to King Henry VIII, and if there was one thing he needed a lot of, it was advice. Cranmer's new friends decided that he was just the person to advise the king, and arranged for the two men to meet. Four years later, in 1533, Cranmer was appointed Archbishop of Canterbury, which really meant that he was head of the newly born Protestant church in England.

Cranmer remained one of Henry VIII's chief advisers for as long as the king lived.

'It's not always easy,' Thomas confided in his best friend. 'I certainly don't agree with all the king does and says, although people think I do because I'm Archbishop of Canterbury. But sometimes the Archbishop's throne is not a comfortable seat to be sitting on.'

Thinking of King Henry's six wives, Thomas's friend was quite sure that what Cranmer said was true.

'I'm sure you advise him well, even when you don't agree with him,' the man decided.

Cranmer said nothing, but he wondered if what his friend said was right.

'My main job is not what I do to support the King,' Thomas said. 'My job is to try to establish a Protestant church in England, a church that is founded on what the Bible teaches rather than on men's traditions. That's my job. And the part of it that's keeping me busy just now is compiling a prayer book. I believe that if people don't have a Protestant Prayer Book, they'll go back to their old Roman prayers. And before they realise what they're doing, they'll be praying to God through the saints once again, rather than through the Lord Jesus.'

If Thomas thought life would be easier after Henry VIII died, he was very much mistaken. Henry's son Edward VI, who was a Protestant like his father, reigned for just a short time then died. His sister Mary, who should have succeeded him, was Roman Catholic. Henry VIII had wanted his relation, Lady Jane Grey, to succeed his son, as she too was a Protestant. When Edward VI died, Cranmer supported Lady Jane Grey's claim to the throne. She reigned for just over a week before Mary was proclaimed queen. And the next thing Cranmer knew was that he was charged with treason and thrown into the Tower of London with a death sentence hanging over his head. It was not carried out.

Four years later, Queen Mary had Thomas Cranmer charged with heresy for his Protestant teaching. Once again he was sentenced to death, this time by burning.

'Can we make him deny his Protestant teaching?' the Queen's advisers asked each other. 'We could tell him that his life would be spared, that he would remain as Archbishop. In fact, we could promise him the moon on a plate if it would make him change his mind.'

Cranmer was brought before them. Brainwashing over his years in prison had taken its toll on him, and he was a greatly weakened man. Promises were made to him, false promises, if only he'd deny his Protestant faith. In the terrible stress of the situation, Thomas Cranmer did what the

Queen most wanted. He agreed that what the Roman Church taught was true.

'Do you agree that the Pope is head of the church?' he was asked.

'I do.'

'Do you agree that the bread and wine are the actual body and blood of Jesus?'

'I do.'

'Sign your name to it!' he was told.

And taking the quill pen in his right hand, he dipped it in ink and signed away the truth.

If Thomas Cranmer thought his signature would save his life, he was wrong. The sentence of death still stood. And when the day came for his burning, a terrible sermon was preached to him, and questions were asked to show the onlookers that the famous Reformer wasn't a Reformer at all, but that he'd gone back to his old Roman faith.

'Master Cranmer,' the preacher said, 'tell all the people what you truly believe.'

'I will,' said the former Archbishop. 'I believe in God the Father Almighty. And I believe every word taught by our Saviour Jesus Christ, and his apostles.'

There was a moment of silence before he went on. 'And now I come to the great thing' he said, his voice growing stronger as he went on. 'For fear of death I signed my name to lies. As for the Pope, I refuse him. He is Christ's enemy!'

The soldiers could hardly believe their ears.

'And the bread and the wine are just that, bread and wine, pictures of the body and blood of Christ, not the real thing.'

The crowd yelled at him for his heresy, and screamed for him to be burned.

Cranmer held up his right hand. 'This hand,' he shouted above the noise, 'this hand, with which I put my name to such lies, will burn first in the fire that will kill me.'

Which is exactly what happened. So ashamed was he of what he had done, when he signed that sheet of paper, Thomas held out his hand to the flames and watched as they lapped around it. Having done something he was desperately ashamed of, Thomas Cranmer went to his death in the sure knowledge that all his sins, even his denial of his Protestant faith, were confessed and forgiven through the Lord Jesus Christ.

FACT FILE

Henry's daughters: When she succeeded to the throne, Mary soon began trying to overturn the reforms to the church that had been put in place during her father's reign, and that of her brother. She executed so many Protestants that she was given the nickname 'Bloody Mary'. However, the changes that she put in place did not last long because she was succeeded by her half-sister, Elizabeth, who was a Protestant, and who regarded Catholics as a threat to the safety of the kingdom. Elizabeth put many of the reforms made by her father back in place, although this brought her into conflict with countries on the continent of Europe.

Keynote: Thomas made a big mistake when he lied about what he believed in an attempt to escape execution. He did something wrong, and it did not do him any good. In the end wrong things we do, don't help us as we think they will. However, Thomas did something about it by admitting that what he had done was wrong and renouncing it. God does not want us to be paralysed by wrong things that we have done in the past. He wants us to ask his forgiveness and to deal with them, with his help.

Think: Thomas knew it was very important for people to realise that Jesus was the only way to God the Father. There was no need to pray through saints. It is a great privilege to be able to pray to God in Jesus' name. Jesus teaches us in God's Word to pray to God as Father. The first part of the Lord's Prayer is 'Our Father, hallowed be your name.' Think about how God is the perfect and best father you could ever have. What does this mean? The word hallowed means - to give honour to and bless. How can you give honour to God's name? How can you glorify him?

Prayer: Lord Jesus, thank you for coming and dying so that we can have forgiveness for our sins. Please forgive me for the bad things that I have done. and give me the courage to face up to them. Amen.

George Wishart

George watched from the window of his home at Pitarrow, in that part of Scotland that was then called Forfarshire. He was searching the road to the south for any signs of his uncle's arrival.

'Will Uncle James be here soon?' he asked his mother. 'I seem to have been watching for ages.'

Mrs Wishart smiled. She too was looking forward to her brother's visit but, unlike her son, she realised that watching from the window would not bring him any more quickly. She was especially glad that he was coming, because since her husband died, she felt the lack of a man's guidance on her young son's life.

'I think I can see him coming!' the boy yelled from his perch at the window. 'I'm sure that's his carriage coming now!'

But it was another false alarm, the fourth that afternoon, for many people travelled the road from Brechin to Stonehaven.

'Wait until you see one turning left into Pitarrow,' said Mrs Wishart, who was beginning to tire of the lad's excitement.

'There he is!' George shouted triumphantly, 'and there's no mistake. His carriage is bumping up our road right now!'

Mother and son were at the door in a flash, and it was hard to say who was the more excited.

'This afternoon is all yours, young man,' James Learmont told his nephew the next morning. 'And all I ask is that we get out into the fresh air together. You choose what we do and where we go.'

As soon as their lunch was eaten, uncle and nephew made for the door.

'Where are we going?' James Learmont asked.

'We're going on my favourite walk and to my special place,' was all George would tell him.

Leaving Pitarrow, they turned west and followed the course of the stream that flowed past the house. It took a sharp right turn almost immediately, then swung left again half a mile later.

'Are we going up the hill?' asked Uncle James.

George nodded. 'The stream starts not far from the top of the hill, and we'll follow it up. Then we'll climb to the top of the hill; it's called Finella Hill. It's not high, but there's a wonderful view.'

James Learmont sat down at the hilltop and looked around.

'You're right, young man,' he said. 'You can see a fair distance from here.'

George stretched his arm out and turned in a circle, telling his uncle the names of the hills all around. 'That's Sturdy Hill to the west, then Cairn o' Mount in the north, and that's the Goyle Hill to the right of it. When he'd turned full circle, he was pointing east, to the sea that shone blue just a few miles from where they sat.

'One day I'll cross the sea,' he said. 'But I'll have to wait a while because I can't leave Mum on her own.'

Mr Learmont caught an edge in George's voice and decided to ask what he knew might upset his nephew.

'Are you missing your dad terribly?' he asked quietly.

The boy nodded.

'Tell me about him,' George said, after a few minutes of silence. 'There are so many things I wish I'd asked before he died, and now I can't.'

Uncle James wondered where to begin.

'You know your dad was a lawyer, but you probably don't know much more about that. His title was Clerk of Justiciary and

65

King's Advocate, which means he was a very important person indeed.'

'I thought he must have been important,' the lad said. 'He kept having private meetings with people, and he was away a lot.'

'What you may not know,' his uncle went on, 'was that your mother – my sister – was your dad's second wife. His first wife died very young.'

George nodded. 'I wondered about that.'

'What else do you want to know?' James Learmont asked.

But George had had enough. He knew his uncle was staying for a week, which would give him time to find out more.

'You said you wanted to go away one day,' said James, as they climbed back down Finella Hill. 'I hope you will, because that's part of your education. Another thing, don't worry about your mother. She's able to look after herself, and I'll do all I can to help her.'

That was like a burden off George's back. He grinned at his uncle and said that he'd leave for Aberdeen that afternoon to book a voyage round the world!

When the time came for George to go to university, he did go overseas. It was while he was studying in Europe that he came in contact with the Reformers. For it was the 16th Century, and the Christian church was in turmoil. Young Master Wishart discovered that new thinking was spreading from village to village and town to town. Like most young people, George was interested in what was new, and he became very interested indeed when he found out more.

'Let me get this straight,' he said to his university friends. 'You're telling me that what the Roman Church teaches is very different from the Bible.'

'That's often the case.'

'So where does the Church's teaching come from if it's not from the Bible?'

The young men looked around to see who would answer. It was a German lad who did.

'The fact is that much of the Church's teaching comes from traditions that go back hundreds of years. Other things just seem to be taken on board to suit the Church's convenience.'

'Like what?' asked George.

'Like indulgences,' said his German friend. 'There's not a word about indulgences in the Bible. But when the Church needs money for some big project, it sells sheets of paper called indulgences that are meant to help those who buy them get in to heaven. It seems to me that has more to do with money than truth.'

'Don't take our word for it,' a student from Switzerland advised. 'Read the Bible yourself and make up your own mind about what is true.'

One of George's subjects was New Testament Greek, and he put it to very good use. It was not long before he was a convinced Reformer, one of the early Protestants. (Protestants protested against the teaching of the Roman Church.)

When George returned to Scotland in 1534 to become a Greek teacher in a school in Montrose, he brought with him copies of the New Testament in Greek for his pupils. He also brought a copy of the Helvetic Confession (an outline of Protestant teaching) that he had translated into English.

'Will you find a nice home for yourself in Montrose?' Mrs Wishart asked, when George travelled the twenty or so miles to Pitarrow for a visit. 'You mustn't worry about money,' she went on. 'The family is well set up, so you'll never have to do without anything.'

'I need nothing grand,' the young man explained. 'I have very simple tastes.'

And it was a very simple life indeed that the teacher decided to follow. He lived in humble lodgings, ate only twice a day, and every fourth day he hardly ate anything at all. None of these things were done to save money – George had no need to do that – rather they were done as disciplines he set on himself.

George Wishart, however, was not destined to spend his life teaching Greek to the boys of Montrose. In 1538, the fact that he was teaching his pupils to read the Bible in the original language – or to read it at all – came to the attention of the Church authorities, and he had to leave Scotland for Cambridge. The story of Wishart's life is very confusing; as some history books tell us, he studied in Aberdeen as a young man, then went to the continent after teaching in Montrose; others assure us that he was in Europe first, then went to Cambridge from Montrose! However, we do know that he was in Cambridge by 1543, because John Foxe (who wrote a famous book about Christian martyrs) met him there. So although there is some confusion about George's life, we do have a good description of what he looked like. Funny thing, history!

Foxe tells us, 'About the year of our Lord 1543, there was in the University of Cambridge, one Master George Wishart ... a man of tall stature, polled-headed, and on the same a round French cap of the best; judged to be of melancholy complexion, black-haired, long-bearded, comely of personage, well spoken after his country of Scotland, courteous, lowly, lovely, glad to teach, desirous to learn and well travelled.' We even know the kind of clothes he wore! 'Having on him for his clothing a frieze gown

69

to the shoes, a black millian fustian doublet, and plain black hosen, coarse new canvass for his shirts, and white falling bands and cuffs at his hands.'

By the following year, Wishart was back in Scotland, preaching the good news of Jesus Christ at every opportunity, and making himself mightily unpopular with the Roman Church. His life was so much in danger that he travelled with a bodyguard, one John Knox, who became Scotland's most famous reformer. It is impossible to state how important Wishart was in the Scottish Reformation, because not only did he preach in many towns and cities, his influence continued through Knox, whose life was changed by Wishart's ministry.

'You can't go preaching where the plague's raging,' a friend told Wishart.

'The plague I preach against is Romanist teaching,' George said. 'As for preaching where the plague is, I can think of no better place. There are people there who will shortly die, and I must tell them to look to Jesus for forgiveness before they do. Otherwise they'll die looking to the Church's teachings and with no hope of heaven.'

'I can't argue with that,' his friend agreed. 'And I'll pray for you and those who hear you preach.'

Hard on Wishart's heels was the most important Romanist in Scotland, Cardinal Beaton. He disliked George Wishart with a passion, and was determined to silence his preaching whatever it took to do that.

On one occasion, Wishart was about to set out to preach in Montrose, when a message arrived from a friend saying that he had taken ill and needed George to visit right away. He prepared to go immediately, and some friends agreed to travel with him for the first part of the journey. They had hardly gone quarter of a mile, when George Wishart reined his horse to a standstill.

'I am forbidden by God to go on this journey,' he said. 'Will some of you be pleased to ride to yonder place (he pointed to a nearby hill) and see what you find, for I see there is a plot against my life?'

Turning his horse round, he rode off in the direction from which he had come. It wasn't long before his friends joined him, with the news that sixty horsemen had been waiting to ambush him, and the letter from his sick friend was a forgery written to draw him into the trap.

'God has spared me this time,' said George. 'This time.'

The more Reformation teaching spread throughout Scotland, the more viciously Cardinal

Beaton tried to stamp it out, and that meant stamping out those who preached it. As others were martyred before him, Wishart no doubt knew what was coming. It would have come as no surprise to him when he was captured and thrown into prison in St Andrews. His Cambridge friend, John Foxe, was not in St Andrews in March 1546 when George was martyred, but he no doubt heard the details from those who were. Foxe records what happened when George was hanged and burnt.

'When he came to the fire, he sat down upon his knees, and rose again, and three times he said these words, 'O thou Saviour of the world! have mercy on me. Father of heaven! I commend my spirit into Thy holy hands.' ... Then he turned to the crowd who had gathered to watch him die, and said to them, 'I suffer this day by men, not sorrowfully, but with a glad heart and mind. For this cause I was sent, that I should suffer this fire, for Christ's sake. Consider and behold my face; you shall not see me change my colour. This grim fire I fear not. I know surely that my soul shall sup with my Saviour Christ this night.'

The hangman, who saw and heard what was happening, knelt down before Wishart and said, 'Sir, I pray you forgive me, for I am not guilty of your death.'

'Come here to me,' George said. And when the man came within reach, George Wishart kissed him.

'That is a token that I forgive you,' he said. 'Do your job.'

The forgiven executioner did his job. He hanged the young preacher and lit the fire below him. Cardinal Beaton watched from the window of St Andrews Castle and thought that was the end of George Wishart. How wrong he was. It was a glorious new beginning. For, as Beaton watched the flames die down, George was beginning eternity in the presence of Jesus.

FACT FILE

Continental travel: George Wishart was not the only Scots preacher to return from university in Europe with new ideas. Many of the Scottish reformers had travelled widely in Europe and were influenced, in particular, by the teachings of John Calvin, a Frenchman who had moved to Geneva. Many Protestants fled to Geneva to escape persecution in other parts of Europe. Geneva seems to have influenced George's clothes as well as his religion, since the white bands that Foxe describes were later referred to as Geneva bands.

Keynote: George was not a poor man, but he still lived a very simple life because he wanted to discipline himself and avoid being distracted from what was really important. He was willing to set aside many comforts, and even risk being infected with the plague, for the sake of telling people the gospel and making sure that they knew what the Bible actually said. We must be careful that the comforts of this life do not take our attention away from trying to please God.

Think: George was not afraid to die because he knew that when he died, he would go to heaven to be with Jesus. That helped him to be very brave when he was about to be executed. He was even able to forgive his executioner! He knew that everything was in God's hands. What difference does knowing that everything is in God's hands make to the way you react, when things go wrong or when sad things happen?

Prayer: Lord Jesus, thank you for giving people in the past the courage to stand up for what the Bible really said, so that we can read it now. Please help me to follow you, even when other people make that very difficult. Amen.

James Chalmers

'When do I start school?' the boy asked his mother. 'How many days is it till I go?'

Mrs Chalmers smiled and wondered if her son would be as keen to go to school every day after he'd discovered what it was like.

'You start school next Monday,' she said. 'And you'll work hard when you go there.'

James grinned. The thought of his first day at school made him feel very grown up, even though he wasn't yet six years old. Despite his excitement, he was more than a little nervous when Monday dawned, and he pulled on his scratchy school jersey and tucked his slate under his arm.

'Beat him if he needs it,' Mrs Chalmers told the teacher, before leaving the boy that Monday.

That gave James a little cause for concern. 'Does Mum expect me to be beaten on my very first day?' he wondered.

James' slate had fine white lines drawn on it. With a scratchy slate pencil, he was taught to write the letters of the alphabet within the lines. And even quite small boys were punished when the tops of their letters went above the lines, or the bottoms of the letters went below them. After the slate was covered with trial letters, they were rubbed out with a damp rag, and the whole process started all over again. Not only that, James had to carry his slate home to practise even more letters. There were many things he would rather be doing.

'Where are you working today?' the boy asked his father, one fine Saturday morning.

'I've some work to do on the prison walls,' Mr Chalmers told his son. 'It seems that the rain's dripping into one of the cells, and the authorities don't want their prisoners wet.'

'May I come with you?' James asked.

'I don't see why not. You're not likely to run away from the inside of Inveraray Prison, are you?'

James laughed at the thought.

'I'll be able to tell the boys at school that I was in jail on Saturday,' thought James. 'But I'd better not tell the teacher. He might think I was there for real.'

So Mr Chalmers and James set off to walk to the prison. James carried their lunch wrapped in a cloth, and his father had a much heavier load: a jute sack with all his stonemason's hammers and chisels inside it.

'Look at the fishing boats on Loch Fyne,' the lad said, when they came out of the trees into the village. 'I wonder if they'll get a good catch today.'

'Did you know that not all boats have red-brown sails like these ones?' asked his father.

'No,' said James. 'What other colours are there?'

Mr Chalmers explained that the Loch Fyne boats were a special kind, and that most fishing boats in other places had lighter coloured sails, and that they were a different shape too.

'How do you know that?' asked the lad.

His father smiled. 'I know that because I was brought up in Aberdeen where there are hundreds of fishing boats. The fish market there is so huge that it makes the one in Inveraray look like a toy.'

'Did Mum come from Aberdeen too?' James enquired.

'No,' his father said. 'She was brought up in Luss, on the shore of Loch Lomond.'

'Where's that?' wondered the lad.

His father pointed over Loch Fyne to the high hills on the other side.

'If you go in that direction, you climb over a high mountain pass called Rest and be

Thankful, then you go down the other side and walk round the head of Loch Long and over a short strip of land to Loch Lomond. Your mother's home is about nine miles from there.'

'One day I'll go there,' James said. 'That would be a big adventure.'

James wasn't an especially bad boy at school; in fact, he did very well there. But despite that, he was sometimes beaten by his teacher; nearly every child was. When he knew he deserved punishment, the boy took it fair and square. But one day his teacher went too far, for he beat James so much that he broke several switches (fine wooden canes) as he did so. Whether the boy deserved any beating at all has been lost in history, but he certainly didn't deserve what he got. After school that day, he went home in a state of rebellion. Storming into the cottage, he told his mother what had happened. Normally, he didn't mention he'd been punished because his parents just punished him again, and he certainly didn't mention when his sisters were punished either. But on this occasion his father and mother realised that more punishment was not due, and they let the boy off.

'It wasn't fair,' James fumed. 'And I hate unfairness.'

'I have a letter to read to you from a missionary magazine,' said Mr Meikle, the minister, at Sunday School one day when James was thirteen years old. 'It's from a missionary in Fiji.'

The letter gripped the teenager as nothing had gripped him before. As Mr Meikle read about the difference the gospel had made in the lives of Fijian cannibals, the boy's heart raced with excitement. Having finished reading, the minister looked over his spectacles, and said, 'I wonder if there is a boy here this afternoon who will become a missionary, and who will take the good news of Jesus Christ to the cannibals.'

'I will,' James said in his heart. 'If God helps me, I'll do just that.'

Before he reached home that day, he knelt by the side of the road and asked God to make a missionary of him. When James told his parents what had happened, their hearts were moved, for they were both Christians, and they had prayed for their son since before he was born.

But there were things to do before thinking of Fiji, things like finding a job in Inveraray.

'Are you working?' a friend asked James, when they met some months after leaving school for the last time.

'Yes,' he replied. 'I've a job in the lawyer's office in Inveraray.'

'That must be interesting,' said the other lad, who was on the crew of a fishing boat.

'It's certainly an eye-opener,' commented James. He would have liked to talk about some of the things he saw and heard in the course of his work, but he thought he had better not.

'There are so many unfairnesses in life,' he thought, as he walked home that day. 'And the more I see of the legal system, I realise it's not always fair either.'

It was November 1859; it was dark, and James and some of his pals were up to no good.

'There's a revival meeting in Inveraray tonight,' one of them said, when they met. 'How about going and making just enough noise that the speaker can't be heard?'

'That sounds like fun,' sneered another.

But one of James' friends heard the plan and made another.

'I've a present for you,' he told young Chalmers, when he 'accidentally' bumped into him. 'It's a Bible. And I'm giving it to you with the suggestion that you go to the meeting tonight not to make trouble, but to hear what is said.'

That's just what James did, and he was so moved and troubled by what he heard, that the very next day he spoke to Mr Meikle, and that kindly minister led him to the Lord. From that day on, young James Chalmers was a Christian worker, and he made plans to become a missionary overseas.

It was hard work for James to train for the mission field, but Mr Meikle helped him in many ways. After long years of training and a marriage, James Chalmers and his very new wife left Scottish shores for the South Sea Islands, via Australia, on 17th October, 1865. Mrs Chalmers was hardly used to being called by that name when they left, for they had only been married two days before sailing! The voyages were not uneventful; they were threatened with shipwreck twice in the time they were at sea. Seven months and three days later, James and his wife arrived at Avarua, Rarotonga, in the South Sea Islands. They were there at last! James was immediately put to work training local men to take the gospel to the remotest parts of their homeland.

It was eleven years later that James' dream of reaching out to the cannibal people came true. That was when he and his wife moved from Rarotonga to the island of New Guinea.

'Life here will be very different,' he told his wife, on the ship. 'The people are ruled by their belief in evil spirits, and there are indescribable acts going on there. Only God can change the lives of the islanders.'

They had no sooner arrived, than the truth of what he had said was obvious.

'Those are human jawbones,' Mrs Chalmers shivered, indicating what some men were wearing as bracelets. 'And the people are painted to look so evil.'

Their new home was soon surrounded by painted men demanding knives, tomahawks and other weapons.'

'You may kill us,' James said, 'but you'll never get weapons from us.'

The next day, the ringleader returned, but this time to say he was sorry! From then on, the new missionary and his wife were shown some strange kindnesses, including being given invitations to many feasts, cannibal feasts among them.

'Is man good to eat?' Chalmers once asked an old man, who by then had become a Christian.

'Sheep and pigs are not good,' the islander replied. 'But man, he too much good.'

Sadly, Mrs Chalmers died after two years in New Guinea. And on a visit home to Scotland, James married again and took his new wife back to the country that had won his heart.

By 1882, James and his wife saw a great change in the people they worked with.

'There are no cannibal ovens here now, no feasts of human flesh and no desire for human skulls,' which was probably why he felt able to write home with an order for 'twelve dozen tomahawks, twelve dozen butcher knives' with the explanation that he was 'going east to try to make friends between the tribes.'

That may seem to be a strange way to make friends, and we can only assume that by then he knew that the weapons were being used on animals rather than humans!

'We're going back to visit Rarotonga,' James told his wife. 'I've not seen the people there since I left thirteen years ago.'

'At every house, men and women came out to join us,' Mrs Chalmers wrote home, soon after they arrived. 'The reception was wonderful! People embraced James as though they thought they'd never see him again on earth.'

It must have seemed to the pair of them that things had changed greatly for the better. No doubt they were very encouraged.

At the turn of the century, a great sadness came upon James Chalmers, when his second wife died. By way of comforting himself, the missionary kept busier than ever. Just a few months later, on 4th April, 1901, he sailed for Goaribari Island with another missionary called Oliver Tomkins, to reach out to the people there. As the boat anchored, three days later, it was swarmed with islanders.

'I promise we'll come ashore tomorrow morning,' James told them.

They kept their promise and were ashore even before they had breakfast.

'Come into the hut,' some men said, pointing to a long tribal hut not far from the shore. 'That's our feast hall.'

James and his friend accepted the invitation, as did a number of islanders who were already Christians. But the welcome that awaited them inside the hut was very different. Going from bright sunlight, the men's eyes were probably not accustomed to the dark before they were attacked. So it may be that they didn't realise what was happening. James Chalmers and Oliver Tomkins were attacked from behind and beaten with stone clubs. As they lay on the ground, they had their heads cut off. Having got rid of the missionaries, the islanders set upon the local Christians, and a terrible massacre followed. Unlike his friends on the mainland of New Guinea, the people of the Goaribari Island were still cannibals. The bodies of the murdered Christians were handed over to the women to be cooked for eating that same day.

When James Chalmers was just thirteen years old, he heard from Mr Meikle about the cannibal peoples of the world, and the thought of working among them made his heart race with excitement. There must have been some who, when they heard that he'd become a victim of cannibalism himself, thought that his life had been wasted. But

James Chalmers knew differently, although he was completely aware of the dangers. Things had changed in many parts of New Guinea, thanks to the work he did there. We know that from a letter he wrote home, not long before he died.

'These people were savages when I came to New Guinea, and a couple of years ago they were still skull hunters. Now they have the finest church in all of New Guinea and they built and paid for it themselves.'

The missionary work, however, continued in New Guinea. Men and women, natives of the islands that James had given his life for, carried on the work. It was through James that they first heard of the Lord Jesus Christ, and they knew that this work had to keep going. They mustn't give up. James had had a great sense of fairness, even as a boy at home in Inveraray. It wasn't fair that those he went to help killed him, but it was worth it to see so many become Christians.

FACT FILE

New Guinea: The easiest way to find New Guinea on the map is to find Australia and look north. New Guinea is not a single country now. The eastern part of the main island is Papua New Guinea, while the western part is part of Indonesia. The climate there is very humid, and the island is home to some remarkable animals. Among the most striking are flying foxes, which are fruit-eating bats with a wingspan of up to 1.5 metres (4.92 feet). They fly out in great swarms to roost on the branches of fruit trees around dusk.

Keynote: James prayed that God would make a missionary of him when he heard about the work with the Fijian cannibals, and his parents were very pleased. But God had to make a Christian of James before he could make a missionary of him. We need to remember that. Before we can do any great things for God, we need a right relationship with him, by putting our faith in Jesus.

Think: How do you think you would have felt if you had landed on an island and found the people with human jawbones for bracelets? Would you have found it easy to love them and to try and help them? That's what James did. Think about who you find difficult to love, and how you can make sure that you do demonstrate love for such people.

Prayer: Lord Jesus, thank you for the people who tell me about you, even when I make it difficult for them. Teach me to love you more than anyone or any thing, and to be willing to give up anything for your sake. Amen.

Dietrich Bonhoeffer

Dietrich and his twin sister, whose name was Sabine, slipped silently from the room they were playing in, at the back of their home in Breslau, to the front of the house, where they could look out at the Catholic cemetery across the road.

'I was sure there would be a funeral this morning,' said Dietrich, who was just ten minutes older than his sister, and therefore felt that he knew significantly more than she did. 'I saw the men arriving to dig the grave.'

Sabine was silent. She knew that she could learn things from listening as well as from seeing. 'I think they're coming now,' she whispered, when she heard the slow clip-clopping of the horse-drawn hearse.

The twins watched as the horse slowed in front of their house then turned in the cemetery gate.

'The dead person must have been important,' said Sabine. 'Look how many people there are!'

Dietrich began to count, but he got in a muddle after he had reached 100, and gave up.

'There you are!' their nursery nurse said. 'I might have known the pair of you would be watching a funeral. I searched the house for you, and, when I saw the cook looking in the direction of the cemetery, I knew exactly where you would be.'

Sabine looked at the ground. She couldn't quite work out why it bothered her nurse when she and her brother watched funerals. They were the most interesting things that happened in their street, so why shouldn't they watch them?

'Come now,' the nurse insisted. 'It's time for your milk and biscuits.'

By the time the youngsters arrived for their snack, everyone else in the house had nearly finished.

'Watching another funeral, were you?' teased Karl-Friedrich. 'Was it a big one?'

'There were over a hundred people there,' Dietrich said. 'I counted.'

'But you've not started lessons with the governess yet,' Karl-Friedrich smiled. 'I don't believe that you can really count to a hundred. Why, I don't think you can even count how many people live in this house.'

'Of course I can,' pouted Dietrich. 'I'll show you.'

Dietrich began to count on his fingers, holding them steady as he did so. Everyone waited for the answer.

'It comes to seventeen,' Dietrich announced.

As his brothers and sisters looked doubtful, the lad went through them one at a time. There were his parents, three older brothers, two older sisters, Sabine, baby Suzanne, the housemaid, parlour maid, cook, governess, nursery nurse and his father's receptionist and chauffeur.'

'But that only comes to sixteen,' said the boy in a puzzled way.

Sabine knew the problem. 'You forgot to count yourself,' she told her twin.

Before they went to bed that night, Sabine and Dietrich had a discussion.

'How long are dead people dead for?' they asked Karl-Friedrich, when they couldn't decide for themselves.

'I think they're dead for eternity,' their oldest brother said. 'At least they never come back to earth again.'

When the twins went to bed, they had plenty to talk about; in fact, they always had plenty to talk about.

'What do you think being dead is like?' asked Sabine.

'It must be like having your eyes and ears shut all the time,' suggested Dietrich.

'But eternity's a long time to have your eyes and ears shut.'

'Let's try it and see,' said her twin.

Sabine and Dietrich screwed their eyes shut and tried not to listen to the sounds in the house. It was difficult, because with such a big family it was always noisy. That's how they were lying when their nursery nurse came in to tuck them up for the night.

'What are you two doing?' she asked.

Dietrich explained about their experiment.

'It's not normal for children to think so much about death,' she said, stomping about the room. 'But this family isn't quite normal. You all think far too much.'

'I can't wait to go on holiday,' Karl-Friedrich said. 'The lake will be warm enough for swimming, and we'll be able to climb and shoot and do lots of other things.'

The Bonhoeffers had a holiday home that they all loved going to. What a hustle of packing had to be done first for so many people! Although they enjoyed all their holidays there, this one was remembered for quite another reason.

'Look!' screamed Dietrich, when they were playing beside the lake.

The children looked to where he was pointing.

'It's Fräulein Lenchen!' the boy screamed again. 'She's drowning!'

Fräulein Horn, the family governess was first to move. Dashing to the side of the lake, she headed right into the water and swam to the middle. Grabbing the nursery nurse, she pulled her to the edge. Dietrich was right there beside the two women. Thumping his nurse on the back, he watched, fascinated, as Fräulein Horn pushed her fingers down her friend's throat, forcing her to cough and begin breathing again. The two women were soaking. Despite this, the governess led the children in a long 'thank you' prayer to God for saving Fräulein Lenchen's life.

The Bonhoeffers' nursery nurse must have been pleased when the family left Breslau and moved to Berlin soon afterwards; at least it would get them away from the cemetery across the road, and all the twins' talk about death. She was especially sensitive, since she nearly drowned herself. Dr Bonhoeffer's appointment as a professor at Berlin University meant they had to move to Germany's capital city.

'This is the best garden in the world!' the children decided, when they moved into their new home. 'It's huge! And there are plenty of places to have dens.'

Hours were spent outside playing games, and hours were spent inside playing music.

All the children were musical, and they often played their instruments together.

'We can't all play at once,' Suzanne said, when she was just old enough to join in.

'Why not?' asked one of her brothers.

Suzanne giggled. 'If we all play, that leaves nobody to be the audience!'

There was much fun and laughter in the Bonhoeffer household. They were a happy crew, although things around them in Germany were not always as happy as they were. And by 1914, when Dietrich and Sabine were eight years old, they found themselves living in a country at war, a war that lasted for four long years.

'Does Walter have to join the army as well as Karl-Friedrich?' Sabine asked. The idea seemed scary to her.

'We should be proud that they're both soldiers for the Fatherland,' said Professor Bonhoeffer.

The night before Walter enlisted, Dietrich wrote words to a popular song and sang them to his brother. 'Now at last, we say Godspeed on your journey,' was the opening line.

The First World War marked the end of the Bonhoeffers' happy home. Both Karl-Friedrich and Walter were wounded. Although the older boy recovered from his wounds, Walter did not. He died during an operation to save his life. And it was as though something died inside Mrs Bonhoeffer. From a lively and happy mother, she slipped into a deep depression that affected her whole family. Even though her husband, who was a psychiatrist, did everything he could to support and help her, it was a long time before she was anything like her former self again.

When Dietrich was in his mid teens, his schoolteacher asked each person in the class what they wanted to do when they grew up.

'You are all very clever,' said Herr Klein-Schmidt, 'so much so that you'll be able to choose from many careers.'

'I want to be a doctor,' said one boy.

Another had decided to be a chemist, and a third told the class he hoped to be a general in the army.

'And you, Bonhoeffer?' said Herr Klein-Schmidt. 'What are you going to do with your life?'

'I want to be a theologian,' said Dietrich.

There was a silence in the classroom as everyone considered their friend's reply.

'I want to study all about God, and all that everyone thinks about God,' explained Dietrich.

'You mean you want to be a minister,' said his teacher, who was half-German and half-Jewish.

'No,' the teenager replied. 'I don't want to be a minister. I want to be a theologian.'

Dietrich's decision produced much the same effect at home. Professor Bonhoeffer had hoped that his sons would study science or medicine, but he respected Dietrich's decision, even if he was more than a little puzzled by it.

Walter's death was the first real shock in Dietrich's life. The second happened just after he started university in 1923.

'My name's Rolf Hoftstag,' a fellow student said. 'And you're Bonhoeffer.'

Dietrich agreed that was who he was.

'I wondered if you'd like to come to join the Hedgehogs,' said Rolf. 'I understand that your father used to be a member.'

He wasn't sure what to do, but because Rolf made no effort to move away, Dietrich agreed to join. The meetings he went to seemed harmless enough, if a little boring.

'Are you a Hedgehog?' Dietrich asked another student he met.

'No,' the young man said awkwardly. 'My name's Sol Friesberg.'

Bonhoeffer was really puzzled. It was as though by telling his name, Sol assumed his friend would know why he wasn't a Hedgehog. Seeing his puzzlement, Sol Friesberg explained that Hedgehogs hated Jewish people, that they were an anti-Semitic organisation. (Anti-Semitism means hatred of Jewish people.) Dietrich was horrified, but he soon discovered that what Sol told him was quite true.

The Hedgehogs were not the only ones in Germany, at that time, that hated Jewish people. Just as Dietrich was discovering about personal faith in Jesus, and as he was committing himself to a life of serving the Lord as a theologian, so others were committing themselves to a life of service to the Fatherland. By the early 1930s, racism, especially anti-Semitism, was sweeping through Germany, and it often erupted into violence. In 1932, the Nazis won 32 per cent of the seats in parliament. Dietrich recognised what was happening and tried to encourage his fellow German Christians to stand up against the state but, in the main, church leaders didn't see what was happening before their very eyes. Some even supported the Nazi cause.

The following year, Adolf Hitler became Reich Chancellor, and the stage began to be set for World War Two. What horrified Dietrich was not the prospect of war with other countries, but what he recognised as a war between the various people of Germany, especially the war that began to be waged against the Jewish people. And when he thought back to his schooldays, and remembered the kindly half-German, half-Jewish, Herr Klein-Schmidt, the thought made him so sad he could have wept.

'I hear that Dietrich Bonhoeffer has been arrested,' a church leader said to his friend in the spring of 1943. 'Is that true?'

'I'm afraid it is,' was the reply. 'He certainly knows how to rub Adolf Hitler up the wrong way.'

'What do you mean?'

'It doesn't help with Bonhoeffer being a leader in the anti-Nazi Confessing Church. Hitler was certainly not impressed when Bonhoeffer took part in the Abwehr resistance circle.'

'Speak more quietly,' the church leader whispered. 'If we're overheard, we could both end up in prison with Bonhoeffer.'

'But I think one of the final straws was when Dietrich tried to help a group of Jewish people escape to Switzerland,' his friend said very quietly.

'You would think Bonhoeffer would realise the only way we can do any good in Germany just now, is to appear to support Hitler. If we don't, we'll be dead, and we won't do any good that way.'

The other man shook his head sadly. 'I'm not so sure,' he said. 'Sometimes I think that the world twenty years from now will think we've done nothing and condemn us. People won't know that we've tried to influence German politics from behind the scenes.'

'Shut your mouth, man!' whispered his companion urgently. 'If you're overheard, you'll be shot!'

'I'll say just one last thing, then I'm going.'

'What's that?'

'I think that Dietrich Bonhoeffer may be right. I think that even from prison, he's an inspiration to people who have more courage than I have. I wish I was as brave a man as he is.'

With that he turned on his heels and walked away, his head bent down and his shoulders drooped in depression.

Although Dietrich Bonhoeffer was in prison, and in solitary confinement, he was not idle, at least not as long as he had a pen in his hand. Letters, thoughts and articles were written, though not all found their way out of prison.

'You must remember to read and memorise Scripture,' he wrote to a friend. 'It will maintain your strength better than anything else … Be sure to pray for all of us here. Some of these men are miserable to the point of death.'

Death was on Dietrich's mind in prison, as it had been when he stood as a child watching funerals. But now he could not count how many went to funerals. 'How many millions have died?' he asked himself, as he thought about the war. 'And how many Jewish people have perished?'

Closing his eyes, he thought of eternity.

On 9th April, 1945, Dietrich was taken from his cell and hanged in Flossenburg. His crime was his participation in the small Protestant resistance movement. Not every Christian would agree with what Bonhoeffer did, or with some of his politically motivated activities, but none can doubt that he died a Christian man, and a martyr to the Christian faith. His theology, for he was a theologian, still influences Christian thinking, especially in some parts of Europe.

FACT FILE

The Nazis: After its defeat in the First World War, Germany became a very poor country, where there was a great deal of unemployment and discontent. The leader of the National Socialist Party (or Nazis, as they were called) was actually an Austrian: Adolf Hitler. He thought that Austria and Germany should be one country, that the Jews were to blame for Germany's loss in the First World War, and that the Jewish culture and race were inferior to that of the German people. Many were attracted to this because it gave them someone to blame, and, when the Nazis came to power in 1933, this led to the Holocaust, in which over 6 million Jewish people were killed.

Keynote: When Dietrich joined the Hedgehogs, he did not realise what their aims were, but it did not take him long to find out. We must be very careful about the organisations that we join and the people that we allow to influence us. Many people find it more difficult to leave such organisations, than Dietrich did. Sometimes we may even have to tell our friends that what they are doing is wrong, and that we cannot go along with it.

 Think: Many people in Germany thought that they should keep quiet about what the Nazis were doing, in order to avoid persecution, and that they could work quietly behind the scenes to oppose Hitler. In the end, however, the two men discussing Bonhoeffer were proved right. History did condemn those who kept quiet, and Hitler turned on many of them. Think about how you can stand up for those who are being picked on and can't stand up for themselves.

 Pray: Lord Jesus, please stop anything like the Holocaust ever happening again. Please give me the courage to stand up for those whom others ignore and pick on. Thank you for showing us how to care for those for whom no one else cares. Amen.

Nate Saint

Rachel looked out of the window and smiled. It had been raining, but the rain clouds were blowing towards the west, and a watery sun had begun to shine.

'It's ideal for fishing,' she told her little brother. 'Does that appeal to you?'

Nate was off like an arrow from a bow.

'I'll go dig worms!' he said, as he slammed the kitchen door behind him.

Fourteen-year-old Rachel smiled. If there was something that always brought a smile to her brother's face, it was the thought of fishing in the creek. Sitting down by the window to read until Nate was ready, she picked up her favourite book, bar none. *Fifty Missionary Stories Every Child Should Know* was just right for any time of day.

'If I've got ages, I can read right through the book,' she told her father. 'And if I only have half-an-hour, I can read one story.'

Mr Saint laughed. 'If you only have two minutes, you can read just a paragraph, because you know what comes before it and happens after it. In fact, I think you could probably close the book and tell me all the stories in it off by heart.'

Before Rachel could show if that was true or not, Nate appeared in the door. His knees were muddy, his eyes shone like stars, and he was in the process of preventing a worm making a bid for freedom over the top of his bait can.

'In you go,' he said. 'And stay there!'

'There might be nine years between Rachel and Nate,' thought Mr Saint, as he watched them head off in the direction of the creek, 'but they get on really well together.'

It was September 1928, and five-year-old Nate was as happy as could be. With a fishing rod over his shoulder, a can of worms dangling from his hand, his big sister at his side, and the thought of an afternoon fishing in the creek, the lad grinned in total satisfaction. If anyone had suggested to the boy that there was anywhere in the world better than Huntingdon Valley, north of Philadelphia, he would have argued the toss!

Two years later, Nate's grin was so big it almost reached from ear to ear, thanks to his brother Sam.

'Do you want to come with me for a flight in a plane?' the older boy asked.

Did he! Hardly big enough to see over the edge of the open cockpit, Nate imagined what he couldn't actually see and thought it was the best day of his life so far. Two years later, Sam let Nate sit side by side with him at the controls of a larger cabin plane.

'Want to take her over for a minute or two?' the older lad asked.

With eyes wide in excitement, and mouth open in concentration, Nate took over the controls. Tugging the wheel gently, he felt the aircraft respond. It was as though he and the plane were one.

'Nate's eleven years old,' Mr Saint wrote to a friend, 'and his main interest is in aviation.'

How right he was. If his son wasn't dreaming about flying, he was talking about it or reading about it! Not only that, he built a six-foot long glider from a drawing he found in a magazine.

'Anyone coming to help me fly her?' he asked, when the glider was finished.

There were times when it was useful being one of a family of seven boys and one girl. It meant there was always someone willing to lend a hand with the latest madcap adventure.

'I'll come,' one of his brothers volunteered, and the pair set off with the glider and flew it like a kite at the local school's athletic field.

Two years later, in the summer of 1936, Nate went to a Christian camp in the Poconos. Having been brought up in a Christian home, the teenager knew that he had to believe in the Lord Jesus for himself, and that he had to tell others about his faith. On a Saturday night, that he would remember for the rest of his life, he told the other campers that he was a Christian. Later that same year, he spoke at a young people's meeting in his own church about what it meant to him to be a Christian. Within a few months, Nate discovered that being a Christian didn't exempt him from problems. He developed a serious bone condition called osteomyelitis that kept him in bed for months.

Europe was at war. America had joined in, and Nate was just the right age for service. Not only that, he already held his Private Pilot's Ticket. Much to his delight he was eventually accepted for the Air Cadet Training Program.

'You ought to see the outfit we get!' he wrote home. 'Complete fleece-lined flying suit and helmet, fleece-lined leather flying boots coated with waterproof vulcanised rubber, plain leather helmet and a beautiful leather jacket and gloves.'

Just as he thought he was heading for the skies, his old medical trouble flared up again, and he was declared unfit for flying.

'I turned twenty yesterday,' Nate told a friend. 'It was a kind of rough birthday present to be told that, instead of going to the airport for my first day of flying, I was going to the base for an X-ray.'

Several weeks in hospital followed, before the young cadet was on his feet again. But there was more to being in the Air Cadet Training Program than flying planes, as Nate was to find out.

'What did you do today?' his friend asked, as they relaxed one evening.

Grinning, Nate replied, 'I took a Tommy gun apart, studied it, and put it together again ... with my eyes closed!'

What the young man didn't know, was that God needed Nate to be a good mechanic, and there was no better training than the Air Cadet Training Program. Though it wasn't always easy to understand why things worked out as they did, Nate Saint knew God makes no mistakes. The picture began to come together when God called Nate to be a missionary. Thinking about it, the young man realised that his flying experience and his knowledge of mechanics went hand in hand. After all, he thought, I might need mechanical help in the back of beyond.

'Dear Nate,' wrote Mr Saint. 'I think you'll find the enclosed article interesting.'

The young man unfolded the magazine and read, 'On Wings of the Wind.' Sitting down, he read on and discovered that it was about the Christian Airmen's Missionary Fellowship, a group of airmen who served missionaries working in remote areas.

'What do I have to offer a group like that?' he asked himself.

And the answer was staring him in the face – he had his Private Pilot's Ticket and a Mechanic's Licence!

'I'll write to the Christian Airmen's Missionary Fellowship,' decided Nate.

And that's just what he did. (The Christian Airmen's Missionary Fellowship became Missionary Aviation Fellowship in 1946.)

'I want to further the cause of Christ in any way I can,' he explained in his letter, 'so count me in and keep me informed of the goings-on.'

Having signed the letter, Nate sat back in his chair and thought about the future.

So it was that having completed his time in the Air Cadet Training Program in 1946, Nate enrolled for Bible School, then dropped out because the Christian Airmen's Missionary Fellowship asked him to come on board right away. There was work to be done in Mexico, and he was the man to do it. But the work for which Nate Saint is best remembered was done in Ecuador. He went there in September 1948 when he was twenty-five years old, and he did not go alone, because he and Marj (Marjory Farris) had been married on Valentine's Day that year. Before leaving for Ecuador, Nate spoke about mission work on the radio.

'During the last war,' he said, 'we saw big bombers on the assembly line, yet we knew that of those bombers many would not accomplish even five missions over enemy territory. We also knew that young fellows ... would ride in those airborne machine-gun turrets, and their life expectancy behind those guns was, with the trigger down, only four minutes. Tremendous expendability! Missionaries constantly face expendability, and people who do not know the Lord ask why in the world we waste our lives. ... Those who have gone to tribes who have never heard the gospel gladly count themselves expendable. And they count it all joy.'

'What's it like flying in Ecuador?' a friend wrote, after the Saints had been there for some months.

'It has its moments,' Nate thought, remembering some of the hair-raising situations the difficult terrain produced. It didn't take him long to decide which one to describe.

'I was flying over Quito just three months after we arrived here. There were two passengers, a mother and her son. Take-off was perfect, but within minutes I knew there was trouble. A strong gust of wind roared over the mountains and slammed into the plane, forcing it downwards. I did my best to control the plane, but it crashed into the ground below. My passengers weren't badly injured, but I spent a month in hospital and another five months in a body cast. Jungle flying can be dangerous,' he concluded, 'but it is what God has called me to do.'

The Saints were not the only missionaries working in Ecuador with the Quetchua people, and Nate often found himself helping Ed McCully, Jim Elliot and Peter Fleming and their wives with their work. In 1955 these young missionaries became convinced that God wanted them to reach out to the Huaorani people, and to tell them about the Lord Jesus. They seemed to hold the same conversation over and over again.

'They are the most dangerous people I've ever heard of.'

'Their name in the local language is Auca, and that means savage.'

'They've killed people who've gone into their villages.'

'They are the fiercest people in Ecuador.'

'Which is why they need to hear about Jesus.'

The young men, their wives, and their children (by then the Saints had two sons and a daughter) prayed about it and felt sure that God wanted them to share the good news with these terrifying people.

In September 1955, Nate and Ed found a Huaorani settlement fifteen minutes by air from their mission station. It was time to make firm plans.

'We won't tell anyone but our wives,' said Jim, when the young men discussed it. 'Otherwise the press and adventurers will try to join us.'

'We'll have to learn some Huaorani from Dayuma.'

Nate smiled, thankful that his sister Rachel had rescued Dayuma after her Huaorani husband was killed.

'I think we should fly over the village regularly,' suggested Nate, 'and lower gifts to the people to show them that we're friendly.'

Nate's inventiveness produced a means of lowering gifts. He discovered that if he lowered a bucket from the plane then flew in tight circles, the bucket remained still enough for one of the Huaorani people to take something out of it. Week after week they circled the village, taking presents with them each time. Soon the Huaorani men responded with gifts by return: a woven headband, carved combs, two live parrots, parcels of peanuts, even a piece of smoked monkey tail!

'We've been in contact with the villagers for three months now,' the young missionary couples decided. 'Now we've got to make contact face to face.'

'We need a fifth man for that,' someone suggested. 'And I think that Roger Youderian is our man.'

A former Paratrooper, Roger was working as a missionary with the Jivaros people, and he was quite at home in the jungle.

'I think we could land on that river beach,' Nate said, when the five young men were making their final plans. 'It's just four miles from the village.'

'Do we take guns?' Ed asked.

'I think we should,' said Peter. 'We could fire them into the air to ward off an attack if necessary. But we'll not use them as weapons, even to save our lives. Agreed?'

'Agreed,' the other four said together.

Having prayed with their wives and families, the missionaries agreed on radio contact details before Nate, Ed, Jim, Peter and Roger climbed aboard the Missionary Aviation Fellowship aircraft for the biggest adventure of their lives. It was Tuesday. They flew in, set up camp, then circled over the village. On Friday a Huaorani man, woman and teenaged girl arrived, stayed a few hours, then left.

'This IS the day,' Nate radioed early on Sunday afternoon, 8th January, 1956. 'I can see ten men coming. It looks like they'll be here for an afternoon service!'

Nate, Ed, Jim, Peter and Roger went to the Huaorani people with the good news that Jesus Christ is the one and only Saviour. The Huaorani men who met them that day at the river arrived with murderous spears. When the five young missionaries didn't contact their wives at 4.30 pm as arranged, the women knew there was something wrong. Their husbands set out on a great adventure, but their greatest adventure of all was in meeting the Lord Jesus when they went home to heaven, killed by the people they went to help.

Less than three years later Rachel Saint (Nate's sister) and Elisabeth Elliott (Jim's wife) were back among the Huaorani people. Today there is a Huaorani church and Bible training college. During the construction of the college, Missionary Aviation Fellowship helped airlift in the building materials. When Nate and Marj's children, Kathy and Stephen, wanted to be baptised, it was two of those who had killed Nate and his four companions who baptised them.

FACT FILE

Access by air: Many of the places that Nate and his colleagues flew to in Ecuador and around the world were totally inaccessible by either road or sea. Before 1900, nobody could access these places because there were no aeroplanes, but after planes had been invented, these inaccessible areas were opened up. The first powered flight was made by Wilbur Wright on 17 December, 1903, but it only flew 9.7 metres (31.8 feet) off the ground. Nate had to climb a lot higher than that to get over the Andes mountains when he was flying in Ecuador.

Keynote: Nate was willing to count himself expendable for the sake of taking the gospel to people in Mexico and South America. He did this because he could see himself as part of a larger plan to reach out to these people. Although he died before that was fulfilled, his sister saw fruit from his labours. God's purposes are always fulfilled in the end.

Think: Nate was disappointed not to be able to go flying in the Air Cadet Training Program, but the mechanical skills he learned during that period proved very useful in later life. He realised that God never makes any mistakes, and that he has a purpose in every experience, although we might not understand it. God is still the same God, and we need to learn to trust him and to seek to serve him, even when we find ourselves in places that we would rather not be.

Prayer: Lord Jesus, it is good to know that you never make mistakes and that you are in control of everything. Please help me to trust you and to follow you in everything that I do, even when it is difficult to understand what is going on. Amen.

Ivan Moiseyev

The snow fell, more snow landing on more snow landing on yet more snow. Only the bright whiteness of the snow made the day seem bearable. Everything else was dull and drab, like a picture with all the bright colours washed out. And it was so very cold.

Vanya (that was Ivan's pet name) stood at the window of his home looking out. He had a choice to make, but he didn't know which of the three alternatives to choose. He could take off his thick gloves and rub his hands together at the risk of them ending up colder than they were with his gloves on, or he could take his gloves off and heat his hands at the little stove and maybe get chilblains again this year, or he could warm his gloves at the stove and hope that the heat would penetrate through to his fingertips. Remembering the terrible pain of last winter's chilblains, he decided on the third option. Keeping his gloves on, he warmed them by the stove and sighed with relief when feeling surged back into his fingers. Then what he knew would happen did happen. It was as though the warmth set his fingers on fire. Oh, the pain of it! Eleven-year-old Vanya tucked his hands under his arms, clapped them together, waved them in the air ... anything to hurry on the process of comfort coming back. Then, as suddenly as the pain began, it was over. Grinning at his mother who had watched the whole performance, Vanya removed his gloves and took a piece of black bread and cheese from the table.

'That's good,' he said, losing some breadcrumbs as he spoke. 'The cold makes me hungry.'

'Why are the winters so cold and so long in Volontirovka?' Vanya asked his mother, who was nursing the baby of the family.

She smiled at her good-looking son. 'That is how God made them,' she said.

'If I made the weather, I'd make freezing winters short and the summers long and hot.'

His mother got up to put the baby to bed. As she passed the window, she glanced outside.

'Come and see this,' she said softly.

Vanya went to the window and looked out. The snow had stopped falling, and pale sunlight was turning the whiteness of the newly fallen snow into shimmering silver.

'What God made is very beautiful,' the woman said.

Vanya's eyes shone like the snow and he had to agree.

Taking another piece of black bread, and sitting down by the stove to enjoy it, the lad watched as his mother wrapped the baby in a shawl, then laid him on a ledge near the stove. Vanya smiled as he thought of the family's sleeping arrangements. At night the two youngest were wrapped tight, then put near the stove where they would benefit from the little heat that was left in it. Then the older children slept on couches and cots wherever there was room in the little house.

'I think we have the coldest of all corners,' Semyon often complained to Vanya.

'Maybe we do,' his brother always replied. 'But the little ones need more heat than we do.'

The cold often kept Semyon and Vanya awake, and they whispered in the darkness to each other.

'What do you want to do when you grow up?' Vanya asked his brother.

Semyon thought of the collective farm on which they lived, a farm that belonged to the state and on which most of the people in the village of Volontirovka worked.

'Well I'm not going to spend my life working my fingers to the bone on the farm, that's for certain,' the boy said. 'I'll make sure I know the right people, then get a job organising the collective farms. Sitting at a desk must be better than slaving in the mud or trying to hack your way through packed ice to dig up winter vegetables.'

Vanya listened to the bitterness in his brother's voice.

'That's why I work hard in Young Pioneers,' went on Semyon. 'The more people who get to know me the better. That's what matters in Moldavia.'

'It's time you boys were going to sleep,' their father said through the darkness. 'Goodnight.'

'Goodnight, Papa,' both lads replied at once. Then they turned round, snuggled their backs against each other for warmth, and dreamed their own dreams.

'Home first again!' Vanya's mother said, as he ran in the door. 'There's bread and cold fish on the table.'

Licking his lips at the thought of the fish, the boy said, 'Mama, there's something I need to ask you.'

Lifting the baby to burp him, the woman waited for what was to come.

'Why does my teacher say that there is no god? He says that people who believe in a god are like men who can't walk and who need crutches to lean on. Are you and Papa like men who can't walk? That's what Semyon says.'

The woman shook her head sadly. Semyon caused his Christian parents a great deal of heartache. He seemed to be taking in all that he was taught by his teachers and at Young Pioneers. It worried her that he would one day become a real Communist, and forget all he'd learned at home about the Lord Jesus Christ being the one and only Saviour.

'It's the other way round,' Vanya's mother said. 'Because Communists don't believe in God, they need Communism to tell them what to do and what to think. Although they can't see it for themselves, they are using Communism as a crutch.'

'Is that what Semyon's doing?' the boy asked.

His mother didn't reply, partly because the baby had just brought up some milk on her shawl, and partly because she was praying for Semyon.

In Vanya's teenage years he asked the questions that all teenagers ask. He wanted to know the whys, hows, wheres, and whats of life. That was how he discovered about Communism from his parents; and what he learned from them was different from his school history lessons. It saddened him that, after the Russian Revolution in 1917, his country should have turned its back on Christianity and tried to build a society that excluded God. And by the time he was sixteen years old, Vanya realised that not only could God not be excluded from the world he had made, Vanya could not exclude the Lord from his heart. Vanya felt God's call to believe in him, and he came to a saving faith in Jesus. That was in 1968, and within a short time of becoming a Christian, he was speaking in church about his faith.

'You'll get yourself into trouble with the authorities,' his friends told him. 'If they discover that you're becoming a preacher, you might find yourself in Siberia working in a mine for more years than you want to think about.'

'The Bible tells us to spread the good news about the Lord Jesus to those who don't know him,' Vanya replied. 'So do I obey God or the Communists?'

'You obey your god if you like,' one of the young men said. 'But don't speak to me again when we meet in the street, because I don't want to end up in Siberia just for being a friend of Ivan Moiseyev.'

Even Semyon, who didn't agree with what Vanya believed, warned his brother to be careful, or he'd get himself into trouble. 'The Baptists are not a recognised organisation,' he said, 'so that makes going to their services illegal.'

Although Vanya knew that Communists only tolerated Christians if they kept quiet about what they believed, he was both unable and unwilling to do that. God had saved his soul, and he was determined to tell others that he could save them too.

Having trained as a taxi driver after leaving school, when Vanya was eighteen years old, he joined the Red Army for his compulsory two years of national service. So from working as a civilian taxi driver he changed to serving as an army chauffeur, not an easy job in Odessa, where the snow had already started for the winter. Vanya's first priority when he moved into barracks was to find a quiet place where he could pray each day. He had to leave his Christian friends at home, but God went with him into the Red Army. It wasn't long before he came up against the army authorities, and it was because he prayed so long one morning that he was late for drill.

'You were late because you were praying!' said the astounded officer. 'There'll be no more of that!'

The result was that Vanya was reported to the Polit-Ruk where he was 'reminded' that the Communists had proved scientifically that God didn't exist. Instead of keeping his mouth shut, the young soldier told the official from the Polit-Ruk what the Bible had to say about the existence of God.

'You need to learn a lesson,' the man said. 'As you seem to like being on your knees, you can get down on your knees and scrub the drill hall and all the corridors in the barracks. That will take you all night. And while you are on your knees scrubbing, you can think about Communist teaching.'

From that day on Vanya was a marked man, and a very close watch was kept on what he did, and to whom he spoke.

It was 1971, and it was cold, very cold. Dreadful news had spread around the barracks about Vanya, and those who knew him couldn't wait to get the story straight.

'What happened to you?' a friend asked him, when they met shortly afterwards.

'Just another punishment for speaking about the Lord,' Vanya shrugged.

'Tell me about it.'

Vanya sighed. 'Corporal Gidenko decided to "bring me to my senses" once and for all. So he ordered me to stand outside all night until I was ready to apologise for talking about my faith.'

'Outside! But it's more than 13 degrees below zero at night,' his friend responded.

'And he made me wear just a cotton summer uniform,' Vanya said. 'The cold was terrible, and I thought I'd freeze to death. But I prayed to God and was warmed.'

'That must have been the longest night of your life,' his comrade said.

Vanya looked at him. 'But it was twelve nights. I stood outside in sub-zero temperatures in my light summer uniform for twelve nights.'

'Are you superhuman?' asked his amazed friend.

'No,' said Vanya. 'I'm just an ordinary human being who believes in Almighty God.'

Soon after that terrible punishment, God spoke to Vanya in a dream, a dream in which he saw and spoke to an angel. Being the young man he was, Vanya shared his dream with anyone who would listen to him. His commanding officers were nearly tearing their hair out!

'If making him stand outside for twelve nights at this time of year doesn't stop him speaking about his god, I really don't know what will,' said one officer.

'That punishment made him worse than ever,' added another. 'It seems that his god sent an angel to comfort him – and he's telling the whole barracks about it!' Then, as an afterthought, the man added, 'Nobody believes it, of course. All the soldiers know it's rubbish.'

But that wasn't the case at all. There were those who through Vanya discovered the reality of God for themselves.

'Don't tell our parents everything,' Vanya wrote to his brother Vladimir on 15th July, 1972. 'Just tell them that Vanya wrote you a letter, and he says that Jesus Christ is going into battle. Tell them that it's a Christian battle, and Vanya doesn't know whether he'll be back.' Vladimir read on to the end of the letter with a lump in his throat. 'Remember this one verse,' Vanya wrote, before signing his name, 'Be faithful unto death, and I will give you the crown of life.'

The following day twenty-year-old Vanya was dead. And having been faithful to the point of death, God did give him the crown of life.

His body was returned to his parents' home for burial. Although they were told that Vanya had drowned, his father and mother wished to see his body. The army officers who accompanied the coffin left before they could do that, perhaps because they had seen the marks of Vanya's last punishments. He had been tortured for his faith before being killed by drowning. It was July when the young man was buried. There was no snow on the ground, and his home village looked at its summer best. Many gathered round to support Vanya's family, some carrying garland Bible texts in the Moldavian and Russian languages.

Soon afterwards, a letter arrived from four Red Army soldiers who had served with Vanya. 'Dear Moiseyev family,' they wrote. 'Don't be discouraged. God has done a great work in the salvation of souls through your dear son and our brother and friend. ... Let them punish us, deprive us of everything on this earth, but they will not be able to take the freedom of Christ out of our hearts.'

Vanya had died and gone to heaven, but God still had his brave Christian soldiers in Russia's Red Army.

FACT FILE

Communist Russia: The Communist Party came to power in Russia in November 1917, after a popular uprising against the increasingly unpopular Tsar and a second uprising against a less extreme government, which was unable to provide the reforms demanded by many Russians. The Communist Party established a one party state in Russia and nationalised land and many of the industries. This often had disastrous consequences. No dissent, either religious or political, was allowed, and many people who spoke against the government were sent to prison camps, known as Gulags, in Siberia.

Keynote: Vanya found that the Communists were telling him to do one thing, while God, through the Bible, was telling him to do another. He chose to tell people about Jesus, even when it meant that he would be subject to very cruel punishments. It is not always easy to tell people about Jesus, but he has given us the responsibility, and he will give us strength and encouragement to do it, just as he did for Vanya.

Think: Although Vanya was far from Christian friends and his parents when he was sent to serve in the Red Army, God was still with him, and he was still able to pray, whatever the Polit-Ruk had to say. They could not stop him by their arguments, any more than the Communists could prove that God did not exist with science. Wherever you are, you can still pray to God and be confident that he will help you.

 Prayer: Lord Jesus, thank you for all that you have done for me and for remaining faithful wherever I am. Please give me the strength not to deny you, even when others try to make me do so. Amen.

Graham Staines

The sun was shining brightly on the Sunshine Coast in Queensland, Australia. From Double Island Point in the north, to the Glass House Mountains in the south, the blue sky was unbroken by a single cloud. As young people awoke that morning, they first checked the piles of Christmas presents at the ends of their beds, then they ran to their windows to see whether they'd be having their Christmas dinner on the beach, by the barbecue or (dreadful thought) in their homes. When Graham looked out on Palmwoods, there was no doubt in his mind that by early afternoon the barbecue would be glowing red, and delicious smells would fill the air. Meanwhile, there were things to do ... and most of them were wrapped in brightly coloured Christmas paper! One parcel after another was opened, and each seemed to be more exciting than the one that went before. But there was something he was especially looking for;

after all, he'd dropped enough hints. It was almost with a sense of relief that he noticed the book-shaped parcel right at the bottom. Graham smiled. 'That's it,' he said, as he unwrapped the book carefully. It wouldn't have been every teenager's choice of books, but *The Flora and Fauna of Queensland* was exactly what Graham Staines wanted. As he flicked through the pages, flowers and insects, trees and animals flashed past him. He could hardly wait till evening. The boy grinned. 'Don't be stupid!' he thought. 'It's Christmas, and there's a lot to enjoy before evening.'

Dinner was round the barbecue, and what a meal to celebrate with. By the end of it, Graham was lying on a lounger dressed in a pair of shorts that were a bit tighter than usual, thanks to what he had just eaten.

'Those barbecued buttered pineapple slices were delicious,' he said. 'But I'm stuffed!'

Although his mind wanted to play some of the games he'd been given for Christmas, all his eyes wanted to do were close. And that's what happened. Minutes later, Graham and the other members of his family were snoozing happily. Strangely, it was the buttered pineapple slices that inspired the boy's dream. He was no sooner asleep than he imagined himself walking through the tropical fruit plantations for which Palmwoods was famous. He pictured vast hands of bananas growing upwards, looking far too heavy to stay on the tree. His dream was so vivid he could smell warm peachiness, he could feel the cosy velvet-covered apricots ... and of course there were pineapples, great big, juicy pineapples. The smell of them seemed to be everywhere. Suddenly wide awake, Graham realised that they were not a dream; more buttered pineapple slices were on the barbecue. Delicious!

Hours later, back in his room with *The Flora and Fauna of Queensland* propped open on the table and a blank airmail letter in front of him, Graham thought how different Christmas would have been for his friend Shantanu Satpathy.

'I guess Baripada in India will have been as hot today as it is in Palmwoods, Australia, but I don't think Shantanu will have had buttered pineapple.'

But the thought of Shantanu sent Graham to his book and his sketch pad. A few days previously he had found a brightly coloured beetle that he'd never seen before. Rather than capture the creature, he drew a detailed picture of it. And he had just looked it up in his new book and wanted to write and tell his Indian pen-friend about it.

'I'd love to see the insects Shantanu tells me about,' he thought. 'I wonder if I will ever go to India, or if that's just a dream.'

Graham laughed aloud.

'My dream about the pineapple slices turned out to be true, so maybe one day I'll go to India after all.'

Having written a long and detailed letter to Shantanu, fifteen-year-old Graham lay on top of his bed and thought teenaged thoughts. And the particular thought that wouldn't go away was a real contradiction to his day. It was Christmas. He'd had a happy day with plenty of gifts that showed he was wanted and loved. Not only that, he'd wandered around the garden in his shorts knowing that he looked bronzed and healthy. So why did the picture he'd seen of Josia Soren keep coming into his mind? Why would the sight of a Mayurbhanj boy with leprosy not go away when he opened his eyes? Why could he see the patches on the lad's skin, his damaged nose and his missing fingertips, whether his eyes were open or shut? Why did the sight of a leprous boy his own age affect him in a way that nothing in his life had ever affected him before?

Lying there on top of his bed, Graham Staines knew what it was to be a boy and to be almost grown up at the same time. The boy in him wanted to weep at the sight of Josia Soren, while the almost man in him made plans about what he could do.

'There must be some treatment for leprosy, if only it could reach those who need it,' he thought. 'And boys like Josia could be trained to do work so that they wouldn't be so poor.' Before he fell asleep, Graham had made all sorts of plans for what could be done for the likes of Josia Soren. But when he finally nodded off to sleep, it was the smell of buttered pineapple on the barbecue that wafted into his dreams.

Nine years later, and after many letters to and from Shantanu Satpathy, Graham sat on top of the same bed in the same room wondering if he was dreaming.

'Am I really leaving for India in a few hours?' he asked himself.

In fact, he almost nipped his arm to check he was awake. India had been his dream for so long it seemed almost impossible that it was now about to become a reality. But it was. The following day, that's where he was! A tingle went from the soles of his feet to the hair on his head when he touched Indian soil for the very first time.

'This is like coming home,' he thought, then his mind immediately turned to his pen-friend.

Graham laughed. 'And in no time at all I'll meet Shantanu! We've written to each other about all sorts of things, especially the plants and animals of India and Australia.

But I wonder what we'll talk about when we meet face to face. I can't imagine that he'll suddenly go on about Asian elephants, and I'll respond with a discourse on the kangaroo!'

Of course it wasn't like that at all, and the pen-friends were soon firm friends who had no problem finding things to talk about.

Although years had passed since Graham first saw Josia Soren's photo, it was one of the biggest influences in all of his life. Graham had become a Christian while still young, and God had used Josia to put a calling into his heart, a calling to help those afflicted by leprosy. Where better to do that than in India where the disease was a scourge that blighted many lives? So, having at last reached India in 1965, Graham Staines just remained there. He joined the staff of the Evangelical Missionary Society of Mayurbhanj in Rairangpur.

'What do I write here?' Graham asked himself, as he filled out an application form for the work permit that would allow him to remain in India. 'I know. I'll say that I'm involved in missionary work, and that I also work with the Mayurbhanj Leprosy Home and Rajabasa Leprosy Rehabilitation Farm.'

Having decided on the words, he had to use small writing to squeeze them into the space provided. In another part of the form,

Graham explained that he 'preached the gospel as and when time permitted.'

Reading through the rest of the application, he came on a request for his 'profession or present occupation'. That caused him some head-scratching, as he'd already put the work he was doing. Thinking through what he was able to do, he picked up the pen again and wrote, 'I'm a missionary trained in carpentry, metalwork and motor mechanics, and a clerk trained in accountancy.'

With all those skills, Graham Staines was a useful person to have around!

'Do you speak the language?' a visitor to Rairangpur asked Graham, after the Australian had been working there for some time.

'What language would that be?' the missionary smiled.

'Em ... whatever they speak here.'

'Well, the people here speak a variety of languages, because they come from a variety of places. But I suppose you could say I speak the language because I've learned Oriya, Santhali and Ho.'

'You must have spent years at university!' was the amazed reply.

Collecting the tools he needed to help a disabled leprosy patient, Graham smiled. 'Yes,' he said. 'I've been at the University of Life.' Seeing the puzzlement in the visitor's face, he explained, 'I've learned the languages by spending time with people who speak them.'

In 1983 Graham met Gladys, the young woman who was to become his wife. She was also Australian, having been brought up just over twenty miles from Palmwoods! But God took them both to India and had them meet each other there. Gladys was a Christian who had already served the Lord in Singapore, Malaysia, Europe, Australia and India. The year they married, the couple moved to another Evangelical Missionary Society of Mayurbhanj Leprosy Home, this one at Baripada. Graham took over the work there, continuing a tradition of serving people with leprosy that had started as far back as 1895. And not only leprosy patients went to him for help.

'People suffering from all sorts of diseases come to Graham,' someone wrote, after visiting them. 'When I was there, they even had people calling at their home looking for treatment for snake bites!'

'What exactly do you do?' the Staines were often asked in letters from people who had never visited the work.

That was a hard question to answer as Graham was so multi-skilled that he did more or less anything that needed doing, from organising the Home, keeping the account books in order, helping patients in their rehabilitation, and teaching them how to make sabai grass products and handwoven goods for sale. He also preached and did outreach Christian work. Whenever he was able, Graham attended baptisms and Christian marriages, as he thought it was important to make a stand with local Christians. And in his 'spare time' he was involved in helping to translate the Bible into the local languages he knew so well. Gladys was very busy too, for as well as helping in the Home she had three children to look after. Esther was born in 1985, Philip in 1988 and Harold in 1992. The Staines were a happy, busy family, who loved where they lived and the work they did.

It was on 22nd January, 1999 that everything changed. Graham and his sons set out for Manoharpur to attend a jungle camp. Jungle camps were annual missionary events.

'They are so excited,' Gladys thought, as she waved goodbye to them. 'The boys just love having time on their own with their dad.'

After a long and exhausting day, Graham parked their station wagon, and then Philip and Harold cuddled down to sleep in the back. To protect them from the icy-cold, night wind, their dad hoisted a straw pad over the roof of the station wagon then settled down to sleep himself. Just after midnight, a group of men armed with sticks, axes and tridents, gathered round the station wagon. Screaming as they circled the vehicle, they hit out at it. The tyres were slashed. The windows were broken. What did they see as they looked inside? Was it the sight of a father praying with his two sons that so enraged them? Whatever it was, the results were terrible. Graham, Philip and Harold were attacked and stabbed with tridents. Straw was pushed under the station wagon, right under the petrol tank, and torched. In seconds the icy wind fanned the flames into an inferno from which there was no possible escape. The attackers watched the fire blaze and chased those who came to help put it out.

'Don't come near, or we'll kill you too,' the death-crazed men screamed to those who lived nearby.

One of Graham's friends, who was visiting Manoharpur, was within shouting distance. He heard the noise and made to race to find out what was wrong, not knowing the Staines were under attack. Grabbing the door handle, he discovered that the key had been turned on the outside. He didn't know what was happening, but he did know he could do nothing to help, whatever it was. By the time the man was freed, the terrible deed was done. All that was left was the charred remains of the station wagon and of Graham and his sons, who loved the Indian people enough to spend their lives serving them.

* * *

'My husband and our children have sacrificed their lives for this nation,' Gladys said later. 'But India is my home. I am happy to be here.'

And Esther, who had lost her father and both her young brothers, said, 'I praise God that he found my father worthy to die for Christ.'

Graham, Philip and Harold died for the sake of Jesus, and for the people of India, and Gladys and Esther remained to serve God and the people of that land. They will meet again one day, and when they do, there will be no more tears or pain, for these things have no place in heaven.

FACT FILE

Leprosy: We read a lot about leprosy in the Bible, and, in the gospels, we find stories about Jesus curing lepers. Now the disease is rarely known in the developed world and, if caught early, can be cured by medicine. However, it is still widespread in India and some other warm and poor countries. The disease tends to affect the extremities of the body. Because it kills the nerves, that means that people with leprosy cannot feel pain. This causes them real problems because they can seriously burn or cut themselves without knowing it.

Keynote: We often look for gratitude or even some reward from those we help. It is tempting to think that Graham did not get much reward for his services to the Indian people, since he and his sons were murdered there. But even if he had no reward on earth, he knew that he was pleasing his Father in heaven, and that he had a reward there which no one could take away from him.

Think: Even at the end of a happy Christmas day in Australia, Graham was thinking about the poor boy in India with leprosy, that he had seen in a photograph. He did not allow his comfort to blind him to the pain and suffering of others. This made Graham pray for these people and look to see how he could help them. Can you think of people anywhere in the world that you would like to help?

 Prayer: Lord Jesus, thank you for the cures for leprosy that are now available. But thank you even more for coming so that we can be cleansed from our sins. Please be with those who are suffering just now and comfort them. Amen.

Quiz

How much can you remember about the ten boys who didn't give in? Try answering these questions to find out.

Polycarp

1. What was used to tie the slaves together in the story that Polycarp's mother told him?

2. What did Polycarp see in his dream?

3. Which person from the Bible is Polycarp said to have met?

Alban

4. Where did the young Alban want to go to watch the chariot races?

5. What did people call London before it was known by that name?

6. Who was the emperor who gave the order to persecute Christians in Britain as well as Rome?

Sir John Oldcastle

7. Which country did John fight in to win his knighthood?

8. What was the name of the group that called him 'Good Lord Cobham'?

9. Where did the government lock John up?

Thomas Cranmer

10. What job did Thomas get as head of the Protestant church in England?

11. Who succeeded to the throne after Henry VIII?

12. Which hand did Thomas put into the fire first?

George Wishart

13. What were the bits of paper called that the Roman Church used to sell?

14. Where was the Scottish school that George taught in?

15. Where was George executed?

James Chalmers

16. Which country did James hear about when he was a teenager?

17. What did the painted men demand of James and his wife when they first arrived in New Guinea?

18. Who went with James to Goaribari Island?

Dietrich Bonhoeffer

19. What was across the road from the first house that Dietrich lived in?

20. Who became Reich Chancellor in 1932?

21. Which anti-Nazi church was Dietrich part of?

Nate Saint

22. What did Nate learn to assemble with his eyes closed while in the Air Cadet Training Program?

23. What day did Nate get married on?

24. How did Nate give presents to the Auca people?

Ivan Moiseyev

25. Where did the baby sleep in Vanya's house?

26. Where did Vanya's friends warn that he would be sent if he did not stop talking about God?

27. What did Vanya have to wear when he was made to stand outside in the cold all night?

Graham Staines

28. Which Australian state was Graham's book about?

29. What did Graham have for his Christmas dinner?

30. How did Graham learn the native languages in India?

How well did you do?

Turn over to find out ...

Quiz Answers

1. A rope

2. Himself being burned at the stake

3. The Apostle John

4. The Circus Maximus

5. Londinium

6. Septimus Severus

7. France

8. The Lollards

9. The Tower of London

10. Archbishop of Canterbury

11. Edward VI

12. His right hand

13. Indulgences

14. Montrose

15. St Andrews

16. Fiji

17. Knives, tomahawks and other weapons

18. Oliver Tomkins

19. A cemetery

20. Adolf Hitler

21. The Confessing Church

22. A Tommy gun

23. Valentine's Day

24. In a bucket suspended from the plane

25. On the shelf beside the stove

26. Siberia

27. His summer uniform

28. Queensland

29. A barbecue

30. By spending time with people who spoke to them.

Start collecting this series now!

Ten Boys who used their Talents:
ISBN 978-1-84550-146-4
Paul Brand, Ghillean Prance, C.S.Lewis,
C.T. Studd, Wilfred Grenfell, J.S. Bach,
James Clerk Maxwell, Samuel Morse,
George Washington Carver, John Bunyan.

Ten Girls who used their Talents:
ISBN 978-1-84550-147-1
Helen Roseveare, Maureen McKenna,
Anne Lawson, Harriet Beecher Stowe,
Sarah Edwards, Selina Countess of Huntingdon,
Mildred Cable, Katie Ann MacKinnon,
Patricia St. John, Mary Verghese.

Ten Boys who Changed the World:
ISBN 978-1-85792-579-1
David Livingstone, Billy Graham, Brother Andrew,
John Newton, William Carey, George Müller,
Nicky Cruz, Eric Liddell, Luis Palau,
Adoniram Judson.

Ten Girls who Changed the World:
ISBN 978-1-85792-649-1
Corrie Ten Boom, Mary Slessor,
Joni Eareckson Tada, Isobel Kuhn,
Amy Carmichael, Elizabeth Fry, Evelyn Brand,
Gladys Aylward, Catherine Booth, Jackie Pullinger.

Ten Boys who Made a Difference:
ISBN 978-1-85792-775-7
Augustine of Hippo, Jan Hus, Martin Luther,
Ulrich Zwingli, William Tyndale, Hugh Latimer,
John Calvin, John Knox, Lord Shaftesbury,
Thomas Chalmers.

Ten Girls who Made a Difference:
ISBN 978-1-85792-776-4
Monica of Thagaste, Catherine Luther,
Susanna Wesley, Ann Judson, Maria Taylor,
Susannah Spurgeon, Bethan Lloyd-Jones,
Edith Schaeffer, Sabina Wurmbrand,
Ruth Bell Graham.

Ten Boys who Made History:
ISBN 978-1-85792-836-5
Charles Spurgeon, Jonathan Edwards,
Samuel Rutherford, D L Moody,
Martin Lloyd Jones, A W Tozer, John Owen,
Robert Murray McCheyne, Billy Sunday,
George Whitfield.

Ten Girls who Made History:
ISBN 978-1-85792-837-2
Ida Scudder, Betty Green, Jeanette Li,
Mary Jane Kinnaird, Bessie Adams,
Emma Dryer, Lottie Moon, Florence Nightingale,
Henrietta Mears, Elisabeth Elliot.

Ten Boys who Didn't Give In:
ISBN 978-1-84550-035-1
Polycarp, Alban, Sir John Oldcastle
Thomas Cramer, George Wishart,
James Chalmers, Dietrich Bonhoeffer
Nate Saint, Ivan Moiseyev
Graham Staines.

Ten Girls who Didn't Give In:
ISBN 978-1-84550-036-8
Blandina, Perpetua, Lady Jane Grey,
Anne Askew, Lysken Dirks, Marion Harvey,
Margaret Wilson, Judith Weinberg,
Betty Stam, Esther John.

CHRISTIAN FOCUS PUBLICATIONS

Christian Focus   Christian Heritage   CF4K   Mentor

Christian Focus Publications publishes books for adults and children under its four main imprints: Christian Focus, CF4K, Mentor and Christian Heritage. Our books reflect our conviction that God's Word is reliable and Jesus is the way to know him, and live for ever with him.

Our children's publication list includes a Sunday School curriculum that covers pre-school to early teens, and puzzle and activity books. We also publish personal and family devotional titles, biographies and inspirational stories that children will love.

If you are looking for quality Bible teaching for children then we have an excellent range of Bible stories and age-specific theological books.

From pre-school board books to teenage apologetics, we have it covered!

Find us at our web page:
www.christianfocus.com

CF4•K
*Because you're never
too young to know Jesus*

TEN BOYS WHO MADE A DIFFERENCE

LIGHT KEEPERS

Irene Howat

CF4·K

Copyright © 2002 Christian Focus Publications
Reprinted 2003, 2004, 2005, 2006, 2007, 2008, 2016,
twice in 2017, 2019, 2020
Paperback ISBN: 978-1-85792-775-7
epub ISBN: 978-1-84550-842-5
mobi ISBN: 978-1-84550-843-2
Published by Christian Focus Publications Ltd,
Geanies House, Fearn, Tain, Ross-shire,
IV20 1TW, Scotland, Great Britain.
www.christianfocus.com
email:info@christianfocus.com
Cover design by Alister MacInnes
Cover illustration by Elena Temporin,
Milan Illustrations Agency.
Printed and bound in Turkey

All incidents retold in these stories are based on true situations.
Where specific information about childhood incidents has been
unobtainable the author has written these paragraphs using other
information concerning family life, hobbies, home life, relationships
freely available in other biographies as well as appropriate historical
source material.

*Cover illustration: This depicts Martin Luther as a young boy growing up in
Germany. He lived in the area of Saxony where both his parents worked hard
so that their son could not only have education, but have food and clothing
and a roof over his head. Gathering wood for the fire, walking miles to get to
the school room and then suffering lashes from the teacher's strap were all part
of Martin Luther's normal school boy life before he went on to become one of
the founders of the reformation.*

For Samuel

Contents

Augustine of Hippo

Augustine raised his arm slowly in order not to frighten the birds roosting on the branch far above his head. Then he slid a stone into the leather band of his catapult, pulled back the cat gut and 'ping'. It flew through the branches and straight for the cluster of birds. There was a dull thud as one landed a short distance away. 'Gotcha!' said the boy. 'You'll roast nicely. Now let's see if we can find where the rest of your family moved to.'

Silently he slid among the undergrowth, taking care not to stand on any brittle twigs that might break and give him away. 'There they are!' he said to himself, seeing birds' shadows cast on to the ground by the bright North African sun. 'I'll try for a double,' he decided. From his leather pouch he took a little pile of stones, looking for two that would fit together in his catapult. They needed to be rounded on one side but flat on the other, and about the same size and weight. 'Perfect!' he whispered. 'These ones are ideal.' Again there was absolute silence until the 'ping,' but this time it was followed by two dull thuds.

Augustine unwound a length of thin creeper from the tree the birds had been on, broke it off and used it to tie together the legs of his three birds. 'Dad can have these two,' he thought. 'That should put him in a good mood.'

'It's me, Mum!' Augustine called as he neared home. There was silence. Dropping his birds on the floor, he went in quietly. It took a minute for his eyes to get used to the darkness after the brilliant sun. Seeing his mother on her knees didn't take him by surprise. Monica was a Christian, and when she wasn't doing all the work of an African mother, she was on her knees praying. Augustine listened. 'Lord, please forgive my child his sins. Please save his soul and use him to tell others about yourself,' she said.

'She's praying for me again as usual,' he thought, creeping back out into the sunlight. 'Maybe I'll become a Christian one day, but I'm too busy enjoying myself to be bothered just now. I wish Mum would stop asking God to convert me until I'm grown-up. It would be so easy to become a believer just to please her, but I want to please myself while I'm young.'

'I had a visit from a member of the Guard today, son,' Monica told her young son, when she joined him outside. 'There's been trouble, and they wondered if you were involved.'

Augustine looked at her. 'What am I meant to have done?' he asked, laughing just a little nervously. 'Because I didn't do it and I wasn't there when I did it.'

His mother looked serious. 'Augustine,' she said, 'I know you weren't involved because you were with me when the theft took place. But I also know that you don't always keep good company, and you do get into scrapes.'

Augustine hung his head, but just for a minute. 'I'm young, Mum,' he said. 'I'll not do anything so stupid that the Roman Guard will come for me. And I promise I will think about becoming a Christian ... sometime.'

'Sometime may not be soon enough,' his mother warned. 'Not everyone lives to grow up.'

A shiver went down the young boy's spine. 'But I will,' he said, defiantly.

'I'm not feeling well,' Augustine whined one day, not so long afterwards.

'What's wrong?' his mother asked. 'Are you feeling sick?' Before he could reply, he was caught in a spasm of pain. He was bent double with the force of it, and it was some minutes before he could speak. 'It's my stomach, Mum,' he said. 'I've got a terribly sore stomach.'

Monica felt his forehead. He was hot, and beads of perspiration were forming as she watched. Another spasm of pain hit him, and he landed on the floor. Within the hour he was tossing and turning. One minute he was roasting and the next he was shivering with cold. His mother washed him to bring his temperature down and gave him sips of water to drink.

'He's in a bad way,' said Patricius, Augustine's father. 'I've made an offering to the gods for him, but maybe you should be praying to your God too.'

'I've been praying to the Lord God for him since before he was born,' Monica said, 'and I've never stopped praying all of today.'

'I don't understand you Christians,' said Patricius. 'How do you expect your God to answer prayers unless you give him animal sacrifices?'

'Mother,' Augustine said weakly. 'I think I'm going to die.'

Monica looked at him and stroked his hand gently. 'Is he dying?' she wondered. 'He's not eaten for days and he's lost so much weight. He's just skin and bone.'

'Please, Mother,' he said, through tears. 'Please get the priest quickly. I want to go to heaven when I die.'

His mother kissed him, her tears mixing with his. 'I'll get the priest,' she said. But when she came back, not knowing whether her young son would be alive or dead, she discovered that he had made an amazing recovery! He was sitting up eating a piece of mango.

'Praise the Lord!' said the delighted Monica. 'Praise the Lord!'

'I don't think I'm going to die quite yet!' Augustine grinned.

Augustine loved his mother, but despite all that she had taught him, he grew up without becoming a Christian. And as if that wasn't bad enough, he went on to live an immoral life. Monica must have been deeply upset, but she kept on praying. Although she was proud of her son's able mind, and that he became a professor across the Mediterranean Sea in Italy, all she really wanted for him was that he should become a Christian. Patricius, who followed Roman gods and was not a Christian, didn't bother about his son's behaviour as that was how people lived in the Roman Empire.

One day in 386, when Augustine was thirty-two years old, he was walking along a road in the Italian city of Milan. He passed a beggar who was sitting on the pavement laughing. 'How can that man laugh?' he asked himself. 'He's sitting there on the street, owning nothing but the clothes he's wearing, and not even sure if he'll have a meal today, and he's happy. The man is laughing!' Augustine walked on. 'And here I am,' he thought. 'I've got a good job, another pretty girl, plenty of money, fine clothes and as much to eat as I want.' He stopped and looked back at the happy beggar. 'And I'm miserable,' he admitted. 'He's happy with nothing, and I'm miserable with everything. What a mess!'

'Would you like to come to church with me?' a friend asked him.

Augustine almost automatically said that he'd rather not, when he remembered the beggar. 'Yes, I'll come,' he said. 'I hear that Ambrose is a good preacher.'

'You can judge for yourself,' his friend commented. Monica, who had moved to Milan soon after her son, heard he was going to church and she prayed, how she prayed!

'He's a good preacher right enough,' Augustine said, as he and his friend left the church. 'I'm going to have to think about what he said.'

For some time he did just that. He wept over it too. 'I just can't take it in,' he told

Monica, one day. 'My sins are so terrible, how can God love me? How can Jesus have died for me after all that I've done?'

'Jesus died for us because we're sinners,' his mother explained. 'He wouldn't have needed to die if we'd been perfect. His blood was shed on the cross for you and for me, and because of that, our sins can be washed away.'

Soon afterwards Augustine was in his garden with a friend. He left his companion sitting under a tree and walked about restlessly. He was in a terrible mental muddle. He heard what sounded like a child's voice saying, 'Take it up and read it. Take it up and read it.' 'Is that a nursery rhyme?' he wondered, but couldn't remember any with those words. Suddenly he realised it was God speaking to him. He rushed back to his friend who had the Bible book of Romans. Opening it up, Augustine read words that told him he should look to Jesus and not live the immoral life he was living. Augustine suddenly knew the truth, confessed his sin and believed in Jesus. When he and his friend went back into the house, Monica learned that all her prayers had been answered.

Augustine became a great student of the Bible and teacher of the Christian faith.

Just eight years after he was converted, he was appointed Bishop of Hippo, the second most important town in North Africa. 'I'm happier now than I've ever been,' he told one of his friends. 'And it's all thanks to that happy beggar who made me realise how miserable I really was, and to my mother's prayers.'

'There is so much odd teaching,' his friend told him. 'Some people say that the Roman Empire fell because they stopped worshipping their gods. Others say that we go to heaven by living decent lives rather than by having faith in God. And there's a man called Pelagius who's teaching that we can be good; our only problem is that we choose not to be.'

'There are more strange teachers around as well,' said a priest who was with them. 'Have you heard of the Donatists?'

Augustine nodded. 'They've got some very funny ideas. They say that the church should be full of people who are absolutely good, that nobody who isn't as good as they are should be allowed in!'

'There's no hope for me then,' his friend said. 'I know myself well enough to know I don't belong in their kind of church.'

'We've got to get things sorted out,' the Bishop announced. 'Or nobody will know what Christians believe. They'll think Christianity is a religion that you can make up yourself – just believe in Jesus and add whatever you like to his life story.'

'I think God gave you such an amazing brain in order that you could think things through for us all,' Augustine's friend said. 'We're in such a terrible muddle.'

'With God's help I'll do what I can. And you,' he told his companion, 'must pray that I'll know the truth when I see it in the Bible and not accept one single teaching that is not in God's Word.'

'I hear that the Bishop's book is nearly ready,' was the news around Hippo in the year 400. Ten years later, the news was much the same. 'I hear that Augustine has written another book,' people said to each other. 'What a mind that man's got!' And the second book was not the last thing he wrote. The Bishop of Hippo spent much of his time studying wrong teachings, then searching the Bible to find out what was true.

'Augustine helped me straighten out my thinking,' a Christian said to his two companions, as they walked through the streets of Hippo in the year 421. 'After the evils of the Roman Empire, I'd been trying so hard to get my congregation to lead good lives that I was almost teaching the same things as Pelagius. How wrong I was to go that far! Of course God expects us to live decent lives, but we don't get to heaven by being decent. We are saved only by faith in Jesus. It doesn't matter how hard we try to be good, we can't be because we are sinners. I have to admit my teaching was not from the Bible. But now the Bishop has sorted me out.'

'And at last I've got an answer for the Donatists,' added their companion. 'Of course we shouldn't try to keep sinners from coming to church. After all, Jesus taught that weeds would grow among the crops till harvest time. That's what it's like in the church. There will always be non-Christians who come, and thank God for that because they might be converted. I'm grateful to the Bishop for making that clear.'

'We all owe a lot to Augustine, even the Romans,' the priest said. 'They thought it was because they'd stopped worshipping their gods that the Empire fell, but Augustine was able to show from the Bible that it was God's judgement, not their gods going in the huff! Maybe now some of them will come to believe in Jesus.'

'Wouldn't that be wonderful!' one of his friends smiled. 'That really would be good news.'

As they walked on, the priest seemed deep in thought. 'What's on your mind?' he was asked.

'I was just thinking how much Augustine has done for the Church. We were all in such a muddle until he came along. We didn't know the Bible and we didn't understand much of what we did know! I think the Church will remember Augustine hundreds of years from now, perhaps even thousands, because he's set us out on the right road.' 'You may be right,' laughed his friend. 'But we won't be here to see it!'

FACT FILE
Mediterranean Sea: The Mediterranean Sea lies between Europe and Africa. It is linked to the open ocean only by the narrow Strait of Gibraltar. It is more than 3,200 kilometres long and covers an area ten times the size of the United Kingdom.

Keynote: When he was young, Augustine and his friends often got into trouble. His mother realised that these friends were a bad influence on him. It is important to choose friends wisely. Ask God to help you make friends with people who trust and honour him. If your friends do not believe in Jesus, pray that God will help you to tell them about him and his love.

Think: Augustine's life before he became a Christian was immoral. He didn't follow God's rules. Look up Exodus chapter 20. Augustine wanted to disobey God's commands as he thought this was more fun. But it was when Jesus came into his life that Augustine's heart changed. What parts of your life need to change? Have you asked Jesus to take control of your life?

 Prayer: Dear God, please help me to honour you in my life. Protect me from sin. I am sorry for the times that I displease you, but thank you for loving me and forgiving me. Amen.

Jan Hus

Jan Hus chose the stones carefully, five of them, about the same size and weight. Then he turned his back to the wind and threw them a few centimetres in the air. 'Can I catch all five?' he wondered, holding his breath. And he did. Next time he threw them a little higher and still caught them. Then he tried higher still and caught them again. 'This is fun,' he said to himself. 'I'll soon be good enough to take on the other boys at fives.' For days and days he practised on his own, until he could throw the stones about half a metre into the air and catch them more times than they fell.

'Where have you been?' his friends asked, when he joined them to play. Jan shrugged his shoulders. He didn't want to tell them he'd been practising fives. That was his secret until he was sure he was good enough.

'Want a game?' one of the boys said.

'What are you playing?'

'Just stones,' he said.

Jan smiled. 'Sure,' he agreed. 'I'll play.' He took his favourite stones from his pocket. The ones he needed were round pebbles, about the size of a blackbird's egg, and he always carried some with him. 'You draw and I start.' Jan took a chalky stone and drew a circle on the ground. He placed a larger pebble in the middle of the circle. 'That all right?' he asked. His friends said it was. All four boys stood in a line about two metres away and they took turns to throw into the circle. Each threw six stones.

'You win!' Jan told his friend. 'Your stone's the one nearest the middle. Let's play again.'

The afternoon passed very quickly because the boys were enjoying themselves so much.

'Jan! Jan!' a voice called from a short distance away.

Jan grabbed his stones and ran. 'I'll have to go,' he shouted over his shoulder. 'That's my mum.'

'Did you beat them at fives?' Mum asked, knowing her son had been practising.

'Not yet,' he grinned. 'I'll wait till I know I'm an expert before I play. I found another good stone today,' he added, holding up a blue pebble. 'You've been down at the river again,' smiled Mrs Hus. 'I used to collect coloured pebbles from the Blanice River when I was a girl. You could give that one to the saint,' she said.

Jan had a sinking feeling. He didn't want to give his stone to the statue of St John. But because he didn't want to upset his mother, he put it on the shelf in front of the carved statue. 'Oops!' he said. 'I nearly knocked it over!'

His mum's face turned white. 'For goodness' sake be careful,' she said anxiously. 'If you break the statue, we could have bad luck for years.' Jan looked at the shelf and wondered. The statue was made of stone; his blue pebble was a stone – could dropping one of them really bring bad luck?

While Jan was still a boy, his father died. All the village of Husinec came to his funeral Mass. The priest read prayers in Latin, and the Mass was said in Latin. There was not much that a boy could understand, and, because he was so upset, Jan needed to understand. After the burial he went back to the church. It was the only stone building there was, and it even had a bell tower. Usually Jan liked the sound of the bell, but when it rang on the day of his father's funeral, it gave Jan the shivers.

'Did you bow to the crucifix?' the priest asked, not unkindly, when Jan entered the church. Jan bowed to the stone figure of Jesus on the cross, then stood waiting to be spoken to.

'What do you want?' the priest asked.

'Please, Father,' Jan said, 'has my father gone to heaven?'

The priest looked shocked at the very idea. 'No,' he said. 'Your father was a good man but not that good. But if you ask the saints, perhaps he'll get to heaven one day.'

Jan felt a terrible emptiness, and when he looked at the statues of the saints all round the church, he wondered how speaking to carved and painted stones could possibly take his father to heaven.

'And remember to bow to the crucifix before you go.'

Hanging his head, he made the sign of the cross and bolted for the door.

'I can't possibly go to university, Mum,' a teenage Jan said, some years later. 'You don't have the money to send me.'

Mrs Hus folded her arms and stood firm. Jan realised his mother meant business! 'Just you listen to me,' she told him. 'A wealthy gentleman has agreed to pay for your education out of the goodness of his heart. You'll go to university and you'll study so hard that he'll be proud of you.' Her arms fell to her side, and Mrs Hus's face lost its fighting look. 'And I'll be proud of you too,' she added, smiling.

Soon afterwards, Jan took his small bundle of clothes and books and went off to Prague University.

'This is a beautiful place,' he said, as he walked round the city streets with another boy from the Blanice Valley.

'I've heard that it's the only place in Bohemia with stone buildings,' his friend said.

'And all these statues too,' Jan said. 'There is stone everywhere.' Jan remembered the games of fives he had played as a young boy at home and all the stones he collected at the river. 'I didn't collect enough stones to make a spire,' he smiled ... and then he remembered the blue pebble at the statue of St John. 'Do you believe that praying to statues can help you?' he asked his friend.

The other young man looked at him. 'If the Church says it, I believe it. Life's easier that way.'

There was a great buzz and worry in Bohemia. Jan was trying to work out why.

'Do you really think the world will come to an end at the turn of the century?' he asked an elderly friend. 'I can't see why 1st January, 1400 will be any different from 31st December, 1399.'

The elderly man shook his head. 'You're young,' he said. 'When you're as old as I am you'll take these things seriously. The Church wouldn't be asking for special collections to get us to heaven if they didn't think the world might end at midnight.'

Fear mounted as the year drew to its close. And as midnight on the last day of the year drew near, some people prayed to the saints, others drank themselves so drunk they didn't know what time of the year it was anyway, and some clung to their families and waited for the end. But it didn't come. Midnight passed, and the new century dawned.

By then Jan Hus was a university professor and in 1400 he became a priest. 'I'm having real problems,' he told his best friend. 'The more I hear of that Englishman Wycliffe's teaching, the less I like what the Church says.'

'So you say,' the other priest commented. 'But you don't explain the difference.'

The two young men sat down on the low branch of a tree. 'Right then,' Jan said. 'I'll try to explain some of the differences. The Church is rich and powerful. For example, who owns most of the land around here?'

'The Church,' his friend agreed.

Jan nodded. 'But surely Christians should give to the poor rather than collecting huge amounts of money for itself. I agree with Mr Wycliffe on that. Then there's another thing: this business of everything being in Latin. What good is that to the people of Bohemia?'

'True,' his friend said. 'But if the priests get the Mass and the prayers right, what does it matter if common people don't understand?'

'It matters because God wants them to know what they're doing. The Bible says that we should have boldness to come to God; there's no mention of going through a priest.'

'That's enough for now,' his friend said. 'My head's spinning with all your ideas.'

Jan Hus was not so easily put off. 'Hear me out,' he said, as they headed for home. 'Mr Wycliffe translated the Bible into English, and we should have it in our own language. And there's the Mass too. Why do we only get bread and no wine in the service? The Bible says that we've to take bread and wine in memory of Christ's death.'

His friend held up his hand. 'Enough is ENOUGH,' he said. 'You sound as though you believe the Bible more than the traditions of the Church!'

Hus grinned. 'I do,' he said. 'But I don't expect the Church to like it.'

Two years later Jan began to preach in the Bethlehem Chapel in Prague. 'I love this place,' he thought. 'It's not controlled by the Church. I can speak to people in their own language.'

Sunday by Sunday he preached in Czech, the congregations sang in Czech and God's Word was read in Czech too. At last the people were hearing the gospel in their own language.

'What a difference it makes when we understand the service!' people said, as they left the church.

'But do you think God hears our prayers when we don't pray first to the saints?' his rather worried companion asked.

'Jan Hus says that praying to a stone statue is no different from praying to a river pebble,' the first man commented. 'He told us that our prayers have to be offered through Jesus alone, not through the saints.'

'I'm not sure about that,' his friend said. 'I always pray to St Christopher when I'm travelling and ask him to keep me safe. I've a whole list of saints I pray to for different things, and I give money to them as well.'

Hus preached about Jesus, telling people that the Bible was the true Word of God and that God didn't tell lies. He explained that the Church had not always told the truth, and that it was still telling people what was wrong.

'How dare you say these things of the Church!' the Archbishop of Prague roared. 'How dare you tell people that the Pope is a mere man and a bad sinner at that – one that lies and deliberately misleads people!'

'I dare to say these things because I don't dare not to,' the pale, thin Jan Hus said. The Archbishop seemed huge next to him as he screamed his next question.

'What do you mean? Explain to me what you mean!'

Jan tried to explain about the Bible and about John Wycliffe, but the Archbishop was too angry to listen.

'Get out!' the furious man roared, his eyes bulging as though they would shoot out and hit Hus. 'You've not heard the end of this!'

The Archbishop of Prague gathered Wycliffe's books and any writings of Jan Hus and had them burned. Then he had Jan thrown out of the Church and banished from Prague.

'If he thinks he'll stop me preaching,' Hus told his friends, 'he's wrong. If I can't preach in the town, I'll preach in the villages. And if he chases me out of the villages, I'll preach on the hillsides and by the rivers of Bohemia.'

As more and more people followed Jan Hus's teaching rather than listening to what the priests had to say, the Archbishop planned how to get rid of him. Even the Pope wanted him out of the way.

'You're not safe anywhere,' a friend told Jan one day in 1414. And he was right. Hus was arrested and thrown into prison. That winter he was taken to Gottlieben Castle, where he was put in a draughty tower, bound hand and foot and left to freeze.

'Dear Jesus,' he prayed, as he sat propped against the stone wall of the tower, 'thank you so much that you're right in this place with me. Please forgive those who have put me here, poor misguided people who think that if the stone I'm leaning against was carved into the shape of a saint it could answer their prayers! Heavenly Father, show them the truth, show them that the Bible is true.'

The winter passed; spring came, then summer. The tower was less draughty, but his jailors were no more kind. In July the

Archbishop sent for him. Jan was taken out of the tower, dragged down the steep stairs, then out into the morning sunshine.

'My beautiful land,' he thought, enjoying the sight of it, and knowing he would soon see an even more beautiful land than Bohemia.

A stake was hammered into the ground and Hus was chained to it. He watched as a bonfire was built around him. Jan saw the lighted torch arrive and the first sparks of the fire fly in the air. He felt the heat come nearer and said before the flames engulfed him, 'The aim of all my preaching, teaching, writing and actions has been to turn people from their sins. And that teaching I seal with my death today.'

As he finished speaking, the flames roared around him. The people who stood by the fire thought they were watching Jan Hus burn. But only his body was there. His soul was in that better land; it was in heaven with the Lord Jesus.

FACT FILE
Prague: This used to be the capital of Czechoslovakia. It is now the capital of the Czech Republic as Czechoslovakia has separated into two countries – the other being Slovakia. Before Czechoslovakia existed, this country was called Bohemia. Prague, which is sometimes called The City of 100 Spires, was built in a broad valley along the banks of the River Vlatva. The traditional heart of the city is the cobbled Old Town Square which is dominated by a monument to Jan Hus.

Keynote: Jan Hus believed that we should have a boldness when dealing with God. We shouldn't feel afraid to pray to God. We can bring all our problems and cares to our loving heavenly Father. The apostle Peter in 1 Peter 5:7 says that we should cast all our cares on God who cares for us. You don't have to ask someone else to speak to God for you.

Think: Jan's main aim in life was to turn people away from their sins and to bring them to know the Lord Jesus Christ for themselves. How has sin harmed your life and the world around you?

 Prayer: Dear God, turn me away from my sin towards you and help me to know Jesus Christ for myself. Teach me to pray to you and cast all my cares on you. Make my main aim in life to praise you and enjoy you forever. Amen.

Martin Luther

Martin peered round the corner of a road in Mansfield in Saxony. 'Are there any goblins coming?' his brother asked from behind. He was younger than Martin and quite happy to let his older brother go first, especially in the dark.

'No,' whispered Martin. 'I think it's safe.' But even though he sounded confident, he was shaking and every bit as scared as his brother.

'What's that!' he screamed, when something touched his leg.

'It was a cat,' the other boy said. 'I thought you'd seen it coming.'

'I don't want to go past the church,' Martin announced. 'We'll go home the long way.'

'I don't like going past the church either,' his brother agreed. 'There are spirits there, and they sometimes run away with children, especially boys.'

'Who told you that?'

'That's what someone told a gang playing near the church. He said that spirits took boys away to work for them, and that they could never get back out of the underworld. They're held prisoners for ever and ever and ever.'

'I think that's nonsense,' the older boy said, but he decided never to go near the church on his own just in case. He didn't want to risk being a prisoner in the underworld.

As he lay in bed that night, Martin thought about goblins and churches, about spirits and priests. Somehow he couldn't separate them out.

'I wish there weren't so many things to be afraid of,' he thought. 'The priest scares me most of all because he says boys are bad and can't go to heaven and that they sometimes spend hundreds of years in purgatory.'

'What is purgatory?' he asked his father the following day.

'It's where we go when we die,' the man explained. 'And we are there until we can go to heaven.'

'But I want to go straight to heaven when I die,' Martin said.

'You'll not do that, son,' Mr Luther said, sadly. 'You've already done too many bad things. Only those who live nearly perfect lives go to heaven right away. And

I suppose they are all Popes and Cardinals and Archbishops.'

'What about bishops and priests?' asked Martin. His father shook his head.

'I expect most of them will go to purgatory.'

Martin was near to tears when he asked, 'How do you get out of purgatory?'

'When people who are still alive say enough Masses or give enough money to the church,' was the upsetting answer.

'Are you awake?' his brother asked.

'Yes.'

'What are you thinking about?'

Martin told his young brother his thoughts, but this only made his young brother ask more questions. 'What happens if families don't say enough Masses? Do people have to stay in purgatory for ever?'

'I suppose so,' Martin said.

'But what if Mum died and Dad was killed down the mine and there was nobody to say Masses for us?'

Because Martin was beginning to feel really quite scared, he decided to pretend he'd fallen asleep and not heard what his brother had said. He grunted, turned round, and lay awake for hours thinking. 'I wonder if we've said enough Masses for my baby brothers and sisters who've died?' he found himself worrying. 'Maybe they're still in purgatory?'

The next morning Martin was slow to get up and his father was not at all pleased. 'You're a lazy, lazy boy!' he said, taking the leather belt off his trousers. 'I've worked hard for you, and all you can do is sleep. When we came to Mansfield, we had hardly a penny. I worked my fingers to the bone to feed and clothe you. I work so hard that I own the mine now. And what do I get? An eldest son who can't get out of his bed in the mornings!'

Martin knew better than to dodge his father's belt, so he took his punishment without flinching. 'Go and help your mother gather wood,' Mr Luther said, as he put on his belt again.

Martin waited until he was out of sight of his home before rubbing where his father's belt had hit him. But he didn't risk stopping long for he knew his father would come after him to check what he was doing. He guessed where his mother would be in the forest because a large tree had blown down and there was plenty of wood to be had from it.

'You've come to help,' his mother said, when she saw him.

'Dad sent me,' Martin told her. 'But I would have come anyway.' He enjoyed collecting wood for the fire. 'Do you know something, Mum. Wood heats you up twice.'

'What do you mean?' his mother asked.

Martin explained. 'It heats you up the first time when you're gathering it and it heats you up again when it burns on the fire!'

'You're an intelligent boy,' the woman said. 'No wonder your father wants you to go to school.'

It was such a long walk to school that, at first, Martin was carried part of the way there.

'What's school like?' his younger brother asked him in bed when they had time to talk.

'It's been a terrible week,' Martin explained. 'The teacher is so cross. He saves up beatings all week and gives them on a Friday. I got fifteen lashes today.'

'That must have been sore,' his brother said sympathetically.

'Why do you think I'm lying on my side?' Martin spat. 'The teacher says I'm so bad that I'll never get to heaven.'

That was the beginning of another sleepless night, and it wasn't just because he was sore from the beating.

After school Martin went on to study at university.

'I'll be a lawyer,' he told his father, 'and you'll be proud of me.'

But a thunderstorm changed his plans. While he was studying law, he went out riding one day, and a furious storm suddenly crashed right overhead. Lightning forked this way and that, blinding in its brightness.

'Help me St Anne!' a terrified Martin cried, 'and I'll become a monk.' He did survive and he did become a monk, though his father was not best pleased.

But even though he was a monk, the fear of spending for ever in purgatory still plagued the young Luther.

'What can I do to make myself good enough for heaven?' he asked himself over and over again, until his mind was nearly bursting.

'I'll say the Lord's Prayer fifty times each morning,' or 'I'll only eat one small meal each day,' or 'I'll wear the scratchiest horsehair vest I can find,' or 'I'll get up at two each morning and pray until daylight,' he thought, and tried them all.

He even went to Rome where he found a building that was supposed to be Pilate's house. When he reached it, Martin got down on his knees, crawled up the twenty-nine steps and stopped to pray on each of them.

'It doesn't matter what I do,' he wept afterwards. 'Nothing makes me feel as though I'll escape purgatory.' He was nearly out of his mind with worry.

One day, while Luther was studying, an amazing idea dawned on him. 'Can this be true?' he said to himself, absolutely brain-blown at what he was thinking. 'Can it possibly be true that we are saved by faith and not by works?'

He went from verse to verse in his Bible, shaking with excitement. Tears of sheer relief flowed down his face. He brushed them off impatiently because they were stopping him reading the Bible!

'It's true!' he said softly. He slid from his high stool and nearly fell. His legs were wobbly with relief, and he felt as though he had lost half his weight. 'It's as if I've been carrying a huge burden that's suddenly gone.'

Sitting down, he thought through what he'd discovered. Had anyone come into the room, they would have wondered what had happened. The serious monk, Martin Luther, was one minute wiping tears from his eyes, and the next jumping up to look at his Bible, then sitting down and smiling more broadly than he had done for years, then striding about saying over and over again, 'It's true! Praise the Lord, it's true!'

Over the months that followed his discovery, Martin did a great deal of studying and thinking.

'The Bible absolutely clearly says that we are saved by faith in God,' he said to himself. 'So why is it that I studied and worried for years and didn't see the truth?'

The answer to that question really upset him. 'I didn't see the truth because the Church has taught me lies all of my life.'

Luther shook his head at the thought then thumped his desk with his fist. 'Every day of my life I've worried about how I'd get out of purgatory and now I discover that there is no such place! It's not in the Bible at all!' He strode about the room, thinking aloud. 'Why has the Church lied? Why? Why? There can only be one reason – that it wanted everyone to be afraid, that it wanted to control us through fear.' His eyes blazed. 'And it's still doing it! What am I to do?'

In 1517 there was an announcement made in Luther's church, and in every other church as well. 'The church of the Holy Father, the Pope, is to be rebuilt. As this will cost a great deal of money, the Holy Father has most graciously decided that there will be a sale of indulgences. Anyone buying an indulgence will have their sins or a loved one's sins forgiven and will therefore go to heaven.'

Martin heard this with astonishment. His head spun as he left the building. 'What's an indulgence?' he asked himself. 'It's only a piece of paper saying your sins are forgiven. How can people believe that by paying money for a piece of paper, God will take them to heaven? Surely ordinary people will have more sense than to believe that.'

Suddenly he stopped, shocked. 'No! They won't! They'll do just what I did for years. They'll believe it because the Church says it. That's terrifying. People will pay out money they can't afford to go to a heaven they'll never see!'

Luther spent a long time in his study preparing a document he knew would cause a storm. When he'd finished writing, he'd made up a list of 95 ways in which the Church's teaching was not from the Bible, most of them to do with purgatory and indulgences. He took the long sheet of paper, some nails and a small hammer and set out for the Castle Church in his town of Wittenberg.

When he arrived at the church door, he didn't go in. Instead, he nailed the list to the door. News of what he had done soon spread through the town.

'I wonder if Luther's right,' one or two people said.

'How dare he say that the money we've spent on indulgences won't take us to heaven!' others fumed.

And a number worried and wept because they just didn't know what to think.

Before long, news of what Martin had done reached the Pope who was not at all pleased with his monk. 'Bring him here!' he demanded. 'There'll be trouble if people listen to what he's saying. Bring him here and I'll sort him out.'

When the Pope's order arrived, Martin Luther refused to go to Rome. 'There's no such person as a Pope in the Bible,' he told a friend, 'and we're certainly not told to obey a man rather than God. So the Pope can say what he likes, but I'm not jumping to attention and obeying him!'

'That's dangerous thinking,' his friend said seriously. Then he smiled. 'But it's true, splendidly true. For so long the Church has lived in fear of Popes, and now we can be free from them.'

As Luther's teaching became well known, people began to gather round him, who already thought as he did. Some had been influenced by an Englishman called John Wycliffe who had lived over a hundred and fifty years before Luther. Nearer home, Jan Hus had made the same discovery in Prague a century later. Followers of Wycliffe and Hus were encouraged that Martin Luther stood up strongly for Bible truths. And some of them were among a group of people who met with Martin on 10th December, 1520, for a bonfire.

Having gathered together many books of Church teaching, which they knew to be untrue, they burned them publicly.

'The Church has led us far from the truth,' one man, who was enjoying the sight of the burning books, said to his neighbour, 'and change has been brewing quietly for years. But it will come soon now. I believe tonight marks a big step in the process of reformation.'

'What is reformation?' his son asked.

'It's change, son,' his father said. 'It's the change that will come as we read the Bible rather than listen to the wrong things the Church has been teaching.'

The fire blazed brightly as book after book was thrown on. And the glow reflected on the faces of those who had the courage to stand near it.

'There's an excitement in their faces,' Luther thought, 'and there's joy too – the joy of being free of the fear of purgatory and sure of the hope of heaven.'

FACT FILE
Rome: Rome is believed to have been founded in 753 B.C. and it has been the capital of a united Italy since the year 1871. The dome of St Peter's, built in 1590, still dominates the skyline. In the year 2016 Rome had a population of 2,869,461.

Keynote: A belief in purgatory is a mistaken belief. When people die, they either go to heaven or hell. There is no place where people go to be purified from sin. It is the blood of Jesus Christ that cleanses us from all sin. His death on the cross means that all who trust and love him will have eternal life and go to be with him as soon as they die.

Think: The Bible says that we are saved by faith and not by works. Martin Luther discovered this and was overjoyed. Think about how perfect Jesus is, yet he had to die to free us from our sins. What does this tell you about sin? It tells you how awful it is. Think how impossible it would be

46

for us as sinful people to ever do anything good enough to get to heaven. Only faith in Jesus saves.

Prayer: Dear God, protect me from wrong beliefs. Give me a clear understanding of what you say in your Word, the Bible. Thank you for sending the perfect Lord Jesus, your only son, to die for me on the cross. Help me to trust in him. Amen.

Ulrich Zwingli

Ulrich, who was aged just five, sat at the table with his father. 'There are hundreds of Zwinglis in the world,' he said.

His father smiled. 'Yes, I suppose there are,' he laughed. 'But mostly they live near here. The area around Wildhaus is the Zwingli part of Switzerland. There are different family names in other parts of the country.'

His face suddenly saddened. 'Do I need to go away to Uncle Barthelemy's in another part of Switzerland?' he asked.

Mr Zwingli straightened his back. 'Yes,' he said firmly, 'you do; and for the very last time I'll explain why. With a houseful of children there's no chance for you to have a good education, and I think you're clever enough and that you'll take to studying and do well in the world.'

'But I'll miss my brothers and sisters, and mother,' he said, then added quickly, 'and you too.'

'You're going, and that's an end of it. As soon as the snows have melted, I'll take you to your uncle.'

Ulrich knew better than to argue with his father. He wasn't the kind of person who lost an argument with his children.

'Will you come and play snowballs?' his brother asked the following morning. Ulrich didn't know whether to enjoy what was left of his time at home or to start feeling sad about leaving, even though the snow was still thick. He decided to enjoy himself.

'You're on!' he said. 'The best snow for snowballs is in the meadow.' The boys ran to the meadow, snow slowing them down as it got deeper. 'I really am going away,' Ulrich told his little brother.

The four-year-old's eyes lit up. 'That's exciting!' he said. 'You'll have lots of adventures. And I'll have the bed all to myself.'

'I don't think so,' the older boy said. 'I think Mother's having another baby.'

April came and the snow began to melt. Mrs Zwingli packed a bag of clothes for her son and presents for the family he was to stay with. Ulrich noticed that his mother looked sad when she was doing his packing, and that made him want to cry.

'You'll like your uncle,' she told him. 'He's a priest and a kind man.'

'Kind?' Ulrich wondered exactly how kind he was. 'Perhaps he won't have a wooden stick like Father's one.'

The bag lay packed and ready for the last of the snow to go. 'We're leaving tomorrow,' his father said, as Ulrich went to bed one night. Ulrich turned to his father, 'But ...'

'No buts,' was the firm reply.

For five years Ulrich lived with his uncle. He was a good man and a good teacher. Ulrich showed everyone that his father was right, for he was clever and he did enjoy studying. Ulrich was especially good at music and could easily have become a professional musician.

'I think you should send the boy to school in Basle,' Uncle Barthelemy told Ulrich's father, when his nephew was ten years old. Five years later, having done very well in Basle, his teacher there recommended to Mr Zwingli that the boy should do even more studying in Berne. But first there was some time to enjoy being back at home.

Ulrich and his friends pulled their wooden sledges up the best slope on his father's farm. 'You go first,' Zwingli shouted. 'And I'll see if I can follow in your sledge tracks.'

The youngest boy went first, then the other. They landed in a heap at the bottom of the hill. 'Watch out, you two!' Ulrich yelled, using his new launching technique. It involved placing his sledge hard against the trunk of a tree then lying flat on it and pushing his feet against the tree trunk with as much force as he could produce. He went off like a stone from a sling. 'Here I come!'

The two at the bottom looked up and saw their friend's sledge almost flying down the slope towards them. They scrambled out of the way only just in time. Ulrich was moving too fast to come to a controlled stop. Instead, he rammed their two wooden sledges, parted company with his own and landed some distance in front. Even then he didn't stop but went on slithering down the hillside. When he eventually came to a halt and clambered back up to his friends, his eyes were shining with excitement and his nose pouring blood. 'That's what I call sledging!'

The older of his two friends looked him in the eye and said, 'That's what I call stupid.'

'What a mess you're in,' Mrs Zwingli told the teenager, when he arrived back home covered in blood. 'Were you like this when you were away studying?'

Ulrich's eyes twinkled as he thought of some of the mischief he'd got up to, the scrapes he'd found himself in, and the fights he'd fought and won. There had been several bleeding noses over the years, and they were not always his!

'You'll have to behave more like a man now that you're going to university in Vienna.' That night Ulrich wrote in his diary, '1498, I must behave more like a man and less like a child.'

By 1506, Zwingli was back in his native Switzerland and working as a priest. For several years he worked away quietly, all the while becoming aware that there were things in the Church of his day that were far from right. 'We must trust in Christ rather than the Church,' he told his congregation. 'The Church is made up of sinful human beings, and it can and does make mistakes, but Christ is the sinless Son of God.'

'You're looking tired,' his friends often told him. 'And you've got bags under your eyes.' 'I don't know why you need to study so much. After all, you've been to two universities.'

Ulrich laughed. 'I study because I both want to and need to. I want to know Greek so I can study the New Testament in the language in which it was written,' he explained.

'But that doesn't seem to do you any good,' the friend pointed out. 'The more you study the Bible, the more unsettled you become.'

'What's on your mind now?' Zwingli's friend asked, realising he wanted to talk.

'It's the Mass,' he began. 'The Church teaches us that the bread and wine in the Mass actually become the body and blood of Jesus; that we actually eat a piece of the Lord's real body and drink some of the Lord's real blood. That is a grotesque teaching.'

'It bothers me too,' his friend, Gunter, said. 'But go on.'

'The bread and wine are just signs of his body and blood, otherwise we're cannibals! The thought makes me ill.'

'We're on dangerous ground,' his friend said. 'We're going to have to be careful.'

'Have you heard of Martin Luther?' someone asked Zwingli in 1519.

'No,' Ulrich replied. 'Who's he, and why should I have heard about him?'

'Read this,' Gunter said, giving him a book by Luther. That night Zwingli read until his candle died, then he lit another, and another. 'This book says just what I think,' he told himself, when the last candle had guttered and he was so tired he didn't have the energy to go for a fourth one. 'But he's a braver man than I am. I'll have to give this some serious thought.' Although he was exhausted Ulrich didn't sleep a wink that night.

The following morning he started reading Luther's book even before he had his breakfast, and by late that afternoon he'd finished it. His mind was in a whirl. 'I'm going to give this to Gunter to read then we can talk all about it.'

It was a week later that the two men settled in front of a log fire in Ulrich's home. They had Luther's book and their Bibles on a table in front of them. 'What do you think?' Zwingli asked.

His friend looked serious. 'This Luther is right,' he said. 'The Church is in a mess. Cardinals and archbishops care only about their own power and many of them are living very wicked lives. The Pope is selling indulgences; telling people all they've got to do to go to heaven is pay up to the Church.'

'The question is,' Ulrich said, 'can we go on as we are, or should we stand up and be counted, like Luther has?'

Zwingli shook his head. For three years he made no decision, but more and more often he found himself preaching against the teachings of the Church.

In May 1522, Ulrich sat down to write to a university friend. 'You'll find it difficult to believe what I'm going to tell you,' he began, 'but I promise you it's true. As you know the Church teaches that we should eat fish rather than meat for four weeks before Easter. Well, some friends and I were at a meeting at a printer's house. We were working on printing part of the New Testament. The printing press had been going day and night for weeks, and the workmen were tired and hungry. The printer's wife bought some sausages because fish was so expensive. She brought in the dish of sausages ... and the smell was delicious! My mouth was watering. But, on with the story ... I didn't eat any but the other men there did, so disobeying the Church's teaching. Although I didn't have any, after I'd thought about it, I decided that there was nothing at all in the Bible about eating fish rather than meat, and that's what I told my congregation.

'Now, you'll never believe what happened. The men who ate the sausages were fined and some of them put in prison!

'That's the last straw as far as the Church is concerned. Since I've read Luther's books, I'm really admiring his courage. Now I've no choice but to break with the Pope.'

'It's so different for us than for Luther,' Zwingli said, when he and his friends were discussing things in the autumn of the following year. 'Our town council is quite happy for us to preach the Gospel of Christ rather than the teachings of the Church. We've such a lot to be grateful for.'

'And have you heard the news?' one of the men said. 'The Council says that all idols have to be taken from churches, and all the bits and pieces of wood that the Church says are from Christ's cross, and the fragments of bone that are meant to be from saints' skeletons. Organs have to go too. But the Council says it has all to be done in an orderly way and without any riots.'

Zwingli wiped his forehead. 'I can hardly believe it!' he said. 'It seems that the Reformation in Switzerland is going to be quite a peaceful affair.'

Not everyone in Switzerland was convinced by Zwingli and his fellow Reformers. Parts of the country seemed to become even more keen on the Roman Church as the Reformation continued. At first there were occasional skirmishes between Romanists and Protestants, but it wasn't long before things became more serious. Catholic armies formed, and Protestant troops gathered too. A peace treaty was drawn up, but it was soon broken.

'What are we going to do?' Zwingli's friends asked him, as they met to talk about the problem.

Ulrich looked surprised that the question was asked. 'What do you mean? We'll get our swords and fight for the truth!'

There was silence in the room. 'Is that the right thing to do?' someone asked.

Taking a deep breath Zwingli began, 'There is right and wrong here, and we are on the side of right. Romanists have gathered their armies and they are ready to advance. Do you hear what I'm saying?' he insisted. 'They are ready to advance, to go into Protestant areas where they will clamp down on the people like never before. We've been holding communion services; they'll change it back to the Mass. They'll insist that people believe they're eating and drinking Jesus' body and blood. Will you not fight for that?' The room was absolutely silent.

Zwingli waited a minute then went on. 'The Pope will force indulgences on poor people. Cardinals and archbishops will grasp back the power they lost, and our people will become slaves once again, slaves to the Church, slaves to superstition and slaves to fear. Are you willing to let that happen? Are you willing to take up your swords for what's right?'

'You might be killed, Ulrich,' someone said.

Zwingli's eyes shone. 'I've shed my blood for fun in the snow. I've shed my blood for the sake of mere arguments when I was young. Do you expect me to be afraid of shedding my blood for the truth of Christ?'

In October 1531, the Romanist army invaded Protestant Zurich. Zwingli was true to his word and fought in the defending army. He fought for what he believed to be true and was killed. But Ulrich did not die in vain as Switzerland went on to play a huge part in the Reformation. Some of his friends felt he should not have gone into battle, rather he should have found a peaceful way of spreading the good news of Jesus. But all of them had to agree that their dead friend had lived up to his motto, 'Do something bold for God's sake!'

FACT FILE
Books: These are an excellent invention. Everything we know and all the thoughts and ideas of human beings may be found in books. The Egyptians were writing books in 2500 B.C. on a type of paper made from a reed called papyrus. These books were made on long strips which were rolled up round a stick when not being read. The Romans were the first to make books like those we know today... but they were still written by hand on parchment. It was not until printing was invented in the 15th century that more than one copy of a book could be made at a time.

Keynote: When Christians take communion, the bread and wine are eaten to remind them of what Jesus did on the cross. They are what we call symbols. Nothing happens to the bread and wine. The most important thing has already happened. Jesus Christ died to save us from our sins and has risen from the dead, victorious.

Think: The church is made up of people who sin. When people become Christians, their sins are forgiven but they are still sinners. Loving and trusting in Christ is just the beginning of God's work in their lives and hearts. Christians hate the sin that they do but they are not totally free of sin until they die and go to heaven. Do you hate sin? Are you upset and ashamed when you disobey God? Do you wish you were more like Jesus? Do you wish you loved Jesus more? These are signs of someone who is a real Christian and is a follower of the Lord Jesus Christ.

 Prayer: Father God, thank you for everything you give me. Thank you for your Word, the Bible, and for the gift of reading. Thank you that your word tells me the truth about my sin and how you want to save me from it. Amen.

William Tyndale

William loved the noise of his mother making butter. She sat beside the wooden churn and turned the handle round and round, then round and round again, for what seemed a very long time to a very small boy.

To start with, there was the swish and splash of milk each time the wooden paddle turned inside the churn. Then the sound changed to a gloop, gloop, gloop.

'That's the milk thickening,' his mother had explained, and, because he was brainy and intelligent, William never forgot it. As the gloops became slower, his mouth watered. Then, all of a sudden, the gloops stopped, and there was a quiet thud. William knew exactly what had happened. The milk had separated into butter and milky water that would be used in his mother's baking. She called it buttermilk.

'May I?' he asked, grinning at his mother. She knew exactly what he meant and she opened the churn and let him take some of the newly made butter on his finger. 'It's lovely,' he said, licking his lips. 'Our cow's milk makes the best butter in all of Gloucestershire.'

When Mrs Tyndale had made the butter into a neat pat, she poured off the butter-milk that was left and started her baking. William sat down to watch.

'Don't you want to go out and play with your brothers?' his mother asked.

'No,' he said. 'I want to watch you and ask you questions.'

'There was never a boy like you for questions,' the woman laughed, 'though often it's only poor answers I can give you. What is it you want to know today?'

Screwing up his face seemed to make questions come into his mind, so that's what William did, and a question was suddenly there!

'What year is it?' asked the eight-year-old.

'It's the year of our Lord 1502.'

'Why do you say the year of our Lord?'

Mrs Tyndale was used to his questions and patient in answering them. 'That's because we count the years from the time of the birth of the Lord Jesus Christ.'

'Who decided we'd do that?'

'Important men in the church did that many years ago.'

'What kind of important men?'

This was getting difficult! 'The Pope and his bishops and archbishops,' his mother explained.

'Were all the bishops in Gloucestershire there to decide it?' the child asked. Mrs Tyndale explained that the bishops in Gloucestershire had not been born when the years were first numbered.

As they were talking, the woman had kneaded her bread, and it was ready to be put somewhere warm to rise. She sat down for a minute to rest.

'Why is it that the bishops and priests use Latin in church?' her son asked. 'I only understand little bits of what they are saying.'

His mother smiled. 'Then you understand more than I do,' she said. 'You seem to have a real gift for other languages.'

William grinned. 'I know some French. The soldier who came to Slimbridge taught me some of his words.'

'Yes, I remember that,' Mrs Tyndale said. 'But sitting here with you won't get the work done. Off you go and play with your brothers.'

'One more question. Please.' His mother nodded. 'Why do we use Latin in church and not our own language?'

'That's just how it is,' the patient woman explained. 'Though it would be easier on all of us if we knew what was being said.'

The older William grew, the more difficult his questions became for his mother. Even his father had problems answering many of them. His brothers Edward and John sometimes teased him, telling him that his brain would burst if he knew the answers. The questions William asked changed as he grew up, but there was one for which he could not find an answer that pleased him.

'Why do we have to believe what the priests tell us when we could read the Holy Book for ourselves if we had it in our own language? They could be talking rubbish for all we know.'

'Shh,' his father hissed. 'When it comes to saying things like that, the very walls have ears. I've told you over and over again that if you want to discuss these things, we must do it out in the fields where there's no chance of being overheard.'

William was around fifteen and just about to go to Oxford University. 'Can we go for a walk then, Father? I need to talk.'

Both wrapped cloaks about themselves as there was a nip in the autumn air. And they set out to walk and talk.

'Why is the Holy Book not in English?' William asked, when he was sure nobody was within earshot.

'It was once,' his father explained. 'Around a hundred years ago a man named John Wycliffe translated the Bible from Latin into English. But the bishops didn't like that because they thought that if people had God's Word in their own language, the Church would no longer have power over them.'

'Have you ever seen Wycliffe's translation?' William asked.

'No. Even though they took hundreds of hours to write out by hand, if any copies were found, they were burned.'

'What!' William was full of rage at the thought. 'How dare they do that!'

'Keep your voice down,' his father said. 'And for goodness' sake be careful what you say when you go to university. People have been burned for saying such things.'

While William was a student in Oxford, he discovered for himself what it meant to be a Christian. And it was no easy thing in those days. After he finished his studies, he became chaplain to a family, and teacher of their two sons. It was while he was doing that for a living that he decided to do something much more interesting with his life ... and very much more dangerous.

William Tyndale decided to translate the Bible into English. And rather than using the Church's Latin Bible, he made up his mind to translate it all from the original Greek and Hebrew languages. 'Mother always said I was good at languages,' he thought. 'I'm going to have to be!'

'It's a terrible thing,' a friend told him, sometime later. 'But if you are serious about translating the Bible into English, you're going to have to go abroad to do it. You'll be found and killed if you stay here.'

'Do you really think so?'

'Have you not heard the news the coachman brought this morning?' his friend asked. William shook his head. 'Seven people have been burnt at the stake for teaching their children the Lord's Prayer, the Ten Commandments and the Apostles' Creed in English.'

'I've no choice then but to go to Germany. Surely I'll get peace there to do the job.'

'And while you're at your translating, there will be people here in England praying that by the time it's finished, God's Word will be able to be read in English here in England.'

By 1525, Tyndale had translated the whole of the New Testament. He wrote to his friend in England telling him the good news. So that no one reading the letter would know what it was about, he used a code that the two of them made up before he left for Germany.

'Listen to this,' his friend told a small group of Christians who had met to pray. 'William says that the first copies should be here within a few months. Isn't that wonderful! The invention of the printing press has made such a difference. It means that copies can be made quickly, not like in the days of Wycliffe when everything had to be written out by hand.'

'How will it be distributed?' someone asked.

'It will have to be from Christian to Christian because if the Church finds out about it, they'll burn any copies they find.'

However, the Church authorities in England did get wind of what was going on, and people were sent to Europe to look for Tyndale. As they travelled from country to country, they bought any Protestant books they could find and burned them all! The King of England also sent spies to look for him. They found Tyndale, but they couldn't persuade him to return to England with them.

'Tell me why I should go back with you,' he demanded of them.

'It's your duty as an Englishman to obey the King's orders,' he was told.

'And is it the duty of an English court to try me and put me to death for giving people God's Word in a language they can read for themselves?'

'Why do you think you'd be put to death?' one of the king's agents asked.

Tyndale heaved a sigh. 'Do you think I don't know that copies of my New Testament are publicly burned? Do you think I don't know that those who trust in the Lord Jesus rather than the Roman Church are tied to a stake, that a bonfire is built around them and they are burned to death? Do you really think that because I'm not in England I don't know what's happening to God's people there?'

The king's agents gave up and, as they left Tyndale's home, one said to the other, 'I don't know where he gets his information, but he certainly knows what's going on at home!'

By 1529, Tyndale had translated several books of the Old Testament from Hebrew into English, but the manuscript was lost in a shipwreck. But by the following year a replacement had been made with the help of his assistant, Miles Coverdale, and smuggled into England.

'I can hardly believe that I'm holding God's Word and can read it for myself,' a new Christian said. 'Look here: it says, "You shall not kill". I don't understand how the Church can kill Christians when the Bible says, "You shall not kill".'

'You know you're risking your life being a believer,' an old Christian man told him.

'If you're caught carrying out your plan, you'll get no mercy.'

The young Christian, his eyes glowing with enthusiasm, shook his head. 'I'm a sailor,' he said. 'And the boat I'm on crosses the Channel several times a year. I'm prepared to risk my life to smuggle Tyndale's translation into England. What have I got to lose? If I die, I go to heaven.'

The next time the young man's boat docked in Antwerp, where Tyndale then lived, a shadowy figure approached him one night, carrying a large package under his cloak. A password was exchanged, and, without another word, the figure followed the sailor on to the boat and down into the hold. It was the middle of the night, and nearly everyone else was asleep, exhausted after their voyage. Only whispers were spoken, but enough was said for the young man to be sure that this was no mere messenger with English Bibles; this was William Tyndale himself. He wasn't content to translate God's Word; he wanted to do all he could to get it to England.

When the package was safely stowed, the two men slunk off the ship. Before they parted, Tyndale put both hands on the young man's shoulders and prayed for his safety and the safe passage of the precious parcel.

As he fell asleep that night, William thought of his trip to the ship, and he broke into a wide smile. 'The Word of God in our own language! I remember mother speaking to me in the kitchen ... she never understood a word of Latin. Now women like her will be able to hear God's Word in their own tongue! Perhaps they'll be able to tell their children about it ... even when they are churning the butter.'

'Thank you for seeing me,' Henry Phillips said, when he first met Tyndale in 1535. 'It's taken me a long time to meet you face to face.'

'I have to be careful,' William explained. 'There are those who would rather see me dead than alive.'

Phillips pretended that the very thought shocked him.

'What is it I can do for you?' asked Tyndale.

His visitor poured out a lying story, saying that he was a Christian in need of help. But he was a spy, and a cunning one. Tyndale fell into the trap that was laid for him. He was arrested and put into prison where he was kept for over a year.

From his prison cell, Tyndale wrote to the governor asking for some of his possessions to be brought to him. The weather was cold, and he asked for his warm coat and cap and a woollen shirt. But most of all what he wanted were candles and his Hebrew Bible, grammar and dictionary so that he could continue his work of translation.

Eventually he was tried and found guilty of being a heretic, someone who spoke against what the Roman Church taught. For weeks after that the prison and Church authorities tried to make William change his beliefs and accept what the Church taught. But they failed miserably.

In October 1536 Tyndale was taken from his cell and strangled. His body was not buried; it was publicly burned.

Just before he died, William Tyndale prayed, 'Lord, open the King of England's eyes.'

He didn't live to see it, but God answered his prayer. Soon after his death, a copy of the Bible in English was placed in every Church in England by order of the King, and ordinary people were encouraged to read it for themselves.

FACT FILE

Printing: This is a method of producing many copies of a document by pressing an inked pattern into fabric or metal. The oldest method of printing is letterpress. This method was used in Japan before A.D. 770. The unusual thing about letterpress printing is that the metal letters have to be arranged in a tray backwards, reading right to left instead of left to right. This is so that when the page is printed, the letters will read the correct way on the paper. The first person in Europe to use this type of printing successfully was Johan Gutenberg in about 1438.

Keynote: As a young man, William Tyndale wanted to know why the Bible was not in English. There are many people groups that still do not have God's Word in their own language. Wycliffe Bible Translators work very hard to translate the Bible into the language of every tribe and nation.

Think: Many people risked their lives so that the Bible would be available in a language that ordinary people understood. They risked their lives to print and distribute God's Word. In some countries Christians still risk their lives to get God's Word to their friends and neighbours. Is God's Word precious to you? Would you risk your life to read it? Would you do anything so that your friends and family could read it for themselves?

Prayer: Lord God, help me to understand and treasure your word, the Bible. Forgive me for disobeying what you say in it. Thank you for all those people who teach and explain it to me. Be with them and encourage them. Amen.

Hugh Latimer

Hugh felt as though he was on top of the world. 'Are you all right?' his father asked. His smile told the answer. 'I'll make a king's horseman of you yet,' he said to his son. Hugh sat as tall as he could, held his head high and nudged the horse to move quicker.

'Not too fast,' came the warning. 'Remember she's not been ridden often and she's not used to you at all.'

'One day I'll ride for the King,' Hugh exclaimed. 'By then she'll go like the wind.'

'Not if you fall from a frisky mount and knock your head off,' his dad laughed. 'Take her out every day for a short time, and she'll calm down soon.'

'Once round the meadow?' Hugh wheedled.

Mr Latimer looked at the pony; she seemed calm enough. 'Once, and take her slowly.'

Hugh pretended he was a soldier riding behind the King. With a straight back and head high, he walked the pony round the meadow. 'He holds himself well,' his father thought as he watched.

'That's enough for today,' Mr Latimer announced, when the eight-year-old pulled the pony to a stop at his side. 'Now give her a treat and leave her to rest.'

Hugh pulled some handfuls of long grass from the side of the ploughed field and fed them to the pony then led her home. 'I think you should go and give your mother a hand with the milking,' the man said. 'If you ask her to fill the wooden buckets only half-full you'll be able to carry them for her. And there might be a white moustache for you at the end of the job.'

The boy grinned. There was nothing he enjoyed better than a cup of warm, frothy milk straight from the cow, and his father often teased him because the froth usually left him with a white, milky moustache.

'I'm glad you've come,' said Mrs Latimer, 'because I've a lot to do before the sun goes down.'

'Dad said I could help carry the milk.'

'And so you can, but the milk I'd like you to carry is a half-bucketful to poor Mrs Fletcher. Her children have whooping cough and they need all the good food they can get. She's a poor widow woman and can't afford to buy extra milk for the boys.'

'It's a long way to Mrs Fletcher's,' Hugh said, looking at the size of the bucket.

'So it is, but I'll make it easier for you by giving you some butter and cheese as well, and a small cabbage from the garden.'

Hugh thought his mum was joking. 'That'll make it a lot easier!' he laughed.

But it did. Mrs Latimer hung the bucket of milk from one end of a short pole. Then she wrapped the cheese, butter and cabbage in a cloth and hung them from the other end.

'Now,' she said, 'you'll discover how easy it can be to carry things.' She hoisted the pole on to Hugh's shoulders. 'Just keep your head held high and you'll hardly feel the weight.'

To his surprise he found out that was true. 'I thought this looked hard when I saw my sisters doing it,' he said to himself, as he reached Mrs Fletcher's, 'but it's not.'

'I'm home!' Hugh shouted, as he neared his father's small farm. 'Watch out!' a voice replied, and he ducked. Without thinking he'd come out of a clump of trees just where his brothers were practising archery. Hugh ducked behind a tree until a voice told him it was safe to come out.

'Your turn,' his brother said. 'If you're big enough to carry loads, you're big enough for this bow.' Hugh looked at his brother's bow.

It seemed huge compared to his own one. 'Stand straight,' the older boy said. 'That's right; your back should be as straight as a soldier's. Now hold your bow firmly. Head up! You need to keep your neck straight and your head high.' Concentrating hard, Hugh pulled the arrow back and held it till his brother told him to shoot. 'Now!' A final pull, then the arrow shot off and headed straight for the target. 'Well done!' his brother laughed. 'You'll make an archer one day.' Hugh grinned. 'The best one in Thurcastone.' 'Maybe the best in England,' added the older boy. 'Maybe.'

'Hugh tries very hard,' Mr Latimer told his wife one day, as they worked together thinning turnips. She straightened her aching back. 'He's not strong,' she said, 'but he's got a good head on his shoulders. He's smart.'

'I think he should go to the university when he finishes school. He'll never be able to work the farm for a living.'

'That would cost a lot of money,' commented Mrs Latimer.

Her husband stood up and stretched. 'We're not rich,' he said, 'but we're not poor either. And if he does well enough, he'd be able to make his own way in the world.'

'I knew he could do it,' boasted proud Mr Latimer some years later when, in 1510, Hugh was paid to work for Cambridge University. 'He studied so hard and did so well that they're willing to pay him.'

'The people in the village thought sending him to university was a waste of money. This will show them they were wrong!' his wife laughed. 'I always knew he was gifted.'

Two years later their youngest son became a preacher and a very eager one.

'What do you think of this new teaching?' a friend asked Hugh. 'There are some who say that the Pope isn't head of the Church.'

'So I've heard. But they'll come to a bad end if they teach that kind of nonsense. Of course the Pope is head of the Church.'

'They say that's not in the Bible,' went on his friend.

'But it's what the Church teaches,' Hugh said. 'And that's just as important as the Bible.'

'There's more and more of that kind of teaching around,' concluded his companion.

Latimer scowled, then said, 'I'll do my very best to stamp out such rubbish!' For some time that's exactly what he did.

'May I make my confession to you?' Thomas Bilney asked Latimer.

'Of course, come to my study,' the priest said. But Bilney believed in the truth of the Bible, and rather than make a confession, he told Hugh what he believed. Latimer listened, because that was what a priest had to do, but soon he was listening because he really wanted to hear what the man was saying. 'Could this be true?' he wondered. That day was the beginning of a great change in Hugh's life. Very soon afterwards he trusted in the Lord Jesus as his Saviour.

'You're going to have to be careful,' one of the university staff warned him. 'You're getting a reputation as a Reformer. Surely you don't believe all that rubbish.'

Latimer smiled sadly at the man. 'Not long ago I thought it was rubbish. Now I know it's the best news in the whole world.'

'What do you mean?' spat out the reply.

Hugh took his colleague by the arm. 'Let's go for a walk and a talk.'

As they strolled along the banks of the River Cam, the new Christian explained what had happened to him.

'What I do is this,' Latimer explained. 'I look at what the Bible teaches and what the Church teaches and, where the two are not the same, I know I should believe the Bible.'

'Why?'

'Because it's God's Word, and he doesn't tell lies.'

'But isn't what the Church says important too?'

'Yes,' Hugh agreed. 'But the Church can be mistaken. God never makes mistakes.'

They walked in silence for a while, as the man thought about what had been said.

'So what does the Church teach that isn't in the Bible?' Latimer's friend asked eventually.

'For one thing it teaches that the Pope is head of the Church where the Bible says that Christ is head.'

'Rubbish!' announced the other man.

'For another, the Church teaches that every time the Mass is held, Jesus is sacrificed again. But the Bible says he was sacrificed once and for all on the cross.'

His companion stopped walking, turned to Hugh Latimer and, with his face red with rage, said, 'You should be burned for saying these things! And from now on you're no friend of mine.' He strode off in the direction of Cambridge.

'What we need,' Hugh said to some men who thought as he did, 'is the Bible in English. People could then read it for themselves.'

'Watch where you say that,' one of them warned Latimer. 'It could get you into trouble.'

And it did.

'What a stupid idea!' a monk said, when he heard the idea. 'Imagine what would happen if common people had the Bible in English. Jesus said that a little yeast makes bread rise and he compared it to what a little sin does in a life. If ordinary folk read what Jesus said, they'd stop putting yeast in bread, and we'd all be eating hard biscuits! Giving men the Bible in English is the stupidest suggestion I've heard in years! In any case, if you did that, they would stop listening to what the priests say.'

'That might be good,' thought Latimer.

Although Hugh was not popular with everyone, some still realised that he was a good priest. Because of them he was made Bishop of Worcester. But he felt he had to resign when the King refused to allow the Roman Church in England to change into a Church that believed and taught the Bible. Many people loved Hugh's preaching, but the bishops and priests did not.

'The time has come to resign,' he told a group of friends who met in his room. 'And that's what I'm going to do.' Hugh took off his bishop's clothes then suddenly did a little skip in the middle of his room. 'That feels better!' he laughed. 'That feels much better!'

'I've come with news for you,' a messenger told Latimer. 'You've to go to London to stand trial for heresy.'

'That's not news to me,' Hugh said. 'I've been expecting it.'

The trial was much as he thought it would be, and he was thrown into the Tower of London.

'That was terrible,' complained one of his friends. 'The court made him out to be a fool.'

'And a heretic.'

'And a traitor to the crown!' added another.

'But did you see Hugh during the trial?' someone asked. 'All the time they were insulting him, he held his head high.'

'I wonder if he'll ever be free again,' one of his friends said sadly.

'At least he has the company of Master Ridley and Dr Cranmer,' the oldest man said. 'But with all three of these fine Reformers in prison, we'll have to work extra hard to preach about Jesus.'

'You're going to Oxford,' barked the prison guard to each of the three men who had been held in separate cells.

'Why?' Ridley asked.

'You'll stand trial there,' he was told. 'And if justice is done, you'll be put to death for the lies you've been telling.'

On 28th September, 1555, their trial began.

'The charge is that you are teaching lies about the Mass,' the Officer of the Court announced. 'Do you deny the charges?'

The men admitted their teaching. 'Will you publicly deny the truth of what you've been preaching?' they were asked.

With his head held high, Latimer said he would not.

'You're an old man,' one of those in court told Hugh. 'For goodness' sake and for the sake of your poor old body just agree with them.'

Hugh shook his head and held it high. 'No,' he said clearly and firmly.

The next day they were asked the same question again. 'No,' the men said. 'We cannot deny the truth of the Bible.'

When they were taken back to their cells, Latimer prayed three things: that God would help him to stand up for the truth till he died; that the Lord would have the gospel of Jesus preached throughout England; and that Elizabeth would become queen and be blessed.

'Guilty!' the Officer of the Court shouted. 'This court finds them guilty!' Then turning to the prisoners, he said, 'You will be burned at the stake for your lies.' A terrible sermon was preached to them, but they held their heads high till it was over.

'Will you deny your teaching?' Latimer and Ridley were asked one last time as they were taken out to be killed.

'I will never deny it,' said both men. The two Reformers were stripped, apart from burial gowns. They gave away all they had with them then walked calmly to the stake.

'Together!' was the command.

Hugh was chained to one side of the stake, his friend to the other. A bag of gunpowder was hung round their necks and the fire lit.

Hugh held his head high and prayed, 'O Father in heaven, receive my soul.'

'Lord have mercy on me,' prayed Ridley.

The fire raged; the gunpowder exploded, and two brave men went to heaven. But their prayers for England were answered, and a Church grew up which began to teach the Bible.

FACT FILE
Tower of London: The Tower of London is beside the River Thames on the east side of London. It has been a palace, a fortress and a prison. Many famous people - queens, dukes and churchmen - have been executed, murdered or imprisoned within its walls. Prisoners are no longer kept in the Tower, and today it is an ancient monument and tourist attraction. As well as being used to house the crown jewels, it is home to a large colony of ravens.

Keynote: Hugh Latimer believed that Jesus Christ was the head of the Church and not the Pope. Jesus died so that those who believe in his name can have eternal life. No one else has ever or will ever do that. Those who believe in the name of Jesus Christ are the Church. Jesus, their Lord and Master, is the Church's leader and head.

Think: Latimer and Ridley both said that they could not deny the truth of the Bible. Think about the Bible for a moment. Who wrote it? Though prophets, disciples and men of God did the actual physical writing, it was God who inspired all the words. God was the one behind it all. Why does that make the Bible special and unique? It is because the Bible is true from beginning to end. God is truth and he cannot tell lies. God wants to bring people to himself. He wants and longs to save you.

Prayer: Lord Jesus, it is sad to think of the violence and hatred that people show to each other. In the past Christians have suffered and died because they believed in you. And that is still happening in some lands today. You suffered, too, so that we can have eternal life. We don't deserve this but we thank you for all that you have done. Amen.

John Calvin

John sat on his mother's bed. She was unwell and found his games tiring, but she enjoyed it when they sat and talked together.

'Tell me about when you were a little girl,' he said.

His mother smiled. 'My father and mother live in a small town right in the north of France. They have an inn, and when I was a girl, people were always coming and going. Sometimes I hid in the kitchen and listened to what the grown-ups were talking about. Most of them were traders on their way to sell things in England.'

'Is my father a trader?' the five-year-old asked.

Smiling at the thought, his mother explained, 'No, he is a lawyer and he works at the Cathedral here in Noyon.'

'What do lawyers do?'

'All sorts of things,' she said. 'Sometimes his work is about buying and selling land.'

'So he is a trader.'

'I suppose in a way he is,' laughed his mother. 'But it's not his own things that he's buying and selling; everything he works with belongs to the Church.'

'The Church must be very rich,' the little boy thought aloud.

'Yes,' agreed his mother. 'I think it is.'

'Shh! Please be quiet,' the woman told John, just a few months later. 'It's not nice to make a noise in a house of the dead.'

'But I want my mother!' he sobbed. 'I don't want her to be dead.'

'Well, you'll just have to get used to it. And you'll have to be quiet too. Your poor father needs peace.'

The child didn't know what peace was, but he knew there was something that he needed to help his sore heart.

'Do I need peace?' he asked the woman who had come to prepare his mother's body for the funeral.

When she looked at him crossly, he went outside to get away from her.

From that day on, life was different for young John Calvin. He did all the things that had to be done, but nothing was ever the same. There was no mother to answer his questions or to kiss him better when he fell and grazed his knees. He must have missed her softness, her night-time kisses and their special times together. Life must have had its sad times for little John Calvin.

'I have something I want to explain to you,' his father told John some seven years later, in 1521. 'An arrangement has been made to give you a job.'

John's face fell. 'But I don't want a job. I want to study.'

His father sat down. 'If you would just listen to what I'm trying to say!'

Calvin took a seat in front of his father. 'This is something that happens in the Church. You are given a job and are paid for it, but you don't actually have to do the work.'

'Why?'

'Because someone else does it for you.'

'So what's the job and why doesn't the other person get the pay?'

'The job is looking after a church, and he does get paid, though not very much. That leaves plenty for you.'

'What do I need the money for?' John asked puzzled.

'Education doesn't come cheap,' his father said. 'The money will help pay for it.'

John puzzled over that. It seemed to him a very odd thing but he was glad to have the money.

When he was fourteen years old, Calvin went off to university, first in Paris where he studied theology (that's the study of God), then, because his father wanted him to, he studied law in another French university. But before he had finished his studies in law, John's father died. He was on his own and could make his own decisions.

'I've decided to go back to Paris to study Greek and Hebrew,' he told a friend.

'That's a dangerous thing to do,' the other young man laughed. 'If you read the Bible, you might become like that man Luther!'

Calvin looked his friend in the eye. 'I don't think I'm as easily convinced as he was,' he announced. 'I was brought up in the Church. It pays for my education. If you think I'm likely to leave it after all that and to start preaching that it's not telling the truth, you can think again.'

'Keep your head on!' said his friend. 'I was only joking!'

Within a very short time, John Calvin had done exactly what his friend had joked about. 'I was absolutely caught up in all the superstitions of the Church,' he wrote later, 'then I was suddenly converted, and God tamed my heart and made me teachable.' When he wrote to his friend to tell him what had happened, the letter that came back was not very encouraging.

'You've made a brave decision,' it read, 'but a very dangerous one. If I were you, I'd prepare to leave Paris, because if you don't go, you'll be chased out. The Church and the King don't like Reformers. Are you quite sure you really are one of them?'

'I'm certain,' Calvin wrote back. 'The Church is full of things that need reform. Think about it. My education was paid for by money the Church gave me to do nothing! And some poor soul did the work and got virtually nothing for it – all because my father was a cathedral lawyer! That can't be right. It's one of many ways in which the Church is wrong. You were right about being chased out of Paris ... this letter is from Geneva which I think will now be my home.'

'What will you do now?' he was asked by a Swiss Christian he met at church.

'The thing I'm best at is studying, so I think that's what I should continue to do,' replied John. 'It's all very well leaving the Roman Church because of all the wrongs in it, but the Reformed Church will also make serious mistakes unless we really know what the Bible says and stick to it. I think that's what God is calling me to do.'

'It's a huge job,' his new friend said, smiling. 'But God only gives work like that to those who can do it.'

'I feel safe here,' John told a Genevan friend in August 1536.

'I know what you mean. It's great that the people here voted to live according to the Bible and to abolish the teaching of the Roman Church in the city.'

'It means I can relax for a while and get on with my writing without worrying about spies tracking me down.'

'I hope you'll be here for more than a while,' another Reformer said. 'We need you to help establish a church in Geneva.'

But two years later Calvin was on the move again. The town council had changed, and he was no longer welcome. 'Moving won't stop my work,' he told his Swiss friends, as he packed up his papers. 'A student can study anywhere.'

'I have never been so happy in all my life,' John said. 'This year in Strasbourg has been wonderful.'

'In what way?' Idelette asked.

'Because,' he smiled, 'you agreed to marry me and you've given me an instant family of children.'

Idelette looked serious, but just for a moment. 'When my husband was dying, it worried him what would happen to the children and to me. I never dreamed that I would love again and that my children would have such a fine stepfather. It's been a very happy year for me too.'

'The only thing is that I don't get the same peace to write,' John said, half seriously.

'You knew what you were taking on!' his wife laughed. 'And you're not doing too badly. You've just finished a book and you're working on another one already.'

'I think the time has come to go back to Geneva,' John told his wife in 1541. 'I've worked out a system of church government that I think the Genevans will approve of.'

They did, even if they didn't carry it out quite as Calvin would have liked.

Reformers came from all over Europe to study with Calvin, many of them former priests in the Roman Church. Their discussions went on for hours and hours.

'I'd like to give you a subject,' a Frenchman said at a meeting one day.

'What is it?' asked Calvin. 'I'll speak on it if I can.'

'Please explain predestination,' the man begged. 'I find it so confusing.'

Calvin stood up, rubbed his chin and began. 'The Bible teaches that before creation God in his great love chose some people to be his own. During their time on earth these people will trust in Jesus and when they die they will go to be with him.

What the Bible teaches is good news – that all those who trust in Jesus will go to heaven. Is that good news?' he asked the Frenchman.

'Yes,' was the reply.

'And that,' his teacher concluded, 'is predestination.'

'My heart is broken,' John Calvin said when, in 1549, Idelette died. 'First, my only son dies as a child, then my wife after just eleven years of marriage.'

'But you have us,' his stepson told him. 'We're your family.'

Calvin put his hand on the young man's shoulder. 'I know,' he said. 'And it's very hard for you all to lose your father, then your mother, when you're still so young.'

'But we're not alone,' the boy said. 'You have us and we have you.'

The man looked up into the strong, young face. 'You're right,' he agreed. 'And God will care for us.'

Some years later a discussion was held about a plan Calvin had for the city.

'It's a very interesting idea,' the Council decided.

'It would be good if Geneva had its own Academy. People would come from all over Europe to study here,' one man said.

'Yes, and that would bring money to the city,' another commented.

'And trade,' added a third.

'Do we agree to go ahead?' the chairman asked, when it came time to vote.

Calvin was very pleased with the result. The Council voted yes. 'I hope it will become the centre of reformed thinking in Europe,' John told his congregation. 'All roads will lead to Geneva.'

'Good morning, gentlemen,' John Calvin said to a class at the Academy in the early 1560s. 'Before we begin, I would like to know where you all come from.'

'I'm German,' one said.

'France,' another called out.

'My home is in Scotland.'

'I'm English,' a voice came from the back of the room.

'Is everyone else Swiss?' questioned Calvin.

'I've come from the Netherlands,' a deep voice said.

'This class is a vision come true,' John told his students. 'You have come from all over Europe, and when you leave, you'll take the Word of God back home with you.'

'It's great to study with you, Mr Calvin,' a former priest told his teacher. 'And all your many books are brilliant. I know I can believe every word you say.'

'That, young man,' John told him, 'is probably the most frightening thing anyone has ever said to me.' His pupil looked shocked. 'You came out of the Roman Church because it was teaching you things that were untrue, and now you're prepared to believe all I say. For goodness' sake use the brain God has given you. I will never deliberately misguide you, but you must check everything I say, everything anyone says, by what is written in the Bible. That is the only source of truth.'

The young man was upset, and Calvin felt suddenly sorry for him. 'Listen to me,' he said. 'I'm just an ordinary human being like yourself, and I, too, can make mistakes. If you ever find yourself thinking that I'm special, ask someone who knows me well. If I have a pain, I'm like a bear with a sore head. And if I go to bed with a stomach ache, I assume I'll die before morning, but I've not done that yet.'

'I really am not well,' John told a fellow teacher. 'I'm not sure that I'll manage to lecture today.' A buzz went round the Academy. 'Was John Calvin ill? Or was this just another of his days of thinking he was worse than he really was. 'He isn't actually looking very good,' one of his students commented. 'And his colour's a bit odd,' added another. They were right. John Calvin was ill and he never got better. Having influenced the Reformation in Europe more than any other man, he died on 27th May, 1564.

FACT FILE

Geneva: This city is now part of the country of Switzerland and has been since 1815. Before that it was French, and prior to 1798 Geneva was an independent city. The International Red Cross was founded in Geneva in 1863 by Henri Dunant, and after World War I the city was chosen for the headquarters of the League of Nations. It is well known for the production of watches, jewellery and chocolate.

Keynote: John Calvin knew that he had good points and bad points and that in the end people shouldn't just accept everything he said as true. Everyone can make mistakes and we all do. It is up to you to make sure that you study the Bible for yourself. Then when you hear someone teaching about the Bible, you will, with God's help, know if they are speaking the truth or not.

Think: 'Take the word of God home with you.' This is an important thing to do. John's students took God's Word home with them from Geneva. You can bring God's Word back to your family if you go to church or Sunday school. You can bring it back to your school. Think about ways you can do this. Perhaps you could start a Christian club at school? Perhaps you could ask your parents to read the Bible with you every morning? How about asking your best friend to come to Christian camp with you next summer?

 Prayer: Thank you God that you never lie. You are always truthful. You are truth. Help me to read your Word, the Bible, and know the truth for myself. Even little children can understand your truth and follow you. Amen.

John Knox

John pulled up his sleeves and lay down on the rocks beside the River Tyne near his home in the small Scottish village of Haddington. He chose the place carefully so that his shadow didn't fall on the water. Because he knew the river well, he knew that under the rocky outcrop on which he was lying there was still water where fish rested as they swam up and down river.

Slowly he slid his hand into the water, so slowly that there wasn't a hint of a splash or ripple. Then he lay absolutely still for several minutes. 'Gently does it,' he thought, as he lowered his hand just a tiny bit and waited yet again. It must have taken him several minutes to get it up to the elbow, but he knew it was worth being patient. One false move and that would be the end of his guddling for fish for the day. Because he had studied the layout of the rocks, he knew exactly where the fish lay.

For minutes he stayed completely still, letting any fish looking in the direction of his hand lose interest in it and settle back down again. 'Go for it!' he said to himself. He made a grab for a cleft in the rock and caught a slithering, swishing, fighting fish in his hand. He scuttled to his feet and looked at his catch. 'Not bad,' he said aloud. 'Not bad at all.'

Leaving the River Tyne behind, John went back to the trees where he'd agreed to meet his friends. They were also guddling for fish, but they spread themselves out along the river, or each would disturb the others.

'Did you catch any?' asked the boy who was already there.

John held up his fish by the tail. 'And here comes Angus,' he added, pointing to a third boy who was waving a fish in the air. 'Let's get the fire going.'

John collected dry gorse, small twigs and some bigger branches as well. With a little bit of effort the gorse was soon sparking into life, and the three boys sat down to wait for their fire to blaze and begin to die down before they cooked their lunch. When all that was left was the glowing embers, they laid their fish on the fire and covered them with the hot red branches.

'Smells good,' said John. 'And I'm starving.'

They chatted until they thought their fish were ready then, using thin green branches they knew would not go on fire, they brushed the embers off their fish and pulled their dinners from the fire. 'Delicious!' Angus said. John licked his lips and wiped them with his sleeve. 'Guddled fish roasted outside on a fire is the best meal in the world.'

'Time to be going,' one of the boys said, when all that was left were three fish skeletons.

'But let's do this again soon.'

John knelt by the ashes and began to clear them up. Thinking they would be cold, he lifted up a handful to scatter.

'Ouch!' he yelled. 'I've burnt myself!'

Although he was brave, he was very near to tears.

'Let me see,' demanded Angus. By the time John had dusted away the ashes, his hand was very red. 'It's so sore,' he said through his tears. 'I've burnt it badly.'

'Go and stick your hand in the river,' Angus suggested. 'That'll cool it down.'

By the time John Knox reached the river, he could hardly see through his tears. The cold water did help, but his hand was very painful for several days, especially in the evenings when his mother lit the fire, and the heat made it even sorer.

'Can we go and have a last guddle for fish?' John suggested to his companions a few summers later. 'It's the last chance we'll have before I go away to St Andrews University.'

'On one condition,' Angus said. 'That you don't decide to cook your hand as well as your fish!'

John laughed. 'No way! When I was a boy, I used to wonder how hot fire was and I discovered the answer that day.'

That conversation came into Knox's mind as soon as he arrived in St Andrews, because right in front of the university was an area of scorched earth.

'That's where Patrick Hamilton was burned at the stake,' he was told. John shuddered at the thought of the pain the man suffered.

'I've heard about that,' he said to his fellow student, 'but seeing where it happened makes me feel sick.'

'All he'd done was preach the Bible,' the other young man commented.

'Not the way the Roman Church likes it preached,' concluded Knox.

After leaving university, John was ordained as a priest and, among other things, he worked as a chaplain to some wealthy families, and tutor to their sons. Nothing much is known about that part of his life, but by the time he comes into the Church's story again, he was a Christian and preaching the gospel fearlessly.

'Will you come with me to hear George Wishart?' a friend asked him in 1545.

'Yes,' Knox said. 'I've heard about him and I'd like to hear what he has to say for himself.'

As they travelled, the two men talked.

'This is a terrible time to live but an exciting one too,' Knox said. 'The Roman Church is in such a mess, and it's not helped here in Scotland by the Queen being a believer in the Roman ways.'

'One day we may even have to leave the Church and follow the European Reformers. They're teaching the Bible while the Church is just preaching traditions. Maybe George Wishart is the man who will lead Scotland through her own reformation.'

When John Knox heard Wishart preach, he was so thrilled that he spent three months going round the country with him telling people to believe in the Lord rather than in the Church. But the following spring Wishart was arrested. John was with him till midnight on the night before he was to be martyred. The thought of his friend being burned at the stake appalled Knox.

'Go home to your family and God bless you,' Wishart told him, as night became morning. 'It's enough that one dies.'

John left and heard later that day that George Wishart had been strangled and his body burned.

'People all know you now,' John's friend said. 'And they're out to get you. The Romanists in Scotland won't stop until you're out of the way.'

'He was right,' Knox often thought over the next nineteen months. 'It was only weeks after he warned me I wasn't safe in Scotland that I was captured, and I've been a slave on this galley ever since. I wonder if I'll ever be free again to preach Jesus to my own Scottish folk.'

A whip hit his shoulder. 'Pull man! Pull your weight!' Taking the oar more firmly in his aching hands, he pulled it towards himself, then pushed it away.

'Pull! Pull! Pull!' the man shouted, until Knox's oar was in time with the others.

As he rowed with every ounce of his strength, he remembered back to his boyhood. 'How I loved the River Tyne,' he thought. 'Now I think I'd rather not see water ever again!'

'Pull!' a voice roared in his ear as the whip hit his shoulder yet again.

'Is that really John?' someone asked, after Knox was released to England. 'He seems so much older and thinner than I remember him.'

'That's what a year and a half as a galley slave did to him,' his companion explained. 'Another few months and I think he'd have died. But we need him alive and well because we need his preaching.'

Knox's freedom to preach only lasted until 1553 when he had to flee for his life. He eventually reached Geneva and met and studied with John Calvin.

'We need you in Scotland,' the messenger said. 'I've been sent to take you back.'

'Is it any safer now,' Knox asked, 'than when I had to leave?'

'Probably not, but we need you.'

John asked the man why he should go.

'The new, young Queen Mary is on the throne. She's a Romanist, and if you don't come back and help us, there's a chance that Scotland will become as Romanist as she is. She's just a young woman,' the messenger concluded, 'and perhaps you'll be able to influence her to believe in the true religion.'

'Perhaps,' said John. 'It seems that I should go back. I've learned such a lot from

Calvin, and the time has come to pass it on to the Church in Scotland.'

On 4th May, 1559, when Knox preached his first sermon back in Edinburgh, it was not to a Church congregation but to an army. The Protestants (those who protested against Romanist teaching) had gathered as an army for fear of a war. Mary, Queen of Scots' husband was on the French throne, and together they had gathered troops against the Protestants. There was a possibility that the young reformed Church could be wiped out. But that was not what happened. England sent troops north, the French troops left and it looked as though things were going well.

'What do you see as the way ahead?' Knox and the reformers were often asked, even by the Scottish Parliament.

Having written a book on the subject, it was John who explained the plan. 'We will worship simply without any of the rituals of the Roman Church. We'll have no idols and no suggestion that the bread and wine are the Lord's actual body and blood. We'll have no bishops ruling over us, and no Pope as the head of the church. Instead, elders will be elected and they'll only serve for one year at a time. They'll help the ministers. And ministers will be elected too, not given jobs by bishops.'

'It was a disgrace before,' one of his friends said. 'Bishops made men ministers because they owed them a favour, not because they were Christians. And if they owed them several favours, they gave them a number of churches. They got the pay for each of them and often did no work at all! Not only that; sometimes they gave their friends' children jobs as priests when they were just eleven or twelve years old!'

'And there should be a church and a school in every parish,' Knox continued, when his friend had finished speaking.

'That's a great idea,' he was told. 'But how will it be paid for?'

'The Church owns hundreds of miles of Scotland. That will be sold to raise the money.'

'How dare that man make decisions for Scotland!' Mary, Queen of Scots fumed. 'I'm on the throne, not him!'

'And how dare you tell me what to do with my life!' she roared on one of the times they met. Mary was so angry that she wept with rage as he left.

'You've gone too far this time,' the Queen told him when, in 1563, he preached against the Mass. 'You've gone one step too far!' She didn't stop from that day until she had him arrested for treason.

'That's the end of him!' Mary announced. 'He'll not bother me again!'

But Knox was set free, and Mary had no peace from the man who wanted Scotland reformed, until four years later when she left the throne to her young son, James.

'Are you comfortable? Do you want me to read to you?' Mrs Knox asked her husband in 1572. He was in bed having suffered from a stroke.

'Yes,' he said. 'I'm comfortable. And I'm just content to think,' he replied. 'You could maybe read to me later.'

'What are you thinking?'

John lay back on his pillows. 'I'm thinking of Scotland,' he said, 'and of the troubled times she's been through. When I started off as a priest in the Roman Church, I never dreamed I'd spend most of my life telling people that much of what the Church taught was wrong and they should look away from the Church to Jesus. I just hope and pray that the new Church, the Church of Scotland, will always preach Jesus, that it won't forget its message.'

'It cost you and the other reformers such a lot to bring reformation to Scotland,' Mrs Knox said. 'All those months on the galley were terrible for you.'

'They were,' he admitted. 'But I'm dying in my bed. Think of Patrick Hamilton being burned at the stake and what it cost him. And my dear George Wishart; think of him being strangled before his body was burned. It didn't cost me as much as it cost them.'

There was a long silence. 'Is he sleeping?' Mrs Knox wondered. John was not.

'You could read to me now,' he said weakly, 'from 1 Corinthians 15 and John 17.'

With tears in her eyes, his wife read, 'Death has been swallowed up in victory. Where, O death, is your victory? Where, O death, is your sting?'

Then from John's Gospel she read Christ's prayer, 'Father, I want those you have given me to be with me where I am, and to see my glory, the glory you have given me because you loved me before the creation of the world.'

That chapter was the last John Knox was to hear on earth. Just a short while later he was with Jesus in glory.

FACT FILE
Mary, Queen of Scots: She was born in 1542, and her father died just after her birth. As a result, she was crowned Queen of Scotland as a young baby. At the age of five she was engaged to be married to the heir to the French throne. However, two years after their marriage in 1558, Mary's husband died, and she returned to Scotland. She married again, but in 1567 her second husband was murdered. Many suspected her of planning the murder so she was imprisoned and forced to give up her crown to her young son James VI. She was finally executed by the orders of the English Queen, Elizabeth I, at Fotheringay Castle on 8th February, 1587.

Keynote: John asked his wife to read the Bible to him before he died. The words were, 'Death has been swallowed up in victory.' This means that because Jesus died for our sins on the cross - and rose back to life again - death has been defeated. Although

Christians die, their souls have eternal life in heaven where death can never touch them again.

Think: John Knox realised that following Christ had not cost him as much as Patrick Hamilton or George Wishart. It cost them their lives. What did it cost John? It meant hardship and a struggle. Do you follow Christ? What does it cost you? Jesus told his followers to take up their cross and to follow him. That means to obey God's Word and stand up for the truth. Don't look back. Don't give up.

Prayer: Lord Jesus, thank you for defeating death. When we think of what it cost you, it is amazing. You suffered like no one else when you took the punishment for our sins. But you rose again, and your power broke the power of sin and death. Help me to believe in you and your power. Give me a knowledge of my sin and of your goodness. Amen.

Lord Shaftesbury

Little Anthony Ashley shivered as he heard his father rage at his three older sisters. 'Had they made a noise?' he wondered. 'Or had they said something without being asked?' There seemed to be so many things that made their father rage, and all of them made six-year-old Anthony shiver. Even his tummy shivered inside himself, and from time to time when that happened, he was sick and got a telling-off for that.

Something touched his arm, and he jumped. His feet actually left the floor. 'It's all right,' a soft voice said. 'Come into the nursery away from the noise.' The child began to relax as Maria soothed him with soft words. But when the nursery door closed behind them, his little legs buckled, and he fell to the floor sobbing. Maria, whose job it was to look after the four Ashley children, sat down and gently lifted the boy on to her knee.

'Why are we all so sad?' Anthony asked, when he looked up at Maria and saw tears in her eyes.

'Your papa and mama are very important people,' she explained, 'and it's just when they are interrupted that they get cross with you.'

He looked at her and knew that she was telling him the truth. But he knew, too, that there were so many important things going on in his parents' lives that he was always an interruption.

'I want to run away,' he said, blowing his nose hard. 'Are you sleeping?' Anthony asked, when he saw Maria's closed eyes.

'No, Master Anthony,' she said. 'I'm praying.'

'Will you pray for me?' he pleaded.

She hugged him close. 'I pray for you all every day, over and over again.'

'Does God hear you?' he questioned.

Maria stood him up in front of her, all the better to look right into his eyes. 'Master Anthony,' she said in a soft but serious voice, 'God hears every word. He hears every telling-off you get and sees every tear you shed. And when you want to run away, there is only one place to which it's safe to run.'

Catching something of the seriousness of the maid's tone, he listened very carefully. 'Where is that?' he asked.

'The only safe place to be is in the arms of Jesus,' she explained.

Anthony looked sad. 'But I can only go there when I die, and that may be a long time away.'

Pulling him back on to her knee and giving him a warm hug, Maria explained that if he puts his trust in the Lord Jesus, the Saviour would keep him safe in his arms through all the hard things he would meet in life.

There was no time Anthony Ashley needed to hear that more than when, just a year or two later, he was sent away to school. Knowing that tears would bring a raging from his father, Anthony just shook hands with his much-loved Maria as he left. That's what his father saw. What he did not see were the tears and the hugs and the prayers the two had had together as Maria dressed the young scholar in his new school clothes. There were no tears when he left for school because, apart from missing Maria and his sisters, he was not sorry to leave home.

'Carry this for me, brat!' an older boy ordered, as soon as he clapped eyes on the new pupil. Anthony looked puzzled. Was he speaking to him? A punch on the cheek made it clear that he was. But before he could pick up the boy's books, he was jumped on by two others who, along with the first thug, gave him a beating much like his father's. As suddenly as it had begun, the assault stopped. 'Get up,' a master roared. The three scrambled to their feet, knowing that if they didn't move quickly, they'd get the master's boot in their sides. But Anthony, not realising that some of his new teachers were as cruel as the children, didn't move fast enough to avoid a nasty and quite deliberate kick. 'Get on your way,' the man growled.

Things went from bad to worse, and sometimes only the memory of Maria helped Anthony to cope. And when he remembered the maid who loved him, her advice came back, and he learned to take all his troubles to God in prayer. But the blows the boys often landed on him were nothing to the blow that came in a letter from home bringing the news that his only real friend had died. Maria, he knew, was with Jesus, but how he longed that she was still with him and that he was no longer in that terrible school. Because Maria was dead, the last thing Anthony wanted to do was to go back home for the holidays.

When he was nine years old, in 1809, his father became the Earl of Shaftesbury, and the family moved out of London to St Giles, the family mansion house in Wimborne, Dorset. At least Anthony could escape from his father's anger in the land around the house. And he was always back on time for meals because in her will Maria had left him her gold watch. Although he lived to be an old man, and a famous one too, that was the watch he always carried.

Three years later, when he was twelve years old, Anthony was sent to Harrow, one of the most famous schools in England.

'I wonder what it'll be like,' he thought as he travelled there for the first time. 'It can't be any worse than prep school. Nothing could be worse than that.'

It wasn't worse; in fact it was far, far better. Soon he made friends, got to know his schoolmasters and settled down to a life that was better than any he had known before. But he never forgot the boy he had been.

'If I have children,' he often thought, 'I'll treat them as Maria treated me. I'll be kind to them, read stories to them and play with them too.' For a minute he tried to imagine his father reading him a story and playing a game with him, but he couldn't.

'What's that noise?' he wondered, as he walked near Harrow School one day. He went to find out and he wished he had not. When he turned a corner, he saw a funeral procession unlike any he'd ever seen before. It was a parish funeral - the dead man had left no money to pay for a coffin – and four drunks were staggering with the cheap coffin often nearly falling off their shoulders. And the songs they sang as they went along were unspeakable. Unable to take his eyes off the scene, the teenager followed the grotesque procession to the grave into which the coffin was tipped like rubbish.

'I don't know how I'll do it,' Anthony promised, 'but I'll do everything in my power to help poor people like that dead man.' As he walked back to school, he shivered at the memory of what he had seen.

Although the Earl wanted his son to go into the army, Anthony went to university, and by the time he was twenty-five years old he was a Member of Parliament.

'It's only by changing the law that things will get better for the poor,' he often said. 'That's the only reason I'm in Parliament.'

'Speaking up for the poor won't make you a fortune,' a friend who had been at university said. 'And it won't make you friends either.'

'I can hardly take in what you're saying,' Anthony told the man who came to see him.

'You're telling me that children as young as five work in factories and coal mines, sometimes for fifteen hours a day!'

His companion nodded. The Member of Parliament sat down, shaking his head in disbelief. 'But what can a child of five do in a coal mine?'

Taking a deep breath his visitor began. 'Let me tell you of a five-year-old girl I met, though she is small and looks even younger. She goes down the mine at four in the morning and is often there till five in the evening. All day she crouches in the pitch-black tunnel just inside a wooden door. When she hears the rattle of coal being brought along the tracks, she pulls the door open and lets it pass. And when it does, it is often pulled by a child not much older than she is. But they can't see each other in the black darkness.'

'But why so young?' Anthony asked.

'The tunnels are narrow and low,' the visitor explained. 'Only children and small women can crawl through them, and only half-starved ones at that.'

To the man's amazement he saw that his story had brought tears to Anthony's eyes. And he was even more amazed when he realised that the Member of Parliament was not ashamed of crying.

'Surely the factory children are better off than that,' Anthony said. 'At least they see the light of day.'

'There are windows in the mills,' his visitor admitted, 'not that the children who work there have time to look up and see them. For half the year they arrive at work in the dark and don't leave until it's dark again for they work the same long hours as the children who are down the mines. The machinery they work with is so loud that they can't hear anything over it and often, by the time they've grown up, they have very little hearing left.'

Anthony thought of his own children, of the long hours they played in the summer sunshine, of the fun and games he had with them. But his companion's story wasn't finished.

'By the end of the day these children are so exhausted that they sometimes have to be carried home, that's if they've survived the day.'

'What do you mean?' the Member of Parliament asked.

'Sadly, many are seriously injured, even killed, by the mill machinery. There is rarely anything done to prevent accidents, and they are too tired to take good care of themselves.'

Anthony shuddered. 'Thank you,' he said to the man. 'You have opened my eyes.'

The following Sunday Anthony was in church with his wife and children. As they sang a verse of a hymn, it was as though the kind man read the words for the very first time.

God gave the rich his riches,
He gave the poor his place;
And each where God has set him
Should sing his Father's praise.

He stopped singing. 'That's not true!' he thought. 'That's just not true! God doesn't want rich people to get richer and poor people to die of hunger. A loving God doesn't want rich children's rooms full of toys and poor children cowering down coal mines! From this day on I will work my heart out for children who are treated less well than animals.' Anthony's son wondered why his father had stopped singing.

Anthony spent years trying to have a law passed by Parliament that only allowed children to work for ten hours a day. Many Members of Parliament were mill owners or mine owners and they certainly didn't want that law to be passed. If it became law, they would have to employ more children, and that would cost them more money. They fought against the Bill every time it came to the House of Commons. But Anthony, who had not been loved as a child, loved the poor children with all his heart. He lost friends; he made enemies; but he struggled on. His father would have nothing to do with him, but his wife supported him all the way. Like Anthony she was a Christian and she too had a heart for children. Eventually, after many struggles, many prayers, and a great many tears, a law was passed.

'What's the most important thing you've done in your life?' one of his children asked Anthony. By then his father had died and he was the Earl of Shaftesbury. But these things were not important to him.

'Was it limiting children's working hours?' his daughter asked. Anthony thought before answering.

'I think,' he said, 'that what was even more important, was encouraging the Christian Church to see that God has not given some the right to be rich and left others to be forever poor. Only when Christians began to accept that, did they become interested in doing anything for the mill children and those who worked down the mines.'

'Is that why you support London City Mission?' asked his daughter.

'It certainly is. The mission was started because Christians saw what was happening to the poor. And it thrills my heart that its missionaries search the darkest corners of London to find those who most need their help, and those who most need Jesus. You see, my dear,' he concluded, 'at the beginning of this century the church was interested in the good folk who attended. It is now beginning to minister to those who are far outside.'

FACT FILE
The statue of Eros in Piccadilly Circus, London, was erected as a memorial to Lord Shaftesbury. However, the Mines Act of 1842 which forbade women, and boys and girls under ten years of age to be employed in coal mines is a more lasting and meaningful memorial. Shaftesbury also helped bring about improvements in health, education and the care of the mentally ill.

Keynote: Shaftesbury was singing a hymn one day when he realised that what he was singing was wrong. It is important when you read books written by people to ask, 'Is this true?' Use your own mind and God's Word to come to the right decision. What does God say about it? Shaftesbury knew that it was wrong to say that rich people were rich and poor people poor and that was that. God tells us to have mercy on the poor. Proverbs 14:31.

Think: Shaftesbury was often frightened as a little boy. However, he thought that you could only go to Jesus when you died. Jesus has promised, 'I am with you always.' Do you worry about the future? Are you frightened of bullies? Are you scared of going somewhere new? Cast your cares on God because he cares for you. Ask God to guide you. Ask him to show you who you should share your problems with. God has many people who love him and who are able and willing to help you.

Prayer: Lord Jesus, give me peace of heart and mind when I have troubles. Give me the strength of character to do the right thing and stand up for others. Help me to love and be obedient to you. May you be the most important person in my life ... the one I love most of all and the only one I worship. Amen.

Thomas Chalmers

Thomas and his older brother William stood on the shore watching six men row their fishing boat out of Anstruther harbour on the east coast of Scotland.

'There's a wind blowing up,' William said. 'They'd better stick close to the shore.'

'I suppose they've got to go where the fish are,' Thomas reasoned. 'And there's been little enough fish lately. They must be getting pretty desperate.'

'What makes you think that?' his brother asked.

'Just something I heard Father say,' Thomas explained. 'When we were coming out of church on Sunday, I heard him telling the elders that, unless the fish came in, there would be starving children in Anstruther.'

'We're lucky we're not among them,' William said. 'There'll be plenty on the table when we get home.'

'And there'll be a telling-off as well if we don't get a move on.'

The boys pushed their hands deep into their pockets and headed for home.

'Listen to the noise!' William laughed, as they reached their door.

Thomas nodded. 'That's one reason I like the shore,' he said. 'It's the only place where there's peace to think!'

'What do you expect,' his brother teased, 'when you've got so many brothers and sisters?' His brother grinned. 'I don't mind the five older ones.'

'I should hope not,' laughed William, who was a year and a bit older than Thomas.

'It's the younger ones that make the noise.'

'I know what you mean,' his brother agreed. 'There are thirteen of us already and another one on the way. I wonder how many more are still to come.'

'None, I hope,' Thomas said. 'There's nowhere we can get peace to study in the whole house.'

William nearly split his sides laughing. 'Since when did that bother you?' he was able to ask eventually.

Thomas Chalmers grinned, pushed the door open and shouted above the noise, 'We're home, Mother. Is it teatime?'

There were bread and oatcakes, hard and soft cheese, a big pat of butter, a bowl of gooseberry jam and a jug of frothy milk on the table when Mr Chalmers said grace. And there were only crumbs when the family had finished the meal.

'Is it true that the fishing's bad?' William asked his father, before they rose from the table.

'Yes,' the man answered. 'And that's not good news for Anstruther. There will be children going to bed with nothing in their stomachs this evening. I hope you're all grateful to the Lord for what you've eaten. It's not every family that can afford it.'

'Could we be poor one day, Papa?' one of the little girls asked.

Mr Chalmers smiled kindly at her. 'We're blessed by having money in the bank,' he explained. 'Poor folk only have what's in their pockets, and when that runs out, they go hungry.'

'Is there nothing we can do to help?' Thomas asked.

'Your mother and I do what we can,' his father said, 'and I hope you'll do that, too, when you grow up and have an income of your own.'

Thomas packed that thought away in his mind, picked up a ball and called for his brothers to come for a game.

Mrs Chalmers watched her sons from the window. She loved these summer evenings when the family was together, even windy ones when their ball went all over the place. 'It's strange,' she thought. 'Thomas is right in the middle of the family but he's the leader of them. Look at him now, keeping them all in order and deciding who should run for the ball when it's blown away. And I'm sure he's got intelligence, though he's not discovered how to work yet. He must have a good brain inside that huge head of his. And what a laugh he has!' She smiled at the thought. 'He can outlaugh, outrun, outplay and outwit most of the boys in the village. But they still get on with him for he's so easy-going.'

'What are you thinking about?' Mr Chalmers asked, seeing the smile that was playing on his wife's face. He nodded when she shared her thoughts. 'He is a grand lad,' the man said, 'but he'll need to pull his socks up and discover how to work. In fact,' he went on, knowing that what he was going to say would surprise his wife, 'I think he should go off to university with William in the autumn.'

The smile cleared from Mrs Chalmers' face. 'But he's not twelve yet,' she said.

'And William is only a year older,' her husband pointed out. 'If the pair of them go together, Thomas might settle down and work. His teacher says he's well able for it.'

A few months later, in the autumn of 1792, William and Thomas Chalmers began their studies at St Andrews University.

'Be sure to write,' their mother said, as she watched them go. William was thirteen, and his little brother was eleven years old.

When they went home for their first holiday, their father was anxious to know what they had learned. And while Thomas told him about maths which he loved, he didn't mention that his chief interests at university were the same as they had been at home – running, football and handball, and that he was getting quite a reputation for his handball. Somehow Thomas felt that was probably not what his father most wanted to hear!

'What do you want to do after you finish at the university?' a local fisherman asked Thomas during that holiday.

'I want to be a minister,' he said, as he had done for some years. 'I don't think I've ever wanted to be anything else.'

'But are you not learning other things that take your interest?' the man wondered.

'Oh yes,' Thomas told him. 'There's maths. I just love maths. But I can do that as well as be a minister.'

The fisherman, who was an elder in the church, wondered about the young Thomas. 'His parents are faithful Christians,' he thought, watching Thomas's back as he strolled along the shore, 'but I don't think that Master Thomas knows the Lord Jesus yet, even though he wants to be a minister.'

When he was fifteen years old, Thomas Chalmers began to study for the ministry, and in 1803 he became minister of a church in his home county of Fife. Just as he thought as a boy, he combined being a minister with lecturing in maths at his old university. But a few years later he had to do some serious thinking when a brother and one of his sisters died and Thomas himself was ill for many months. It was as he was getting better that he realised his priorities had been all wrong. He wrote to a friend, 'I resolve to devote every talent and every hour to the defence and illustration of the gospel.' And that's just what he did.

In 1815, Thomas left Fife with his young wife Grace to become a minister in the great city of Glasgow.

'We have to do something for the children who live around the church,' he told his elders. 'Many of them know nothing about the Lord Jesus. And we need to visit everyone who lives in the area. I reckon that's over eleven thousand people.'

The elders gasped but agreed it had to be done.

'First things first,' their minister said, 'how do we go about reaching the children?'

The men talked about it, prayed about it and decided to arrange a Sunday evening school for them. There were thirteen at the first meeting. Two years later there were 1,200!

One Sunday, after he had returned home from the class, Thomas sat in front of the fire thinking. 'It's a strange thing,' he smiled at the memory. 'I remember William and I talking when we were boys, and I said I hoped that thirteen other children were all we would have in the family. And here we are with a family of 1,200 children in the church, all started off from a little group of thirteen. When I was young I thought thirteen was a terrible lot of children. How things change!'

'Are you aware, brothers,' Chalmers told the elders of his church, 'that many of the children who come to our classes can neither read nor write?'

The men nodded seriously. 'But what can we do about that?' the bravest of them asked, knowing that when their minister saw something needing to be done, he usually found a way to do it.

Thomas looked the man in the eye. 'We can open schools for them,' he said. 'God doesn't only care for the souls of these children; he's interested in every part of them, their education included.'

Some of the elders caught the vision right away, others took longer, but within quite a short time schools were set up for nearly 700 children.

If Chalmers' elders wondered what their minister would think of next, they didn't have long to wait. 'We must discuss the care of the poor,' he told the men at a church meeting.

'This city is full of poor people,' one elder thought. 'And anything we do will just be a drop in the ocean.' But he listened to what Thomas was saying, and even he began to catch his minister's vision as he heard what he had to say.

'At present,' Chalmers said, 'the poor are provided for from the poor rate levy. But if we think back to the Bible, we'll realise that collections for the poor should be made within the church and deacons should use that money to make sure that the really poor have what they need. Not only that, the deacons should know the people well and their families too, so they can help families care for their own instead of being dependent on others.'

'But surely that's not the job of the church,' one elder wondered aloud.

'But surely it is,' Thomas Chalmers boomed. 'Have you not read the Bible?'

'You couldn't have put another person into the church today,' Grace Chalmers told her husband after a special service in 1823. He smiled. 'When I was young, I used to wonder how many children could be packed into one house! But I discovered that as many as came could be fitted in somewhere.'

Suddenly Thomas looked serious. 'The church was built to hold 1,700,' he said, 'and it's reckoned that over 3,000 were there today, and all to say goodbye to us.'

There was a long silence before he continued. 'I'll miss the Glasgow people so much. I wouldn't leave unless I was sure it was God's will for me to lecture at university.'

His wife nodded her head. 'I know that,' she said. 'And I'll miss them too.'

Although Thomas Chalmers moved away, he didn't forget the people of Glasgow or the lessons he had learned as their minister. He remembered the poverty and sickness he had found in Glasgow's alleyways. He remembered the children who could neither read nor write, and the men who couldn't find work. He remembered mothers who starved themselves so that their children had bread to eat. And he knew that Christians should do something about it.

As the years passed from the 1820s through the 1830s to the early 1840s, and Chalmers became more and more well known, people began to listen to what he had to say and to take seriously the problems of the poor. It was as though the Church began to wake up; as though it rubbed its eyes and saw what Scotland was really like, then shook itself and did what it could to help.

But while good things were happening in the Church, there were things going on that worried Thomas Chalmers and a number of others.

'We just can't sit and let this happen,' he said to a minister friend, as they discussed the situation. 'Congregations should be able to choose their own ministers. Landlords have no right to put men in churches when the people don't want them!'

'I agree,' his friend replied. 'But what can we do about it?'

'We can pray,' Thomas announced. 'And we can ask God to guide us through the next General Assembly.'

When that large annual meeting of the Church of Scotland was held in May 1843, Chalmers and around 400 others who agreed with him, felt the right thing to do was to walk out. Having left the Assembly Hall, they gathered in another building where they established the Free Church of Scotland with Thomas Chalmers as its first Moderator.

'It's a sad time,' a young minister said, 'but it's an exciting one too.'

'Yes,' his friend agreed. 'There's a great sadness over Scotland, but a great opportunity is opening up.'

The two men didn't realise that Thomas Chalmers was walking behind them and could hear what they were saying.

'Yes, my good friends,' he said, drawing alongside them, 'it's an opportunity to do more than choose our own ministers. It's a God-given opportunity to be like the early church and to have a real concern for the people of Scotland.'

'That's something we've learned from you, Dr Chalmers,' the young man said.

'I don't know where you learned it,' he said. 'But just don't forget it. We won't be a Church worth the Christian name if we do.'

FACT FILE
School: In the United Kingdom in 1870, schools only taught reading, writing and arithmetic. In 1872 in Scotland you could be educated until you were thirteen. In 1914 more than 70,000 children spent half the day at school and the other half working in a factory. In 1944 free secondary education for all was provided.

Keynote: Thomas Chalmers did not have a saving faith in Jesus Christ when he started to study for the ministry. It was only after his illness and the death of his brother and sister that things changed. He realised that there was no point in preaching unless you preached about the forgiveness of sins that Jesus has made available by his death on the cross. That's what he meant when he said, 'I resolve to devote every talent and every hour to the defence and illustration of the gospel.'

Think: It is important to have a real concern for the people of your own country and area. Think about what it needs. Are there poor people who need help? What can you do? There are definitely people you know who do not know about the Lord Jesus. How about talking to them about what you learn at Church, Sunday school or youth group? You could start a prayer group to pray about your town or country.

Prayer: Father God, please be with the people of my town and my country. May this land be a place which honours and obeys your Word. Be with those people who run the country and make decisions. May they be people who love you. Help the churches in my country to be worthy of the name of Jesus Christ. Help us all to obey your Word. Amen.

QUIZ

How much can you remember
about the ten boys who
made a difference?

Try answering these questions
to find out ...

Augustine of Hippo

1. Which continent did Augustine live in as a young boy?

2. What was Augustine's mother's name?

3. Which book of the Bible was Augustine reading when he became a Christian?

Jan Hus

4. In which city did Jan go to university?

5. Which English preacher did Jan Hus agree with?

6. What happened to Jan in Gottlieben Castle?

Martin Luther

7. What did Martin Luther's father work as?

8. What was Martin going to be before the thunderstorm?

9. Martin wrote a list of ways in which the Church wasn't obeying the Bible. How many points were on this list?

Ulrich Zwingli

10. Which country was Ulrich Zwingli from?

11. When Ulrich and some other men were at the printing house, what did the printer's wife bring them to eat?

12. Which German Reformer did Ulrich Zwingli admire?

William Tyndale

13. What language was used in churches when William was a young boy?

14. What language did William translate the Bible into?

15. What did Henry Phillips do to Tyndale?

Hugh Latimer

16. In which university did Hugh Latimer become a teacher in 1510?

17. What was the name of the other man who was sentenced to death alongside Hugh Latimer?

18. Who did Latimer pray for before he died?

John Calvin

19. Which of John Calvin's parents died when he was a young boy?

20. What did Calvin study in Paris?

21. Which city did Calvin eventually settle in?

John Knox

22. What was the name of the village in which John Knox was born?

23. What was the name of John's friend who was martyred?

24. Who became very angry with John Knox when he preached against the Mass?

Lord Shaftesbury

25. What was the name of the maid who looked after Anthony when he was a little boy?

26. What did Anthony become when he left university?

27. Name one of the missions that Anthony supported when he grew up.

Thomas Chalmers

28. What was the name of the fishing village that Thomas lived in as a boy?

29. What was the name of the city that Thomas went to work in, in 1815?

30. How many children came to the Sunday school after two years?

How well did you do?

Turn over to find out...

Answers:

1. Africa

2. Monica

3. Romans

4. Prague

5. Wycliffe

6. Imprisoned then killed

7. A miner

8. A lawyer

9. 95

10. Switzerland

11. Sausages

12. Martin Luther

13. Latin

14. English

15. Betrayed him

16. Cambridge

17. Mr Ridley

18. Queen Elizabeth I

19. His mother

20. Theology

21. Geneva

22. Haddington

23. George Wishart

24. Mary, Queen of Scots

25. Maria

26. A Member of Parliament

27. London City Mission

28. Anstruther

29. Glasgow

30. 1,200

Start collecting this series now!

Ten Boys who used their Talents:
ISBN 978-1-84550-146-4
Paul Brand, Ghillean Prance, C.S.Lewis,
C.T. Studd, Wilfred Grenfell, J.S. Bach,
James Clerk Maxwell, Samuel Morse,
George Washington Carver, John Bunyan.

Ten Girls who used their Talents:
ISBN 978-1-84550-147-1
Helen Roseveare, Maureen McKenna,
Anne Lawson, Harriet Beecher Stowe,
Sarah Edwards, Selina Countess of Huntingdon, Mildred Cable,
Katie Ann MacKinnon,
Patricia St. John, Mary Verghese.

Ten Boys who Changed the World:
ISBN 978-1-85792-579-1
David Livingstone, Billy Graham, Brother Andrew,
John Newton, William Carey, George Müller,
Nicky Cruz, Eric Liddell, Luis Palau,
Adoniram Judson.

Ten Girls who Changed the World:
ISBN 978-1-85792-649-1
Corrie Ten Boom, Mary Slessor,
Joni Eareckson Tada, Isobel Kuhn,
Amy Carmichael, Elizabeth Fry, Evelyn Brand, Gladys Aylward,
Catherine Booth, Jackie Pullinger.

Ten Boys who Made a Difference:
ISBN 978-1-85792-775-7
Augustine of Hippo, Jan Hus, Martin Luther,
Ulrich Zwingli, William Tyndale, Hugh Latimer,
John Calvin, John Knox, Lord Shaftesbury,
Thomas Chalmers.

SOME BOOKS IN THE TRAILBLAZERS SERIES

For a full list of Trailblazers, please see our
website: www.christianfocus.com
All Trailblazers are available as e-books

Martin Luther: Reformation Fire
by Catherine Mackenzie

What made an ordinary monk become a catalyst for the Reformation in Europe in the 1500s? What were the reasons lying behind his nailing of 93 theses against the practice of indulgences to the door of the Schlosskirche in Wittenberg in 1517? Why was Martin Luther's life in danger? How did his apparent kidnapping result in the first ever New Testament translated into the German language? Discover how a fresh understanding of the Scriptures transformed not only his own life but had a huge impact upon Europe.

ISBN: 978-1-78191-521-9

CHRISTIAN FOCUS PUBLICATIONS

Christian Focus | Christian Heritage | CF4K | Mentor

Christian Focus Publications publishes books for adults and children under its four main imprints: Christian Focus, CF4K, Mentor and Christian Heritage. Our books reflect our conviction that God's Word is reliable and Jesus is the way to know him, and live for ever with him.

Our children's publication list includes a Sunday School curriculum that covers pre-school to early teens, and puzzle and activity books. We also publish personal and family devotional titles, biographies and inspirational stories that children will love.

If you are looking for quality Bible teaching for children then we have an excellent range of Bible stories and age-specific theological books.

From pre-school board books to teenage apologetics, we have it covered!

Find us at our web page:
www.christianfocus.com

CF4·K
Because you're never too young to know Jesus

TEN BOYS WHO MADE HISTORY

LIGHT KEEPERS

Irene Howat

CF4•K

Copyright © Christian Focus Publications 2003
Reprinted 2004, 2005, 2007, 2008, 2010, 2012, 2014, 2016,
2017, 2019, 2020
Paperback ISBN: 978-1-85792-836-5
E-pub ISBN: 978-1-84550-844-9
Mobi ISBN: 978-1-84550-845-6

Published by Christian Focus Publications,
Geanies House, Fearn, Tain, Ross-shire,
IV20 1TW, Scotland, Great Britain.
www.christianfocus.com
e-mail:info@christianfocus.com
Cover Design by Alister MacInnes
Cover Illustration by Elena Temporin,
Milan Illustrations Agency
Printed and bound in Turkey

All incidents retold in these stories are based on true situations.
Where specific information about childhood incidents has been
unobtainable the author has written these paragraphs using
other information concerning family life, hobbies, home life and
relationships, freely available as well as appropriate historical
source material.

*Cover illustration: This depicts Robert Murray McCheyne as a young lad. He
was a very active child despite his ill health. In later years he would practice
gymnastics and the parallel bars amongst other things. He even hurt himself
quite severely when showing a young boy how to do a particular gymnastic
manoeuvre on some poles in the garden. Read all about this in chapter 5.*

for
Ali and Mo

Contents

Samuel Rutherford

Samuel stood looking at the burn marks on the wall high above him.

'Jedburgh Abbey was burned down by the Earl of Surrey's army about ninety years ago,' his teacher told the boys. 'In 1523, to be exact. Since then it has been occupied several times. In fact, from what is left, it is hard to imagine how magnificent the building once was.'

'Sir,' said Samuel. 'Was the church roof originally much higher? It seems so low compared with the rest of the building.'

'Good thinking,' the teacher said. 'The roof was very high before the great fire. But rather than replace it after it was burned down, it was lowered, and internal walls were built to make the church smaller. Of course, the Latiners' Alley, where the school meets, was originally inside the great abbey.'

The teacher surveyed his pupils.

'How,' he asked the youngest boy, 'did the Latiners' Alley get its name?'

The boy looked puzzled, then he grinned.

'Sir,' he said. 'Is it because that's where we learn Latin?'

'Quite right,' smiled the teacher, and that's what we're going to do now.'

Glancing all around him, Samuel tried to imagine what Jedburgh Abbey must have looked like before the Earl of Surrey's army did their worst.

As they walked home to the village of Nisbet after school that afternoon, Samuel and his brothers discussed what they had been told.

'Will we go by the road or along the Jed Water?' James asked.

'Let's go by the river,' suggested George.

The three brothers left the road and dropped to the right towards the riverbank.

'I like history,' Samuel commented. 'It makes sense of things.'

'Let's pretend to be the Scots' army spying on the Earl of Surrey's troops,' George said. 'I reckon we could get all the way to Bonjedward without being seen from the road if we kept to the bushes.'

His brothers thought that sounded a very satisfactory way of returning home after a day at school. For over a mile they dodged from bush to bush and rock to rock. Even though they could see people walking on the main road and on the track to the other side of the Jed Water, nobody called their names and shouted hello. They were very pleased with themselves, if a little dusty and covered in grass.

'Just quarter of a mile to go,' whispered James, as they neared Bonjedward.

'What did you say?' asked a voice from the far side of the copse they were hiding in.

The boys felt like burst balloons. They had been so pleased with their spy act, and just before reaching the village they had been discovered. An old man came round the copse to where the boys were crouching.

'Hiding, are you?' he asked.

Samuel decided it was better to explain what they'd been playing at than to seem very foolish. Old Mr Ker smiled when he heard their story.

'I'm going home to Bonjedward,' he told them. 'And if you walk with me, I'll tell you some more of the history of the area. And it's every bit as exciting as the Earl of

Surrey's attack on the Abbey, because I saw it with my own two eyes.'

The boys got to their feet immediately and joined the old man on his walk along the riverbank.

'When I was a boy,' he said, 'there was a great battle just four miles from here, at Ancrum. I was six years old at the time, and I'm seventy-six now, but I remember it as though it was yesterday. King Henry of England sent an army that landed at the port of Leith before entering Edinburgh, where he set the city on fire. It was said that the fires didn't go out for four days.'

The boys' eyes danced with excitement.

'His army marched south, and some Scots families joined them on the way.'

'Why did they do that?' George asked.

'I suppose it was join them or be killed by them,' Mr Ker explained. 'By February 1545, the great army had reached Ancrum Moor and camped there. Do you know where the battle site is?'

'Yes,' James told him. 'It's just three miles up the road from here.'

Pleased that they knew where the battle site was, Mr Ker went on with his story. 'News went round that the English army had set fire to the Tower of Broomhill, burning to death an old woman, her family and her servants, who were locked inside. So the Scots forces were in a real mood for battle. They were an odd assortment of men, but rage drove them on. With cries of "Remember Broomhouse" they surged towards the English. Very cleverly they timed the battle for late afternoon when the setting sun would dazzle their enemies' eyes. The Scots fought with a fury and scattered their enemy, or what was left of them, for 800 English troops died on Ancrum Moor.'

The old man, seeing that his audience was captivated by his tale, looked for the perfect finishing line.

'That was my earliest memory,' he said. 'The cries of "Remember Broomhouse" and the clash of swords. Your earliest memories will be tamer than that, I'm sure.'

James and George looked at their brother, wondering if he would tell Mr Ker his story.

'Would you like to know my earliest memory?' Samuel asked.

'I would indeed,' said the old man.

'There is a well in the village of Nisbet,' the lad said. 'The water in it is about three feet deep. I was playing there with my friends one day when I sat on the edge of the well and fell in. They ran for help, knowing I would drown if I didn't get out. But while they were away, a lovely man dressed in white came and pulled me out of the well. I was safe on the grass beside the well when my friends came back with help.'

'A lovely man dressed in white,' Mr Ker repeated. 'Who was he then?'

'I didn't know him,' Samuel said.

'Was he an angel?' asked the old man.

Samuel shook his head and smiled. 'I didn't know him,' he repeated. 'But that's my earliest memory.'

By the time the boy had told his story, the four of them had reached the village of Bonjedward. The boys left Mr Ker there and walked the last stretch of the Water of Jed to where it joined the River Teviot. Then they turned east and walked the mile along the grassy bank of the Teviot to their home, passing the well on the way.

By the time Samuel was seventeen, he was a student in Edinburgh. Soon after he graduated in 1621, he was made a professor. But he resigned just four years later and spent his time studying theology. In 1627, he moved to the parish of Anwoth and became minister there. We don't know when Samuel became a Christian, but his heart was just full of love for the Lord Jesus by the time he had grown up.

'What do you think of the Solway coast?' one of his church members asked, not long after he arrived in the area.

'It's a fine part of Scotland,' Samuel told him. 'And the church is in a beautiful place, with the hill beside it, trees around it, and the sea within walking distance. I already love the place and I'm growing to love the people too.'

The man was about to say more, but Samuel excused himself.

'There are two lads over there herding the sheep. I'd like to talk to them.'

With that Samuel was off to make friends with the youth of his congregation.

The man watched him go. 'Rutherford's nothing to look at,' he thought, 'just a little fair-haired man. But there is something about him I like.'

'Hello there,' Samuel called out to the boys. 'I'm the new minister. What are your names?'

'I'm Thomas,' one answered.

'And I'm Archie,' said the other.

'Well, Thomas and Archie,' Rutherford smiled, 'I've got news for you.'

The boys looked interested.

'The Lord Jesus himself knew about herding sheep,' he told them. 'He's the best shepherd of all and he loves you both more than you'll ever know.'

The boys liked their new minister immediately.

'Goodbye, boys,' Samuel said. 'It's good to meet you.'

'Mr Rutherford is different from many ministers,' commented a local farmer.

'In what way?' asked the farmer's brother, who was visiting him.

'Most ministers preach about hell's fire and try to frighten us into becoming Christians.'

'So they do,' the other man said. 'And there's nothing wrong with that.'

The farmer ignored what had been said.

'Mr Rutherford preaches about the love of God rather than the fires of hell. He makes God's love sound so ... so ... so lovely.'

'Lovely!' his brother said crossly. 'That message will not make much of an impact. You need hell shouted from the pulpit to make people listen.'

'We do listen to Mr Rutherford,' the farmer told his brother. 'It's almost as if he wants us to fall in love with the Lord Jesus.'

'I've never heard anything so sloppy in all my life!' the other man announced.

But the farmer knew that he had fallen in love with Jesus, and his life had been changed completely.

Samuel worked hard in Anwoth, even though things were far from easy for him.

His young wife died after a year of illness, and two of his children died there too. In 1636, he published a book showing that we are saved through God's grace and special choice. Unfortunately the church authorities didn't like that at all, and he was called before the High Court! The court exiled him to Aberdeen.

'I long to be in Anwoth,' Samuel thought, as he looked out over the grey, granite buildings of Aberdeen. 'I long to see my dear people and to tell them about the love of Jesus.'

He sat at his table and began to write a letter to one of his congregation. It was the first of many letters that went from Aberdeen to Anwoth. And so beautiful were his letters, and so full of love, that people kept them, and they were collected into a book which is still being read today, over three-and-a-half centuries after they were written!

Scotland in the 1630s was in great confusion. The king was trying to make the church in Scotland like the church south of the border, and not everyone was happy about it. In 1638, there were so many comings and goings that Samuel was able to slip out of Aberdeen and make his way back to Anwoth.

'Every mile is a mile nearer Anwoth,' he thought, as he travelled from the north-east of Scotland to the south-west. 'And every mile is a mile nearer my dear people.'

But Samuel was not back in Anwoth long before the Church of Scotland held a General Assembly and broke free from the king's church once again. Not only that, but the Assembly appointed Samuel Rutherford as a Professor of Theology in St Andrews University.

It was with a very sad heart that he said goodbye to the people he loved, and rode away from Anwoth.

Five years later, Samuel found himself in London. A great assembly of ministers was held there, and he was invited to join them. They had the job of working out exactly what the Bible taught, and putting the teachings together in a book that became known as the Westminster Confession of Faith. They also compiled the Larger and Shorter Catechisms. All of these are still in use today!

'It's good to be home in Scotland,' Samuel told his colleagues, when he arrived back from London. 'I much prefer the fresh sea air to the awful smell of the River Thames.'

'Have you made plans for what you'll do now?' he was asked.

Rutherford nodded. 'Yes,' he said. 'I'll teach my students, of course. But there's a book that needs writing, and I think I'm the one to write it.'

'What will it be about?' queried his colleague.

Samuel thought for a moment before answering. 'It will be about the relationship between the king and the church. God is the King of kings, and the king of the country needs to know that.'

The other university teacher shook his head.

'Are you wise to think of writing a book on that subject?' he asked. 'It won't be popular.'

He did write his book, and the king didn't like it one little bit. Rutherford was charged with treason in 1661 and summoned to appear in court. Samuel, who was by then very unwell, refused to go. When the summons was delivered to him, he answered the messenger, 'I must answer my first summons; and before your day arrives, I will be where few kings and great folk come.' By the day that had been set for his trial, Samuel Rutherford had answered God's summons to go to heaven, where he met the King of kings, whom he had loved deeply and served faithfully.

FACT FILE

The Covenanter: During Samuel's life there was a lot of disagreement between the king and the church in Scotland about the way that they should worship God. Many of those who disagreed with the king were persecuted by government soldiers. These people were called the Covenanters, because some of their leaders had signed a protest about what the king was doing. This protest was called The National Covenant. It said that they would obey God rather than the king. The Covenant was signed in Greyfriars Kirkyard in Edinburgh.

Keynote: Samuel got into a lot of trouble because he resisted the king's attempts to control the church. He was willing to go through this because he knew that God was the King of kings and was more important than any human leader. There are still countries where Christians are persecuted. They know that God is more important than any government. Although Samuel suffered greatly, God gave him the strength and help that he needed to get through the difficult times.

 Think: Samuel believed that God is the King of kings. That means that he is most important, and that we should all do what he tells us in the Bible. When we don't do this, we sin. Sin displeases God. Jesus came so that we could be forgiven for our sins, but also so that we can learn to obey God more and more each day. Do you try to obey God? Who can help you to find out more about what God wants you to do?

 Prayer: Lord Jesus, thank you for your love. You are perfect, and in charge of everything. Thank you for those who suffered in the past so that we would be able to worship you in the way that the Bible tells us. Help those Christians who are suffering for you today. Amen.

John Owen

The two boys stood side by side on the bank of the stream.

'I dare you,' William said to his friend.

John looked at the rushing water. Then he looked behind him to see how good a run he would get at it.

'OK,' he said. 'I dare you too.'

Taking one last look at the stream to find a good solid edge from which to leap, John turned and strode back over the rise of grass.

'Ready?' asked William.

John nodded.

'Go!'

John Owen pelted down the rise and over the grass to the stream. Measuring his paces perfectly, he arrived at the water's edge on a left stride, catapulted over, and just managed to reach solid ground with his right foot before throwing himself forward and landing flat out on the grass. Grinning from ear to ear he lay there, not turning to watch the inevitable, just enjoying imagining it. He could hear his friend thudding down the grass bank. He enjoyed the seconds of silence when he was in the air and the anticipation of the almighty splash that would surely follow. And he wasn't disappointed.

'You all right?' he asked, rolling over on to his back, all the better to see William stagger out of the stream, dripping from the top of his head to the soles of his feet.

'You've been practising!' the soaking lad fumed.

Scrambling to his feet, John pulled off his jacket and threw it to his friend.

'I'm sorry,' he said. 'But I couldn't resist it when you dared me.'

By the time they'd got back to the village of Stadham, they were the best of friends again.

When they parted, John raced through the village to his home.

'Where's Dad?' he called, as he went in the door.

His mother looked up from her mending. 'He's in his room working on Sunday's sermons,' she said. 'You'd better not disturb him.'

John grumped, and sat down at the table.

'Have you finished the work Dad gave you to do?' his mother asked.

Looking guilty, the boy admitted he had not.

His mother tried not to smile. 'I suggest you get out your books and do it before your father comes through. He may be your kindly minister, but he's your schoolmaster too.'

Taking his books from a shelf on the wall, John settled at the table and began his mathematics. It wasn't that he didn't like working, far from it. But it was a glorious day, one that just begged him to run and jump and kick stones around with his friends.

'Do I need to go to school in Oxford?' John asked his father, later that day. 'There are still loads of things I could learn from you.'

His father, who was the minister in the small village of Stadham, explained that a teacher in Oxford, a Mr Sylvester, would be able to teach him much more.

Having lost that argument, John tried a different one.

'Oxford is miles away,' he said. 'And I won't know anyone there.'

Mr Owen smiled. John really was stretching it! Oxford was only six miles away. His son had one last shot.

'There'll be nothing for a boy to do in Oxford!' he said, though he was already feeling quite excited by the challenge.

Smiling broadly, Mr Owen assured his son that there would be plenty to do in Oxford. There would be mathematics, Latin, Greek, history, English grammar, and plenty else besides.

'And there's the River Thames,' John's father concluded. 'It may not be the mighty river it is when it flows through London, but it is still deep enough to soak your friends.'

John's neck grew red, then the blush crept up his face until he could not help but smile.

'You heard about William?' the boy asked.

His father grinned back. 'Yes,' he replied. 'I heard about William!'

So young John Owen left home for Oxford, and Mr Sylvester's school, where he studied hard and did very well indeed.

In November 1631, when he was just fifteen years old, John Owen became a student at Queen's College, Oxford.

'I'm really enjoying my studies,' he wrote home to his father and mother, towards the end of his first year. 'But it is very hard work. I only allow myself four hours sleep a night. But in case you think your son's life is all work and no play, occasionally I take time off to practise my jumping, throwing the bar and bell-ringing. Of course, I have my regular music lessons, which give me a break from my books. By the way, did I tell you that my music teacher taught the king to play the flute?'

During John's student years, what he had learned at home about the Lord Jesus became real to him, and he knew that Jesus was his Saviour. At the same time there were changes in the university that he found impossible to live with.

'How can the Chancellor do these things?' he asked himself. 'This is a Protestant university, yet he's bringing in all kinds of Romanist things. The chapel service last Sunday was a Mass!'

John agonised over this and discussed it with his friends.

'Owen!' a fellow student called after him one day. 'I want to speak to you.'

The two young men walked along the bank of the Thames.

'Have you heard the news?' John's friend asked, then rushed on to tell what he had heard. 'Anyone objecting to the Romanist innovations the Chancellor is bringing in is to be expelled from the University!'

Suspecting that might happen, John had already thought the issue through.

'In that case I'd better pack my things and go home,' he said. 'Because what the Chancellor is bringing in is against what the Bible teaches, and I'm not prepared to accept it.'

On leaving Oxford, John Owen became a private chaplain for a time before moving to London. He also became an author.

'What a year 1643 has been,' he told a friend that December. 'In July I moved here to Fordham in Essex, and in the few months since then I met and married Mary.' He grinned. 'I think coming to Fordham was a good move!'

John grew to know the area around Fordham very well as he visited the homes of his people. From house to house he went in the hamlets round the parish, from Rose Green to Gallows Green and from there to the quaintly named Seven Stars Green, then east to Eight Ash Green. Sometimes, as he crossed and recrossed the River Colne that flowed right through his parish, he smiled at the memory of his exploits with William back home in Stadham.

'Here's the minister coming to catechise us,' children called to their parents, when they saw him coming.

The parents and children would go into their homes and listen to John Owen's teaching then answer the questions he asked them on the Christian faith.

'I've been asked to preach before Parliament,' John told his wife, in the spring of 1646.

'You'll only do that once in your life!' Mary said, smiling at the thought of what her husband had been asked to do. 'It's the people of Fordham who'll hear most of your sermons.'

But just a few months later, the people of Fordham said goodbye to their minister, as he moved five miles away to Coggelshall. Soon he had a congregation of nearly 2,000 people which gathered in the market town to hear him preach.

These were troubled times in England, and John found himself in the centre of things. King Charles I was accused of being a traitor, tyrant and murderer. At a trial before the High Court of Justice, he was found guilty and sentenced to death. On 31st January, 1649, the king was beheaded. The following day, John preached before Parliament. He was back there again three months later. On that occasion, Oliver Cromwell heard him preach. No king succeeded Charles I, and Oliver Cromwell became the military ruler of the country. Although he made some bad mistakes, Cromwell was a Christian and he liked Owen's preaching. The day after Cromwell heard John preach, the two men met again.

'Sir,' said Cromwell, 'you are the man I want to get to know.'

'That will be more to my advantage than to yours,' answered Owen.

Taking John by the arm, Cromwell spoke to him quietly and urgently.

'I'm leaving with my troops for Ireland soon,' he said. 'And I want you with me as chaplain.'

On the ship to Ireland, John Owen talked over the events of the previous day with one of the soldiers.

'I've never seen anything like it,' the soldier said. 'Twelve thousand soldiers spending a whole day in prayer, fasting and reading their Bibles, apart from when they were listening to three sermons being preached.'

'It was a day to remember,' Owen said. 'There's never before been one like it.'

Cromwell's troops did what they set out to do in Ireland and then returned home. The following year they were mobilised again and headed north to Scotland. John Owen was commanded to accompany Cromwell, now as an adviser as well as chaplain. Having fought and won the Battle of Dunbar, the English troops stormed Edinburgh, and Cromwell put his preachers in the city's churches. John Owen took the services in St Giles.

'How dare Cromwell put one of his men in our pulpit!' an elder said, as he went into church the first Sunday.

'Thank goodness it's Mr Owen and not another of Cromwell's men,' he thought the following week.

And the next Sunday, as he took his seat in church, the elder found himself looking forward to what John Owen had to say. 'He may be Cromwell's chaplain,' he told his wife, as they walked home after the service, 'but he preaches about the Lord Jesus Christ and makes me want to listen.'

Oliver Cromwell had removed all the Roman Church practices from Oxford University, and he was so pleased with John Owen that he appointed him Vice-Chancellor and Dean of Christ Church. Cromwell was clever; he knew that the university had been nearly ruined and that his friend would put it to rights again. And that's just what the new Vice-Chancellor helped to happen.

'What do you think of Mr Owen?' one student asked another, as they fished in the Thames one Saturday.

'He's a good man,' his friend answered. 'He doesn't only preach the Bible, he actually lives a good Christian life.'

'What makes you say that?' queried the student.

His friend recast, letting his cork float settle in the water before answering.

'My father died not long after I came to Oxford,' he said. 'And until my uncle sent me some money, I had nothing at all to live on. Somehow Mr Owen heard about that and he gave me enough to see me through.'

Although Owen's work kept him very busy, it didn't stop him writing. He wrote many books that were popular in his own day and that are still read today. John didn't find it easy to say things in just a few words, so his books can be heavy reading. Someone has suggested that they are easier to understand when read aloud, because then it sounds as though John Owen is speaking.

In 1657, a majority of Members of Parliament voted to crown Cromwell as king.

'That's not right,' John thought. 'He is a good military ruler but not a good king. I hope he has the sense to know that.'

But Cromwell thought differently and he wasn't pleased with John. Owen and several others drew up a petition against Parliament's ruling, and Cromwell was forced to stand down. Instead, in a very grand ceremony, he was made Lord Protector. John was not even invited to the ceremony. Three years later, when Charles II was crowned king, Owen was forced to resign his job and leave Oxford. Although he was not legally allowed to preach, he continued to do so when he could. Of course, no law could stop him writing his books.

London went through terrible times in the mid-1660s. The Great Plague hit the city and at its height, in September 1665, more than 8,000 people died each week. Then the Great Fire of London roared through the streets. While many ministers the king approved of fled the city in terror, John Owen and others who thought as he did (they were called Puritans) were soon back in London preaching the good news that Jesus saves.

Although John Owen was one of the cleverest men of his time, his friends were not all grand people. One of them, John Bunyan, was a tinker who had spent time in prison for his faith.

'I hear you wrote a book in prison. What's it about?' Owen asked his friend.

'It's a story, a kind of fantasy, about the Christian life,' Bunyan explained.

'May I read it?' enquired John.

Bunyan gave 'The Pilgrim's Progress' to his friend, and John Owen was so impressed by it that he asked his publisher to produce the book. That was a wise decision as 'The Pilgrim's Progress' is probably the best-known Christian book of all time. John Owen knew that God could use tinkers as well as professors to teach people about the Lord Jesus Christ.

FACT FILE
Pilgrim Fathers: John Owen was a Puritan, and there were times when the government made life very difficult for Puritans. In 1620, some of them decided to set sail for America in a ship called 'The Mayflower'. They landed on the coast of Massachusetts and settled in a place that they called Plymouth.

The voyage and the first winter were very difficult, and half of those who set out on the voyage had died by the spring of 1621. However, none of them wanted to return to England. Their condition improved as time went on. There are still people in America descended from these 'Pilgrim Fathers'.

Keynote: Although Cromwell was a brave and successful soldier, John Owen wasn't afraid to tell him when he thought that he was making a mistake. It is important to get on with our friends, but we need to remember that true friends are ready to give and take correction when they do something wrong.

We need to be careful, however, that we give correction in the right way. Even when we do this, as John did, our friends might be upset. But it is important to tell them the truth all the same. It is also important to accept correction in the right way. If someone points out to you that you have made a mistake or are doing something wrong, you should thank them for telling you.

Think: The teaching that John received from his father and from Mr Sylvester helped him to do great things for God later in life. John benefited from going to Oxford as his father told him he would, even though he did not want to go at first. Think about times when you have been told to do things that you didn't want to do, but which later proved to be good for you. Remember these, and John's example, the next time that it's sunny outside but there is a room to tidy inside, or other work to do.

Prayer: Thank you, Lord Jesus, for those who teach me, and especially for those who teach me about you. Please help me to listen to them carefully and to use what I learn in a way that pleases you. Please help children who do not have anyone to teach them about you. Amen.

Jonathan Edwards

Jonathan lay absolutely still on the grass, hardly daring to breathe. Just in front of him was what he had hoped to see. A tiny spider climbed up a twig on a low bush, then it stopped and seemed to rub all of its legs together. A moment later, it swung to another branch, and the boy could see just the faintest glint of sunshine on the very first strand of a web. He was fascinated. Quite unaware of the time, Jonathan lay there, watching the spider go back and forth and up and down, then round and round the web until the job was done. Even though he was stiff from lying still, he didn't move a muscle as the spider worked.

'How does the spider produce the threads that make the web?' he wondered. 'How does it manage to swing up through the air as well as down? And how do the strands of the web stick together?' Later, as he walked back to his home in New England, Jonathan tried to work it out. 'I think that when the spider was rubbing all its legs together, it was making some kind of juice flow, and that the juice doesn't dry immediately when the spider threads it between the branches. If it did dry immediately, the web wouldn't stick together; every strand would dangle separately.'

'Where have you been?' one of Jonathan's cousins asked, when he arrived back home.

'I was spider-watching as usual,' replied the boy.

'Again!' his Stoughton cousins said together.

'May I come with you next time?' asked Jonathan's younger sister.

He looked at her and doubted that she'd stay still enough to see anything.

'Yes,' he said. 'You can come with me first thing tomorrow morning before school. I saw a brilliant web being made today, and we'll see if it has caught anything by morning.'

His sister grinned.

'But you'll have to be quiet and still,' he warned her.

Early the following morning, Jonathan and his sister went back to the spider's bush. There had been a heavy dew, and the sun was just beginning to shine.

'Shh,' he told his little sister. 'Follow me and don't make a noise.'

At first she couldn't see the web at all. But when her brother pointed to it, she thought she'd never seen anything more beautiful in her life. Dew hung from the strands of the web like diamond drops, each one reflecting the light of the morning sun.

'Where's the spider?' the girl asked.

'I don't know,' Jonathan replied. 'But we'll see her if we come back later when the web has had time to dry out.'

As they walked back home, Jonathan's mind was busy.

'Water is heavy,' he thought. 'I wonder what the weight of all the dewdrops on the web would be. It must be very strong not to break under their weight.'

'We'll have to hurry or we'll be late for school,' the girl said, as they walked through the wood.

The pair of them broke into a run and arrived back just in time.

Having dashed into the kitchen to wash their hands, Jonathan and his sister arrived in the schoolroom red-faced and breathless. Their father, who was also their teacher, smiled. 'I hear you've been spider-watching,' he said, as they sat down on their benches.

School was held in a room in Jonathan's home. His father, Timothy Edwards, was a minister and schoolmaster. And the pupils were mainly family. There was Jonathan and his six sisters, their seven Stoughton cousins, and some boys from the village. After school that day, Mr Edwards went for a walk with his brother-in-law, Captain Thomas Stoughton.

'Thanks for showing me the essay Jonathan wrote about spiders,' Captain Thomas said. 'That boy has a remarkable mind.'

Mr Edwards nodded. 'He seems to be able to work things out for himself rather than just accepting what other people say.'

'I agree,' the Captain said. 'But it's more than that. He can also explain his thinking to other people.'

'There's something I want to ask you, Dad,' Jonathan said after tea one evening.

Mr Edwards shook his head. 'You always have things you want to ask. I've never met another boy with so many whys in his brain.'

But as the man could see there was something troubling his son, he made sure they had time to talk. Jonathan didn't only want to understand spiders, he wanted to understand life. And he wanted to understand the Bible too, not just accept what his father taught and preached. That night they discussed some very difficult questions, and the boy's mind turned them over and over again as he tried to go to sleep.

'Is every word in the Bible true?' he asked himself. 'Is it really God's Word speaking to us?'

He fluffed up his pillow to make himself more comfortable.

'And is Jesus actually God's Son?'

When he awoke the following morning, even more questions had appeared in his mind than had been there the previous evening.

Before Jonathan left home for college in 1710, when he was thirteen years old, he realised for himself that what he had been taught was true, and he put his trust in the Lord Jesus as his Saviour. After that he thought of spider-watching as exploring the wonderful world of nature God made.

Yale College, where Jonathan studied for the ministry for four years, is now very famous, but then it was a new college, just two years older than Jonathan Edwards. During his studies there, the boy from New England had a difficult time. There were a great many arguments about what people believed, just as there are today. Jonathan's sharp mind helped him work out what the Bible really said. That did not make him Yale's most popular student, even though he graduated with two degrees, one in 1720 and the other in 1723.

'I think you should accept the offer of working with Grandfather Stoddard,' Timothy Edwards told his son, four years later. 'And when he is no longer able to work, you'll most likely become the minister of his congregation in Northampton.'

The young man shook his head. 'I'm not sure,' he said, thinking of his grandfather, his mother's father. 'He's a fine old man, but I don't agree with all that he says.'

'But you could still work with him,' his father insisted. 'And Northampton would be a good place to begin family life with Sarah.'

Jonathan thought of his young wife and prayed about what he should do. Eventually he decided that going to Northampton was the right thing to do. Two years later, Grandfather Stoddard died, and Jonathan took over his big congregation.

'Tell me how you spend your days,' a visitor asked Jonathan Edwards, after he had been in Northampton for some years.

'I get up at 4 am,' Jonathan said, 'and I reckon to spend thirteen hours a day studying. In the afternoons, I take some exercise by chopping wood, fencing or whatever else needs to be done. And if the weather is good, I often ride out to a place where I get peace to study. After tea, I spend an hour with Sarah and the children, before taking my candle and getting back to work again.'

'How many children do you have now?' his friend asked.

Jonathan smiled as he thought of his young family. 'We have five, and another on the way.'

Eventually, John and Sarah had eleven children, eight girls and three boys.

Jonathan's ministry was not always easy, because he disagreed with some of the things his grandfather had taught. But in 1734, the town of Northampton was buzzing with news of what was happening in the church.

'Did you hear that a young rogue was converted? Last week he was cursing his way down the street, this week he's singing hymns!' one neighbour said to another.

'And Abigail Hutchinson too, though she's a frail young thing, has changed completely! She's so full of joy,' her friend replied.

A man coming along the road heard what the two women were saying.

'The most remarkable conversion story I heard was about Phebe Bartlette.'

'Phebe?' one of the women said. 'But she's just a baby.'

'Not quite a baby,' corrected the man. 'She's four years old and she's become a Christian.'

The two women walked a little further along the road.

'Is that Mr Baker?' one asked, puzzled at the sight.

The man heard his name and smiled.

'It is indeed,' he said, 'though you've never seen me sober before. But I'm a Christian now and I've given up the drink for better things.'

The taller of the two women nudged her friend. 'Cross the road,' she whispered, out of the corner of her mouth. 'Greta the Gossip's coming our way.'

But before they could cross, Greta was right beside them.

'I want to apologise for all those years of gossiping,' the old woman said. 'I've been a nasty bit of work, but from now on you'll not hear another word of gossip from me. And if you do, please tell me to stop talking about people and talk about Jesus.'

Before the two women could think of what to say, Greta had spotted someone else she wanted to apologise to, and was off.

For months the news was about people becoming Christians. News spread, and visitors began to go to Northampton to see for themselves what was happening there.

Many went home changed, and the things that happened in Jonathan's church began to happen in many other places too. The years 1734 to 1736 were exciting times for the Edwards family. And in 1740, when Jonathan invited the famous preacher, George Whitefield, to preach in Northampton, the same wonderful things began all over again.

Ten years later, Jonathan and Sarah sat on either side of the fire in their little living room. It was dark, and the candle was nearly done. All the children, who were still at home, were sound asleep in bed.

'Just a decade ago,' Jonathan said, 'people were being converted, the church was growing, and it would have been full if we'd had a service every night of the week.'

Sarah smiled. 'I remember it well,' she said. 'Those were the good days.'

'And today the congregation voted for me to leave Northampton,' added her husband sadly. 'I'm not surprised though; it's been coming for some time.'

'You did the right thing,' Sarah assured Jonathan. 'Because what Grandfather Stoddard taught was sometimes a little different from the Bible, you had no choice but to tell the people the truth. Your father once told me that you'd been like that since you were a little boy. You worked things out carefully in your mind, then explained your thinking to other people.'

Jonathan smiled for the first time that day.

'I used to watch spiders for hours,' he said. 'Then I worked out how they made their webs and explained it to the others at school. I imagine that's what he was thinking about.'

'It was indeed,' laughed Sarah. 'He told me about the spiders!'

It was some months before Jonathan got another job, and when he did, it was in a very spidery place! He became minister to the River Indians or Housatonics in the remote small town of Stockbridge, about sixty miles from Northampton. He also worked with the Mohawks and Iroquois. Jonathan Edwards wrote many books while he was at Northampton and he continued to write in Stockbridge. He was quite famous by this time, and visitors came all the way to his new home to talk with him.

'Is this where you write your books?' one asked, as they sat in the living room.

'No,' said Jonathan, 'there are still too many children at home to have peace to write in the living room!'

'May I see your study?' enquired the visitor, a little cheekily.

The minister smiled. 'Only if you are short-sighted,' he joked, 'because the walls will be very near your nose in all four directions. 'Come and see for yourself.'

Jonathan opened the door to his study. 'Don't get lost,' he laughed.

His guest went through the door into what looked just like a cupboard. The study the famous author wrote in was just seven feet long and three-and-a-half feet wide!

'You'll certainly get peace in there,' the man said. 'There's no room for company.'

'That's where you're wrong,' Edwards told him. 'If you look up to the ceiling corners, you'll discover that I have the company of some rather fine spiders!'

Jonathan studied the Indians' language, though his children learned it much more quickly than he did. For seven years he worked among the Housatonics and other Indian peoples, and many of them became Christians. He also helped to keep the peace when war threatened the area around Stockbridge. At the end of 1752, he was asked to become Principal of the college that is now the famous Princeton Theological Seminary. Just three months after moving there, before Sarah was able to join him, Jonathan Edwards fell ill and died. Amazingly, some of the books he wrote in the 1700s have never been out of print since the day they were first published!

FACT FILE
Spiders: Jonathan watched spiders very carefully and was very interested in how they spun their webs. Spiders' webs are made of silk which comes out of glands in the spider. The silk becomes sticky when it comes into contact with the air. Spiders use their silk for many purposes – even making threads to swing on – but the most common use is to make webs to catch insects.

The silk is very strong and stretchy. As well as the many uses that spiders have for it, some telescope manufacturers use it to make the cross hairs on their telescopes.

Keynote: Jonathan realised the importance of studying the Bible closely and really looking to see what it has to say. When he was preaching to people, he was careful to stick closely to the Bible. It is still important that we stick to the Bible when we are trying to learn about God. We need to know it well in order to do that.

Remember Jonathan's enthusiasm for studying the Bible as you hear it read and explained and as you read it yourself.

Think: When Jonathan had questions about parts of the Bible that he did not understand, he asked his father about them. He realised that he could not work it all out for himself. We can all learn from others when we are trying to understand the Bible. Think about people you could go to with questions about the Bible, and think carefully about what you learn in the Bible, just as Jonathan did.

Prayer: Lord Jesus, thank you for all of the amazing things that you have created. Thank you for spiders, birds, insects and animals. Thank you for your Word, the Bible, and for all that it has to teach us about you. Please help me to study it carefully so that I can know you better and love you more. Thank you for those who can explain the Bible to me. Amen.

George Whitefield

Mrs Whitefield looked at her four-year-old son and wondered if he would survive the night. His body was covered with measles spots, and his face was red with fever. She washed him gently to try to bring his temperature down, but all night the fever raged.

'Is George going to die?' an older brother asked.

His mother shook her head. 'Don't say such a thing. Go and pray that he'll get better.'

But in her heart she nearly despaired of her little son. The following day things were no better, and a woman came to help with nursing the lad.

'You have six others to think about,' she told Mrs Whitefield. 'You see to them, and I'll do what I can for this poor mite.'

George struggled to speak, and the nurse bent toward him to hear what he was saying.

'He wants water,' she announced to the child's sister. 'Get me a cup of water for the boy.'

Mrs Whitefield did what she was told. She had been up all night and was too tired to argue. All day she was busy with her six older children, all boys apart from one girl. Every time she had a minute, she ran through to see if George was still alive.

'Is it my imagination?' she wondered, as the afternoon wore on, 'or is his fever going down at last?'

By evening it was clear that the boy was a little better, and the following morning proved it.

'I want a drink!' George announced crossly from his bed. 'I'm thirsty and I want a drink!'

His mother nearly wept with joy that her youngest son would live. But something was different about him, and she couldn't quite work it out.

'George's eyes are funny,' his sister said, a week or two later. 'They don't both look in the same direction.'

While the boy recovered from measles, he was left with a squint in his eye. And because he had such very dark eyes, everyone noticed the squint.

Two or three years later, young George was out playing with his friends when a stranger approached them on horseback.

'Let's be highwaymen and ambush him,' the boy suggested. 'Run up the lane and get handfuls of stones.'

George was very much the leader of the gang, and his friends did exactly what they were told.

'Your money or your life!' George Whitefield yelled, as they pelted the stranger with small stones.

The man reined his horse to a standstill.

'Cheeky scoundrels!' said the rider, sliding off his horse in a flash.

Before George knew what was happening to him, he was being held very firmly by the ear.

'Take me to your father,' the man demanded.

'I don't have one,' George mumbled.

This was too much for the angry man. 'What do you mean you don't have one? Everybody has a father!'

'Please sir,' one of the other boys said, 'George's father died when he was a baby, and he can't remember him.'

The stranger was kinder than the boys deserved. Feeling sorry for the fatherless boy, he told them to behave themselves in future or they would come to a bad end, then he mounted his horse and rode on.

But George didn't take the man's advice and he didn't get any better. His dares went from bad to worse, and he was so often in trouble that his mother nearly despaired of him. Even though she loved him dearly, he even stole from her purse when he wanted to play cards for money. And he wasn't just a pest at home, he was known in the town as a troublemaker.

'I dare you to do the meeting-house!' one of George's friends said, on a Sunday when they should have been at church but were not.

George knew exactly what 'doing the meeting-house' meant, and it sounded fun.

'Come on, you lot!' he said, 'and see if I can shout louder than old man Cole.'

They ran along the streets till they came to the meeting-house where Mr Cole was preaching his sermon.

George strode in, walked up the aisle and shouted at the top of his voice, 'Old Cole! Old Cole! Old Cole!'

The minister tried to preach through the noise, but George outshouted him, and he had to stop. The old man bowed his head and prayed for the lad. Thinking that he had won the shouting match, George lost interest in the game and left the meeting-house to look for some other mischief to get up to.

Seven years later, in 1732, he was a very different George Whitefield. His mother married again, but not very happily. And although he had left school at fifteen, he was now about to become a student at Oxford University. Because he was poor, he had also to work as a servant there. Within a year he became a member of the Holy Club, where he met Christians who had a great influence on him. Two of them, John and Charles Wesley, became very famous preachers. It was in Oxford, in 1735, that George took all his sins to Jesus, even his stone-throwing and his disrupting the meeting-house services, and he asked the Lord to forgive him. God answered his prayer, and George began a new life as a Christian. Less than four years later he was a minister.

Returning to London, George thought he would be able to preach in some of the city's churches. But because he was friends with the Wesley brothers, who were not Church of England, many churches would not have George in their pulpits!

'I hear there is a Welshman who preaches to crowds in the open air,' Whitefield told the Wesleys. 'Do you think I should be doing that too?'

Soon afterwards, George preached at his first open-air meeting. Despite it being a cold February day, over 200 people came to listen. Before long the crowds coming to hear the new preacher had grown to upwards of 35,000, and their singing could be heard two miles away!

'What a mess you're in,' a friend said, seeing George immediately after he had preached to a huge crowd at Moorfields, near London.

His friend grinned. 'I was honoured with having stones, dirt, rotten eggs and pieces of dead cat thrown at me.'

'Doesn't sound much of an honour,' his friend commented. 'I thought everyone who went to an open-air service would be above that sort of thing.'

Shaking his head, George assured his companion that he was wrong there, and that some people just went to make mischief. Deep in his heart, he knew that if open-airs had taken place in Gloucester when he was a boy, he would have been right in the thick of it making all the mischief he could.

As they walked along the road, his friend questioned him further about what happened at his open-airs.

George grinned. 'You know some people say I should have been an actor rather than a preacher?'

The other man said he thought that might be a good idea!

'You may be right!' the preacher laughed. 'One day I was preaching about Jesus calming the storm at sea. I painted as vivid a picture as I possibly could, so much so I could almost feel the salt spray in my face. And I obviously wasn't the only one who got carried away because, just as I reached the climax of the sermon, an old sailor in the crowd jumped to his feet and yelled, "To the lifeboats, men! To the lifeboats!"'

Whitefield's friend laughed heartily and said that perhaps he should have been an actor after all!

On 1st August, 1739, the Bishop of London denounced the young preacher and banned him from every Church of England building. Two weeks later, George was on his way to America. The Wesleys were already there and they wrote asking him to join them. He had been there for a time in the previous year and had established an orphanage and school for poor children. By the time he returned a year later, he had collected a large amount of money for the orphans.

'Why do you bother yourself with these fatherless children?' an American woman asked him one day.

George stopped what he was doing and looked her in the eye. 'I was a poor, fatherless child myself,' he said. 'I ran wild and could have become the worst rogue in Gloucester. If God had not saved me, I'd not be here in America preaching the gospel. I'd be back in England in a dark prison cell.'

Very embarrassed, the lady rifled about in her bag and found some money to go towards the orphanage.

'Thank you, Ma'am,' said George. 'And who knows, perhaps God will raise some preachers from among these dear orphan lads.'

In March 1740, the foundation stone was laid of Bethesda, the main part of his orphan home in Savanah.

George Whitefield led a travelling life. He had no settled church and he preached where he was invited. In a day when travelling was not easy, and journeys could take many months, he travelled the length and breadth of England, as well as Scotland, Ireland, Wales, Gibraltar, Bermuda and America.

'What was your biggest open-air?' he was asked one day.

'I couldn't begin to guess,' he replied, 'but I suppose over 40,000.'

'And your smallest?'

George smiled. 'I remember the smallest one well. I was on my way across the Atlantic, and the ship we were on was so buffeted by a storm that the sails were tattered and the gear was a mess. My pulpit was the swaying deck, and the congregation was just thirty people, some looking more seasick than others. I remember on that voyage my blanket was a buffalo hide and, although my quarters were in the driest part of the vessel, there were nights when I was drenched through more than once.'

'I don't know why you go back and forward across the Atlantic,' his friend said, after hearing that story.

'I do,' Whitefield replied. 'I go because people ask me to preach the good news of Jesus. But there's another reason besides that.'

'Oh,' said the other man, 'what's that?'

George's eyes grew soft as he thought of Savanah. 'My wife and I only had one child, a boy, and he died. But I have a home in Savanah that's full of orphan children I think of as my own. Many of them never knew their fathers, as I never knew mine. And I'd happily cross the Atlantic Ocean to see the smiles on their faces when I arrive.'

'I suppose it is worth endangering your life then,' his companion said, although he was not quite convinced.

It was in Ireland, not in a storm at sea, that George Whitefield nearly lost his life.

In 1756, he was preaching on a green near Dublin, when a mob among the people who wanted to listen, started to throw clods of earth and stones at the preacher. When the crowd dispersed, the mob grew and threatened to take his life. He had a half-mile walk to safety, and all the time he was pelted with stones from every direction. A riot was soon in full swing, and blood poured from George's head as he tried to get away. Eventually, he staggered to a minister's door, and the murderous mob disappeared. The minister found an almost unconscious Whitefield on his doorstep. Lifting him to his feet, he helped him into the house and looked after him.

'Now I know what the Lord's apostles felt like when they were stoned by angry crowds,' he told his friend, when he felt a bit better.

George continued his travelling ministry, preaching to bigger and bigger crowds on both sides of the Atlantic Ocean, until he left for America for the last time in September 1769. He went to upgrade his orphanage to Bethesda College, and he was especially looking forward to seeing some English people there. Whitefield had taken twenty-two orphans to America fifteen years before, and he was interested to see what kind of young men they had grown into. Having spent the winter at Bethesda, he travelled north to preach. Huge numbers of people gathered to hear him, and he preached his heart out.

A year after arriving in America, while he was staying with a friend, a large company came to the house to meet him. They talked until late at night. George, who was ill and tired, said goodnight and was about to go to bed when one of the visitors asked him to give them just a short talk. By then Whitefield was actually on the stairs with a candle in his hand! He turned round and preached until the candle went out, then climbed the stairs wearily and went to bed. George had preached his very last sermon, and he died without ever getting out of bed again. But that was not the end of the man; his work went on at Bethesda, and many of those who had heard him preach became preachers themselves, and continued to tell people the good news that Jesus Christ is the Saviour of all who trust in him, even rogues and rascals like the young George Whitefield.

FACT FILE

Transatlantic Travel: It was very dangerous for George Whitefield to cross the Atlantic in a ship, but at that time it was the only way to get to America from Europe. Not many people made the trip. Even a hundred years after Whitefield, many people who left Britain to go to America knew that they would never come back to their homes. Today, however, it is much easier to travel between Europe and America. An aeroplane can complete the journey in less than seven hours.

Keynote: George travelled all over the world, sometimes taking great risks so that he could preach about Jesus. This is not the behaviour that might have been expected from the boy who shouted down the preacher in the meeting-house. God is able to change all sorts of people and make them into his servants.

In the book of Acts we read about a man called Saul who was

very angry with Christians and did lots of bad things to them. But God spoke to him and turned him into one of the greatest missionaries ever.

Think: As well as preaching, George took care of many orphans. He did this because God had taken care of him although he was fatherless.

Think about some of the good things that God has done for you. How can you follow George's example by showing thankfulness and helping others? Remember that God loves us and invites us to come to him as children to their father.

Prayer: Lord God, thank you for being so good and kind to us. Thank you for inviting us to call you 'Father'. Please help us to love you as we should, and to try our best to help others. Please watch over all the children whose mums and dads have died, and help them to know you as their heavenly Father. Amen.

Robert Murray McCheyne

'It's snowing!' Robert yelled, as he looked out of the window. 'Look, the hills are white!'

'We have a great view from this part of Edinburgh,' his older brother David said. 'Although we live just a few minutes' walk from the centre of the city, from here we can see right over the Firth of Forth to the snowy hills of Fife.'

'But we won't be able to see them for long,' Robert laughed. 'The snow's getting heavier. Look at the size of the snowflakes!'

'You'll be wanting to go sledging before long,' said David.

Robert's love for anything sporty was almost a family joke.

'If there's a tree, Robert will swing from it,' Mr McCheyne often commented. 'If there's a hill, he'll be the first to climb it, and whenever he sees water, he wants to be in for a swim. There's just no stopping the boy!'

By the end of that afternoon, Robert's sledge was covered in snow, and so was he.

Despite a bath when he came in, and a rubdown with a warm towel, the following day the boy was in bed with a chill.

'I worry about Robert,' David told his father. 'He's so often ill.'

'I know,' Mr McCheyne agreed. 'But he bounces up again and before long he's running about all over the place.'

'How are you feeling?' asked David, sitting down on his brother's bed.

Robert, who was still shivery, ignored the question and pointed to a picture in the book he was reading.

'Look at this,' he said. 'Did you know that ants can carry leaves much bigger than themselves, even leaves that weigh much more than they do?'

David admitted that was news to him. Then he burst out laughing.

'What's so funny?' Robert asked.

'I was just remembering back five years. You were four years old and in bed unwell. We were looking for something to interest you so we taught you the Greek alphabet. In just one week you learned to read and write all the letters.'

'And I still remember them,' the boy said. 'Alpha, beta, gamma, delta ...'

'OK,' his brother laughed. 'I believe you.'

When David took a cup of hot milk to his brother a short time later, Robert was told to sit up and listen.

'I've written a poem for you,' David said.

'A boy was in bed with a bug,
all warmly wrapped in a rug.
His brothers were doing their best
to keep him in bed for a rest.
They taught him alpha and beta
and because he wasn't a cheater
he learned the letters well,
and that's why he can tell
that bed is the best place to be
if you want some time to be free
to study in peace and quiet.'

Robert smiled. 'That's great!' he said. 'But the last line doesn't rhyme with anything.'

'Well, I had to get you this milk! I can't do everything, you know,' David told him.

Although Robert was often off school because of illness, he worked very hard and did well in his studies. And he was not only noticed because he worked hard.

'I remember McCheyne as a tall, thin lad with a pleasant face,' a friend wrote many years later. 'He was bright and serious yet fond of play and he lived a good life. I especially remember his tartan trousers, which I both admired and envied.'

'Will you come on a walking holiday?' Robert asked his friend Malcolm, when they were teenagers.

Malcolm agreed, and they planned to explore the countryside around Dunkeld in Perthshire. All went well until they crossed the hills to Strathardle, and a mist came down.

'I can't see where we're going,' Robert said, as the mist turned into fog that seemed to grow thicker by the minute.

'Let's keep going downhill and we'll maybe get below the fog level,' suggested Malcolm.

The boys slithered and skidded down the hillside, but the fog had reached the valley too.

'I can hear running water,' Robert said. 'If we find the river and follow it, we'll reach safety.'

'I don't think we should do that,' Malcolm decided. 'It's not only foggy, it's dark now. If you fell and broke your leg and I went for help, I'd never be able to find you again. I think we should bed down in the bracken and try to get some sleep.'

'Travelling adventures are fine when everything goes well,' Robert thought, as they tried to get to sleep. 'But it's not so good when things go wrong.'

The next morning dawned bright and sunny, and the two boys woke to the sound of moorcock, grouse and loudly rumbling stomachs!

When Robert Murray McCheyne was just fourteen, he became a student at Edinburgh University. Four years later, in 1831, the bottom fell out of his world. His brother David became ill, and it was soon clear that he would not get better. David was a Christian, and his love of the Lord Jesus made a deep impression on his younger brother.

When David died, Robert's heart broke. Much later he wrote to a friend, 'This day, eleven years ago, I lost my loved and loving brother and began to seek a Brother who cannot die.' So it was through David's death that Robert began to search for Jesus, the friend whom the Bible says, sticks closer than a brother. And like all who seek Jesus, Robert found him as his Saviour, Brother and Friend.

When Robert graduated from university in 1835, all he wanted to do was to introduce others to Jesus. After a short time assisting a minister in central Scotland, Robert became minister of St Peter's Church in Dundee. Soon his church was full of people every Sunday. They came from around the church and from other parts of Dundee as well.

'Why do you think so many people have started going to hear the new minister at St Peter's?' asked a man who lived near the church but who never went inside it.

One of Robert's elders was passing at the time and answered the man's question.

'Mr McCheyne loves the Lord Jesus with all his heart, and his preaching is just full of that love.'

The man snorted. 'At least that's different from all the others who preach about hell's fire every Sunday.'

'How do you know what other ministers preach when you're never inside a church?' the elder asked.

Winking and tapping his ear, the man answered, 'I hear as much by hanging around outside a church as most people hear who go in to the service.'

Speaking gently and seriously to the old man, the elder said, 'Then you'll no doubt have heard that when Mr McCheyne mentions hell in his sermons, the tears often run down his cheeks at the thought of anyone going there.'

'I have 170 girls and 70 young men in my Bible Class,' Robert wrote to his brother William, six months after moving to Dundee. 'I use what I call the Geographical Method of teaching. I give them out some place, such as the Sea of Galilee, and get them to look up where it is mentioned in the Bible. Then I draw a map, as we used to do at school. I also read passages about the place from history books and from modern travellers. I find this interesting, and they seem quite delighted with it. You'll find my map of the Sea of Galilee in with this letter, and you mustn't smile at my map-making!'

Perhaps one of the reasons why Robert liked teaching young people was that he was still young himself. And his father would not have been surprised to know that he continued to enjoy gymnastics even after he was a minister.

On one occasion Robert came home covered in cuts and bruises. Eliza, his sister, lived with him at the time. She was shocked to see his injuries.

'It happened when he was visiting his friend,' she told a neighbour. 'Apparently Robert put up some gymnastic poles in the garden and challenged his friend's son to a trial of skill.'

'The boy must have been delighted with that,' the neighbour smiled.

Eliza nodded her head. 'I'm sure he was!'

Amused at the idea of her minister doing gymnastics, the neighbour waited to hear what happened next.

'Robert went first to show the boy what to do,' explained Eliza. 'He was hanging by his heels and hands six feet above the ground when the poles snapped and he landed with a tremendous thud.'

The neighbour, suddenly realising that things might have been serious, was concerned.

'He was winded, cut and bruised,' Eliza concluded. 'God was good to him. He might have been killed.'

On that occasion Robert had to rest for some days because of his injuries, but other times he had to take to his bed because he was ill. Although he was athletic and really enjoyed exercise, he was never strong. His hard work wore him down, and more than once Eliza was very worried in case he would not recover. But as soon as Robert was fit to be up and dressed, he was always back to work.

In 1839, Robert Murray McCheyne was asked to go with a small group of others on a fact-finding trip to the Holy Land. It was the first time any ministers of the Church of Scotland had done such a thing.

'Are you well enough for such a long journey?' Eliza worried.

Her brother's eyes shone with excitement. 'If God wants me to go,' he said, 'he'll give me the health and strength I need.' His face broke into a wide smile. 'Eliza,' he said, 'I just can't believe that I'll walk where Jesus walked, and see the Sea of Galilee, the Mount of Olives, and other places the Lord saw when he was alive on earth!'

Realising that there was no possibility of persuading her brother to back out of the trip, Eliza set about getting his clothes prepared and buying medicines for him to take with him just in case.

The places the little group of ministers visited read like a travel brochure. Robert's diary records their journey by sea to London, then across the English Channel to France before travelling overland to Italy, before continuing to Valetta, Alexandria and eventually the Holy Land. Having left Dundee in March, they reached Jerusalem in June. Robert wrote to tell his mother about it.

'This is one of the most privileged days of my life,' he wrote. 'I left my camel and hurried over the burning rocks. In about half an hour Jerusalem came into sight!'

For more than a week the men camped at the foot of Mount Carmel and explored the area, paying special attention to the Jewish people they met on their travels. They were introduced to a Jewish Christian who was able to give them a vast amount of information. The man was delighted to learn that the Church in Scotland had sent ministers all the way to the Holy Land to find out the best way to tell Jewish people about Jesus the Messiah.

Although at one point on the journey Robert became so ill that his companions thought he would die, he recovered enough on the way home to be able to visit many Jewish areas of Eastern Europe. They even went as guests to a Jewish wedding. Knowing that his sister would be interested, he drew a picture of the bride's dress and sent it to her! The wedding was much more pleasant than another incident Robert described.

'Two evil-minded shepherds made signs that I should follow them,' he wrote. 'When I refused, things became quite ugly. I could have run away, but I knew my heart wouldn't stand it. I raised my stick, but I didn't want to hit out at them. Eventually, I sat down. That confused them, and they went away!'

Nine months after leaving, the travellers returned home, and the information they brought with them was used to plan how to reach Jewish people with the good news that the Messiah they were waiting for had come, and that his name was Jesus.

When Robert returned to Dundee, he discovered that God had done a wonderful work in his congregation while he was away. Many people, adults and children, had become Christians.

'Doesn't your brother mind that it was when another minister was preaching that this all happened?' someone asked his sister.

Eliza shook her head. 'He is just delighted to see his dear people trust in Jesus.'

For nearly three years, Robert looked after his congregation in Dundee, and thrilled each time someone became a Christian. It was a special delight to him when children and young people trusted in Jesus, because they would have their whole lives to live in his service.

In 1842, when Robert was 29 years old, he became ill once again, but this time he did not recover. He had never been strong and he had worn himself out. After he died, a letter arrived for him. It was from someone who had heard him preach just the previous week. The letter read, 'I heard you preach last Sunday, and God blessed what you said to my heart. But it wasn't just what you said that meant so much to me, it was how you said it. I saw in you a beauty of holiness that I've never seen in anyone before.'

By the time that letter arrived, Robert Murray McCheyne was enjoying all the beauty of his Saviour in heaven.

FACT FILE

Dundee: Robert was a minister in Dundee and he went to the Holy Land. But he wasn't the only person from Dundee to travel far and wide. In the past, Dundee was a thriving port that traded with other cities in Northern Europe and beyond. It was best known for trading in jute, which is used to make sacks. Another citizen of Dundee who is well known is Mary Slessor. She went out as a missionary to Calibar in Africa in the 19th century. You can read about her in *Ten Girls who Changed the World.*

Keynote: Although Robert was very young when he died, God used him to make a great impact on many people. (His sermons are still being read today.) He suffered from illness a lot when he was a minister but he trusted God, even for the strength to make the difficult journey to the Holy Land. God has promised to make us strong in him, even when we are weak. We can see that he fulfilled that promise in McCheyne's life, and he can do so in yours too.

Think: Two shepherds threatened Robert. He knew that his heart was too weak to let him run away. He did not want to hit them with his stick. When he sat down, however, they ran away. Think about how you can respond to threats in the same way: by trying to avoid a fight rather than win one. Do you think that Robert's example only applies when people are going to hit you?

 Prayer: Lord Jesus, thank you for the health and strength that you have given me. Help me to use it to serve you, and to trust you to give me the strength to be the kind of person that you want me to be. Please watch over those who are ill and help them to remember that you love them. Amen.

Dwight L. Moody

The Moody brothers rushed round the little farmstead at Northfield, hiding anything of value they could find.

'Put Dad's tools in the bushes!' one shouted.

Another ran for the cowshed. 'I'll take the new calf into the woods and tether it to a tree.'

Dwight, who was just four years old, was given some small things to hide among his wooden bricks.

'Don't tell anyone they are there,' he was warned.

The boy hadn't a clue what was going on, but he felt important at being given something special to do.

There was the rumble of a cart coming along the track.

'Now, don't any of you be saying a word,' Mrs Moody instructed her children. 'I'll do all the talking.'

A horse and cart drew up in front of the little house.

'You know what I've come for,' the visitor said, as he jumped down from the cart.

'I know very well,' agreed Mrs Moody, 'but I can't believe you've the heart to take away my husband's horse and buggy, and his cows as well, when he's only been dead four days.'

The man avoided looking Mrs Moody in the eye.

'I've come for the furniture too,' he said.

The woman's eyes filled with tears, but she was absolutely determined that he wouldn't see them. Picking up Dwight, she turned towards the house and strode in.

'I suppose I should be grateful that the law of Massachusetts prevents you taking the house as well,' she called, without turning around.

Striding into the house and lifting two chairs at once, the man turned and looked at the widow.

'I suppose you should,' he said, and continued on his business.

The Moody children watched later that afternoon, as the cart began to move, piled high with their belongings.

'I'll be back for the horse and buggy,' the man shouted as he left.

Mrs Moody gathered her children around her.

'I kept the things safe among my bricks,' Dwight said.

His mother hugged him.

'So you did,' she agreed. 'And we still have your father's tools and a calf. We'll win through yet. You see if we don't.'

One month later there were two more Moody children to care for. That's when the twins were born. They never knew their dad.

In 1843, two years after his father had died, Dwight had work to do as some of his older brothers had already left home.

'I'm glad we kept you,' the boy told his favourite cow. She was the one that had been hidden in the woods. 'And now you've given us a fine calf as well as gallons of milk to drink. Mum says your milk makes the finest butter and cheese in the state.'

Mrs Moody had been able to get one or two more cows in the time since her husband died, and Dwight's job was to look after them.

'Let's go,' the boy told the beasts. 'If you're wanting some new, green grass you're going to have to walk to it.'

Striding out in front of them, and leading the way, Dwight headed for the meadow. When the cows stopped for a drink, he climbed on to a rugged fence to wait for them. Taking a long blade of grass between his thumbs, the boy tried to see how loud he could whistle. Suddenly, the fence gave way under him, and he clattered to the ground. The nearest fence post was dislodged, fell on top of him and pinned him down.

'Help!' the lad shouted, when he got his breath back. 'Help!'

But even as he shouted, he knew there was nobody near enough to hear him. Trying as hard as he possibly could, he pushed against the fence post, but he couldn't make it move at all. The problem was leverage. His heavy boots were caught among the bars and he couldn't loosen his legs to help him lever the post off his back. Dwight was desperate.

'God,' he yelled, 'help me lift these heavy rails.'

As soon as he had prayed that prayer, he was able to get himself free. For a while after that he often prayed, but somehow he got out of the habit.

Eleven years later, by which time Dwight had decided that religion was boring and only for old folk, he set out by train for the city of Boston.

'I'll miss Mum,' he thought, as the train rattled along, 'but I won't miss working on the farm. I'll make her proud of me. One day I'll go home with enough money in my pockets to give her an easy life. Dwight L. Moody will make his name in Boston.'

Suddenly Dwight broke into a broad smile as he remembered that the name he'd been given at birth was Dwight Lyman Ryther Moody. Ryther was the name of Northfield's doctor. But when the doctor didn't give baby Dwight the gift of a sheep (that was the custom when a baby was called after someone), Ryther was dropped from his name!

On arrival in Boston, Dwight headed for a shoe shop his uncle owned and asked for a job.

'If you work for me, you'll do it on my conditions,' his uncle told him, when he eventually agreed to take his nephew on. 'And one of these conditions is that you go to church and Sunday school every week.'

'No problem!' the lad said, trying to hide his amusement and irritation. 'You'll find I'm a hard worker,' he added, being much more interested in earning money than religion.

To Dwight's surprise he didn't find church as boring as he'd expected. He began to wonder if there might be something in the Christian faith after all. Over the months, the thought bothered him when he wasn't busy working or enjoying himself.

In 1855, a year after he'd arrived in Boston, special services were held in his church. Dwight's Sunday school teacher decided to speak to all his pupils about the Lord. Arriving at the shoe shop to discover his pupil was in the back premises, he went though to see him. Putting his hand on Dwight's shoulder, he asked him to trust in Christ who loved him enough to die on the cross for him. Right there, in among piles of shoes, laces and boxes, the young man from Northfield put his faith in the Lord Jesus and became a Christian. He was nineteen years old. Before long he was on the move to Chicago. But although he was now a Christian, Dwight's main concern was still to make money.

'Why don't you go out into the alleys and streets to see what boys you can bring in?' asked the man in charge of the mission church Dwight attended.

That was a challenge, and Moody liked a challenge. Remembering how poor he had been as a child, Dwight was not embarrassed to be seen with the poor children of Chicago. When he arrived back at the mission, he had eighteen barefoot and ragged lads trailing behind him.

'Will you be back next week?' Moody asked his young friends after Sunday school.

'Only if you are,' the oldest one replied.

Dwight screwed up his face.

'I'll be here next time,' he assured them, then added, 'but my work often takes me away. You can come when I'm not here though.'

He knew from the looks on their faces that they would only attend Sunday school if he were there to bring them in.

It was 1858, and Dwight and a friend were deep in discussion.

'You think we should get what?' his friend asked in amazement.

Moody grinned. 'I think we should get an old railway truck and use it for our own mission Sunday school.'

Because he had a way with his friends, by the following Sunday the truck was theirs and an enthusiastic group of boys were desperate to explore it.

'In you come,' yelled Dwight over the noise. 'And bring your friends next time.'

They did, and before long the truck was bursting at the seams. A man Dwight knew, heard about it and gave him a building to replace it.

'I went to see the new Sunday school,' someone said, soon afterwards. 'There was no lighting in the house, and Moody had tried to light it with half a dozen candles. I found him with a candle in one hand, a Bible in the other, and a child on his knees that he was trying to teach. There were twenty-five to thirty there altogether, and they were as poor lads as you would find anywhere in Chicago.'

Before long, girls started attending too. The number grew and grew, eventually becoming too big even for their new building, and they had to move again.

'How many do you have in your Sunday school?' Dwight was asked, when it was about two years old.

Moody grinned. 'It's hard to count when children swarm like bees, but the last estimate was 600!'

Eventually, Dwight found he could not hold down a job and do the children's work, he loved so much, as well. Giving up his work, he decided to live on his savings, believing that when his money ran out, God would provide him with all that he needed. 'And if that doesn't happen,' he told his friends, 'I'll take it as a sign that I've to go back to work.'

That didn't happen. From 1860 till the end of his life, Moody never had another paid job.

In November that year, a very important visitor went to Chicago: Abraham Lincoln, the President-elect. He accepted an invitation to visit Dwight's school.

'I was once as poor as any boy in the school,' Lincoln told the children, 'but I am now President of the United States, and if you attend to what is taught you here, one of you may yet be President.'

Abraham Lincoln's visit came at a difficult time as the American Civil War was in full swing. Dwight was against slavery, but he was also a pacifist. He believed it was wrong to enslave other human beings, but he also believed that fighting was not the way to settle a difference. Dwight's belief about not fighting did not stop him from wanting to help the soldiers who were fighting for the abolition of slavery. He was all for doing what he could for them.

In a letter to his brother, he wrote about the work he was doing.

'I have some 500 or 800 people that are dependent on me for their daily food and new ones coming all of the time. I keep a saddled horse to ride around with, to hunt up the poor people and then I have a man to wait on the folks as they come to my office. I have just raised money enough to erect a chapel for the soldiers at the camp three miles from the city. I hold a meeting down there every day and one in the city so you see I have three meetings to attend to every day beside calling on the sick. And that is not all. I have to go into the country about every week to buy wood and provisions for the poor, also coal, wheatmeal and corn.'

Although Dwight was incredibly busy, he still found time to fall in love. He and Emma were married in 1862, and they went on to have a family.

After the Civil War, Moody became very well-known as a preacher, and not just around the city of Chicago. He travelled as far as the United Kingdom, where huge crowds of people went to hear him. Eventually, he teamed up with another American, Ira Sankey, who was a Christian singer and songwriter. When he sang, people were so moved that they often wept. The names Moody and Sankey were linked together, and they became as famous in the 1870s as television stars are today.

'Have you heard Mr Moody preaching?' people asked, on both sides of the Atlantic. 'His grammar is poor, but he can fairly pack a punch in his preaching.'

'And Mr Sankey's songs are so catchy I find myself singing them as I work,' others commented.

The duo visited city after city and preached and sang to halls crowded with people. So popular were Sankey's hymns, that they were printed and sold in millions. Had there been golden discs in the 1870s, Ira Sankey's walls would have been covered with them.

Although Dwight became famous, he was nowhere happier than back in Northfield, Massachusetts. Partly that was because it was home, but also because he had built two schools there, one for girls and the other for boys. He had never forgotten what it was like to be a poor lad, and he was always conscious of his own lack of education. Before he died, he also founded a college in Chicago to train Christian workers.

Dwight Moody was a great man but he wasn't perfect. Perhaps his children knew that better than anyone else. When he was grown up, one of his sons said that sometimes his father lost his temper with them. 'Then after we had gone up to bed, we would hear his heavy footsteps, and he'd come into our room and put a heavy hand on our heads and say, "I want you to forgive me; that wasn't the way Christ taught."' Only great men can ask their children to forgive them.

FACT FILE

American Civil War: Moody had a visit from Abraham Lincoln during the American Civil War. This broke out in 1861, soon after Lincoln was elected president. There was a lot of disagreement between the Northern and the Southern states about how much power the central government should have and about slavery.

The war lasted until 1865, and 600,000 men were killed. The Northern states won the war and managed to prevent the Southern states from breaking away and forming their own 'Confederacy'. Slavery was abolished shortly after the end of the war.

Keynote: Moody's love for little children can be seen in the number who attended the Sunday schools that he was involved in.

Jesus loved children too and told his disciples to let the little children come to him. This shows us that we are never too young to start learning about God and about all the amazing things that he has done for us. That was part of the reason that Moody was so enthusiastic about getting children to come to his Sunday school.

 Think: When Moody was a boy, he thought that religion was boring and didn't really want to go to Sunday school. But, when he did go to one in Boston, he found it more exciting than he had expected.

Think about the chances that you have to learn about God. Do you go to church and Sunday school expecting to learn new and exciting things every time? The children around Moody certainly seemed to do so.

 Prayer: Lord Jesus, thank you for those who teach me about you and all that you have done. Thank you for all the exciting things that there are to learn about in the Bible. Please help me to listen carefully and to try and learn these things as well as I can. Amen.

Billy Sunday

The night was dark apart from the brightness of the sugaring fire, and young Billy Sunday was feeling good.

'I just love sugaring-off nights,' he told his grandfather.

The old man smiled. 'So do I, son,' he said, 'especially as I built this old sugar cane mill myself.'

'It's very clever,' Billy said. 'I like watching the horse going round and round in a ring and working the mill that crushes the sugar cane until the sticky, thick sap comes out. But best of all, I like when the sap is boiled and skimmed, and we have to keep the fire going until all the sugaring-off is done.'

'You're a great help,' his grandfather said, 'especially when you feed the fire to keep the sap a-simmering. By this time of night, after a day on the mill, my poor old bones are aching so much I'm grateful for your help.'

'I've learned a lot from you,' Billy told the old man. 'You've taught me how to cut wood, build fences, care for horses and milk the cows. And I can help with the crops too.'

Mr Sunday looked down at the eight-year-old. 'I had to teach you, son,' he said, 'after your poor papa died just before you were born. Your mama couldn't teach you men's things.'

Billy swelled with pride at the thought of being a man.

'Tell me about my papa,' he asked, after a few minutes of staring into the firelight.

A sad look crossed his grandfather's face. 'It was in the summer of 1862, four months before you were born, that your father marched off to the sound of the fife and drum to be a soldier. And he never came back.'

'But he wasn't killed in a battle, was he?' queried the boy.

'No, he died of an illness before the battle had a chance to get him.'

'I would have liked to have had a papa,' young Billy said.

Grandfather Sunday nodded. 'And I would like to have had a son. But you and your brothers have been sons to me, and I've been all the father you've ever had. And that's enough for now; the fire needs more wood, and I'm too stiff to get up.'

Billy jumped to his feet and pushed fresh wood under the sugaring vat.

But two years later, Billy's life as a country boy came to a sudden end.

'Sons, I have something I've got to tell you,' Mrs Sunday said to Billy and his brother Edward one day.

The tone of her voice made the boys look at each other.

'I'm going to send the two of you to the Soldiers' Orphans Home at Glenwood. You've had all the schooling you can have here.'

'But how will we get there?' Edward asked. 'And how often will we get home?'

Edward, who was twelve, knew better than Billy what a huge change was about to happen in their lives.

It was one o'clock in the morning when the boys were put on a train at the local Ames Station.

'Goodbye,' Edward said, hugging his tearful mother.

Then it was Billy's turn, and when he said 'Goodbye,' he realised that he had never had to say goodbye to his mother before. She had always been there for him. When the train chugged out of Ames Station, the boys could not see their mother for the darkness. It was four long years before they saw her again; four long years before they had another long hug from their mother.

Living away from home and family was very hard, but eventually there came a day when Edward and Billy finally returned home. However, things weren't easy then either as they both had to look for work.

Billy did a number of different jobs before going to work in Nevada for Colonel John Scott, who was once Lieutenant-Governor of Iowa. He got that job because he could scrub stairs until they were squeaky clean. And while he worked for the Scotts, Billy went to high school where he became well known as a runner. Some time later he took up baseball, and right from his first game it was clear he was a winner.

'Are you Billy Sunday?' he was asked, after a baseball game.

'That's me,' he said. 'But who are you?'

'My name's Anson, and I'm told you have a future in baseball,'

Billy grinned. 'I can sure play the game,' he agreed.

Anson shook Billy by the hand. 'I'm told you're better than that. In fact, I'm here to persuade you to come to Chicago to join the White Stockings.'

Young Billy Sunday could hardly believe his ears. The White Stockings! They were in the National League! It didn't take him long to make up his mind that he should move to Chicago.

Quite soon after he moved, Billy and his baseball friends came across an open-air preacher when they were out walking one day. They sat down on the grass to listen to what he was saying. Billy was so interested that he went time and time again to hear the preacher. What he heard about God there was no different from what he had learned from his mother, but somehow it suddenly made sense to him. Billy asked the Lord Jesus to be his Saviour and promised to serve him all of his life.

'I guess the guys in the team will laugh at me now,' he thought. 'But I'm not going to hide that I'm a Christian.'

Instead of laughing at him, Billy discovered that his teammates treated him with real respect.

The White Stockings certainly respected Billy's baseball.

'Tell me about your famous save,' a friend asked, having missed a memorable afternoon.

Billy grinned. 'OK,' he said, 'this is how it happened. I saw Charley swing hard, and heard the bat crack as he met the ball square on the nose. As I saw it rise in the air, I knew it was going clear over my head into the crowd that overflowed on to the field. I could judge within ten feet of where the ball would land, so I turned my back on it and ran, and as I ran, I yelled, "Get out of the way!" The crowd opened like the Red Sea for the rod of Moses. And as I flew over the dirt, I prayed to God to help me. Jumping the bench, I stopped where I thought the ball would fall. Looking back, I saw it going over my head. I jumped and shoved my left hand out. The ball hit it and stuck! I was going so fast I fell under some horses, but I hung on to the ball. You should have heard the crowd yell!'

Billy's friend laughed aloud. 'I can just see it!' he said. 'What a catch!'

'Billy Sunday's speaking at the Young Men's Christian Association,' one boy told another. 'Would you like to come?'

His friend looked surprised. 'You mean the Billy Sunday, the baseball player?'

'The very one! Are you coming?'

'Try to stop me!'

Right from when he became a Christian, Billy wanted to tell other people about the Lord. He was as enthusiastic when he was talking about Jesus as he was when playing the game. And before long, he was well known for his preaching too.

In the spring of 1888, Billy was sold by the Chicago White Stockings to the Pittsburg team. This was a great move for baseball, but it meant that he and his girlfriend would be separated, but not for long. They were married that September and lived in Pittsburgh for two-and-a-half years until Billy decided to give up baseball and become a full-time preacher.

'Funny,' Billy said to his wife one day, 'I thought preachers only preached. It didn't occur to me that I'd spend my time putting up tents, organising great choirs of singers, and touring shops, offices and factories!'

His wife smiled. 'That's because you're not a regular preacher,' she said. 'Regular preachers stand in the same pulpit every week; you go all over the place and take your tent with you!'

'Jesus told the paralysed man to take up his bed and walk,' Billy commented. 'It seems he's telling me to take up my tent and preach.'

Along with another well-known preacher, Billy toured several states of America.

'Tell me about your father,' Helen asked her dad one day, several years later.

Helen was Billy's only daughter. She had two brothers, George and little Billy Junior, and then there was a baby on the way.

'I never knew my papa,' Billy explained. 'He died just months before I was born.'

'It must have been sad not to have had a dad,' said Helen.

'I didn't know any different,' her father explained. 'And my grandfather was very good to me.'

'Is it because you didn't have a dad yourself that you try to do so much with us?'

Billy gave a sigh of relief and hugged his dark-haired daughter. What she said pleased him a lot, because he was away from home so often he sometimes felt as though he was neglecting his children. But Helen at least didn't seem to think that was the case.

'Want a game of ball?' he asked.

Helen and George were up like a shot!

'Were there really ten thousand at the meeting?' George asked his father, when he heard the news.

'There really were,' laughed Billy. 'And there were some outside that couldn't get in.'

'Did you really have electric light?' the boy queried.

'Yes we did! The place was bright as a summer's day, so bright the light almost dazzled me when I was preaching!'

'I'd love to see electric light,' George said wistfully.

'You would?' said Billy. 'Then get your sister and brother and I'll show you what it looks like.'

Billy took the children with him to the building in which he'd been preaching and asked the caretaker to switch on the lights.

'How did that happen?' George gasped. 'Nobody did anything!'

Billy explained that electric lights worked from a switch, and he even allowed the children to switch them on and off.

'You're a great dad,' Helen said, squeezing her father's hand.

Billy thought back to his own childhood and to his four long years in the orphan school, and returned Helen's hand squeeze with lots of love. As they walked back home, George asked his father where his next preaching meetings were to be. Billy told him and said he was going there by train.

'I love travelling by train,' George said.

Billy thought back over the years to his first train journey and told his children about when he was sent away to school and didn't see his mother for four whole years.

'That must have been an awful train journey,' Helen sympathised.

'It was,' agreed Billy, 'but I made up for it long ago with many happy train journeys. I guess that was the start of my travelling.'

Billy Sunday spent his life going from place to place holding Christian campaigns. The meetings he spoke at grew until the average attendance was more than 20,000. Over the years he spoke to several million people. But not all of them went to hear the good news about Jesus.

At one meeting in Springfield, Illinois, a man jumped out of the crowd brandishing a great whip that he used to lash Billy Sunday across the knees. But the poor man had forgotten how athletic the preacher was, and he must have got the biggest surprise of his life when Billy leapt off the platform and on to him before he could lash out at anyone else. For the next few weeks, Billy had to preach at his meetings holding himself up with crutches, not because of the damage the whip did, but because he sprained his ankle when he'd landed on the attacker!

'Did you hear what Billy Sunday said?' John asked his friend one day.

'What was that?' Tom asked.

'He says that if you live wrong, you can't die right.'

'Well that's true enough,' Tom said. 'He has a real way with words.'

Puzzled by the expression on his friend's face, John asked if Tom had ever heard Billy Sunday preach.

'I sure have,' his friend replied. 'And if I hadn't, you wouldn't see me here today.'

'Why's that?'

'I'll tell you why,' Tom said, sitting down on a wall at the roadside. 'You know me as a respectable businessman, and so I am. But when I went to hear Billy Sunday, I was a broken-down drunk. And if there is something that man can't abide, it's drink.'

'I know,' John said. 'I've heard him speak on the subject.'

'So have I,' Tom told his friend. 'And my life has never been the same since. That night I asked the Lord Jesus to wash away all my sins, and he did just that. Over the months that followed, Jesus helped me give up drink and build up my business again. I thank God for Billy Sunday, and I thank the Lord Jesus for what he's done for me every day of my life!'

In 1935, when America's baseball preacher died, there were men and women, boys and girls, right across the country who thanked God for Billy Sunday, and who thanked God for the message of Christ's love and salvation that he had brought to them.

FACT FILE

Baseball: Billy Sunday played baseball for the Chicago White Stockings, one of the most famous baseball teams in America. (Today they are usually called the Chicago White Sox.)

Baseball has been played in America since 1839, and the first organised club was founded in 1845. Today it is played by a large number of professional clubs across America, and by lots of amateurs in America and beyond. Although Billy was paid to play for the White Stockings, players today receive much more money than they did in the past. Baseball is a big business in America.

Keynote: Billy was afraid that his teammates would make fun of him because he had become a Christian, but he decided to tell them anyway. He found that they actually respected him rather than laughed at him.

It is not always easy to let people know that we believe in Jesus

Christ, but Jesus has suffered so much for us. He even died on the cross for us. We do not have any right to be ashamed of him.

 Think: Billy had heard the gospel message from his mother many times before, but it made sense to him in a new and exciting way when he listened to the open-air preacher. This shows that we should keep listening to explanations of what God has done, even when we haven't understood the message in the past. Think about the parts of the Bible that you find hard to understand. Who could explain them to you again?

 Prayer: Lord Jesus, thank you for using all sorts of people in your kingdom. Help me to remember how great you are, and not to be embarrassed to tell my friends that I believe in you. Thank you for all the different people who preach your gospel. Please help me to listen to you carefully. Amen.

Charles H. Spurgeon

Charles was positively jumping with excitement.

'We're nearly there!' he said. 'It's just two more miles to Stambourne!'

His father smiled.

'Does it feel as though you are coming back home when you come here?' the man asked.

Ten-year-old Charles thought about that.

'I suppose it does, in a way,' he said. 'After all, I did stay here with Grandad and Grandma until I was five, and I've been back for every summer holiday since then.'

'True enough,' commented Mr Spurgeon. 'But what do you like best about it?'

The boy laughed.

'I love Grandad and Grandma, and I love the house too,' he explained. 'It's so big and rambling that I can always find hideaway places. My favourite part in the house is a secret.'

'Even to me?' asked his father.

'I suppose not,' Charles laughed. 'It's a little, dark room off one of the bedrooms. There are shelves of books all the way around it and piles of them on the floor. Going in there is like entering a treasure chest.'

'Have you found any treasures there?' queried Mr Spurgeon.

'Yes,' the lad said, excitedly. 'There's a book full of stories about people who were killed because they were Christians. But my favourite book of them all is 'The Pilgrim's Progress'. Christian – he's the main character in the story – had all kinds of adventures. In one of them, he has to walk between roaring lions to get where God wants him to go. He's scared stiff, but then a man who lives nearby shouts to him and tells him to stay right in the middle of the path and he'll be safe because the lions are chained and they can't reach the middle of the path. So he does that, and walks right between the lions! You should see the drawings in the book, Dad,' he added, 'the lions are really ferocious!'

Mr Spurgeon smiled at his son.

'I know,' he said. 'I read that book when I was about your age, and I remember the lions well.'

Charles's grandfather was a minister, and during that summer holiday he had a representative of the London Missionary Society staying with him for a short visit while he was taking some meetings near Stambourne. His name was Richard Knill.

'Mr Knill's very interesting,' Charles told his grandfather. 'I like listening to the stories he tells.'

'He is indeed,' old Mr Spurgeon agreed. 'And I think he enjoys your company too.'

'How do you know that?' the boy enquired.

His grandfather smiled. 'I know because he was asking which room was yours. I think you'll be getting an early morning call tomorrow and an invitation to go for a walk with your missionary friend.'

The following morning, Mr Knill did knock at Charles's door, and they did go for a walk in the garden before breakfast. As they walked, Mr Knill spoke to the lad about God's love. Before they returned to the house, the missionary prayed with Charles, asking God that the boy would soon know the Lord, and that he would grow up to be God's faithful servant.

'This child will one day preach the gospel,' Mr Knill told Charles's grandfather, 'and he will preach it to multitudes of people.'

In 1848, when Charles was fourteen years old, he was sent to a Church of England school at Maidstone.

'What's your name?' one of his teachers asked, soon after he arrived.

'Spurgeon, sir,' the boy replied.

'No, no,' the teacher responded. 'What's your name?'

'Charles Spurgeon, sir.'

Shaking his head, the teacher said, 'I just need your Christian name lad.'

'Please, sir,' was the reply. 'I'm afraid I don't have one.'

'Why is that?' asked the man.

Charles answered what he knew to be true. 'It's because I don't think I'm a Christian.'

While he was not a Christian when he went to school at fourteen, he became one the following year.

One Sunday, Charles was on his way to church when a terrible snowstorm forced him to shelter in a little church he had never been in before, and it wasn't one that appealed to him.

'The minister didn't arrive,' he told someone later. 'I suppose he was snowed up. One of the men in the church took his place, and at first I thought he was very stupid. He had to stick to the text he'd taken from the Bible because he seemed to have nothing else to say. His text was, "Look to me, and be saved, all the ends of the earth." He kept repeating, "Look! Look! Look!"'

'That must have been pretty boring,' Charles's friend commented.

'It was at first,' the boy replied, 'but then he really made me look to Christ. He made me think about Christ on the cross, then dead and buried and raised from the dead, and now alive forever in heaven. After about ten minutes he stopped because he'd run out of things to say.'

His friend smiled. 'That must have been a relief.'

Charles ignored the comment and continued. 'When he'd finished, the man looked right at me and spoke right to me.'

'Embarrassing or what?' his friend laughed.

Again Charles ignored him.

'Young man,' he said, right to me, 'look to Jesus Christ. Look! Look! You have nothing to do but to look and live!'

'And?' asked his friend.

'It suddenly all made sense. It was as though a wonderful light had been switched on. I became a Christian that day, and I now know for sure that Jesus is my Saviour.'

Charles' friend looked at him. 'Are you being serious?' he asked.

'Never more so,' said Charles. 'I've never been more serious and I've never been happier.'

Just two years later, in 1851, seventeen-year-old Charles became pastor of a small church, and two years later he moved to New Park Street Chapel in London. Before long he was the talk of the town, and the church became far too small for all the people who came to hear him preach.

'This is a terrible time to be a minister in London,' thought Charles, in 1854, as he walked home after a funeral. 'Now that cholera is sweeping through the city again, it just seems to be one funeral after another. And the disease hits people so hard and so suddenly that most die within hours of becoming ill. While I know that the Christians in my congregation go home to the Lord when they die, my heart breaks at the thought of those who die without hope.'

A horse trotted along the road, and as it passed, the young minister saw that it was trailing a cart full of rough coffins, no doubt full of more victims of cholera. He turned away from them and found himself looking into the window of a shoemaker's shop. There was a card in the window, and he read it aloud.

'If you make the Most High your dwelling – even the Lord, who is my refuge – then no harm will befall you, no disaster will come near your tent.'

As he read the verse, which comes from Psalm 91, a great peace flowed through Charles's heart and mind. He knew he could go on, and he knew that, having God with him, he should not fear any evil. In fact, God gave him a very precious gift to encourage him, as he married Susannah[1], a young woman in his congregation. Their life together was a most beautiful love story.

Thomas Medhurst, who was converted through Charles's preaching, started preaching himself as soon as he became a Christian. That was around 1854. Spurgeon worked with him for part of each week, training the younger man as well as being helped by him. Soon other young men came for training. By 1861, he had 20 students; two years later there were 66, and some of the following years topped over 100! That was the beginning of The Pastors' College.

'Tell me about your students,' a visitor asked Charles, in the mid-1870s. 'Are they all from London?'

Spurgeon smiled at the thought.

'One man walked from the highlands of Scotland to study here, but the rest come from all over England, and beyond.'

---

1. Susannah Spurgeon's story is included in *Ten Girls who made a Difference.*

'That's all very well for those who can spare the time to study,' the visitor commented. 'Not everyone is free to do that.'

'True enough,' Spurgeon agreed. 'That's why we run evening classes too. Between one and two hundred people attend them.'

As the college was growing, so the congregation was growing too. In fact, New Park Street Chapel was bursting at the seams. In 1856, which was the year The Pastors' College began, work started on the building of a huge, new church, the Metropolitan Tabernacle. It was opened in 1861.

'I'm told that there were 6,000 people in church today,' Susannah commented to her husband, one Sunday evening. 'I'm sure that's right because the place was absolutely full.'

Charles was relaxing on one side of the fire with four-year-old Thomas nearly sleeping on his knee. And Susannah was on the other side, with Thomas's twin brother, Charles.

'And,' went on Susannah, 'I hear that your sermons are being printed in more than twenty languages, including Russian, Chinese, Japanese and Arabic.'

'That's all true,' her husband said. 'And I'm really grateful for that. But I hope and pray that people are more anxious to hear what God has to say than what I have to say.'

'Yes, indeed,' agreed Susannah. 'But I still think it is good to remember the ways in which God is using you.'

'Only so long as it doesn't make me proud,' added her husband seriously.

Susannah grinned. 'I'll soon tell you if it does!'

Charles took the sleepy Thomas and put him to bed, and his twin was soon sound asleep beside him. Tired out after preaching, Spurgeon suggested an early night for them too. Before they went to bed, the pair of them continued to think through the things they had to thank God for.

'We should thank God that as well as the 6,000 who hear you preach, your sermons are being sent all round the world,' said Susannah. 'They are also being printed every week in some American newspapers! Did you hear how many of your leaflets were given out to university students?'

Spurgeon shook his head.

'I understand that it was over 150,000.'

Kneeling by his chair, Charles commented to his wife. 'I wanted an early night, but you've reminded me of so many things to thank God for that we might be on our knees praying for quite some time!'

'It's all very well for famous preachers to stand up in church and talk week after week after week. All they do is talk, they don't actually get down to the business of helping people in need,' said John Smith, who had been invited to go to a service in the Metropolitan Tabernacle. 'You show me a man that does good works, and I'll come and hear him preach.'

The old man who had invited the stranger in smiled. 'Then let's go for a walk together. I'll tell you some of the things Mr Spurgeon has done, and I'm quite sure you'll want to come to the service this evening.'

It was 1873, and Charles had been the old man's minister for twenty years. As the two men walked, the story that unfolded kept John Smith interested for the whole afternoon.

'Charles Spurgeon has always been generous to the poor, often leaving himself poor as a result. He encouraged the congregation to help too, and said that the Metropolitan Tabernacle should take up some work with children. In the church magazine, *The Sword and Trowel*, he suggested the opening of a Christian school. A lady called Mrs Hillyard saw the article and wrote saying that she thought the church should open an orphanage, and that she would give £20,000 towards it.'

'That's a lot of money,' commented John Smith.

'So it is,' the old man said. 'When Mr Spurgeon went to visit Mrs Hillyard and saw that she lived in a very ordinary house, he thought she'd made a mistake in the letter. "We've called about the £200 you mentioned in your letter," Spurgeon said. "Did I write £200?" Mrs Hillyard replied. "I meant £20,000." The minister questioned the lady carefully to see if her money should be left to some family members, but there were none. So the £20,000 was accepted and used to open the Stockwell Orphanage for Boys.'

'You were right,' John Smith said. 'Your minister does seem to live like a Christian as well as talk like one. I will come along to the evening service with you.'

That was John Smith's first visit to the Metropolitan Tabernacle, but it was not his last. He was still attending in 1880, when the Stockwell Orphanage for Girls was opened. There were many people in London like John Smith, men and women who were brought by friends to hear Charles Spurgeon, and others who came just out of interest. Often they came with no faith, and many left having found Jesus Christ as their Saviour. Among them were some of the hundreds of children who lived in the Stockwell Orphanages.

FACT FILE
Cholera: Spurgeon was a minister in London during several cholera epidemics in the mid-19th century. Cholera is an infectious disease that can spread very easily through contaminated water supplies. Getting clean water was a real problem in cities at that time because they had grown so quickly. Once the connection between dirty water and cholera was discovered, laws were passed to encourage new water supplies and reservoirs to be developed.

Keynote: Spurgeon was a very famous man. You might even call him a superstar preacher. Many people came to hear him preach, and many more read his sermons. But he realised that these were things that should make him thank God rather than be proud of his own ability. We need to remember to thank God for all our successes, and to remember that they come from him rather than ourselves.

Think: John Smith was impressed with Spurgeon because he was living out the things that he told other people to do. Spurgeon was willing to make himself poor so that he could help other people. It is important that we believe the things that we read in the Bible, but it is also important that we obey it. Think of ways in which you can put the Bible teaching you have received into practice.

Prayer: Lord Jesus, thank you for all the skills and talents that you have given me. Thank you for the chances that I have to help others. Please help me to know you as my Saviour, just as Spurgeon did, and teach me to give praise and thanks to you for all the good things that are in my life. Amen.

Aiden W. Tozer

'I don't believe it!' Mr Tozer said, as the lamb was born. 'This little thing has got three ears!'

His son came running at this interesting news and watched as the newborn lamb nuzzled its mother. But the sheep edged away from it and pushed the tiny creature aside.

'I must have given her a fright when I shouted for you,' the farmer told Aiden. 'Let's give the pair of them some peace to get to know each other. You check on her in half-an-hour.'

Aiden went back to give his pig a new bed of straw. Her ears twitched when the boy spoke to her. 'I remember when you were young,' he told the sow. 'You were half-starved and looked fit for nothing. You'd never know that now,' he added, clapping the sow's sturdy shoulder. 'You've grown into a fine old girl.'

Having replaced the pig's bedding and filled her water trough, Aiden went back to see how the new lamb was getting on.

'She'll be licked dry by now and full of her mother's first milk,' he thought, as he crossed the field.

But she was not. The lamb was standing alone, wet and miserable, and the sheep was a good distance off and looking cross. Aiden picked the little thing up and took her to the sheep. The lamb tried to nuzzle her mother, but every time they got close, the ewe nudged her baby away. Aiden took off his jacket, picked up the lamb and wrapped it round her.

'She doesn't seem to want you,' he told the tiny creature, 'I wonder if she doesn't recognise a lamb with three ears.'

'What have you got there?' Mrs Tozer asked, when the boy took his bundle into the kitchen.

'It's a lamb with three ears,' he explained, 'and her mother won't accept her.'

'Bring the poor creature here,' said the woman, 'and let me have a look at her.'

Aiden handed the lamb over.

'She's shivering with cold and fright,' the boy commented. 'Will I heat some milk for her?'

'There's no need to do that,' explained Mrs Tozer. 'Your brother is milking the cows, and the milk will still be warm. Go and get some for her.'

Taking a jug from the shelf, Aiden went to the cowshed and collected some milk. He put it into a bottle they kept for orphan lambs, and very soon the bottle was empty and the lamb was full. She stopped shivering too.

'May I look after this one?' the boy asked.

'She's all yours,' laughed Mrs Tozer, 'and she'll make a good sheep, I'm sure. Look how you rescued that scraggy pig and built her up to be a good 'un.'

'Aiden's got a kind heart,' Mr Tozer told his wife that night, after the children had gone to bed. 'But he can pick a fight in an empty field. I reckon he's the most argumentative boy in La Jose, Pennsylvania!'

'He's just like my mother,' said Mrs Tozer. 'And that's not a compliment.'

Just then Aiden came into the room. He had woken up and wanted to check how the lamb was.

'Did you hear what we were saying?' his father asked.

The boy had, but wondered whether to admit it or not.

'You did, didn't you?'

He bowed his head.

'I just don't understand you, son,' his father said wearily. 'You're as gentle as can be with helpless creatures, and as argumentative as a bear with a sore head with other people.'

Aiden opened his mouth to argue with his father but decided that would not be a good idea.

Not long afterwards, Aiden and his sister Essie were swinging high up in their apple tree. The gloriously sunny day had brought the boy out in a very good mood, so good that he started to sing a Sunday school song.

'Is there any room in heaven for a little lad like me?' he sang aloud. 'Is there any room in heaven for me?'

From the other side of the bushes under the tree, his neighbour's voice yelled back, 'If there's going to be any room for you in heaven, you'll have to mend your ways.'

Essie started to giggle but stopped as soon as she saw the thunderous look in her brother's eyes.

'I dreamed our house burned down,' Aiden told his parents one morning at breakfast time. 'I wonder what the dream meant.'

'You're getting as bad as your grandma,' Mr Tozer said. 'She's forever telling us the meaning of her dreams.'

But that dream made a deep impression on young Aiden, so much so that he worked out how he could save his brother and sisters if the house were to go on fire. Just a few months later, that's exactly what happened. Ten-year-old Aiden carried out the plan he had made and led his younger brother and his sisters to the safety of the woods.

Even his next-door neighbour admitted that the boy was a hero that day in 1907!

'I've made a decision,' Aiden announced some time later. 'I hate my name and I don't want to be called Aiden ever again.'

'But it's a good name,' his mother protested. 'You were called after the storekeeper, and his wife's a good friend of mine.'

'I don't care!' the boy said crossly. 'From now on I'll not answer to Aiden ever again! I'll just answer to AW. My initials are much better than my name.'

And from then on, that's what he did. Aiden Wilson Tozer was AW for the rest of his life.

One day, when AW was not quite eighteen, he was in town and came upon a crowd at a busy street corner.

'I wonder what's going on here,' he said to himself, as he pushed his way through the crowd, till he stood in front of an elderly man who was speaking about Jesus.

'If you don't know how to be saved,' the preacher shouted, 'just call on God, saying "Lord be merciful to me a sinner."'

The words spun round in AW's mind. As he walked home, all sorts of things went through his head. He remembered the arguments and fights he'd been in. And at the same time he remembered what his father's mother had told him about the Lord.'

'Am I really a sinner?' AW asked himself. 'Do I really need to be saved? Am I that bad?'

When he arrived home, he went into the attic to sort himself out. And by the time he climbed down the stairs, he was a changed young man. He had asked God for forgiveness and had become a Christian. That very day his parents noticed a difference in him, and before long he was the talk of the town.

'I don't know what's happened to AW,' a neighbour told her husband, 'but he's as kind to people now as he's always been to animals, and that's saying something!'

In 1919, AW became pastor of the Alliance Church in Nutter Fort, West Virginia and went there to live with his young wife, Ada. In the ten years that followed, he was a minister in Ohio, Indiana and Chicago. By the time they moved to Chicago, where they were to remain for over thirty years, there were seven young Tozers: six boys and a baby girl.

'The elders offered me an increase in my salary,' AW told his wife, after a meeting at the church. The children were young at the time, and Mrs Tozer had to work very hard to make ends meet.

'You didn't accept it, did you?' she asked.

AW smiled. 'No,' he assured her. 'I didn't, though you would have had no trouble spending it I'm sure. But when we were married, we promised each other and the Lord that we'd rely on him for all our needs, and he's never let us down.'

Thinking of the children's shoes that were becoming too small, Mrs Tozer nodded agreement. 'The Lord will supply all our needs,' she said firmly. 'And I look forward to seeing how he does it.'

Just then she noticed that the knees of AW's trousers were wearing thin. Mrs Tozer smiled. 'Some people wear through the seats of their trousers by lounging around,' she thought. 'But my husband wears through the knees by spending so much time in prayer.'

AW went through to his study and knelt by his chair. He also knew the children needed shoes, and he prayed that God would provide them.

'Thank you, Father, for giving all we need,' he finished, knowing for a certainty that God would hear and answer his prayer.

'Dad,' his eldest son said, as they walked to the railway station to meet a friend off the train, 'why don't we get a car? You travel miles and miles to preach at meetings.'

'We don't have a car because we don't need one,' AW said.

His son thought about that. 'Can we only have things we need?' he asked. 'Can we not sometimes have things just because we want them?'

AW strode along beside the boy. 'I hope we do give you treats,' he said, 'but I don't feel the need for them myself. All I need is my family about me, enough food to eat, warm clothes to wear and my books.'

His son thought about that as they neared the station. 'It's quite true,' he decided. 'Dad does only buy what is absolutely necessary for himself, though we do get treats from time to time.'

Although the boy didn't know it, his parents had so little money that they didn't even have a bank account.

'What's Dad doing?' Rebecca asked her mother, when she came home from school one day.

'I'll give you three guesses,' one of her brothers teased. 'In fact,' he went on, 'I'll give you three things to choose from. Is he writing a book, or is he writing a book, or is he writing a book?'

Rebecca pretended to think about the answer, and then she grinned. 'I think ... I think he's writing a book.'

'First prize to Rebecca Tozer,' her brother laughed. 'She got the right answer first time!'

'How many has he written now?' she asked.

The boy shook his head. 'I've no idea, but it must be more than a dozen.'

'His older brother looked up from his homework. 'Much more,' he said, then looked down again.

For once the young Tozers were wrong. Their father was not writing a book; he was writing a letter. It was in reply to one he had received from a boy he had met at a youth camp. AW was a favourite of the young people at Christian camps.

'I greatly enjoyed meeting you at Canby Camp,' he wrote, 'and hope to hear good things about you as the years go on. Learn to discipline yourself like a prize fighter or big league ball player. Most boys are too soft and don't like to do anything they don't enjoy doing. Sometimes we have to do what we don't like, and that is good for us. Abraham Lincoln was a good example of a man who started young to learn everything he could. If he had wasted his time loafing, he would not have become the great man he was.'

AW signed the letter and folded it into its envelope.

'It's strange,' he thought. 'A letter to a boy I met at camp might be every bit as important as the book I'm going to work on now, if it helps show him how to live for the Lord.'

It was a summer evening, and he worked until the sun had nearly set before going through to be with his family.

'Does everyone's father work as hard as you do?' his youngest son, Stanley, asked.

Mrs Tozer wondered what the answer to that question would be.

'I don't suppose they do,' AW told the boy. 'But not everyone has the best news in the world to pass on, and it seems a shame to waste any time by not doing it. If you had good news, you'd want to pass it on right away, wouldn't you?'

'If my team won a ball game, I would tell everyone I met,' Stanley agreed. 'So that's why you spend so much time in your study preparing sermons and writing books, and why you go to camps as well.'

'That's right,' said his father.

'But will you never take a holiday, ever?' the boy asked. All his friends' fathers took holidays with their families.

'I've never had a holiday. I don't feel the need. A preaching tour or young people's camp is better for me than a holiday.'

Stanley thought about that and decided that if he had children he would take them on holidays that weren't all about work.

AW had already prepared his Sunday sermons one week in May 1963, when he suffered a heart attack. The sermons were never preached, because he died late that evening. When the news broke, Christians in many countries of the world remembered the man who had taught them how to live for Christ. And many others looked at the row of books on their bookshelves written by AW Tozer. Some people had two shelves of his books, for he wrote over forty. That was quite amazing because AW never went to college; he just studied God's Word, the Bible.

FACT FILE

Publishing: AW was very well known because of the large numbers of books that he wrote. Many ministers and preachers have been able to reach thousands of people through books. These are people whom they could never have spoken to in person.

In fact, some people regard the development of the printing press as one of the major factors that helped the Reformation in the 16th century. The printing press allowed lots of books to be produced at once for the first time. Until then, every copy had to be written out by hand.

Keynote: AW never felt the need of a holiday because he was so enthusiastic about spreading 'the best news in the world'. When people have good news, they want to share it with others, especially with their friends.

The whole purpose of AW's efforts in preaching, camps and books was to tell people the good news about Jesus. In doing that, he was fulfilling one of the main jobs that Jesus left with his disciples just before he ascended to heaven.

Think: AW wrote to the boy from the camp about the need for discipline. Sometimes we need to do things that we don't want to do at the time. We do them knowing that they will be good for us in the future.

AW used training to be a baseball player as an example. In the Bible Paul used the example of a runner in a race. Think about ways in which you can discipline yourself and try hard for God.

Prayer: Lord Jesus, thank you for being willing to leave the glory of heaven to live and die so that people can be saved from their sins. Thank you for those who tell us about you, and for the effort that they put into doing this. Please help me to try hard to discipline myself in serving you. Amen.

Martyn Lloyd-Jones

Martyn Lloyd-Jones looked out the window of the train.

'Are we nearly there?' he asked.

His father smiled. 'We've a long way to go yet. But we're just coming up to a very important stage in the journey.'

The boy looked out the window. 'We're not in anywhere,' he said.

'We are,' Mr Lloyd-Jones told his son. 'We're in Wales, and before very long we'll cross the border into England.'

Martyn sat with his nose nearly touching the train window. A few miles further on his father told him that they were crossing the border.

'But it looks just the same,' the lad said, sounding a little disappointed. 'It's just hills and trees and fields like we have at home.'

Mr Lloyd-Jones smiled at his son. 'Not quite the same,' he said, in his lovely Welsh accent. 'There's nowhere in the world quite like Wales.'

Martyn didn't want to argue with his father, but to his eight-year-old eyes England looked much the same as home.

'Wake up,' Mr Lloyd-Jones said, giving his son a shake. 'We're nearly in London.'

Martyn jumped, then looked out the window as the train snaked through the suburbs and into the centre of the city.

'There are a lot of houses here,' he said. 'There must be thousands of people in London.'

'Millions,' corrected his father. 'And there's the river,' he added, pointing to the left.

'That's the Thames!' Martyn said excitedly. 'In geography we learned that the first people to live here came to trade on the River Thames.'

'You're a clever boy,' his father told him, then laughed. 'Maybe one day you'll come to London. A lot of Welsh boys come here to work.'

Martyn shook his head. 'I don't think I will. There are too many people here already.'

When they climbed out of the train and tried to walk along the crowded platform, Martyn thought back to what he had said. 'There are too many people here already' just seemed to describe the station platform perfectly. It was exciting, but he was glad that he would be catching a train back home on Saturday, after they had been to the agricultural show.

On Friday, something happened to change their plans. One of the most important men in their home village of Llangeitho, in Cardiganshire, sent them a message to say he was in London to buy a car and he would give them a run home!

'Wait till I tell my brothers!' thought Martyn.

His father laughed. 'Imagine the pair of us arriving back in Llangeitho in the squire's car! It'll be like royalty coming to town.'

But it didn't turn out to be quite like that. Although the car was a grand one, it was not in good condition. Their first puncture happened before they left London, the next one not long afterwards, and there were others after that. When they eventually drew near their home village, Martyn whispered to his father.

'How many miles is it from London to here?'

'About 300,' his father whispered back.

'And how long has it taken us to come by car?'

His father winked at him. 'It's taken from 5.30 pm on Saturday till 9 pm on Monday. You can work out how long that is for yourself.'

'That's you home safe and sound, if rather later than expected,' announced the squire from the front seat of the car.

Martyn's brothers couldn't wait to hear about London and about the car journey home. He told of his travels and adventures, punctures and all.

'I'm not going back to London,' he finished. 'There are too many people there already, and it's too far away from Llangeitho.'

Six years later, in 1914, Martyn was back in London, though he longed to be home in Wales. His family had moved for business reasons. From a small town where everyone knew everyone else, and all that was going on, the three Lloyd-Jones boys found themselves strangers in a vast city at war. However, there was a little of Wales in London, at Charing Cross Chapel, and that's where the family went to church.

'What subjects interest you?' one of his new school teachers asked Martyn.

'I like history and English, Sir,' the teenager replied. 'But my best subject is science, and I want to study medicine.'

The teacher nodded his head. 'You'll have to work hard if you hope to be a doctor.'

Martyn did work hard, both at school and in his father's dairy business. At the age of sixteen he became a medical student at St Bartholomew's Hospital in London, one of the most famous teaching hospitals in the world. It was while he was a medical student there, that Martyn began to think seriously about what he believed.

'I don't know exactly when I became a Christian,' he told a friend at church. 'Over a period of time it just became clear to me that what the Bible says is true; that I needed a Saviour and that he is Jesus Christ.'

'Can you not remember a day when you decided to become a Christian?' asked his friend.

Martyn shook his head. 'No,' he said. 'I cannot. Some people, like the Apostle Paul, have sudden and dramatic conversions. I did not, and that doesn't make me any less of a Christian.'

In January 1927, Dr Martyn Lloyd-Jones married Dr Bethan Phillips[2]. They met in church. Bethan was also of Welsh descent.

'What does your wife think of you giving up medicine?' a colleague asked Martyn, on hearing that his friend had made that decision.

Lloyd-Jones shook his head. 'I'm not giving up medicine,' he corrected. 'I'm taking

---

2. The Story of Bethan Lloyd-Jones is included in *Ten Girls who made a Difference*.

up preaching. Bethan and I have discussed this and prayed about it, and she is as clear in her mind as I am that we are doing the right thing.'

'But you're a very clever doctor,' objected his colleague. 'It seems such a waste.'

Martyn took a long breath before answering.

'My patients have medical problems, and I can often help them. But they also have a spiritual problem that no medicine can help. They have the problem of sin, and sin is a terminal disease. They will die of it. But if they accept the Lord Jesus as their Saviour, they will rise again and spend forever in heaven with him. Is that not better medicine than aspirin?'

His colleague had nothing more to say.

Soon after their wedding Martyn and Bethan Lloyd-Jones set off for their new home in the Welsh town of Aberavon, where Martyn became minister of Sandfields Church.

'Dear Mother,' Martyn wrote, after they had been in Sandfields for a year, 'God has been so good to us since we came here. The church is growing, and not only with respectable people who want to come and hear the gospel. Some well-known drunkards were converted, and the difference in their lives was so marked that they were the talk of the town. Of course, that brought more people in, and some of them have since become Christians. Ordinary working men and women are finding their way to Sandfields, and many of them are really searching for the truth. Bethan runs a Bible class for women, and I have one for men.'

Not only did Martyn's reputation as a teacher spread through Aberavon, people all over Wales heard about the young doctor turned minister.

Having moved to London as a boy the year the First World War broke out, Martyn, Bethan and their two young daughters moved back there just months before the outbreak of the Second World War. He was to become one of the two ministers in Westminster Chapel. Although the war was raging all around them, the congregation continued to meet for worship every week.

'I can hear a flying bomb,' a lady thought, during one Sunday morning service.

The noise of the bomb grew louder and louder, then there was the dreaded silence.

'It's very near,' she worried, as she waited to hear from which direction the explosion came.

There was a minute of silence between flying bombs cutting out and landing.

Suddenly there was a terrific explosion. The flying bomb had landed not far from the church. Everyone in the building closed their eyes, many in prayer and some in terrible fear. The building shuddered, and a fine, white dust fell from its walls and ceiling and covered the whole congregation.

Opening her eyes, the woman looked round in shocked amazement at the white covered people around her.

'I'm in heaven!' she thought. 'I've died and gone to heaven!'

But as the people in the congregation began to rub the dust out of their eyes, she realised that she was still very much on earth!

Every Friday night, the Doctor (as Martyn was most often called) held discussion classes in Westminster Chapel. Eventually too many people were attending for discussions to take place, and he started preaching instead. Some of the sermons the Doctor preached on Friday evenings are now published in books that are read in many countries of the world.

Martyn Lloyd-Jones also became involved in Inter-Varsity Fellowship, an organisation for university students. He was often asked to speak at students' meetings.

'I believe in the theory of evolution,' a student told Martyn before a meeting.

'Then you are a brave man,' the Doctor replied. 'I would not like to base my life on a theory which is not based on truth, when I could base it on the Word of God who never tells lies.'

The student looked shocked.

'You're a doctor,' he said, 'and you've studied science. How can you then ignore what scientists tell us about how the world was made?'

'Young man,' said Martyn, 'if I want to know about something, should I ask the person who made it or someone else who had only used it?'

'The maker, I suppose,' agreed the student. 'But you can't ask God questions about how he made the universe.'

'I don't need to,' the Doctor replied. 'God has told us how he made it. Go home and read the first few chapters of the Bible and you'll find out for yourself.'

An hour later, as Martyn finished his talk to the students, he told them that he had just one more thing he wanted to say.

'It seems that some of you are in danger of making science your god, and that is a very dangerous thing to do. Science is the process of discovering what God has made in his wonderful creation. All science does is find out about God through what he has made. Nothing science discovers will ever prove that God doesn't exist. If it seems to do that, it is not true science; it is a lie.'

The Doctor sat down. And there was one student in the audience who was very quiet. He knew that it was because of him Martyn had said what he did.

'I need to go home and think about this,' the young man said to himself. 'And I'd better read the beginning of the Bible too. I might even go along to Westminster Chapel.'

The following Sunday, the student headed for the City of London. He had thought about what the Doctor said, and wanted to hear him preach.

'What kind of people will go to his church?' he wondered, as he walked along the road. 'I imagine they will all be well off and clever.'

There was a surprise in store for him, and he told a fellow student about it the next day.

'The place was packed! There were some very wealthy looking people there,' he said. 'But there were one or two faces I knew from the theatre too. I didn't think actors and actresses went to church! And there were a lot of very poor people, some just off the streets.'

In that one visit to Westminster Chapel, the student found out a great deal about the Doctor. Although he was by then a very famous preacher, Martyn Lloyd-Jones cared for everyone, rich or poor, famous or quite unknown. And all kinds of people came to church and became Christians through his preaching.

The Doctor did not just make an impact on those who attended Westminster Chapel and university students. He helped set up an annual conference for ministers, and his encouragement greatly helped a new publishing house and a Christian library

'Books can go where people cannot,' he told Bethan. 'And the ministers who come to the Westminster Conference and use the Evangelical Library will be here long after I'm in heaven.'

Thirty years after moving to Westminster Chapel, because he became ill, the Doctor felt it was time to retire. But that did not stop him preaching. He was a doctor of souls, and for another thirteen years he continued to preach to people suffering from sin-sickness.

It was in 1981 that the time came for him to die.

'Don't pray for healing,' he told his family. 'Don't try to hold me back from the glory.'

And when he died, he left his family here on earth and went to meet his lovely and loving Lord Jesus in heaven.

FACT FILE
The Blitz: Martyn was pastor in Westminster Chapel during the Second World War. At that time London was a very dangerous place to be. From mid-1940 until mid-1941, Nazi planes dropped bombs on many cities and towns in Britain, but London was the most heavily bombed. People had to put blankets over their windows at night in case the light would attract the attention of the bombers.

Keynote: Martyn did good work as a doctor. Doctors can help lots of people by using medicine to cure illnesses. But Martyn also knew that the most important disease that we suffer from is sin sickness. No medicine can cure this. What we need is to be forgiven through Jesus' sacrifice for us. Martyn decided that he should tell people about this, even if it meant that he could not work as a doctor anymore.

Think: All sorts of people came to Martyn's church, even people whom we might not expect to go to church at all. The good news about Jesus is for everyone. Martyn mixed with all sorts of people, and he really loved them. The gospel is for everyone. This means you too.

 Prayer: Lord Jesus, thank you for coming to seek and to save all sorts of people. Help me to understand what you have done. Please help me to be kind to all the different people I meet, and to realise that they are all valuable in your sight. Amen.

QUIZ

How much can you remember
about the ten boys who
made history?

Try answering these questions
to find out ...

Samuel Rutherford

1. What did Samuel fall down when he was a little boy?
2. Where did Samuel serve God as a minister?
3. What did he want for his congregation?

John Owen

4. How old was John when he started studying at Oxford?
5. Which church did John preach in after the Battle of Dunbar?
6. Which disasters hit London in the 1660s?

Jonathan Edwards

7. What was the town where Jonathan first served as a minister?
8. What happened between 1734 and 1736 and again in 1740?
9. Can you remember the names of any of the Indian tribes that Jonathan became a minister to?

George Whitefield

10. Why did George have a squint in his left eye?
11. Why did George start preaching in the open air?
12. Name three of the places where George went to preach.

Robert Murray McCheyne

13. Where did Robert go to university?
14. What was the name of his brother who died while he was at university?
15. Where did Robert go on a fact-finding trip in 1839?

Dwight L. Moody

16. Which city did Dwight go to so that he could work for his uncle?
17. Which American president visited one of Dwight's schools?
18. What was the name of the singer he teamed up with as he toured around preaching?

Billy Sunday

19. What had happened to Billy's father?
20. Which baseball team did Billy first play for?
21. Which invention intrigued Billy's children?

Charles H. Spurgeon

22. What was Charles' favourite book when he was young?
23. How old was Charles when he first became a minister?
24. What was the name of the big church that was built to replace New Park Street Chapel?

Aiden W. Tozer

25. What was wrong with the lamb whose mother did not want it?
26. Why did the knees on AW's trousers wear out?
27. Why didn't AW have a car?

Martyn Lloyd-Jones

28. Which part of the UK was Martyn from?

29. What did he want to be when he was young?

30. What was the name of the big church in London that he was minister of?

Answers:

1. A well.
2. Anwoth.
3. That they would fall in love with Jesus.
4. 15.
5. St Giles, in Edinburgh.
6. The Great Plague and the Great Fire.
7. Northampton.
8. Lots of people were converted (there was a revival).
9. River Indians/Housatonics, Mohawks and Iroquois.
10. He had a very bad attack of measles when he was a little boy.
11. Many of the churches would not let him preach in their buildings because he was not a member of the Church of England.
12. Any of – England, Scotland, Ireland, Wales, Gibraltar, Bermuda and America.

13. Edinburgh.

14. David.

15. To the Holy Land (Israel).

16. Boston.

17. Abraham Lincoln.

18. Ira Sankey.

19. He died of an illness that he caught in the army before Billy was born.

20. The Chicago White Stockings.

21. The electric light.

22. The Pigrim's Progress.

23. 17.

24. The Metropolitan Tabernacle.

25. It had 3 ears.

26. Because he spent so much time on his knees in prayer.

27. He didn't need one.

28. Wales.

29. A doctor.

30. Westminster Chapel.

Author Information:
Irene Howat

Irene Howat is an award-winning author who lives in Scotland. She has published many biographical books for all ages and is particularly well-known for her biographical material. She has written many books about the lives of different Christians from around the world. She has also written a biographical work about her own life entitled: *Pain My Companion*. Irene has many other interests including painting, dog walking and editing her Church's young people's magazine called *The Instructor*.

Start collecting this series now!

Ten Boys who used their Talents:
ISBN 978-1-84550-146-4
Paul Brand, Ghillean Prance, C.S.Lewis,
C.T. Studd, Wilfred Grenfell, J.S. Bach,
James Clerk Maxwell, Samuel Morse,
George Washington Carver, John Bunyan.

Ten Girls who used their Talents:
ISBN 978-1-84550-147-1
Helen Roseveare, Maureen McKenna,
Anne Lawson, Harriet Beecher Stowe,
Sarah Edwards, Selina Countess of Huntingdon,
Mildred Cable, Katie Ann MacKinnon,
Patricia St. John, Mary Verghese.

Ten Boys who Changed the World:
ISBN 978-1-85792-579-1
David Livingstone, Billy Graham, Brother Andrew,
John Newton, William Carey, George Müller,
Nicky Cruz, Eric Liddell, Luis Palau,
Adoniram Judson.

Ten Girls who Changed the World:
ISBN 978-1-85792-649-1
Corrie Ten Boom, Mary Slessor,
Joni Eareckson Tada, Isobel Kuhn,
Amy Carmichael, Elizabeth Fry, Evelyn Brand, Gladys
Aylward, Catherine Booth, Jackie Pullinger.

Ten Boys who Made a Difference:
ISBN 978-1-85792-775-7
Augustine of Hippo, Jan Hus, Martin Luther,
Ulrich Zwingli, William Tyndale, Hugh Latimer,
John Calvin, John Knox, Lord Shaftesbury,
Thomas Chalmers.

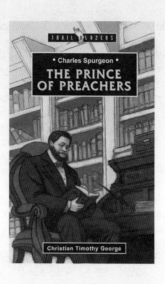

Charles Spurgeon
The Prince of Preachers
by Christian George

Charles Spurgeon was a simple country lad who went on to become one of the best known preachers in London, Europe and the world. Caught in a snowstorm one day when he was a teenager, he crept into the back of a church and the words "Look unto Jesus and be saved!" changed his whole life. Charles spoke words that touched the hearts of rich and poor alike. His fame became so widespread that it is reputed that even Queen Victoria went to hear one of his sermons. Charles was more concerned about the King of Kings – Jesus Christ.

ISBN: 978-1-78191-528-8

OTHER BOOKS IN THE
TRAILBLAZERS SERIES

For a full list of Trailblazers, please see our
website: www.christianfocus.com
All Trailblazers are available as e-books

CHRISTIAN FOCUS PUBLICATIONS

Christian Focus | Christian Heritage | CF4K | Mentor

Christian Focus Publications publishes books for adults and children under its four main imprints: Christian Focus, CF4K, Mentor and Christian Heritage. Our books reflect our conviction that God's Word is reliable and Jesus is the way to know him, and live for ever with him.

Our children's publication list includes a Sunday School curriculum that covers pre-school to early teens, and puzzle and activity books. We also publish personal and family devotional titles, biographies and inspirational stories that children will love.

If you are looking for quality Bible teaching for children then we have an excellent range of Bible stories and age-specific theological books.

From pre-school board books to teenage apologetics, we have it covered!

Find us at our web page:
www.christianfocus.com

CF4•K
Because you're never
too young to know Jesus

TEN BOYS WHO USED THEIR TALENTS

Irene Howat

CF4•K

Copyright © Christian Focus Publications 2006
This edition printed 2006
Reprinted 2007, 2008, 2010, 2012, 2014, 2016, 2017, 2019, 2020
Paperback ISBN: 978-1-84550-146-4
E-pub ISBN: 978-1-84550-846-3
Mobi ISBN: 978-1-84550-847-0

Published by Christian Focus Publications,
Geanies House, Fearn, Tain, Ross-shire,
IV20 1TW, Scotland, U.K.
www.christianfocus.com
email:info@christianfocus.com

Cover design by Daniel van Straaten
Cover illustration by Elena Temporin,
Milan Illustrations Agency

Printed and bound in Turkey

All incidents retold in these stories are based on true situations. Where specific information about childhood incidents has been unobtainable the author has written these paragraphs using other information concerning family life, hobbies, home life, relationships freely available in other biographies.

Cover illustration: Ghillean Prance and his mother used to row a boat on the loch near Dunvegan Castle on the Isle of Skye. His mother would sing Gaelic songs to attract the seals towards them. Ghillean's interest in nature was fostered from a very early age and when he became a Christian he truly appreciated the wonder of creation.

Dedication
for Steven and Stuart

Contents

Wilfred Grenfell

'Kick it to me!' Wilfred yelled to his older brother.

Alfie dribbled the ball down the side of the football pitch, dodged the boy who was marking him, sighted his brother to his left and kicked the ball in his direction. Wilfred, being smaller and faster, ran with it between two members of the team they were playing, squared up to the net and kicked for all he was worth.

'Goal!' several dozen boys screamed together. Even the supporters of the other team had to admit, it was a good one. After all, Wilfred was only ten years old.

'I want to be a footballer when I grow up,' he told his father.

Mr Grenfell smiled. 'That would be a turn-up for the books,' he said. 'We've had ministers in the family; we've had teachers in the family, but we've not yet had a footballer.'

'But I don't need to be a minister or a teacher, do I?' Wilfred asked, horrified at the thought. 'I mean, I can still be a Grenfell and do something else, can't I?'

'Of course you can,' laughed his father. 'But it would be good if we could see you putting effort into your schoolwork. Remember, footballers need to count their goals.'

Wilfred was not stupid, nor was he lazy. His problem was purely and simply that he couldn't sit still. Had his teachers allowed him to move about in the class, he might well have done better in his young days at school. But, in 1875, when Wilfred scored his best goal so far, school desks were in straight lines, and boys were expected to have straight backs and silent tongues in the classroom.

'What are you doing, Wilfred?' his teacher asked one day, when he noticed that his pupil was more interested in something on the floor than in what he was being taught.

'I'm sorry, Sir,' the boy said. 'I was watching an earwig.'

'Perhaps you would like to come and tell the class about earwigs then.'

Wilfred was on his feet in an instant.

'The common earwig is between half and three-quarters of an inch long, and brown. It's the most common member of the *Dermaptera* family and its Latin name is *Forficula auricularia*. Although earwigs like dark places, there is no real evidence that they enter the human ear other than by chance.'

Had the teacher not been new to the class, he would have been less surprised. All Wilfred's friends knew that he could talk all morning about insects.

Alfie, who was very clever with his hands, made wooden cases in which Wilfred could display the insects he collected. Each specimen was caught carefully in order not to damage it. But, sadly, each insect that reached his beautifully arranged collection was well and truly dead.

'What do we have here?' asked Mr Grenfell, looking at a set of butterflies. 'I know this one. Isn't it a tortoiseshell?'

'That's right. It's *Aglais urticae*. The tortoiseshell butterfly is common all summer in England; then it hibernates from October until April, depending on the weather.'

'And the others in your collection?'

'The next one is the Red Admiral, *Vanessa atalanta*, which arrives here from the Mediterranean in late spring. Red Admirals eat nettles. We often see them on the buddleia bush in the garden.'

'I suppose that's why buddleia is nicknamed the butterfly bush,' Alfie said.

'Got it in one,' laughed Wilfred.

'I think we should forget the insect collection for an afternoon and plan our next sail,' suggested Alfie, who then began singing an old sea shanty about a drunken sailor.

'Somehow I don't think it would be a good idea to be drunk and a sailor,' laughed his brother. 'If you were sailing a boat as small as our one, you'd probably end up very wet indeed, maybe even very drowned!'

'Let's have a look at the map.'

Mr Grenfell watched his two growing-up sons. Why was it, he wondered, that Wilfred could discuss insects in great detail – and in Latin – when he had very little interest in his school subjects? And how was it that he could spend ages studying maps with a view to planning sails during the holidays, when he wasn't interested in his geography lessons?

'I may be a headmaster,' the man thought, 'but I don't think I understand my younger son very well at all.'

'What a cough you have,' Wilfred's teacher said. 'You should see the school matron.'

It was 1881. The boy was sixteen years old and a pupil at Marlborough School in Wiltshire.

'Take this,' Matron said, giving him a spoonful of foul-tasting, brown liquid. 'A few doses of this will soon sort you out.'

'Or kill me,' thought Wilfred. 'It's Disgusting with a capital D!'

But the medicine did not cure the cough, which grew worse and worse.

'Here's Wilfred coming,' his friends said, before he came into sight. 'I'd know that cough anywhere.'

Taking their doctor's advice, Wilfred's parents sent him off to stay with his aunt in the South of France.

'The warm air there will do him the world of good,' said the doctor. 'A term away from school won't cause any problems, I'm sure.'

Mr Grenfell wasn't quite so sure. He just shook his head when he thought of Wilfred's school marks and the regular 'Could try harder' and 'Could do better' that was written in his exercise books.

'I'm having a wonderful time,' Wilfred wrote home to Alfie. 'Aunt's friend has two teenage daughters, and they're so interested in nature study. Yesterday we collected frogs from the wild and brought them into the miniature ponds in the garden. Mind you, we've had to put nets over the ponds to keep the frogs in. And there are butterflies here that I've never seen in England. How many different butterflies do you think there are? I'll bring some specimens back with me ... if I can ever tear myself away from here to come home.'

But come home he did, and was not best pleased to be back at school.

'What are you going to do with your life?' Mr Grenfell asked his son when he was eighteen years old.

'I've decided to be a doctor,' he said. 'That's what I'm going to do.'

'A doctor? We've never had a Doctor Grenfell in the family,' his father replied. 'Do you know how much studying that involves?'

Wilfred found training to be a doctor very hard work indeed. His head was fairly buzzing with medical information as he walked along a London street in 1885. Suddenly, he heard the sound of singing, and he followed it into a huge tent.

'Who's he?' the young man wondered. Then he remembered hearing about a famous American preacher called D.L. Moody and that he was in town.

During the meeting a man prayed a very long prayer. Wilfred was becoming so bored that he was about to leave when he was amazed by Mr Moody, who interrupted the prayer, saying, 'Let us sing a hymn while our brother finishes his prayer.'

Wilfred stayed! By the time he left that meeting, he had come to know the Lord Jesus Christ as his Saviour. As he walked home, Wilfred decided to try to be the kind of doctor Jesus Christ would want him to be.

Not too long afterwards, Wilfred was in the middle of a bunch of noisy young boys. He shook his head and smiled. His minister had asked him if he wanted to be a Sunday school teacher. 'Yes, I'd love to!' he'd exclaimed. Now he was finding out that teaching noisy young lads wasn't as easy as he had thought.

'Sit down and listen,' he told his class, over and over again.

But they seemed quite unable to sit still.

'What are they like?' Wilfred said to himself, after one particularly noisy class, and the answer came into his mind right away. 'They're exactly the same as I was. What they need is to get rid of some energy before they'll sit and listen.'

That was how the East End Boys' Club was born. Not only did they have games together at their weekly meetings, they also went sailing with Wilfred and Alfie and had a marvellous time. They learned that it was good to train their bodies to serve the Lord, as well as training their minds and souls.

No sooner was Wilfred back in London than he realised how much he missed the sea.

'I really don't like big cities,' he thought. 'In fact, I'm not at my happiest on dry land at all. But I don't suppose there are many medical practices at sea!'

Not long afterwards there was a surprise in store for Dr Wilfred Grenfell.

'I think I know of a job that would suit you very well,' said Dr Treves. 'I'm a member of the National Mission to Deep Sea Fishermen. We're looking for a doctor to help with the work. We're presently equipping a medical ship, and we need a doctor on board to serve the deep-sea fishermen in the North Sea.'

Wilfred's pulse raced as his heart beat fast with excitement.

'It won't be easy,' added Dr Treves. 'Deep-sea fishermen can be a rough lot of men.'

Easy or difficult, this was the job for Dr Wilfred Grenfell. He took the train to Yarmouth where the *Thomas Gray* was being fitted out as a medical ship. It looked grand tied up to the quay, but it seemed smaller and frailer a few months later when, in 1888, after a stormy sea voyage across the Atlantic, the crew first sighted the fishing fleet.

'Hoist the blue banner,' the captain shouted. 'That'll let them know we're here.'

Before long, Wilfred's first patients were being helped to transfer from trawlers that had drawn alongside.

There were horrible burns from fires on the wooden ships, broken bones held together with makeshift splints, rotten teeth to be extracted, injuries from drunken falls and brawls, as well as all sorts of illnesses.

Once men's medical needs were seen to, they were offered books to read, a brief rest and a change of clothes.

They also heard about the Lord Jesus Christ and how he could save their souls for heaven. Life at sea was rough and tough, and the *Thomas Gray* was a welcome addition to the fleet.

For three years Wilfred worked among the fishermen. On shore, he went round churches telling people about the work of the National Mission to Deep Sea Fishermen.

'I could almost feel the wind whistling through my hair,' one lady said, after hearing him speak.

'And I began to feel seasick,' her friend laughed. 'I've never heard anyone tell such vivid stories. We really must give some money to help with Dr Grenfell's work.'

In 1892, after hearing about the fishermen who spent all year round off the coast of Newfoundland, Wilfred felt the Lord was leading him there. As they sailed towards St John's, a strange light lit the sky.

'It looks like the whole town's on fire,' one of the sailors said. And it was. Reaching harbour as quickly as they could, they set out to help in the devastation. Wilfred had plenty of burns patients that day.

'We needed you, Doctor,' the governor of the colony said, by way of thanks.

And that's just what Wilfred felt. There were plenty of doctors in England. He was needed here.

From St John's, in Newfoundland, Wilfred headed north among the difficult currents, icebergs, fjords and cliffs of Labrador. In one settlement after another, he found people in need of his help.

'We've never had a doctor here,' he was told, and he could see that himself from badly set bones, wounds that wouldn't heal, and young people old beyond their years.

He knew they'd never had a minister either, so as he worked as a doctor, he also chatted to people about the Lord.

During the years that followed, Wilfred worked among the fishermen and visited settlements. But, in 1899, he decided that Labrador was where he should be rather than among the fishermen. In the summers, Wilfred sailed up and down the wild coastline. Winters were spent travelling by dog sled. Once, in April 1908, when he was on his way through thick ice to reach a boy who was ill, he and his dogs were trapped on ice that broke off and floated out to sea! Three of his dogs lost their lives that day, in order that Wilfred and his other dogs could be saved.

'That was six months ago,' Wilfred concluded, having told a group of Christians back in England about his adventure. 'God was very good to me that day.'

God was also good to him on the voyage back to Labrador, for that was when he met Anne MacClanahan, who became his wife. He spent much of that voyage telling her what his hopes and dreams were for Labrador.

Years later, Wilfred and his wife revisited those dreams.

16

'Just think of it,' he said, smiling. 'It's 1927, and the International Grenfell Mission has helped to build six hospitals, five schools, nine nursing stations and an orphanage.'

'And it has allowed women to sell the crafts they make, over the long winter months. Some of their lovely work is on the other side of the Atlantic Ocean now,' Anne smiled.

'Most important of all,' Wilfred added, 'men, women, boys and girls have heard about Jesus, and many have put their faith in him.'

Anne smiled. 'There are people in this cold, wild place who feel as though they've walked along the warm, sandy shores of the Sea of Galilee, for I've never heard a story-teller like you. Of course, that's also why the Mission has been able to do so much. When you tell people in Britain or America about the hardships in Labrador and Newfoundland, they feel so chilled and hungry and ill that they're willing to open their hearts and their wallets to give money for the work to go on.'

The work did go on, even after Wilfred Grenfell died in 1940, two years after his wife.

FACT FILE

Discovery: John Cabot, in the ship *Matthew*, first sighted the lands of Labrador and Newfoundland on June 24th, 1497. In the year 1583, Sir Humphrey Gilbert reached the harbour of St John's with letters from Queen Elizabeth I authorising him to take possession of Newfoundland.

Keynote: Wilfred Grenfell wasn't that great a scholar. He would rather kick a football around than sit still in class. Earwigs were more interesting than algebra. But he knew a lot about the natural world and showed himself to be intelligent as well as hard-working. Sometimes we can feel that we aren't as successful as we could be. Perhaps we wish we were smarter or that we knew more facts? God has given us all different abilities. Some people are smart and organised, some are good at looking after others. Wilfred was good with practical, hands-on things. We should thank God for our abilities. We shouldn't covet the talents that other people have. Instead, we should work hard at developing those talents God has given us.

Think: When Wilfred was asked what he was going to do with his life, he said that he was going to be a doctor. His father reminded him that he would have to do a lot of study – and Wilfred wasn't well known for being a good student. However, he did his best although it was hard at first. For years, God had been preparing him for mission work at sea and in inhospitable regions. Think about what God is preparing you for – right at this moment. You may go on to study at college or university; you may take up a trade or learn a skill. You may even have a hobby or favourite pastime that God is planning to use in the future to bring others to trust in his Son, Jesus Christ.

 Prayer: Lord Jesus, thank you for gifts and talents. Thank you that you are planning my future and that I am safe with you, whatever happens. Help me to use my time, strengths, body and mind – everything about me – to honour you. Amen.

C.S. Lewis

'Dinner time!' Mum called. 'Come on, Clive, or it will be cold.'

Four-year-old Clive was looking at a picture book. He found it so interesting that he didn't even hear his mother calling. Warnie, his older brother, was sent to fetch him.

'Come on,' he said. 'I'm starving.'

'I'll just finish this book,' Clive replied. 'There are only three more pages.'

Warnie decided to resort to serious tactics. 'There's a spider climbing up the back of your chair,' he said quietly.

His little brother was off the chair and in his mother's arms in a split second. He hated spiders. In fact, Clive's definition of a nightmare was to dream about spiders!

'Don't do that, please,' said Mrs Lewis to Warnie, when she eventually calmed Clive down enough to hear what had happened. 'You're three years older than he is, quite big enough to know not to give your brother a fright.'

'But I was hungry,' wailed Warnie. 'And dinner would have been cold if we'd waited till he'd finished the book.'

Mr Lewis shook his head. 'It's cold anyway with all this fussation.'

Just a few weeks later, Clive was in tears again, this time for a very good reason.

'Why did Jacksie get run over by a car? Why didn't the car stop?' the boy wept. 'I loved him. He was the very best dog in the whole wide world.'

'I'm sorry, dear,' said his mother, holding him in her arms. 'I'm afraid the car driver didn't have time to stop when Jacksie ran out in front of him. It really wasn't his fault.'

For days, Clive talked of nothing but Jacksie, and for weeks he kept forgetting he had been run over and would expect him to come, tail wagging, for a rough and tumble.

Then, quite out of the blue, Clive made an announcement.

'My name's not Clive now. I'm called Jacksie. And if anyone calls me Clive, I'll not answer.'

Although he was only four, Clive had made up his mind. He totally refused to answer to any other name from then on. He was Jacksie, then Jacks, and eventually Jack for the rest of his life. However, he used his real name when he became an author. Today he's known as C.S. Lewis. As that is how he's remembered, we'll call him C.S. for the rest of this story.

'Does Warnie need to go away to school?' C.S. asked his father.

'I'm afraid that's what we've decided,' Mr Lewis said. 'We think the school we've chosen in Watford is the best place for him to go.'

C.S. wailed, 'But that's across the sea in England?'

'My dear boy,' smiled his father. 'You make Belfast sound as though it's at the South Pole. England is just a short sail across the Irish Sea.'

'Watford feels as far away as the South Pole,' C.S. sulked. 'I just don't want Warnie to go. I'll miss him.'

C.S. missed his brother very much indeed because the boys were very good friends. Warnie's absence allowed more time for reading, and among his favourite books were those written by Beatrix Potter.

'Look at Peter Rabbit's blue jacket,' he said to his mother. 'Do you remember the story of Benjamin Bunny, when Peter lost his jacket and was wrapped up in a red cotton handkerchief?'

Both Mrs Lewis and C.S. knew the story so well that they were able to say it by heart together.

'Peter was sitting by himself. He looked poorly, and was dressed in a red cotton pocket-handkerchief. "Peter," said little Benjamin, in a whisper, "who has got your clothes?"'

Mother and son fell into a fit of giggles.

'I think you should put on your jacket now,' said his mother. 'It's a nice day for a walk.'

But C.S.'s time at home was as short as Warnie's, and he joined his brother at school in England when he was nine years old. The following year, their mother died.

'Are we going to Boxen today?' Warnie asked his young brother one Saturday afternoon. They had done their team games and were free till teatime.

'Yes, please,' C.S. grinned. 'I like Boxen better than here.'

Boxen was their imaginary world. Its inhabitants were animals, and its rulers were animals too. Teachers and pupils, kings and servants, soldiers and fishermen – all were animals.

C.S. suggested, 'How about designing a Boxen army uniform. I think it should be a royal blue jacket with silver epaulettes and buttons, and dark blue trousers with a silver stripe down the sides.'

'What will they wear on their heads?' asked Warnie.

'You choose,' C.S. said. 'I chose everything else.'

Although Boxen was an imaginary place, it seemed very real indeed to the brothers, and they loved pretending to go there.

Being a soldier was not a game in 1917 when C.S. joined the Somerset Light Infantry, the year before the end of the First World War. He arrived in the terrible Somme Valley in France on his nineteenth birthday. Paddy Moore, C.S.'s best friend, was killed in action. Before the war, C.S. had studied at Oxford University for a year. After he recovered from his war wounds, he returned there to study.

'Do you believe in God?' C.S. was asked by one of his friends, after he became a Fellow of Magdalen College, Oxford, where he taught.

'I did as a boy,' he replied. 'But then I lost what faith I had. And it would have been hard to believe in a loving God in the Somme. In a strange way, I think I feel angry at God for not existing because I think he should.'

C.S. shuddered at the memory of his war years. Every time he thought back to the Somme, he remembered Paddy, the young man who, like millions of others, never came home.

'What are you writing?' Warnie asked his brother. 'Another poem?'

'Yes, actually,' C.S. replied. 'Another poem.'

'It looks rather long for a poem,' teased Warnie. 'Are you sure it's not a detective story?'

C.S. was writing a very long poem. In fact, it was so long it was published as a book!

'You writers,' Warnie laughed. 'Look at the length of books your friend Tolkien writes.'

'Don't his Hobbits remind you of Boxen and the characters we invented to live there?' C.S. asked.

'Of course they do,' his brother laughed. 'If you'd taken up writing sooner, you might have written *The Lord of the Rings* yourself!'

Among C.S. Lewis's friends were a number of Christians, and the men often had long discussions together. What they said, and the kind of lives they lived, made C.S. think very seriously.

'I give in,' he said eventually, in 1929. 'I admit that God is God.'

Having admitted that in his mind, C.S. Lewis knelt and prayed. But it was another two years before he became a Christian.

'Let's visit Whipsnade Zoo,' suggested Warnie in 1931. 'We'll go on my motorbike and you can travel in the sidecar.'

It was a sunny morning as the pair of them sped from Oxford, south towards London. C.S., sitting in the sidecar, had time to think as he looked at the countryside through which they were passing. And something happened during that journey that changed his life. He had news for Warnie at Whipsnade.

'When we set out,' he said, 'I did not believe that Jesus is the Son of God, and when we reached the zoo, I did.'

By then Warnie and C.S. had bought The Kilns, a large house near Oxford, and this they shared with Paddy Moore's mother.

'I just love it here,' said Warnie, as the brothers walked through the grounds.

'It has everything: tennis court, a pond, woods and an orchard – eight acres of England that's ours to enjoy.'

When the Second World War broke out, children from the cities were sent to the countryside for safety. They were called evacuees. In September 1939, several of them arrived at The Kilns. The quietness there seemed very strange to them after the hustle and bustle of London.

'Do you really swim in that pond?' one of them asked C.S.

'Every morning,' he replied. 'I go out in the punt to the middle, then dive in – first asking the moorhens to move over and make room, of course.'

'Yuck!' said another. 'The water's brown!'

'And when I come out, I'm pink,' laughed C.S. Lewis. 'Or blue, if it's wintertime. Let me tell you a story about the birds and animals that live in and around the pond.'

'You're good at telling stories,' a girl said.

'Course he is,' snapped her friend. 'He writes books, doesn't he?'

There was never any argument if C.S. offered to tell the evacuees a story. They were always willing to curl up around his chair and listen.

'That's an interesting old wardrobe,' commented one of the evacuees. Then she grinned mischievously. 'May we go inside and see if there's anything behind it?'

'By all means,' said C.S. Lewis.

As the children scrambled into the oversized wardrobe, memories of Boxen came into C.S.'s head. 'I wonder,' he thought. 'There might be the beginnings of a story right here in the wardrobe.'

C.S. Lewis worked at Oxford University for twenty-nine years, and over that time he wrote many books. Some were very learned, others were stories, and many taught about Jesus Christ. It was in 1950, that his famous children's books began to be published.

'I have our evacuee children to thank for the idea,' he thought, when The Lion, the Witch and the Wardrobe,' was published. 'They made me think of a world behind a wardrobe.' Then he smiled. 'But I suppose it really goes further back than that – right back to Boxen and the characters Warnie and I invented for our secret world.'

In 1954, C.S. Lewis moved from Oxford to become a professor at Cambridge University.

'How many Narnia books have you written?' a boy asked C.S. Lewis the following year. 'I've collected the first four, and I'm saving up for the others.'

The author thought for a moment. 'So you have *The Lion, the Witch and the Wardrobe*, *Prince Caspian*, *The Voyage of the Dawn Treader* and *The Silver Chair*.'

'That's right,' nodded the lad.

'And you've still to get *The Horse and his Boy*, *The Magician's Nephew* and *The Last Battle*.'

The child's eyes shone. 'Wow! You mean I have three more still to read?'

'I tell you what,' said C.S. Lewis. 'You give me your address and I'll send you a copy of *The Horse and his Boy*, then you'll only have to save up for another two.'

'Oh thank you,' he grinned. 'Thank you ever so much!'

'May I ask you a question before I go?' said the boy.

'You've already asked me one,' C.S. laughed. 'But feel free to ask another.'

It took a minute for him to realise what he meant, then he could hardly speak for giggling.

'In the Narnia books, is Aslan meant to be Jesus?'

'That, my lad, is a very big question. Why do you ask?'

The child screwed up his face as he tried to think what he meant.

'It's just that Aslan did the things Jesus did. He overcame evil and he rose from the dead too. And he seems ... so ... beautiful and good and so powerful.'

C.S. looked very serious. 'If you think Aslan is like Jesus, then the Narnia stories will be more than just stories to you. You will understand them in a special way. But remember, Jesus is not like Aslan. Jesus is higher and holier and much more amazing than any storybook character could ever be.'

Although C.S. Lewis wrote many books for children, he had no children of his own. He shared his home with Warnie and Paddy Moore's mother until Mrs Moore died in 1951. Shortly after her death, he met an American writer, Joy Gresham, who had two young sons. Five years later C.S. and Joy were married. For the first time, the storyteller had boys at home to tell stories to. Sadly, Joy only lived for three years after they were married.

When the boy, to whom C.S. Lewis had sent the book, was some years older, he read *The Lion the Witch and the Wardrobe* to his young brother. This is my favourite bit, he said, as he turned over a very worn page.

'Aslan stood up, and when he opened his mouth to roar, his face became so terrible that they did not dare to look at it. And they saw all the trees in front of him bend down before the blast of his roaring, as grass bends in a meadow before the wind. Then he said, "We have a long journey to go. You must ride on me." And he crouched down, and the children climbed on to his warm, golden back. ... That ride was perhaps the most wonderful thing that happened to them in Narnia. ... This is a mount that doesn't need to be guided and never grows tired.'

The boy remembered what C.S. Lewis had said, and saw a deeper meaning. A psalm from the Bible came into his mind. 'My help comes from the Lord, ... he who watches over Israel will neither slumber nor sleep.'

In November 1963, he heard on the news that C.S. Lewis had died. And the young man remembered the quiet storyteller he had once met, and whom he would never, ever forget.

FACT FILE
Chronicles of Narnia:
C.S. Lewis' books are famous the world over. The final title in the Chronicles of Narnia, *The Last Battle,* won the Carnegie Medal for Children's Literature. C.S. Lewis dedicated *The Horse and His Boy* to David and Douglas Gresham who were later to become his stepsons. Lewis didn't just write children's books. *Surprised by Joy* is the autobiography of his early life that focuses on his conversion.

Keynote: C.S. Lewis had an amazing imagination. As a child, he and his brother invented imaginary worlds to live in. Years later, Lewis would invent another world called Narnia. Our imagination is a gift from God. We may not write books or poems, but we can be creative in other ways. We should take care of our minds and bodies. Our imagination can be tarnished if we keep looking at things that do not please God. Our bodies can be damaged and spoiled if we do not follow God's laws.

Think: Lewis was asked if he believed in God. He answered that he had done once. He had questions and doubts and couldn't understand how there could be a God of love when he remembered the awful fighting during the First World War. There is a lot of evil in the world. Today we can see war on our T.V. screens. Perhaps you wonder how a God of love could allow such awful disasters to happen throughout the world? When you think about how the world began and how it all went wrong, then you will realise that the horrible things that happen in our lives are a result of sin. Our disobedience of God has spoiled the beautiful world. It is only Jesus Christ who can deliver us from sin and bring us back to a right relationship with God.

 Prayer: Lord God, when we have questions and doubts about you, help us to bring our worries to you. Help us to read your Word so that we can learn and know the truth. Help us to find out about you and about who you really are – a merciful, faithful and just God.

James Clerk Maxwell

James stood by the front door of his home,
locking then unlocking the door key. Each time
the key turned, he listened for the click and
tried to picture what was happening in the bit
of the lock that he couldn't see. Deciding to
discover if the puzzle was any clearer from
the other side, the four-year-old opened the
heavy door and was about to go out.

'Come away from there,' said a voice behind
him. 'We don't want you wandering out to the
stream. There was so much rain last night
that there's more than enough water to wash
away a young boy like yourself.'

Slowly, James turned round, for his mind
was still on the puzzle of the lock.

'I'll not go near the stream,' he told Maggie.
'I'm just going on to the doorstep to look at
the outside of the lock.'

'You're a strange boy, and no mistake,'
Maggie said. 'I've looked after children all of
my working life, and I've never met one like
you for wanting to know how things work.'

'Good morning, Ma'am,' Maggie smiled, when James's mother appeared on the scene. 'The young master is about his investigations again.'

Mrs Maxwell smiled down at her lad. For someone so small, she thought, he was interested in a great many things.

'Is it time for my lessons?' James asked.

'I think we'll do nature study today,' said his mother, who was also his teacher. 'Some interesting things may have been washed down the stream in the storm last night. Let's go and see what we can find.'

Wrapping her cloak around her, Mrs Maxwell walked down the path to the trees at the foot of the front garden of Glenlair and watched as her son clambered down the bank to the stream that ran through the trees.

'I love nature study,' the boy said, picking up a sparkly stone and holding it like a special treasure.

'You know what I've told you over and over again,' his mother reminded him. 'Look up ...'

James joined in, for he knew exactly what she was going to say. 'Look up through nature to nature's God.'

'Who made the sparkly stone?' asked Mrs Maxwell.

'God did,' he laughed. Then, as he looked around at the rolling hills of Kirkcudbrightshire, in the south-west of

Scotland, he added, 'God made everything I can see, and all the things I've still to discover.'

'We have visitors today,' said Mrs Maxwell, three years later. 'Mrs McMillan is coming with Thomas. Think of a game to play.'

James was ready with his favourite toy when the carriage arrived at the door.

'What's that?' asked Thomas, who lived in the nearby village of Twynholm.

'It's my magic spinner,' James explained. 'If you watch it when it spins, you'll see a story.'

Puzzled at the very idea, Thomas watched as James spun the disk that was covered with drawings he had done. At first it looked like a blur of grey. Then, quite suddenly, when it was spinning quickly enough, he could see a dog jumping over a gate. All the little pictures James had drawn, merged into a moving story!

'Are you going to do any tricks today?' Thomas asked later.

James, who had been teaching his dog tricks, held up three fingers. 'How many fingers am I holding up?' he asked.

Toby barked three times.

'And how many this time?'

Toby barked ten times, and James was holding up ten fingers.

'Let me try,' said Thomas, holding up four fingers.

There was silence for a few seconds, and then Toby barked once. James wouldn't tell his friend how to make Toby count. He only told his mother after a great deal of persuasion.

'I taught him to bark each time I blink. So if I hold up seven fingers, I blink seven times, and he barks seven times.'

A dark cloud crept over James Clerk Maxwell's happy childhood in 1838 when he was just seven. His mother, who was also his teacher, companion and friend, became ill. She still taught him, especially from the Bible. By the time he was eight years old, he could say the whole of the 119th psalm by heart – all 176 verses of it!

'I've brought you some tadpoles,' James said, as he went into his mother's room. 'Look, Mum, you can see their squiggly, wiggly tails. I think nature's wonderful.'

Mrs Maxwell, who spent most of her time in bed now, looked at the jar of tadpoles and smiled. 'If you forget everything else I've taught you, James,' she said, 'don't forget this. Look up through nature to nature's God.'

Something told James that what had been said was of terrific importance. 'I will, Mum,' he said. 'I promise you that I will.'

And it was not long afterwards that Mr Maxwell told his son that his mother had gone to heaven.

'Oh, I'm so glad,' James said. 'Now she'll have no more pain.'

Thinking that he was doing the best thing for James, Mr Maxwell hired a tutor to teach him at home. Had he known what an unkind man the tutor was, James's father would never have given him the job. In fact, he was so unkind that James often ran away from him.

'Oh! Come and see this!' Maggie yelled to the other servants. 'Come to the window and see this. If it wasn't so pathetic, it would be funny.'

James had run away from his tutor to the pond in the garden. Having put a half-barrel into the water, the boy had climbed into it and paddled out to the middle of the pond. His tutor grabbed a garden rake and was reaching as far as he could to try to haul his pupil back, but James always managed to paddle just out of reach.

'I hope the horrible man falls in,' said Jeannie, the kitchen maid.

'And I would hope that too if it wouldn't put him in a worse mood than ever.'

It took two years before Mr Maxwell realised how unhappy his son was. But, when he did, the unkind tutor was sent packing. And so was James, who was sent to school in Edinburgh. He wasn't alone in the city, for he stayed with his aunt there. Laughed at because of his country clothes, and teased because of his Kirkcudbrightshire accent, James found school annoying and boring and spent the weeks looking forward to his father's Saturday visits.

'I've a treat for you today,' Mr Maxwell said, one Saturday. 'We're going to a lecture at the Edinburgh Royal Society.'

'What's that?' James asked, but his father just grinned and told him it was all about wasp.

'What about wasp?' the twelve-year-old asked, thinking his dad was talking nonsense.

'How do you spell wasp?' asked Mr Maxwell.

'W … a … s … p.'

'That's right,' the man laughed. 'W is for wait, a is for and, s is for see and p is for please. So wasp is short for wait and see please.'

'I'll remember that,' James laughed. 'Aunt always says I've to wait and see when I ask what's for dinner. Next time I'll tell her we're eating wasps.'

The Edinburgh Royal Society lectures were often on very interesting scientific subjects, and they became the highlight of

James Clerk Maxwell's young life. When he was fourteen, a paper he wrote was read to the Society. It had to be read by a university professor because James was thought to be too young to read it himself.

In 1847, when he was sixteen years old, James became a student at Edinburgh University. But after a while there, Mr Maxwell realised that it would be better for his son to go to Cambridge University to get a thorough grounding in mathematics. The thing that bothered him most was that Cambridge was not well known for its Christian approach to science. After much thought, and no doubt many prayers, Mr Maxwell agreed that James should move south, to Cambridge. There he continued experimenting with anything and everything that came to hand.

'What are you doing?' his friend asked him one day, having watched James take the college cat into his room every day for over a week. 'Are you troubled with mice?'

James laughed and told his friend that he was doing an experiment, and to come and see. Sitting down, he watched James lift the cat 30 cm off the ground then drop it. The cat's feet were up in air, but the cat spun round and landed on its feet. Next time, he dropped the cat from 25 cm off the ground. Again the cat spun round and landed on its feet.

'You are quite mad!' his friend laughed.

'Not at all,' said James, grinning. 'I've even proved that a cat dropped from just 5 cm above ground level can twist round and land on its feet. Now, isn't that interesting?'

While a student, James often thought of his mother's words as he did his experiments. 'Look up through nature to nature's God.' But instead of just accepting what his mother had taught him, James examined everything with a scientist's eye, and found for himself that he believed in God, the God who made the wonderful world that he so much enjoyed exploring.

Having completed his studies in Cambridge, James Clerk Maxwell moved in 1856 to Aberdeen in the north-east of Scotland where he taught in Marischal College. James was not a brilliant lecturer, possibly because his mind moved too fast. But, after lectures, his students loved to stay behind because he did experiments with them. They could understand him better then! Science was not the only thing James enjoyed at Marischal College, because that's where he met Mary Dewar – her father was College Principal. They fell in love and were married. Even before they married, they studied the Bible together, and they continued that throughout their married life.

Four years after moving to Aberdeen, James and Mary went to live in London when James became Professor of Physics and Astronomy at King's College. For a long time, James had been interested in the planet Saturn, and in the rings that surround it.

'How is it that the rings around Saturn hold their shape?' a student asked.

Another student shook his head. 'There are so many theories about that, I don't know which to believe.'

'Well,' said Professor James Clerk Maxwell, 'from a maths and physics perspective, the only way that Saturn's rings can remain as stable as they are, is if they are made up of numerous, small, solid particles rather than being formed from gases.'

The students knew not to argue and went off to think about what their professor had said. Nothing has been discovered since then to disprove Maxwell's theory of Saturn's rings.

James Clerk Maxwell's main area of interest became electricity and magnetism.

'I owe so much to Michael Faraday,' Maxwell told his students. 'What I have discovered is based on what he discovered before me. That is the nature of science. Each discovery builds on what has gone before.'

'What part of Mr Faraday's work most interests you?' he was asked.

Maxwell's eyes lit up. 'I'm working on his theories of electricity and magnetism, and how electricity travels through space. But it is a massive piece of research. It will take years to complete ... if I live long enough.'

In 1865, James and his wife moved back to Glenlair, his family home, where he set up a laboratory and continued his experiments free from the teaching commitments he had in the south. For the following six years, he worked on electricity and magnetism. During those years he went, from time to time, to Cambridge to meet with fellow scientists working in the same field. Then, in 1871, he moved back to Cambridge where he became Professor of Physics.

'No one has explained the laws of magnetism and electricity as Maxwell has,' a man in the Edinburgh Royal Society said to a friend. 'His mathematical brain has done a fine job. Who else, but a mathematician, could have calculated that the speed of propagation of an electromagnetic field is approximately the speed of light, and that light is therefore an electromagnetic phenomenon. The light we can see is, consequently, only a small part of the entire spectrum of electromagnetic activity.'

'Excuse me,' said his friend. 'You're talking to an ordinary human being, not a scientist.'

The man laughed. 'All right,' he said. 'In words that any mere mortal will understand, I believe that James Clerk Maxwell's calculations and experiments have opened the door to things that we cannot even begin to imagine, but which will be common 100 years from now. And the interesting thing is that he has no time whatever for those who tell us that all we see around us has evolved, rather than having been created. I heard him say in a lecture that we should look through nature to the God of nature. And what wonderful things he has discovered by doing just that.'

That man was to be proved quite right. Although James Clerk Maxwell's theories are difficult to understand, his work provided the basis from which we now have radio, television, radar and satellite communications.

FACT FILE

King's College: James Clerk Maxwell became Professor of Physics and Astronomy at King's College, London. This college was founded by King George IV and the Duke of Wellington (then Prime Minister) in 1829. Two other famous people who attended this college were John Keats the poet, and Florence Nightingale. James' work in the field of electricity and magnetism was a continuation of another scientist's work. This man was Michael Faraday, who was also a Christian.

Keynote: James' mum told him to look through nature to the God of nature. The Bible tells us this too. In Psalm 19:1 it says, 'The heavens declare the glory of God.' Look at the world around you with fresh eyes. You will see wonderful scenery and amazing animals, birds and plant life. There are fields and gardens, mountains and jungles and some places that human beings haven't even discovered yet – and they were all made by the Lord God.

Think: Think about a beautiful bird and then think about how intricate it is. Look in the mirror – you may not think you look that stunning – but think for a minute about the eyes you are using to look at yourself. They are amazing. We see thousands of different images on a daily basis as well as being able to see things near and far. There are so many colours that our eyes can pick out. Can you honestly believe that these wonderful things were made by chance? Of course not – they were designed. Creation proves to us the existence of the Creator.

 Prayer: Lord Jesus, we know that you are our caring creator and that we have you to thank for our wonderful world. It is amazing that you, the all-powerful creator, came to earth as a tiny, helpless baby, and that you died on the cross to save your people from their sins. We worship you and praise you for this wonderful truth.

Ghillean Prance

Dunvegan Castle looked enormous from the small boat on the loch. Ghillean looked at its ramparts against the deep blue sky and smiled.

'What are you thinking about?' his mother asked, returning his smile.

Ghillean looked from the castle to the sparkling waters of the loch, and to the seals sunning themselves on a rock before he answered.

'I was thinking that this must be the best place in the world,' said the boy. 'There is so much to see and do.'

Mrs Prance, who was staying with her cousin at Dunvegan House, just along the loch from the great castle, agreed with her six-year-old son.

'And if this is the best place in the world, what would be the best thing you could do right now?' the woman asked.

Ghillean grinned. He didn't need to think about the answer to that question.

'I'd like you to sing a song to the seals that would make them come alongside.'

Very quietly Mrs Prance sang a Gaelic song, fitting the rhythm of the song to the slow movement of the oars. Two seals turned their heads in her direction and seemed to stop to think if they should be bothered moving. Then, as though the same thought entered both their minds, they lumbered into the water and swam towards the boat.

The boy watched entranced as they followed the boat, caught up in the beauty of his mother's song. The Gaelic air ended, and Mrs Prance laid down the oars.

'They are such waddlers on land,' she commented. 'But in the sea they are as agile as can be.'

'Keep singing or they'll go away,' Ghillean said. 'They've come to hear your song.'

Once again his mother started to sing, leaving the boat to drift in the sparkling waters.

Fear a' bhàta na hòro èile
Mo shoraidh slàn dhuit's gach
Àit' an teìd thu!

Suddenly there was only one seal near the boat. The other one had felt the need to dive for a snack.

'Where's he gone?' asked the lad.

'I don't know,' laughed his mother. 'But he'll have to come up for air soon.'

As though she was determined to join in the fun of the day, the seal swam under the boat and broke water on the other side.

'There she is!' Ghillean said. 'She's playing tricks on us.'

Just along the shore from the jetty was one of the boy's favourite places. There was a shallow shingle beach bordering on the road. And it looked as though an artist had splashed pink, white and yellow all along the roadside.

'Spring is my favourite time of year,' commented Mrs Prance as they reached the shingle. 'The sea pink's flowers are like fairy lollipops.'

'What does the white campion look like?' Ghillean asked.

'I don't know,' laughed his mother. 'What do you think?'

The lad studied the white flowers before deciding they looked like the lacy mats on which his godmother served her home-made scones.

'And the yellow vetch,' said Mrs Prance, 'what do you think it looks like?'

As Ghillean studied the plant closely, his mother smiled at the pleasure her son found in nature.

'I think,' said Ghillean, 'that the flowers look like rabbits' faces with long ears, and the leaves are like zip fasteners...' He paused for effect. 'The curly tendrils look as though they're reaching out to catch me!'

'I think we should be heading back home for tea or Cousin Margaret will be reaching out to catch us both!' concluded his mother.

A year later the Prance family moved from Dunvegan on the Isle of Skye in Scotland to a lovely house surrounded by 50 acres of woodland in the English county of Gloucestershire. Ghillean and his sisters were happy there to start with. There was plenty of exploring to be done, trees to be climbed, and hide-and-seek just asking to be played. But their joy in their new surroundings was not to last. Mr Prance died in 1946, when Ghillean was just nine years old. His young heart was broken. When he felt a need to be alone, he took himself into the woodland and looked at the trees, birds, flowers and insects. It was easier for the boy to look outside of himself than to look into his sad heart.

'What are you doing today?' Mrs Prance asked some time later.

'I'm going to read my favourite book,' said Ghillean.

'Now, I wonder what that will be,' his mother smiled. 'May I guess?'

Her son grinned. He knew that she would never guess the amazing book he had discovered.

'Is it *Uncle Tom's Cabin*?'

Ghillean shook his head.

'Is it *Kidnapped*?'

'I knew you would never guess,' Ghillean laughed aloud. 'My favourite book is Gilbert White's *Natural History of Selborne*.'

Mrs Prance looked puzzled. 'I know the one,' she said. 'It's an old book that's been in the house as long as I can remember. Tell me about it.'

Ghillean ran to fetch the book, raced back to the sitting room where his mother had made herself comfortable on the settee, and crash-landed beside her.

'I take it you really do like this book when you are so keen to show me it,' Mum laughed.

Turning the pages slowly one by one, Ghillean showed his mother picture after picture of plants and birds, trees and insects.

'You see, Mum,' the boy said, 'this book is full of things I know about. The trees in our wood are here. There are drawings of the wild flowers, and descriptions of the birds too. When I found a beetle I'd not seen before, I looked it up and discovered what kind it was.'

Mrs Prance watched her son's enthusiasm and realised that he was expert beyond his years in the study of nature.

'Nature study is a lovely hobby,' she said. 'It's a hobby you'll be able to continue with whatever you do for a living.'

By the time Ghillean went to boarding school, aged twelve, his particular interest was in wild flowers. And, much to his surprise and delight, one of his masters was every bit as keen as he was. Mr Bill Wilson was so keen on botany (the study of plants) that he spent weekends, even some holidays, taking pupils on trips to find rare plants. Not only that, but Ghillean had several aunts, two of whom were keen botanists, who did all they could to encourage the boy in his interest. They also began to teach him about plant families, and they called plants by their Latin names rather than their English ones.

'How many names can one plant have?' the lad laughed, when he and his aunts were looking through a book together. 'Up in Dunvegan we called that plant sea pink, though I knew it was also called thrift. Now I've discovered that its botanical name is *Armeria maritimae*.'

As Ghillean climbed through his teenage years, his interest in plants became more than just a hobby. And, by the time he had to decide what to study at university, there was no decision to be taken. Ghillean Prance would go to Oxford and study botany.

'Would you like to come to a tea for new students?' a member of the Christian Union asked, within a few days of the beginning of term.

'Yes, thanks,' Ghillean answered.

The student who invited him seemed a nice sort, and going to university is a good time to make new friends and discover interesting, new things. Another invitation followed soon afterwards.

'Would you like to come to church next Sunday evening?'

Once again, Ghillean accepted. And at that Sunday service he heard a sermon like none he'd ever heard before. Three weeks later, the first year botany student became a Christian. Jesus was his Saviour and Friend.

Botany took on a whole new meaning. Not only was Ghillean learning new and wonderful things about plants, he was discovering more and more about the great Creator God who made every one of them. The young botanist looked with wonder through his microscope at the amazing detail God put into even the most insignificant of plants. Not only did Ghillean study botany, he also studied his Bible. To his delight, his two studies came together as he read verses like: 'Come and see what God has done, how awesome his works on man's behalf!' It seemed to him, as he looked at plants under the microscope, that he was discovering awesome works of creation, all made by God to benefit and delight mankind.

In July 1961, Ghillean married Anne, whom he had met at a beach mission a few months after he became a Christian. Several exciting field trips later, the Prances moved from England to America, where he began work with the New York Botanical Garden. Although he was based in New York, much of his time was spent on plant-hunting expeditions in the Amazon Basin, in Brazil.

'Even if we have to watch every penny we spend,' Anne said, after she'd been left alone in New York with their two daughters, while he was away on an expedition, 'we must go back as a family. It's lonely being left behind.'

That was why the Prance family moved to South America and made their home in Brazil.

'I've been asked to assist in the Amazonian Research Institute,' Ghillean explained some time later.

'What will that involve?' asked Anne.

'We're to set up a university course in Amazonian botany for Brazilian students.'

Anne didn't need to ask if her husband would like to do that ... Of course he would.

Ghillean invited one of his colleagues from New York to come and lecture to the students on ecology, the science of looking after the earth and all that lives and grows.

'I think we should take the students to see the Trans-Amazonian Highway,' one of the men suggested.

That was agreed, but no one could have guessed the outcome. The Trans-Amazonian Highway cut through hundreds of miles of rainforest ... and left utter devastation. Ghillean, Robert Goodland, and the students could hardly believe what they were seeing.

On their return, the two men wrote articles about what was happening, and they made such a fuss that people began to listen to what they were saying.

'What does it matter if a few miles of trees are hacked down?' some said.

But if they said it to Ghillean Prance, he told them exactly why it mattered. Land treated in that terrible way could never be the same again. People, animals, birds, trees, plants and insects, all were badly affected by the disastrous road project.

'And the thing is,' he would say, 'the plan to build villages along the highway for settlers from other parts of Brazil isn't even working. They don't know how to live there.'

The Indian peoples were of great interest to Ghillean Prance. And if anyone suggested that they were 'primitive', he was quick to correct them.

'I've learned more from my Indian friends about plants than from any of my Oxford University professors,' he insisted. 'They understand and care for the natural world in a way that we don't. And they treat it with a respect that planners and developers have long forgotten.'

In his years working in the Amazon Basin, Ghillean worked along with fourteen different tribes of Amazonian Indians, making good friends among them and learning new things from them.

In 1987, the Director of Kew Gardens near London retired. The Royal Botanic Gardens, Kew, are the best-known gardens in the whole world.

'Would you consider applying for the job?' six different people asked Ghillean, all in the space of seven days!

He did apply. But a week before he flew to England for his interview, a hurricane hit Kew, a hurricane so severe that it destroyed over a thousand trees. Ghillean wondered if there was anything left of the great gardens at all. There was. Although 1,000 trees came down, over 9,000 still stood tall and strong. The interview went well, and Ghillean Prance became Director of the Royal Botanic Gardens. The Prance family said goodbye to Brazil, to New York, and headed east across the Atlantic Ocean to England.

'Does that remind you of Brazil?' someone asked Anne one day, as they stood beside the giant water lily *Victoria amazonica* in Kew.

Anne smiled. 'Yes, it does. And let me tell you about it. My husband would spend all night in revolting, smelly, still waters studying the lily, and in the mornings he brought me two things. One was a disgusting bag of smelly clothes to be washed, and the other was a sack of water lily flowers. I had to cut each in half and count the number of beetles I found there.'

'I didn't know you were interested in insects,' her companion laughed.

'I'm not. But I did become something of an expert beetle-catcher!'

'Could you sum up your personal vision for Kew in just a few words?' asked a journalist, who was writing an article about the new director.

'Yes,' said Ghillean, 'I think I can. My vision for the Royal Botanic Gardens, Kew, is that they lead the world in thinking about conservation. We are facing a most serious environmental crisis, and we must do all in our power to prevent it. The earth belongs to the Lord; he made it. Our job is to look after it for him.'

The journalist glanced up from his notes.

'Do you really believe God made the earth?' he asked.

Ghillean smiled, 'I do,' he said. 'I most certainly do.'

FACT FILE
The Amazon:
The Amazon rain forests are being destroyed at near record levels. 8,000,000 hectares of rain forest are being destroyed every year. The figure is the second highest on record, 6 per cent higher than the previous twelve months. Deforestation was worst in the state of Mato Grosso where vast swathes of land have been cleared to grow crops.

Keynote: It is important to remember that God has given us his creation to look after and not to squander and destroy. He has given us resources to use and make use of, but these are not to be used without thought or used in a selfish and greedy way. In the book of Genesis, Adam and Eve are given the task of looking after the Garden of Eden. It is sad to see how sin has indeed destroyed so much of God's creation. The destructive effect that humanity has had on the land and living creatures is just one part of that.

Think: Can you think of some ways that you can look after the plants and animals in your world? You can feed birds in the winter months and help keep your environment clean by tidying away rubbish in bins. But you should also consider recycling. Try and reuse paper and then put it into a recycling bin. Do you leave the tap running when you brush your teeth? Do you leave the lights on in the house when you don't need to? These are just little things but they all contribute towards helping to look after the world that God has given us.

Prayer: Dear Lord, thank you for the world that you have given us. Thank you for water and food that we need for daily life. Thank you for the colours and the beauty that we see all around us. We know that you care for your creation, as your Word tells us that not even a sparrow falls to the ground without your knowledge. Your love for sinners meant that you sent your son to die for them on the cross. We thank you for that and ask that you will help us to tell others about you, about your love for people and the world.

Paul Brand

'I have to go out for a while,' Mrs Brand told her young son. 'You look after Connie.'

Paul's eyes opened wide. It was dark, and he wasn't at all sure about being left.

'You won't really be alone,' said his mother. 'God will look after you. But he needs you to help look after your little sister.'

Paul was four years old, and Connie two years younger. As he lay awake, the boy thought about things.

'I wonder if Mum will be able to help whoever is sick. She's very clever, my mum.'

He smiled as he thought of the times his mother was called to help sick people in their own village or one of the other communities in the Tamil Nadu, and of how often her patients got better.

'You all right?' asked Mrs Brand, when she returned in the fragile light of early morning.

'Yes,' Paul said. 'God was with us, and Connie's still asleep.'

'Mum, are you a real doctor?' Paul asked the following morning, as she cleaned a cut on his knee.

Mrs Brand smiled. 'No,' she explained. 'I'm not a real doctor. I've not done full medical training. But the people I treat are real patients. God kindly allows me to help them.'

'Is Dad a real doctor?'

Mrs Brand smiled. 'I'm sorry to disappoint you,' she said. 'Dad's not a real doctor either. Come, let me explain.'

Sitting outside their little home on stilts in the village of Kollimalai, high in the mountains of South West India, Mrs Brand told her children how it came about that they were growing up there.

'Dad and I both felt that God was leading us to come here to serve the people and to tell them about the Lord Jesus Christ. That's why we left England for India. And in order to be of help to the people here, both of us did a course in tropical medicine. You see, many of the diseases here are different from those in England, which means that our training in tropical medicine was very helpful. But, of course, there are things that we don't know about that real doctors understand.'

Paul, a very intelligent little boy, was full of questions.

'What diseases do people in England not have that we have here?'

'Well,' his mum said, 'they don't have bubonic plague, blackwater fever or malaria. Cholera is very rare in England now, though it was a real problem till the end of last century.'

'What about influenza?' the child asked, remembering what had happened a few months before in a village near Kollimalai.

'Yes, they do have influenza, and sometimes people die of it.'

Mrs Brand's face looked suddenly sad. 'Do you remember when influenza hit the mountain village above us last year?'

Paul nodded.

'Every single person in the village died,' she said. 'Not one survived. Back in Britain, when influenza strikes, some people die but never a whole town or village.'

'Why does it happen here then?' the lad asked.

'I suppose it's mainly because the people here are poor and underfed and not really strong enough to fight against diseases.'

Paul smiled, much to his mother's surprise, as it seemed a sad topic to smile about.

'I think you know just as much as a real doctor,' he said. 'And I think Dad does too.'

It was ten days later, and there was great excitement in the village of Kollimalai, especially in the Brand home.

'Dad should be home today,' Paul told his sister.

The very word 'Dad' made the little girl smile. She saw him first. 'Dad! Dad!' she yelled in the local language.

Mr Brand was no sooner home than people crowded round to see him, including a man who had just arrived in the village with a bundle of rags. Pushing past the local villagers, the man handed the bundle to the missionary. It was Connie who first yelled 'Baby', for it was she who noticed the tiny hand sticking out of the bundle.

'What do we have here?' asked Mr Brand gently.

He was told that the baby's mother was ill and that it seemed the baby was dying.

The baby was undressed from its hot wrappings, then washed and had his poor sticky eyes cleaned. He was fed tiny drops of boiled, cooled water and wiped with a clean, damp cloth over and over again to bring down his temperature.

'Look, Dad,' said Paul, who was most interested in what was going on. 'The baby's eyes are opening. Can I do anything to help him?'

'Yes, you can,' said Mr Brand. 'You can do two things. You can sit beside him and pray for him – with your eyes open – because I want you to tell me if he sicks up any of that water.'

Paul did exactly as he was told. The lad would have been very surprised if anyone had told him so, but that afternoon he was doing exactly what his parents went to India to do – he was caring for the bodies and the souls of the people of the Tamil Nadu.

The Brand children were a year or two older when they saw something that remained with Paul for the rest of his life. Three strangers came slowly up the mountain one day looking for Mr Brand. The missionary always welcomed people whoever they were, but Paul was aware that these people received a different kind of welcome from usual.

'What's Dad doing?' the boy wondered, as he watched.

Then he screwed up his face. The three strangers had white patches on their dark skin, and it looked as though the ends of their fingers had fallen off.

'Look at their feet!' he exclaimed. 'No wonder they can't walk properly.'

The men had hardly any toes at all.

Paul watched, fascinated by the horror of what he was seeing and at his father's unusual response.

'Why's Dad putting on gloves?' he wondered.

Mr Brand took a basin of water and washed the poor, deformed feet, then rubbed ointment on to them. At one and the same time his son tried to see what was going on and tried not to look because it wasn't very nice at all.

'Here comes Mum to give them a basket of food,' Paul told Connie. 'But she can't like the look of them either because she's not going near.'

Having had their feet dressed in strips of cloth, the men hobbled off, taking the food with them.

'I'll go and take the basket to Mum,' said Paul, trying to be helpful.

'No!' Mrs Brand's voice rang out, when she saw what he was about to do. 'Don't touch that!'

The boy felt confused at his mother's response, and very much more confused when he saw her lifting the basket with a stick and putting it on the fire to burn! Meanwhile, Mr Brand scrubbed his hands in hot water and with strong soap, took off his clothes, scrubbed again then dressed in clean clothes. Only after all of that were Mr and Mrs Brand able to relax and explain what the problem was.

'These men have leprosy,' Mr Brand told the children.

Paul shivered. He'd read about people with leprosy in the Bible, and knew that no one went near them apart from Jesus who made some of them better. That night, as he lay in bed with his mosquito net tucked firmly under his mattress, he thought of his parents, and of how kind and brave they were as they tried to be like Jesus.

Not long after that, the family went home to England for a while. Paul and Connie remained there to go to school when their parents went back to India. Every day, Mr and Mrs Brand wrote part of a letter to their children. When it was long enough, they posted it to the two young folk they loved most in the world. Sadly, in 1929, Mr Brand died before his children could see him again. He died of blackwater fever, one of the diseases that exist in India but not in Britain.

When Paul left school, he didn't think he wanted to be a doctor, but some years later God showed him that that was exactly what he should do with his life. By 1940, the Second World War was raging, and Paul had plenty to keep him busy.

'There's been a huge bombing raid tonight,' he was told. 'Everyone to Accident and Emergency.'

'What damage glass can do,' Paul thought, as he picked tiny shards out of a little boy's face and arms. Then he began work on his hands.

'Poor lad,' he said, 'he's obviously put his hands up to shield his face. Look at the mess they're in.'

It took ages to pick the glass out of the lad's hands, and that gave Paul time to think.

'You know,' he told a friend afterwards, 'hands are absolutely beautifully made.'

Paul Brand married Margaret in 1943, and God led them to live in India and to bring up their family there. He also used Paul's previous experiences to do very wonderful things. Having seen leprosy as a boy, he now saw it through the eyes of a very fine surgeon.

'What's your name and what age are you?' Paul asked a new patient who came to his clinic in 1951.

'Sadagopan,' the boy said. 'And I'm eight.'

'Tell me what's happened to you.'

'I can't feel anything with my fingers,' said Sadagopan. 'And I have white patches on my body and ulcers on my feet.'

'Are they sore?'

'No,' the lad said. 'I couldn't walk on them if they were sore.'

'How did you get here?' Paul asked.

'I was told you could help me so I walked for days to get here.'

The doctor looked at Sadagopan's feet and could see the terrible damage that walking to the hospital in Vellore had caused.

Paul Brand put an arm around the boy and took hold of his damaged hands. Sadagopan was shocked and speechless. The doctor had touched him! That night the weary boy slept peacefully, smiling occasionally in his sleep.

'Sadagopan,' Paul said. 'I want to explain what I can do for you.'

The lad, who by then loved Dr Brand very much indeed, listened carefully.

'I'll put you to sleep, then operate on your hands. I can cut them open with special instruments and work right inside them.'

'That won't make them better,' said Sadagopan quietly, 'it will be very sore.'

'I think I can help you to use what's left of your hands,' said Paul. 'And I think I can help you to prevent more damage to your feet.'

The boy looked utterly disbelieving.

'And you won't feel anything at all during the operation, but there will be times when you'll be sore as you get better. You would have to be very courageous.'

Sadagopan, brave boy that he was, agreed to let Paul do what he could for him.

The surgeon operated several times on his patient's damaged hands and was able to give him useful movement again. Paul also had special shoes made for Sadagopan. They didn't rub and cause more damage, and helped the boy to walk without hurting his feet.

'Look at Sadagopan,' a nurse said some months after he'd arrived at Vellore Christian Hospital. 'He looks a different boy.'

'In what way?' asked a stranger, who'd not seen the lad before.

The nurse explained. 'When Sadagopan came here, the only life he could expect was that of a beggar, and he knew it. He was just a sad scrap of humanity.'

'Really?' gasped the stranger, looking at the boy weaving a basket and laughing at a joke as he wove.

Sadagopan was just one boy whose life was completely changed by what Dr Brand was able to do for him. To Sadagopan it seemed like a miracle, and that is how very many people have felt in the years since Paul began his pioneering surgery.

'When I think back to Dad's treatment of leprosy,' Paul told a friend one day, 'I realise how much things have changed. Then nothing could be done apart from applying cream to the ulcers. And people were scared to do even that, in case they caught the disease themselves. At least Dad did what he could.'

'So what made the difference?' his friend asked.

'I suppose it was the realisation that it wasn't the disease that damaged hands and feet, but that people did it themselves because the disease made them lose feeling. As they didn't feel pain, they could stand on burning embers, or a snake, and not feel the injury. And because they didn't feel the injury, they didn't know to treat it, and their situation just went from bad to worse.'

What Paul Brand didn't tell his friend was that it was he who convinced doctors that was the case.

'You see,' Paul said, 'God designed the human body so that it is able to survive because of pain. Pain is the body's warning system to tell us that something is wrong and we should do something about it.'

Margaret Brand, who was also a medical missionary, worked on the prevention of blindness in those who suffered from leprosy. After doing over 3,000 operations in the hospital at Vellore, Paul and Margaret moved to America in 1966, where he worked on rehabilitation. Rehabilitation is helping people to make the very best of anything they are able to do: helping ill or injured people to walk, to use their hands, to work ... to live.

In the summer of 2003, Dr Paul Brand died and went to heaven. There he was welcomed by Jesus, who himself reached out and touched and healed those suffering from leprosy.

FACT FILE
Leprosy:
Leprosy is a medical condition, also known as Hansen's Disease, after Armauer Hansen, a Norwegian doctor who was the first to view the leprosy microbe under a microscope in 1873. It is neither hereditary nor flesh-eating. Many think that it is a disease of the past, but leprosy still affects hundreds of thousands of people around the world. Most leprosy cases arise in Asia, South America and Africa. In 2017, 210,671 new cases were diagnosed - that's 577 new cases each day, about one every two minutes.

Keynote: There are many diseases and illnesses that are difficult to cure, and there are still many that are incurable. When Jesus was on this earth, leprosy was an incurable disease and people didn't know anything about it. If you had the disease, you were forced to leave home and people wouldn't even come near you. But one day Jesus healed ten lepers from their disease. Can you imagine how these men must have felt? But only one of them came back to thank him. Make sure that you follow that man's example and thank God for your health.

Think: Even when we are sick, God is still with us. We can pray for a cure, but this may not be something that we will receive. God's answers to our prayers can be 'Yes', 'No' or 'Wait'. When we are suffering, we can pray to God to help us. He can give us the strength to carry on – even though we are ill, even though we may never get better.

Prayer: Lord Jesus, thank you for your love and mercy. Thank you for how you showed this love to all people – sick and healthy. Help us to show your love to others. Help us to be loving and caring to people in hospital and old folks' homes. Help us to be welcoming to boys and girls from other countries and to show friendship to people who are lonely and afraid.

Johann Sebastian Bach

'Let's play hide-and-seek,' said Johann Sebastian to a friend. 'This house is great for it!'

So, while Johann ran to hide, the young boy began the long count to fifty.

'Will I hide in the grain store or in one of the students' rooms?' wondered Johann Sebastian. 'No, I know, I'll hide in Dad's music room.'

Tiptoeing along the corridor, Johann reached the music room and crept in. Looking around, he made up his mind where to hide.

'I'll lie down here behind the harpsichord. And if I pull this rug over myself and put Dad's trumpet on top, he'll never find me.'

'Forty-nine, fifty!' yelled Johann's friend. 'And here I come!'

Footsteps were heard running upstairs to where the students lived, downstairs to the grain store and along to the sunny room in which the family played music together. But Johann could not be found anywhere.

'He wouldn't dare go into his father's music room,' thought the boy. 'He'd be skinned alive if he damaged anything there.'

But, having failed to find his friend, the boy opened the music room door and waited – a little scared to go in.

'Aaaa ... tishoo!' exploded from under the rug behind the harpsichord. And as it did, a trumpet crashed to the ground.

'Caught you!' yelled the boy. 'But I'm off before your dad comes to see what the noise is.'

Music was everywhere in the Bach home, in the German town of Eisenach. Herr Bach, Johann Sebastian's father, was court trumpeter to the Duke of Eisenach, and he taught music students. Some even stayed in their home. The Bach family were famous for music. Johann Sebastian, who was only seven years old, already had his own little violin, and he was learning to play the harpsichord.

'Your uncle would like to teach you to play the organ too,' Herr Bach said, when his son had finished his violin practice. 'Would you like that?'

The boy thought of the magnificent music his uncle played in the St Georgenkirche in Eisenach, and said 'yes' right away.

'I'm starting at the Latin Grammar School next term,' Johann Sebastian told his friend the following year, 1693.

'You'll only study the Bible there,' the lad laughed. 'They are so proud that Martin Luther used to be a pupil, they're not interested in anything else.'

Everyone in Eisenach knew about Martin Luther. In the early 16th century he had studied the Bible and discovered that the church was teaching very wrong things. He'd also taught Bible truths in a day when people were burned at the stake for doing so. Luther was not martyred for his faith, but the Pope had many of his books burned as a warning to others. That period of church history is called the Reformation, and Martin Luther was one of the most famous Reformers.

'Of course they study other things,' laughed Johann. 'We study Latin at least, because it's called the Latin Grammar School.'

The boys from the school made up the choir of the St. Georgenkirche, and before long Johann was a member.

'The music makes my skin tingle,' he thought. 'God must enjoy listening to it.'

Johann's skin tingled especially when he sang solo. As the notes soared higher, he felt he was reaching up to God himself.

'Have you heard the news?' the boys at school asked each other just a few months later. 'Johann Sebastian's mother has died.'

'Imagine losing your mother when you're nine,' one friend said sadly. 'Who would look after you?'

'I suppose Herr Bach will look after him, and his servants will always be there to help,' someone answered. 'But it must be horrible.'

Before a year had passed, the same group of boys were standing outside the school before classes began.

'It's terrible news about Johann's father dying. I wonder what will happen to him now.'

'That means he's an orphan. But I suppose he'll go to stay with one of his big brothers.'

'We'll miss him. But I won't miss the arguments we have. The annoying thing is that most of the arguments are about music, and he's usually right!'

Johann Sebastian went to live with his brother, Johann Christoph, and his wife in Ohrdruf. There were fourteen years between Johann and his older brother.

'I'm glad you're able to teach me music,' the young boy told his brother. 'You're a great teacher.'

'The Bachs are all great teachers,' Johann Christoph smiled. 'And they are all great pupils, you included. I hope you'll be as good a pupil at your new school.'

The boy did work hard at the Ohrdruf Grammar School, studying theology, Latin and Greek. Of course, much of Johann Sebastian's time was taken up with his music.

'It's very good for young musicians to copy what the old masters wrote,' Johann

Christoph told his brother. 'For tomorrow I'd like you to copy out this page by Jakob Froberger. Do it so carefully that you'll be able to play from it.'

Copying music became rather a hobby for Johann Sebastian, because he could hear the music in his head as he wrote.

'May I copy this piece?' he asked one day. 'It's new music, and I really like it.'

'No,' his brother said firmly. 'I want you to stick to the old masters.'

But Johann really did like that piece of modern music. So he went to the music room late at night and copied it by moonlight. It took him six whole months. Was his brother pleased with his enthusiasm? He most certainly was not!

'I like Martin Luther's hymns,' said Johann Sebastian. 'He says what I believe. The words make me want to write music for them.'

'Do that then,' he was told. 'See if you can write music to fit these words, though Martin Luther wrote his own tune for this hymn.'

The boy read the words aloud.

> *'Glory to God in highest heaven,*
> *Who unto man his Son has given!*
> *While angels sing with pious mirth*
> *A glad New Year to all the earth.'*

Sitting at the organ he played Luther's tune, then made an arrangement of his own. Before he laid his pen down, Johann Sebastian wrote across the bottom of the manuscript paper the words, 'To the glory of God.' Young though he was, he wanted his music to praise his Lord in heaven.

'Are you serious?' a friend asked one day, when Johann suggested that they walk to Lüneburg to hear the great organist Dietrich Buxtehude. 'Do you know how far that is?'

'It's a mere eighty miles or so,' laughed Johann Sebastian.

'And a mere eighty miles or so back, making it a mere 160 miles round trip!' his friend said. 'That's serious walking.'

The pair of them did go, and all to hear someone play the organ wonderfully well. Bach was just fifteen years old at the time.

Over the years that followed, the young man worked as a professional musician in various parts of his homeland. Bach lived in Lüneburg and then in Weimar before moving on to Arnstadt in 1703, where he began to focus on the organ.

'The Arnstadt organ is splendid,' he wrote to one of his brothers. 'It has two manuals and twenty-three speaking stops. And I love being responsible for the congregation's music.'

Three years later, his letters were less enthusiastic. 'The choirboys are awful! They shuffle about and don't learn their parts. One even spoke back to me the other day. And, would you believe it, some of the people in the congregation don't like my musical arrangements. They say they are "too ornamental!" The truth is that they just don't want to understand them.'

Not surprisingly, Johann Sebastian applied for another job and moved to Mühlhausen in 1707. While he was there, he married another Bach, his cousin Maria Barbara. In those days, professional musicians moved from place to place. They sometimes served as church musicians or worked for grand families who had their own musicians. Once, an employer put Bach in prison for a month to prevent him moving to another job. For five years Johann Sebastian worked for Prince Leopold of Anhalt-Cöthen, who had an orchestra of eighteen players. Bach was his Capellmeister[*1], the highest rank of musician at that time.

'I can't take it in,' Johann Sebastian said in a trembling voice. 'When I went away with the Prince and the orchestra, I left behind a dear wife and a happy family. Now you're telling me that Maria Barbara is dead, that my children are motherless.'

He sat down heavily. It was as though the last forty-three years had rolled away and he

---

1. Capellmeister: The director of an orchestra or choir, formerly belonging to a German prince.

had once again just lost his mother. He knew exactly how his children felt.

'Come,' he said to them later that evening, 'let's make music together.'

The family took their instruments, as they had done so often in the past, and played music that allowed them to feel all the sadness of those who had lost someone they loved.

'Your mother is with the Lord,' Johann Sebastian told his children. 'She is with Jesus, where she will be happier than ever.'

'But she was happy here,' said his youngest son.

Bach smiled at his memories. 'Yes,' he said. 'She was. We had a very happy family life.'

There were to be happy days again in the future, for Johann Sebastian married again, and their new stepmother, Anna Magdalena, brought laughter back into their lives.

'Tell us about Leipzig,' Bach's children asked, before they moved there.

'Well, it's the second most important city in Saxony, with about 30,000 people living there. It's a very beautiful city and very forward-thinking. You'll never guess what you'll see there?'

No one could guess.

'The streets of Leipzig are lit up at nights,' their father told them. 'And another wonder in Leipzig is the great, new library that has just opened.'

'I think street lights are more wonderful than that,' his daughter laughed.

At the end of May 1723, a North German newspaper carried an interesting account of the Bachs' removal. 'Last Saturday at noon, four carts laden with goods and chattels belonging to the former Capellmeister to the Court of Cöthen arrived in Leipzig, and, at two in the afternoon, he and his family arrived in two coaches and moved into their newly decorated lodgings in the school building.' The family that travelled in those coaches were Johann Sebastian, his wife, and four children, aged 8, 9, 12 and 14. The great musician and composer's new job was as Director of Choir and Music in Leipzig.

'What a huge amount of music the Director has written,' one choirboy said. 'Most of it from the Bible.'

'I know,' his friend agreed. 'I was studying the Bible for school the other day, and when I turned the page, I realised I knew it already because I'd sung it in one of his cantatas.'

'That's a nice easy way of doing your homework,' Johann Sebastian laughed.

'I'm sorry, Sir,' the boy blushed. 'I didn't know you were there.'

The Director of Music smiled at his pupil. 'Don't worry. It's my hope and prayer that my music leads people to think about the Lord. Although it never occurred to me that it could help you young scamps with your homework.'

That afternoon, as Bach completed work on a new piece of music, he stopped before putting his pen down. Then he wrote at the bottom, 'This work is written to the glory of Almighty God.'

'It's not always easy finding boys to sing in the four churches here in Leipzig,' he said to his wife that evening, after he told her the homework story. 'I have fifty-four boys to choose from. Of them seventeen are good, twenty are getting there, and the other seventeen can't sing the music.'

'But remember they're learning about the Lord as they practise,' Anna Magdalena said.

'True. I'll try to remember that, especially when I'm working with the seventeen who can't sing the music. Perhaps that will help me to be more patient with them.'

'I'm really tired,' said Johann Sebastian in 1747. 'It's a privilege to be invited to play for King Fredrick the Great of Prussia, but I think I'm getting too old for travelling.'

'The concert will begin soon,' he was told when he arrived. 'You are just in time.'

'Your visitor is here, your Majesty,' announced a courtier.

The king's eyes lit up. 'Old Bach is here,' he said.

The concert was cancelled, and King Fredrick and the great composer spent the evening together. The king was especially delighted because Johann Sebastian composed a fugue based on a simple tune Fredrick himself had written.

'Blindness is a great trial,' Bach said, less than two years later. 'And the two operations haven't helped at all.'

'If you tell me what to write, I'll take down your music. You can still play it because you know it in your head and heart. It just needs to be written down for other people,' Anna Magdalena said.

It was to his wife that he dictated the notes of his very last composition, a piece of choir music with title, 'Before thy throne I now appear.'

Shortly afterwards the great Johann Sebastian Bach, aged 65, died and appeared before the throne of his God in heaven.

FACT FILE
The Reformation: Bach's ancestors showed a great loyalty to the Reformation and to the teachings of Martin Luther. At some point prior to 1597, a baker named Veit Bach left Hungary for Germany. This was in order to protect his Protestant faith against the increasing persecution in Hungary. Veit established himself once again as a baker, and, from then on, future generations of the Bach family became great musicians, the greatest, of course, being Johann Sebastian Bach.

Key note: The Bible today is written in many different languages, but originally it was written in Hebrew and Greek. If you look at a copy of a Latin Bible, Romans 16:27 and Jude 25 have the words 'Soli Deo Gloria'—'to the only God be glory.' This was to become Bach's motto. He would sign all his works with the initials SDG. It didn't matter if they were deep theological works or light-hearted ones – they were all written to the glory of God.

Think: Is there a difference between doing work in a church and doing work somewhere such as a hospital, shop or sports hall? Is one job better than another? Is one job holier and more virtuous than the other? In the Bible, God tells us that we are to do everything as if we were doing it for God. And we are to do it with all our might.

Prayer: Thank you, Lord, for work and employment. Thank you for learning, teachers and books. Help me to appreciate the gift of education, when so many children do not have it. Help me to do all that I can for your glory. You are the one who gives me strength and intelligence. I thank you for providing for me in so many ways. Help me to trust in you, even when it seems that life is a struggle, times are hard and money scarce.

Samuel Morse

At four years old, Samuel Morse was already at school. Usually, when school ended for the afternoon, he raced home and forgot all about it, but not today.

'Did you have a good day at school?' his father asked.

Papa was a minister in Charlestown, Massachusetts, and he was very interested in his son's education.

Samuel held his head low.

'Something wrong?' Papa asked.

The boy nodded his head.

'Do you want to come into my study to talk?'

His father's study was where serious things were talked about. Samuel thought for a minute and then went with his Papa into the study. Jedidiah Morse sat down on one side of the fire and told his son to sit on the other. Samuel perched himself on the edge of his chair and swung his legs, for they didn't quite reach the ground.

'Tell me about it,' said Papa, then he sat and waited till his young son was ready to talk.

'On my way to school this morning, I found a pin on the road,' Samuel began, looking straight into his father's eyes. He had been taught to be open and truthful. 'I pinned it on my shirt to play with later. Then, when Old Ma'am Rand was working with the other boys, I remembered about the pin. I was so bored.'

Mr Morse would normally have reminded Samuel not to call his teacher old, and that clever children should never be bored ... but he let it go. There was obviously something else coming.

'As she wasn't watching me, I decided to do a drawing of her ... on the chest of drawers ... with my pin. It was a very good drawing, very like her.'

'Go on,' said Papa, seriously.

'You know Ma'am Rand is disabled and can't chase us. Well, when she saw me, she told me to go to her desk. I thought she was going to beat me with the cane. But ....'

'But what?' Papa asked, after a long silence.

Samuel looked into his father's eyes once more.

'She pinned me to her dress so that I would have to stay there right beside her all day. I couldn't do that, Papa,' he said, his eyes beginning to fill with tears. 'So I pulled myself away … and it only made a little rip in her dress. She laid into me with her cane and hit me here,' he concluded, rubbing his shoulder.

There was some serious talking done in the study that afternoon, and some praying, before Samuel Morse and his father went to join the rest of the family for dinner.

It was the year 1795, and Samuel Morse paid the price of being a talented artist.

Samuel was thirteen years old when he decided to keep a diary.

'What will I write in it?' he wondered. 'I want it to be special.'

The teenager spent some time thinking about it and then made a list of things he would record.

'I'll write about what happens at home and school, local news, the books I read and the weather. I'll put some drawings in too. Then, when I'm old, I'll read it and see how much I remember about being young. Perhaps one day I'll have a son, and he can read it too and discover what his father was like as a boy.'

As he sat back and wondered how to begin, he laughed out loud.

'I'd better watch my spelling,' he said to himself. 'When I was at Phillips Academy in Andover, my school report gave me five bad marks for spelling … and another eighteen for whispering. At least I can't spoil my nice new diary by whispering to it.'

The three Morse boys had a happy childhood in a fine Christian home. They had freedom to play wild and adventurous games, though they had to do their lessons first. But there was sadness too. Over the years, a further seven children were born, either dead or so sickly that they died as young babies.

'I now write to you again to inform you that Mama had a baby, but it was born dead and has just been buried,' Samuel wrote to his brothers. 'You now have three brothers and three sisters in heaven, and I hope you and I will meet them there at our death.'

Samuel knew a great deal about life and death, even though he was just fourteen years old, and he trusted in the Lord Jesus that he would go to heaven when he died.

'Why must I go to Yale College?' Samuel asked his father. 'That's not where my friends are going.'

'I know,' Mr Morse agreed. 'But you'll get the best education. What's taught there is based on the best book of all, the Bible.'

'Then it must be good,' the boy agreed. 'And I suppose I'll make new friends when I get there.'

Samuel was still fourteen when he began his studies at Yale College, and he did make friends very quickly, even with some of the members of staff.

'Science is fascinating,' Samuel wrote to a friend in Charlestown. 'My professor says that Christians should not be afraid of studying science as they are studying God's wonderful world. When I see you, I'll tell you what happened in science class the other day.'

When they did meet, Samuel's friend could hardly believe what he heard.

'Professor Day made us stand in a circle holding hands,' the boy remembered. 'The idea was that an electrical current would pass round the circle, going right through each one of us.'

His friend's eyebrows rose.

'Well, he joined us up to a generator ... and switched it on. Immediately, every one of us left the ground amid cries and screams that could be heard all though the College! We were pretty shaken when Professor Day switched off the generator. I don't know what we were meant to learn from the experiment, but I learned something I'll never forget.'

'What's that?' asked his friend.

Samuel laughed. 'Electricity is a powerful force ... for it forced us all off the ground!'

'Papa, I know you don't think I'm good enough,' Samuel said, when they were discussing his future, 'but I really do want to be an artist.'

'It's not that I don't think you're good,' admitted Mr Morse. 'You are. You wouldn't be able to sell your portraits if you were not. It's just that I don't think you realise how hard it is to be a successful artist. Many try it, but few succeed. If you had a nice steady job like a bookseller, you could paint in your free time. Art's a wonderful hobby, you know.'

Samuel despaired of convincing his father, but his Heavenly Father understood. The teenager prayed that God would show him what to do with his life. Meanwhile, he did what his father suggested. For a while after leaving Yale, he worked as a bookseller, spending most of his free time painting.

'You know,' Mr Morse said to his wife after a while, 'I wonder if we are being fair to Samuel. He's so keen to paint, and he does seem to be very talented.'

'But we can't afford to train him,' his wife objected. 'On your minister's salary it's hard making ends meet as it is.'

'God will open the way if that's what he wants,' the minister said. 'And the more I pray about it, the more I feel that is what he wants the lad to do.'

Mr and Mrs Morse searched for every saving they could make and sent their gifted son to London to study art.

'That's very bad, Sir,' Morse's art teacher in London said, shaking his head. 'The skin looks the colour of mud.'

Samuel looked at the painting – one he was pleased with - and saw it through his teacher's eyes.

'Here, let me show you,' Mr Allston said.

Wiping part of Morse's palette clean, and using fresh paint, Mr Allston demonstrated to his pupil how to create a good flesh colour. Although Mr Allston rarely paid Samuel a compliment, he taught him a very great deal. His young student became a great artist.

War broke out in 1812. It sometimes took Samuel's letters a long time to reach home.

'I'm glad that we know he's a Christian,' Mrs Morse said, 'for he's safe in God's hands.'

'Yes,' agreed her husband, 'the famous Mr William Wilberforce seems to have made a huge impression on our boy. Parents have no greater joy than knowing that their children are trusting in the Lord Jesus, and that they're among God's people.'

They were quite right. Samuel took his faith seriously. He kept a diary and each day answered these questions: How did I pray? Did I feel weighed down with sin? Did I pray like the self-righteous Pharisee? Have I received blessings for which I've not been thankful?

Three years later, Samuel returned to America and married Lucretia Walker, but, after just seven years of marriage, his young wife died. Samuel, who was away painting at the time, did not know about her death for some days. When he returned home, it was to discover that his children had no mother.

'I wish there was a way to get a message from one place to another,' he thought sadly. 'It's terrible not to know when your family needs you.'

Samuel was so sad that he nearly gave up painting. He had always been interested in making things, even inventing a machine that could cut three-dimensional marble copies of sculptures. For the middle years of his life, Samuel Morse travelled in America and Europe painting, though inventing was never far from his mind.

'I want to paint historical pictures,' he said to himself, 'but the only way I can earn enough money is to paint portraits. Not my favourite subject. Why are people willing to pay to see their own faces on a wall, when they can see them perfectly well in a mirror?'

The artist laughed out loud. 'It's just as well they do,' he thought, 'or I'd go hungry.'

In 1832, Samuel Morse was sailing to New York, where he'd been appointed as a professor of painting and sculpture.

'What are these men saying?' he asked, when he overheard a discussion. Moving closer to the men who were talking, he listened. They were having a discussion about electricity.

'Can electricity only be conducted through a short length of wire?' Morse asked, after he'd joined the group.

'No, not at all,' Charles Jackson answered. 'It can pass through any known length of wire.'

'If that's the case,' he said, 'then why can't information be transmitted by electricity.'

That night, as Samuel Morse tried to fall asleep in his cabin on the packet-ship[2] *Sully*, his mind went back to his young wife's death. 'If the family had been able to get in touch with me, I could have been with Lucretia when her dear heart failed.'

From then on, Morse concentrated on inventing the electric telegraph rather than painting. He found someone to fund his research and a congressman to advise him.

'If a message can go ten miles without stopping, I can make it go round the world,' he said, and that's what he set out to do.

'You think a message from that contraption can go round the world?' a visitor laughed.

Morse looked at the first telegraph model. It was made of such odds and ends as an artist's canvas stretcher, the wheels of a wooden clock and a length of carpeting.

---

2. Packet-ship: a ship that regularly carried packets of letters, passengers etc. between ports.

'I do,' Samuel said, 'or one based on the same idea.'

In September 1837, an updated model transmitted a message in code through 1,700 feet of wire running back and forward across a room.

'It's the beginning,' Samuel said. 'One day it will cross the world.'

At first, each letter of the alphabet was represented by a number. The person receiving a message had to count the number of taps to decide what letter was being relayed.

'There must be a simpler way than that,' Samuel thought, his notebook in his hand, as usual.

Scribbling possible codes, one after the other, he sat back and looked at the sheet.

'Dots and dashes,' he said. 'That would work. Each letter could have a simple combination of dots and dashes, and that could be passed along as short and long bursts of electricity in the telegraph. Now, how do I work out the code? The most common letters should have the shortest codes, and the least common should have longer ones. Each number could have a dot/dash code too!'

On 24th May, 1844, after many ups and downs (mostly downs for financial reasons), a cable was laid from the city of Baltimore to the Supreme Court Chamber in the Capitol Building in New York. Everyone in the Chamber held their breath, wondering if the whole thing was a waste of time. Morse tapped out a series of dots and dashes that transmitted all the way to Baltimore. There was silence in the great Chamber, but not for long. An identical series of dots and dashes arrived back and was printed out on a paper ribbon, in order that those gathered in the Supreme Court Chamber could see for themselves. And the message? It was from the Bible. 'What hath God wrought!' or, to put it in modern words, 'What a wonderful thing God has done!'

'It's God's work,' Samuel Morse said. 'He alone could have carried me through all my trials and enabled me to triumph over all the obstacles.'

And, in 1872, God carried him home to heaven.

FACT FILE
Uses of Morse Code: Morse code can be used to help severely disabled people communicate. If they have a minimal control of movement, they can use Morse code while blowing and sucking on a plastic tube. People with severe motion disabilities, who are also deaf and/or blind, can receive Morse code through a skin buzzer. Through the use of this code and modern technology, disabled people can obtain access to the Internet and electronic mail. Stroke sufferers have been known to communicate with Morse code by blinking their eyes. Prisoners of War have even used Morse code in this way to pass on secret messages while they were being shown on T.V. by their captors.

Keynote: Samuel first thought of using electricity to pass on information after having suffered a great tragedy in his life. He realised that, if he had been able to get in touch with his family, it may have been possible for him to be at home with his wife before she died. Sometimes, good things do result from painful and tragic events.

Think: Some people might look on the death of Jesus Christ as just a tragic event. Jesus' suffering certainly was awful. But why do Christians celebrate the death of Jesus Christ and remember that day by calling it Good Friday? This is simply because Jesus' death freed his people from the power of sin and hell. It is through his death that sinners can be saved.

 Prayer: Thank you, Lord Jesus, for your death on the cross. Show me my sin, so that I will realise I need to repent and turn to you for forgiveness.

George Washington Carver

'Goodness gracious me! What do we have here in the barn this early in the morning, but a boy, and a hungry one at that.'

George looked set to run away.

'Don't go, boy,' the kindly woman said. 'At least wait and have your breakfast with us.'

The thought of food made up George's mind.

'Thanks, Ma'am,' he answered. 'I'm mighty grateful to you.'

Over breakfast the boy told his story.

'My dad and mum were enslaved in a plantation near Diamond Grove. I never knew my dad. Some say he was killed in an accident hauling logs just after I was born.'

'Poor boy,' cooed the woman. 'You'll have another piece of warm bread.'

George took the bread and talked as he ate.

'When I was just a lil' tiny baby, raiders carried off my mother and me, as well as some others from the plantation. Mum held me fast and wouldn't let me go. But the Master came and traded me back, so I never saw my mother again.'

'If that's not the worst story I ever heard,' breathed the woman. 'To lose both your father and mother, before you could remember them, is a fearful bad start to a boy's life. What happened to you after that?'

George, who by now was warm and comfortably full, relaxed.

'The Master's name is Carver, and they call me Carver's George, for I ain't got no other name that I know of. He was good to me and treated me kind. I called them Uncle Moses and Aunt Sue.'

'Did you work for them?'

'No,' the boy admitted, 'not exactly work. Because I had neither father nor mother to keep me at it, I spent most of my time exploring the world around me. The Master didn't seem to mind. He called me the Plant Doctor because I knew so much about the plants that grow around Diamond Grove.'

'You mean you heal the sick with your plant concoctions?' asked the woman, fascinated by what she was hearing.

'No,' he laughed. 'I mean, if there's anything wrong with growing things, I usually know how to help them grow better.'

'But if your master treated you kind, why've you run away?'

'I ain't run away,' George explained. 'Years past someone gave me a spelling book, and I taught myself to read. Now I want to go to school. Master said I could leave and that the nearest school was at Neosho, eight miles away. So I packed my things in this bandana and I'm on my way to school.' There was a pause, and then his voice grew quieter. 'But when I came last night, it was too dark to find the school, so I found your barn instead. Thank you kindly, Ma'am, for the use of it.'

'I think you can call me Aunt Mariah; everyone does. And you don't have far to look for the school, for there's one especially for black children on the other side of the fence.'

George's eyes opened wide in surprise.

'And,' said Aunt Mariah, who could sum up a situation in less time than most, 'you can live here and help out at those times you're not at school.'

On his first day at school, when asked his name, the boy did a quick turnaround. Instead of saying he was Carver's George, he gave the name George Carver.

'And what age are you?' he was asked.

'I don't rightly know,' the boy replied. 'But I'm told I might be ten. I think I was born in 1864.'

'I don't know what you did at the Carvers' place,' said Aunt Mariah, after George went to live in her home. 'But while you're here,

107

you'll join us in reading the Bible, in praying and in singing to the Lord. There's no real joy to be found in anyone else but Jesus. Seeing as you can read, I've a gift for you. Here, boy.'

George took the Bible from her hand and held it as the treasure it was.

'Why, thank you, Aunt Mariah,' he said, not knowing whether to laugh or cry. 'Sorry,' he spluttered, wiping tears from his eyes, 'I just ain't that used to getting presents.'

George worked as hard as he could for kind Aunt Mariah while studying at Neosho school. Then he moved away to further his education. He was about twelve or thirteen years old, though George never did know his birthday.

Not long after leaving Aunt Mariah, the teenager saw something he was never to forget. He saw an African American prisoner being beaten to death and his body burned in a fire. George, who was as dark-skinned as that poor prisoner, ran away from the terrible scene until he could run no longer. But he knew, even then, that he would never be able to run away from the memory of it.

The next time he saw Aunt Mariah, he was a successful businessman who had sold his laundry business to pay to go to university.

'Goodness, gracious me!' the good woman said, when she heard his story. 'And you've come all the way back here to tell me. God bless you. Now, let's get to what's even more important. Are you following Jesus?'

Smiling widely, the young man assured Aunt Mariah that he certainly was. 'And I've you to thank for that,' he concluded.

'Don't thank me for anything, George Carver. Everything good comes from God.'

From Aunt Mariah's home, George went to Diamond Grove to tell Master Carver that he had gone to school and that he was now on his way to university. But when he arrived at the university, a terrible disappointment was in store. They took one look at his face and turned him away.

It was not until he was thirty years old that George became a university student, and it was at Simpson College, a Christian university in Indiana, Iowa. That was in 1894. A minister, who befriended the young man, persuaded him to put that nasty experience behind him and to become a student after all. Unlike at the previous university, he was welcomed by all the students and faculty. George felt at home amongst them no matter what their skin colour was or his.

'What a beautiful painting!' a teacher said, when he looked at George's work. 'That flower is exquisite.'

'Thank you, Sir, but it's just a poor copy of a lovely thing the Lord has made.'

'A poor copy it is not. In fact, I've never seen finer botanical painting. I can almost smell the scent from the bloom.'

'Thank you kindly, Sir. And I thank the Lord for all the good things that grow.'

'Would you let us exhibit your paintings?' George was asked, some time later.

He took a little persuading, but eventually four were sent to an exhibition in Cedar Rapids. All four were selected for the World's Columbian Exposition in Chicago.

'George,' said the College Principal, 'you could become a world-class botanical artist. You have a great gift.'

'Sir, I thank you for that, I really do, but I don't believe that's what the Lord wants me to do with the rest of my life.'

'What do you think you should be doing?' he was asked.

'I believe the good Lord wants me to become an agricultural scientist. That's not so far distant from being an artist. You know, it takes the same eye for detail.'

'Whatever you do, you'll do it well,' the Principal said, shaking George's hand.

After further training, George was appointed as Director and Consulting Chemist on the Agricultural Experiment Station of Tuskegee Institute in 1897.

'My job title is three times longer than my name,' said George, who by then called himself George Washington Carver.

The Tuskegee Institute was founded in 1881 by an African American man for his own people. The founder, Booker Washington, 'wanted his fellow blacks to be of such practical and social value that even white people would come to feel that blacks were necessary for the happiness and well-being of the community.'

If that was the aim of Tuskegee Institute, Professor George Washington Carver was just the right person to employ. After all, even as a child he was known as the Plant Doctor. Everyone, no matter what their colour, needs to know how to grow their crops.

'Can you give me advice?' he was asked over and over again. And the problem was often the same. Poor farmers worked poor soil, and both the farmers and the soil just grew poorer.

'Your soil is like a workman,' George told them. 'You need to feed it and rest it to get it to work for you. The problem is that because you're growing the same crop on the same land every year, it has used up all the nutrients in the soil, and there's nothing left to help the next crop grow.'

'That makes sense,' a farmer agreed. 'But it's always been cotton that's grown in these parts in the past.'

'It is,' George agreed, 'but it needn't always be in the future.'

Weekly lectures were arranged at which Professor Carver spoke about rotating crops instead of growing the same ones on the same fields, and about the composition of the soil, and how to decide what would grow best on the kind of soil each farmer had.

'For example,' he said, 'if you have three fields, try growing three crops, say sweet potatoes, peanuts and cotton one year. The following year grow the same crops, but put the sweet potatoes in the peanut field, and so on, and the next year use that field for cotton.'

'Bring in a soil sample,' he told them, 'and I'll analyse it for you. If you know the kind of soil you have, you can work out the best crops to grow. Not every crop likes every kind of soil.'

At first, only African American farmers brought samples of their soil. As time passed, however, their crops were so much improved that white farmers started to bring theirs too. Then a strange thing happened. George's scientific farming methods were so successful that one year the farmers had such heavy crops of sweet potatoes and peanuts, that they couldn't find buyers for them.

'What will we do?' the farmers asked. 'Everyone has enough of their own, and the shops just don't want any more.'

'Give me time, please,' George said. 'Let me talk it over with the Lord.'

Going into his laboratory at the Tuskegee Institute, George told his Heavenly Father all about the problem. Then he sat down and thought very, very hard. As he scribbled idea after idea, the pages of his notebook began to fill up. He was able to give the farmers ideas about other ways to use sweet potatoes and peanuts. By the end of his life he had found 300 different uses for peanuts and 150 new uses for sweet potatoes!

'If you can grow the crops,' he told the farmers, 'there will always be a use for them.'

'One day, I went into my laboratory and asked God to tell me what the universe was made for,' he told an audience, who thought that was a strange thing to pray. 'And God said, in my heart, that I was asking for knowledge that my little mind could not possess. So I asked God what man was made for, and he still told me that the answer was too big for me.'

Some of his audience smiled, thinking this was a joke.

'Then I asked the Lord what the peanut was made for, and God told me how to turn it into shampoo, vinegar, coffee, printer's ink, milk, butter, salads, face powder, a cure for dandruff, soap and many other things besides. You see,' he concluded, 'until now we have always thought that the great Creator gave us three kingdoms: the animal, the vegetable and the mineral. Now he has added a fourth – the synthetic. That shows us how one thing can be made into something quite different. Think of it. From peanuts we get butter – peanut butter.'

'Did I hear that your fame has travelled all the way across the Atlantic?' a farmer asked him one day in 1916. 'I read in the paper that you'd been elected a Fellow of the Royal Society of Arts of Great Britain. Congratulations!'

'Thank you, Sir,' said Professor Carver, in his usual kind and humble way. 'But I only discover what the good Lord has made.'

Seven years later, in 1923, George was recognised in his homeland, when he was awarded the Springarn Medal by the Attorney General of Kansas.

'The wonder of the medal is that it marks the contribution that the black population has made to national prosperity,' George was told by one of his fellow professors. 'And that's just what Tuskegee is all about. Would you ever work anywhere else?' he asked his friend.

George Washington Carver smiled. 'I've been offered other positions, but I've never taken them. This is where I believe God wants me to be.'

Sadly, towards the end of George's life, race relations were the cause of much sorrow in the United States of America. When he wanted to see the flowers in a park in Montgomery, George had first to check if there was a sign forbidding black people from entering. There didn't seem to be one. So that humble gentleman went in to look at the flowers God had made. Seeing him, the park keeper rushed up to where he was and shouted, 'What are you doing here? Don't you know blacks ain't allowed? Get out!'

But, in 1943, when George Washington Carver died and went to heaven, he heard the gentle voice of Jesus welcoming him home.

FACT FILE

$1,000,000: George Washington Carver declined an invitation to work for a salary of more than $100,000 a year (almost a million today) to continue his research on behalf of his countrymen. Carver did not patent or profit from most of his products. He freely gave his discoveries to mankind. Most important was the fact that he changed the American South from being a one-crop land of cotton to being multi-crop farmlands, with farmers having hundreds of profitable uses for their new crops.

Keynote: Carver did not profit from his products. 'God gave them to me,' he would say about his ideas. 'How can I sell them to someone else?' In 1940, Carver donated his life savings to the establishment of the Carver Research Foundation at Tuskegee, for continuing research in agriculture. This should remind us in a very small way of Jesus Christ who gave up the glories of heaven to come to earth to suffer and die to save sinners.

Think: What do you think makes a job or career worthwhile? Is it the salary? Is it the prestige or importance? Is it that you have to be clever before you can do that career or that you have to be physically strong? It is wrong to think of someone as more important because of their job or how much they earn. Remember that whatever you have, you have because God gave it to you. We have no right to be proud in our own abilities when they have been given to us as a gift. But we must work hard to make the most of these abilities and to use them for God's glory.

Prayer: Dear Lord, help me to appreciate others for the variety of jobs they do. Help me not to be proud in myself, but to be thankful for your gifts. Thank you, Lord, for all your people who work to bring glory to you and help to others.

C.T. Studd

'Keep your back straight, and push your feet forward in the stirrups,' said the groom, on C.T. Studd's first hunt.

C.T. did exactly as he was told.

'Now, let's see the three of you,' said Mr Studd, striding up to where his young sons were waiting to go on the hunt. This was C.T.'s first time, and he was just six years old. Two of his brothers, J.E.K. and G.B., were with him. They had names (Charles, Kynaston and George), but they were still quite young when they came to be known by their initials.

The boys looked very smart in their hunting gear, even though they had to be strapped on to their mounts because they were so small.

The Master raised the hunting horn to his lips, blew hard ... and they were off, their hounds racing along beside them.

'I think the Studd boys were born in saddles,' the groom told his wife, as he described the chase to her that evening.

'They're game for anything,' she agreed.

'That's just as well,' laughed her husband, pulling off his riding boots, 'for the Leicestershire fences are reckoned to be the stiffest in England. It's a pity that Salamander's win was before the boys were old enough to enjoy it,' the groom thought aloud.

'Maybe 1866 won't be the only year that one of Mr Studd's horses wins the Grand National,' said his wife.

The groom shook his head. 'None of the horses he owns just now has what it takes.'

His wife laughed, 'Remember what you called Salamander when the horse first came here? An exhausted scarecrow!'

Hallaton Hall, in Leicestershire, was not to be home for much longer, as they moved shortly afterwards to Wiltshire.

'You bowl,' J.E.K. said, 'and I'll bat first.'

C.T. rubbed the ball in his hands and polished it on his trouser leg before running and hitting the stumps with a better overhand ball, than most boys his age could manage.

'Getting some practice?' Mr Studd asked.

'Just trying out the new ground,' J.E.K. laughed. 'It's really good.'

On moving to Wiltshire, Mr Studd had decided to have one of his paddocks made into a cricket ground, and a very good one too.

J.E.K. said, 'Thanks for doing this, Dad.'

Mr Studd smiled. He had made a large amount of money working in India, and now it gave him great pleasure to spend it – especially on horses and his new cricket ground.

'Will we take part in the country house cricket this year?' C.T. asked his father.

'I think we should let the ground settle for a year, then organise matches and cricket weeks as from the beginning of next season.'

When C.T. was thirteen years old, his father became a Christian. As Mr Studd realised that horse racing and betting went hand in hand, he sold most of his racehorses. Three of the best ones were given to his oldest sons for hunting. Then he cleared one of the largest rooms in his very grand house and had it made into a room for Christian meetings. Life was changing for the Studd family.

One of Mr Studd's friends asked C.T., 'Are you a Christian?'

The boy tried to dodge the issue. He was home from boarding school to play cricket, not to discuss religion! But the man persisted and talked for a while about Jesus Christ. Later that day C.T. asked the Lord to be his Saviour. But he didn't tell his two brothers what had happened.

'Dear Father,' he wrote, when he was back in his room at Eton, one of the most famous schools in England. 'I am writing to tell you that I have become a Christian. I know that is what you've been praying for.'

A few days later, a letter arrived from Mr Studd to his three sons.

'My dear boys, I'm so delighted that you've all become Christians. Praise the Lord!'

As the boys passed the letter to each other, their faces broke into smiles. Each had written to tell their father of their conversion, but they had been too embarrassed to tell each other. All three had become believers on the very same day. Just two years after his conversion, Mr Studd died.

C.T., J.E.K. and G.B. all went on to play cricket for Cambridge.

'Did you hear the result of the Cambridge versus The Gentlemen of England match?' one don asked another.

'What was it? Did the Studds do us proud?'

'They did indeed. We won fair and square, with the three brothers making 249 out of a total of 504.'

'You don't get better than that,' laughed the don.

But things did get better than that.

'Congratulations on being picked for the English team,' said J.E.K. 'We'll be at the Oval[3] cheering you on.'

---

3. The Oval: The U.K. national cricket ground.

C.T. grinned. 'I'll be needing it.'

It was 1882, C.T. was 20 years old ... and England lost. A few days later, the following mock obituary appeared in a newspaper.

In Affectionate Remembrance of English Cricket, which died at the Oval on 28th August, 1882. Deeply lamented by a large circle of sorrowing Friends and Acquaintances. R.I.P.

N.B. – The body will be cremated and the ashes taken to Australia.

The following year, C.T. was in the test team that went to Australia to even the score. They won! A number of Melbourne ladies put some ashes into a small, silver urn and gave it to Ivo Bligh, the English Captain. Some believe that they were the ashes of the ball used in one of the games, or of the bails[4]. While no one knows for sure, England and Australia still play for the 'Ashes' in the 21st century.

'I'm ashamed of myself,' C.T. said. 'I've been a Christian for six years, and I've kept it to myself instead of sharing the good news of Jesus. As a result my faith has grown cold.'

But it was not to remain like that. Two old ladies were faithful in prayer for C.T. Studd, and God answered their prayers. When G.B.

---

4. Bails: The small wooden bars placed on top of cricket stumps.

was so ill that he was thought to be dying, God brought C.T. back to his senses.

'Will you come and hear Mr Moody?' he asked his friends a short while later.

It was through the American preacher, D.L. Moody, that C.T.'s father had become a Christian. Several young men went with C.T., and a number were converted.

'When Mr Moody left for England,' he said later, 'I wanted to know what my life's work for the Lord Jesus Christ was to be. I wanted only to serve him, and I prayed for God to show me.'

God did show C.T. Studd what he wanted him to do. In fact, he showed seven young men at Cambridge that he wanted them to serve him in China with the China Inland Mission. They became known as the Cambridge Seven. In February 1885, the Cambridge Seven sailed for China.

'We have the length of our voyage to learn to be Chinese,' one of them said, as they sailed.

'Having our hair in a pigtail will seem strange at first, I'm sure. And so will wearing Chinese clothes.'

China Inland Missionaries have to live as much like the Chinese people as they possibly can.'

'Shanghai, 1st April, 1885,' C.T. wrote at the top of his mother's first letter from

China. After telling her about a meeting the previous evening, he went on, 'I have been laughing all day at our unusual appearance. We put on the clothes this morning, then were duly shaved and pigtailed. The other three had their moustaches off. It all took some getting used to.'

The following three months were spent travelling 1,800 miles by the Yantse and Han Rivers to where they were to work. And they worked very hard indeed, serving the Chinese people and telling them about the Lord.'

'Now that I'm twenty-five,' said C.T. in December 1887, 'I'm due to inherit my share of my father's money. And what a wonderful time I'm going to have giving it away.'

C.T. believed that he should not keep his fortune for himself, and that the Lord would provide for his needs. His father had left him £29,000 – an absolutely huge sum of money at that time. 'I'll give £5,000 to Mr Moody, £5,000 to Mr Müller for his orphan and mission work, £5,000 to help the poor in London, and £5,000 for the work of the Salvation Army in India. I owe that money to India. That's where Father made his wealth.'

'What will we do with the money that's left?' he asked his wife-to-be.

Priscilla smiled. 'Charlie,' she said. 'What did the Lord tell the rich young man to do?'

'Sell all he had,' C.T. replied.

'Well then, we'll give it all away, then start clear with the Lord at our wedding.'

'Life is not easy,' Priscilla admitted in a letter home. 'For the past five years we've not gone out the door without being called foreign devils, and sometimes we are spat on by the people for whom we care so much.'

Nor was it easy for them as a family. They had five children when they were in China, four girls and a boy. Their little son died when he was just one day old. Not only that, but C.T., who suffered from asthma, seemed to be getting worse as time went on.

'We believe the Lord is calling us back to England,' C.T. and Priscilla told the China Inland Mission in 1894.

'Our work on the way out was to learn to be Chinese,' Priscilla said, when the matter had been decided. 'On the way home our work will be to try to teach the children some English. They don't know a word of the language.'

But that was just the beginning of the Studd girls learning a new language for, six years later, the Lord called their parents to be missionaries in India.

'My father wished that one of his children would take the good news about the Lord Jesus back to India, where he worked when he was young,' C.T. explained to his daughters. 'It was his way of thanking the Indian people.'

'Are we going to stay in this part of India for ever?' his youngest daughter asked. 'I like it here at Tricot.'

But six months later they were on the move. C.T.'s asthma was especially bad, and it was thought the climate of Ootacamund in South India would suit him better. For the next five years he was minister of the Union Church in Ootacamund, and the Studds saw many people become Christians.

'How happy father would have been,' C.T. thought, as he watched the church fill.

Just a short time later C.T. and his wife were the happiest parents of all. All four of their daughters became Christians and were baptised on the very same day.

'This is goodbye to India,' Priscilla thought, as the coast of the land she had grown to love faded into the far distance. 'I wonder if it's also goodbye to overseas missionary service.'

For a few years it seemed that was the case, though C.T. Studd travelled far and wide speaking at meetings. Many people went to hear him, who knew him as a famous cricketer rather than a Christian. And some who went to hear about the Ashes came away having put their faith in the Lord Jesus Christ. As they listened to C.T. speaking about Jesus, people realised that his enthusiastic spirit, which had made him throw everything into his cricket, now made him throw absolutely everything into serving the Lord.

'Cannibals want missionaries,' C.T. read in a Liverpool shop window in 1908.

Although he was severely asthmatic, the Lord used that sign to call C.T. to work in Africa. It took time, a great deal of planning, and hours and hours of prayer.

'It will mean you remaining in England while I'm there,' C.T. reminded Priscilla.

'I know,' she replied quietly. 'But if that's God's will, he'll give us his strength.'

On 15th December, 1910, C.T. sailed without Priscilla for Khartoum. After months of trekking through malaria and sleeping sickness country, C.T. knew where his heart lay.

'In the Congo, between the Nile and Lake Chad, there are so many people who have never heard of Christ. I believe that God wants me to spend the rest of my life here, telling them about his Son Jesus.'

Although it was hard for Priscilla, she also wanted the Lord's will more than she wanted her own. And it was a comfort to her that when C.T. came home to England for a time, he took one of their daughters back with him to be a missionary and to marry a missionary.

'The work will go on after we've gone home to heaven,' she thought, as she prayed day after day for the land of Congo.

After twelve years of sacrificing time together, Priscilla spent two weeks with her husband at Ibambi, where he worked in the Congo.

'Look how they love one another,' people said, when they saw the couple together. 'They must love us very much indeed for Bwana Mukubwa[5] to stay here when his wife is thousands of miles away.'

That was the last time C.T. and Priscilla saw each other on earth. She died in 1929.

'Bwana Mukubwa has a busy day,' one of his Congolese friends said on Sunday 12th, July 1931. 'Today's meeting will last many hours.'

The next day C.T. did not feel well, and the following Thursday he died and saw his wonderful Lord Jesus face-to-face.

5. Big Boss

FACT FILE
Cricket: Cricket's most likely birth-place is the Weald, an area of dense woodlands and clearings in South East England that lies across Kent and Sussex. The game was probably devised by children of the Weald's farming and metalworking communities. The game's origin seems to have been in Norman or Saxon times (i.e., before 1066). The original implements may have been a matted lump of sheep's wool as the ball, a crook or other farm tool as the bat, and a wicket gate or tree stump as the wicket.

Keynote: When C.T. Studd realised his funds were low one day, he praised God because he realised that God trusted him. God knew that C.T. would trust him to provide. Perhaps you feel unsure about the future. Maybe you have worries and doubts. It is good to remember the lives of people like C.T. Studd. They are examples to us of how we should trust in God for all our needs – today and in the future.

Think: C.T. Studd wanted to know what his life's work for the Lord Jesus Christ was to be. He wanted to serve him. He prayed for God to show him what he should do. If you are wondering what the future holds for you, first make sure that your eternal future is secure. Trust in the Lord Jesus to save you from your sin. Then pray to God as C.T. did. Your life should be placed in his hand for today, tomorrow and eternity. He will show you what he wants you to do.

Prayer: Lord Jesus, thank you that I can trust you always. Help me to trust in you for the future. I do not know what will happen, but help me to follow you. Whatever I do – if I stay at home or travel to the other end of the world – may I do it for your glory. May I obey you in every area of my life.

John Bunyan

John watched his father at work and grinned. He liked to hear the clink, clink of his dad's metal tools against the pots and pans he was mending, for then he knew where his father was. When the clink, clink turned into a silence, John usually stopped whatever mischief he was up to and pretended to be the good son that John and Margaret Bunyan hoped he would be. But today his father, a tinker to trade, was busy, and the noise of his mending went on for hours. Today John was free!

'Coo, coo' said John, from behind a bush.

His friends, who were passing by, recognised the signal and ducked behind the bush.

'You don't sound anything like a pigeon,' said one of the boys.

John didn't reply; he just aimed a kick in the right direction.

'Old Mother Taylor's apples are ready,' John told his friends. 'It's time for a feast.'

133

They knew that Mother Taylor was poor and hoped to sell apples to buy things she needed. That might have stopped some of the boys from stealing, but it didn't stop ten-year-old John Bunyan. Because he was the ringleader, the others did what he said. However, that year, 1638, the English summer had been so sunny that apples reddened on the outside before sweetening on the inside, and the boys suffered very sore stomachs.

'This place is a dump,' announced John, looking round the village of Elstow. 'As soon as I'm old enough, I'm packing up my things and leaving here for good.'

'Going all the way to Bedford?' laughed an older boy. 'You'll make it there and back in time for your dinner.'

'Are you going away to London to make your fortune there?' teased another boy, who was much older and bigger than John. He wouldn't have teased him if they'd been the same size, for John could put up a good fight when he chose to.

'You could always be a lawyer,' laughed another. 'After all, you've been at school.'

A vision of his school days came into John's mind, but he knew that he'd forgotten nearly everything he learned there. John Bunyan stuck out his tongue at his tormentors and ran off to find someone smaller than them to annoy.

'I'm going to tell Dad about you,' said John's younger sister Margaret. 'Everyone is talking about you. Old Mother Taylor told me you swore at her.'

'Don't you dare,' hissed the boy. 'Or I'll tell Dad things about you.'

'What things?' Margaret demanded.

'Things I'll make up,' laughed the boy. 'And they'll be worth a sore smacking!'

Margaret was right about John having a bad reputation. He was well known for his swearing and lying. In fact, mothers in Elstow told their young sons not to go near John Bunyan. He was a bad influence.

What people did not see was that, deep inside himself, John was a seriously disturbed boy. Dreams of hell upset him badly. He pictured demons and evil spirits bound up with chains for judgment, and he could just see himself among them. The sight of anyone reading the Bible or praying hit at John's heart so hard, that he fought against it by doing something he knew to be wrong. Strangely, if he saw a person he knew to be a Christian doing something unkind, or saying something untrue, John was really upset. Poor boy, he really was in a mess.

'What's that moving in the grass?' one of his friends asked, as they walked near the village.

'It's an adder,' said John, picking up a stick to hit the snake.

His blow just stunned the creature. Seeing that, the young fool picked it up to do some showing-off.

'I'll teach this thing to be poisonous,' he said. And, holding the snake in one hand, he prised its mouth open and pulled out its fang with the other.

'You wouldn't catch me doing that,' said one of his friends.

'Too right,' added another.

In 1644, influenza swept through Bedfordshire. Hundreds of people were sick, and death struck in many homes. John Bunyan's was one of them. First his mother died, then just a month later, his young sister died too. John was nearly sixteen years old but, when his mother and sister died in such quick succession, he must have felt for a while like a little lost boy.

'I told you I was going to leave Elstow,' John told his friends, 'and I'm going now.'

This was just weeks after the family's terrible sadness.

'I'm going to join Cromwell's Parliamentary Army.'

The English Civil War was raging at that time, and John took sides with Cromwell against the King. Although Oliver Cromwell was a Christian, and each of his soldiers was given a Soldier's Catechism[6], young John Bunyan wasn't in the least interested.

'You're a very lucky young man,' his sergeant said one day.

'Don't I know it,' agreed John. 'That might have been me.'

'What happened?' asked a soldier, who was just passing by.

John told his story.

'I was meant to be going with some others to help in a siege. Just as we were preparing to leave, someone came and asked if he could change places with me. That was fine with me, so off he went. But ...' he paused for effect ... 'the poor man was shot in the head by a musket ball and died. That was a lucky escape.'

'For you,' said the soldier, 'but not for him.'

For three years, John fought with Cromwell's men and then he returned to Elstow, where he married. His first child, a daughter named Mary, was blind. John's wife had come from a Christian home and she had brought two Christian books with her when she was married. Although John's reading was poor, he ploughed his way through parts of them from time to time. His wife also sometimes persuaded him to attend church.

6. A catechism is a book of Bible questions and answers.

After the services, however, he forgot it was Sunday and went off to play sports with his friends. Once, his minister preached on the commandment to keep Sunday special. John was very impressed ... right until after he'd had his lunch ... then he headed off to his sports again. During the game, it was as though God spoke directly to John. He dropped his bat and felt ashamed of himself. But, just as suddenly, he decided that he was so bad that God couldn't save him. Picking his bat up again, he played furiously till the end of the game.

From then on, John Bunyan's life was a total confusion. One day, he wanted to learn about the Lord, the next he decided God couldn't possibly be interested in him. He tried for a time to live a good life; he even studied the Bible and his wife's Christian books. But he knew he wasn't a believer, and he was still scared of judgement.

'You coming to bell-ringing tonight?' John was asked, as he walked home from work one day.

Bell-ringing was one of his hobbies.

'I'll be there,' he said. 'Try and stop me.'

But that night he felt uncomfortable. What if one of the bells fell down on him? He knew he wouldn't go to heaven if he died.

'I'll stand here and ring the bell,' he said, pulling himself back against the wall.

The other bell-ringers looked at him with amused expressions.

As he walked home, it occurred to him that next time he went bell-ringing the steeple might fall down on top of him.

'That's it,' he decided. 'No more bell-ringing for me.'

Not long afterwards John, who was by now a tinker like his father, went off to Bedford to work one day.

'Look at them,' he thought. 'They've nothing better to do than gossip.'

As he drew nearer the little group of women, he realised they were talking about their faith. And they seemed to be saying that the Lord Jesus was their Saviour and Friend. John, who never hesitated to burst into other people's conversations, listened to the poor, ragged women and wondered about their joy and grace. From then on, he looked for excuses to work in Bedford just in order to hear what these women were saying.

'I think that young man is seriously looking for God,' one of the women decided, and the others agreed.

'You should meet our minister, John Gifford,' they told him, when he next came along their road. 'He'll help you find Jesus.'

What a surprise it was to John to discover that Mr Gifford had once been as wicked as himself, having gambled, drank and spoken against the Lord for years before becoming a Christian. The two men became firm friends, and twenty-five-year-old John Bunyan, tinker and troublemaker, became a believer in the Lord Jesus Christ. He was the talk of Bedford and Elstow yet again, but this time for the very best of reasons.

In 1655, John Gifford died, having lived long enough to hear his friend preach the gospel. John Bunyan became well known for his preaching. Because he had been so well known in the area before – for bad reasons – people went to hear him and were amazed at the change in the man. And how different life was in his home, than what it used to be. His wife, who by then had three children, must have praised the Lord for the change in her husband. Three years later, however, Mrs Bunyan died, just after their fourth child was born. It was a really hard time for John, as he struggled to work as well as look after his four children. Over a year later, he married again, and his new wife – Elizabeth – was a fine Christian woman.

After Cromwell's death, Charles II reigned as King of England.

'I promise that people will have liberty of conscience to worship as they see fit,' he said, and some people believed him.

Before long those whose consciences made them worship differently from the King found soldiers at their doors, and discovered what it was like inside prison cells.

'Will you use the King's Book of Common Prayer?' Elizabeth asked her husband.

'No,' he replied. 'I'll only use God's book, the Bible.'

The couple knew what that meant and were not surprised when trouble brewed.

It was November 1660, and John Bunyan was preaching at Lower Samsell, about twelve miles from their home in Bedford. When John arrived, he discovered that a warrant had been issued for his arrest.

'I think we should cancel the service,' someone said.

'No, no,' said the preacher. 'I won't have the service cancelled just because of that.'

The service went ahead but was interrupted by a constable striding into the church and thrusting the warrant into John's hand. The following morning John found himself a prisoner in Bedford Jail. It was two months before he was called to answer to his charge. John finished his reply by saying, 'If I am out of prison today, I will preach the gospel again tomorrow – by the help of God.' Not surprisingly, Preacher Bunyan spent a very long time in prison.

While he was a prisoner, John worked on two things. He made leather laces to support his wife and children, and he began writing books. Of course, he was very well known, especially because he was in prison so long.

'If only the King thought about it, he'd set me free,' John said to his wife when she visited him. 'The longer he keeps me in prison, the better my books sell.'

Elizabeth, who supported her husband in all he did, smiled at the joke of it.

'It's quite true,' she said. 'The King keeps you here to stop you preaching the gospel, and because you're here, you have time to write about the gospel.'

'Things seem more relaxed in the country now,' John said to a fellow prisoner, after twelve years spent mostly in prison.

'Do you think they'll set us free then?'

And that's just what happened. John Bunyan was released in 1672 and was free to preach for four years before being imprisoned again. It was in 1678 that his most famous book was published. *The Pilgrim's Progress* sold over 100,000 copies in its first ten years. It has never been out of print in all the years since then. It's second only to the Bible in the number of copies that have been sold. *The Pilgrim's Progress* is the story of a man called Christian who sets out to find his way to heaven. In many respects it's the story of

142

John Bunyan's life, as it describes the people who helped him and those who tried to hold him back. The names John chose for the characters and places in the book describe them well. There is the Giant Despair and Doubting Castle, among many others. *The Pilgrim's Progress* has since been translated into many different languages, rewritten for children, illustrated, published in cartoon form and made into films. In fact, there is a version of *The Pilgrim's Progress* for nearly every age of reader. John Bunyan could never have imagined that when he wrote it over 400 years ago!

FACT FILE
The Pilgrim's Progress
This book is an allegorical novel and is regarded as a great classic of literature. An allegorical story is a fictional story with a deeper and hidden meaning. *The Pilgrim's Progress* is about a man on a journey – but the deeper meaning is about how someone can get to heaven by believing in Jesus Christ. Some famous people who have read and enjoyed *The Pilgrim's Progress* include: The artist Vincent van Gogh; The preacher Charles Spurgeon; the poet Samuel Taylor Coleridge and the novelist John Buchan.

Key note: John Bunyan is described as a tinker and a troublemaker... but he was brought from being a trouble maker to being a preacher of God's Word. Jesus tells us in his Word that he did not come to save the righteous, but to bring sinners to repentance. Jesus also tells us that it is not the healthy who need a doctor, but the sick. We just have to realise that all have sinned and have fallen short of God's perfect standard. There is no one who is good – no, not one.

Think: John Bunyan said, 'If I am out of prison today, I will preach the gospel again tomorrow.' Bunyan spent a long time in prison. The apostle Peter was also imprisoned for preaching about Jesus Christ. Peter was also told not to preach but he refused. The Pharisees and religious authorities could not stop these disciples of Jesus preaching about the One they loved. Where do you find it hardest to stand up for Jesus? If you were in prison for your faith, how would the Bible help you to cope? Think about Christians who suffer for their faith in countries such as Afghanistan, Iraq, Myanmar and China. Pray for them and ask God to give you the courage and faith to stand up for Jesus Christ and his Word.

Prayer: Dear Lord, thank you for the example you give us. You suffered for us. Your love was so great that you were willing to die for us. Give us a love for you and your Word so that we can stand strong too. Help us to follow your example and forgive those who persecute us.

Quiz

How much can you remember
about the ten boys who used
their talents? Try answering
these questions to find out.

Wilfred Grenfell

1. What was the name of the American preacher that Wilfred went to listen to?

2. What was Wilfred once trapped on with his dogs?

3. What two areas did Wilfred work in - both of these are now part of the nation of Canada?

C.S. Lewis

4. Can you name the series of chronicles that C.S. Lewis wrote - and which became worldwide best sellers?

5. What was the name of the imaginary world that C.S. Lewis invented as a young boy?

6. What was C.S. Lewis travelling in when he believed in Jesus Christ for the first time?

James Clerk Maxwell

7. What scientist did James Clerk Maxwell owe a lot to?

8. Who should we look to through nature?

9. What area of Scotland did James grow up in?

Ghillean Prance

10. What castle could Ghillean and his mother see from the boat?

11. What was Ghillean's favourite book when he was a boy?

12. Where did Ghillean go on plant hunting expeditions?

Paul Brand

13. What disease infected 500,000 people in 2005?

14. What disease killed Paul's father?

15. What country did Paul go to in 1943?

Johann Sebastian Bach

16. What two instruments was Johann playing when he was seven years old?

17. Who used to be a pupil at Johann's Latin Grammar School?

18. What words did Johann use to sign all his work?

Samuel Morse

19. Why did Samuel's father choose Yale College for his son?

20. What did Samuel want to be before he became a scientist?

21. What was the first coded message that Samuel Morse sent from the Capitol building in Washington to Baltimore?

George Washington Carver

22. George's parents were slaves on a plantation. What was the name of that plantation?

23. What did Aunt Mariah give George as a present?

24. How many different uses did George discover for peanuts?

C.T. Studd

25. What sport did C.T. play for England?

26. Which other members of C.T.'s family became Christians on the same day as he did?

27. Why did C.T. believe that he should give away his fortune?

John Bunyan

28. What is the name of the jail where John Bunyan was kept in prison?

29. What two things did John Bunyan work at during his stay in prison?

30. Who was John Bunyan's military commander during the civil war?

How well did you do?

Turn over to find out...

Quiz Answers

1. D. L. Moody.
2. A sheet of ice.
3. Newfoundland and Labrador.
4. *The Chronicles of Narnia*.
5. Boxen.
6. The sidecar of a motorcycle.
7. Michael Farraday.
8. God.
9. Kirkcudbrightshire.
10. Dunvegan Castle.
11. Gilbert White's *Natural History of Selborne*.
12. The Amazon Rainforest in Brazil.
13. Leprosy.
14. Blackwater fever.
15. India.
16. Violin and Harpsichord.
17. Martin Luther.
18. 'To the glory of God.'
19. They based their education on the Bible.
20. An artist.
21. 'What hath God wrought,' or 'What a wonderful thing God has done.'
22. Diamond Grove.
23. A Bible.
24. 300.
25. Cricket.
26. His two brothers.
27. He believed that God would provide for his needs.
28. Bedford Jail.
29. Making leather laces and writing books.
30. Oliver Cromwell.

Author Information:
Irene Howat

Irene Howat is an award-winning author who lives in Scotland. She has published many biographical books for all ages and is particularly well-known for her biographical material. She has written many books about the lives of different Christians from around the world. She has also written a biographical work about her own life entitled: *Pain My Companion*. Irene has many other interests including painting, dog walking and editing her Church's young people's magazine called *The Instructor*.

Start collecting this series now!

Ten Boys who used their Talents:
ISBN 978-1-84550-146-4
Paul Brand, Ghillean Prance, C.S.Lewis,
C.T. Studd, Wilfred Grenfell, J.S. Bach,
James Clerk Maxwell, Samuel Morse,
George Washington Carver, John Bunyan.

Ten Girls who used their Talents:
ISBN 978-1-84550-147-1
Helen Roseveare, Maureen McKenna,
Anne Lawson, Harriet Beecher Stowe,
Sarah Edwards, Selina Countess of Huntingdon,
Mildred Cable, Katie Ann MacKinnon,
Patricia St. John, Mary Verghese.

Ten Boys who Changed the World:
ISBN 978-1-85792-579-1
David Livingstone, Billy Graham, Brother Andrew,
John Newton, William Carey, George Müller,
Nicky Cruz, Eric Liddell, Luis Palau,
Adoniram Judson.

Ten Girls who Changed the World:
ISBN 978-1-85792-649-1
Corrie Ten Boom, Mary Slessor,
Joni Eareckson Tada, Isobel Kuhn,
Amy Carmichael, Elizabeth Fry, Evelyn Brand,
Gladys Aylward, Catherine Booth, Jackie Pullinger.

Ten Boys who Made a Difference:
ISBN 978-1-85792-775-7
Augustine of Hippo, Jan Hus, Martin Luther,
Ulrich Zwingli, William Tyndale, Hugh Latimer,
John Calvin, John Knox, Lord Shaftesbury,
Thomas Chalmers.

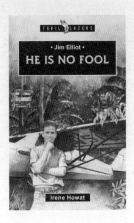

Jim Elliot: He is no Fool
Irene Howat

ISBN: 978-1-5271-0465-5

Jim Elliot and four other young men were in the middle of doing God's work when they were brutally killed, by the very people they had come to rescue. However, Jim had realised that there was nothing more important than Jesus and that was why he was there. These young men knew the dangers but still went ahead with their plans to reach out to the Auca Indians.

After their deaths the work carried on thanks to Jim's wife, Elizabeth Elliot and Nate Saint's sister, Ruth Saint. Many Auca Indians came to know Jesus Christ for themselves and the church is still growing in that area of Ecuador today.

Elisabeth Elliot: Do the Next Thing
Selah Helms

ISBN: 978-1-5271-0161-6

Although she is best known for her time on the mission field in Ecuador, Elisabeth Elliot went on to become a vibrant role model for valiant, godly women all over the world. Follow her journey from the jungles of the Amazon, where she faced the tragic death of her first husband, to the lecture halls and radio shows of the culture wars, where she stood as a strong defender of God's Word.

CHRISTIAN FOCUS PUBLICATIONS

Christian Focus | Christian Heritage | CF4K | Mentor

Christian Focus Publications publishes books for adults and children under its four main imprints: Christian Focus, CF4K, Mentor and Christian Heritage. Our books reflect our conviction that God's Word is reliable and Jesus is the way to know him, and live for ever with him.

Our children's publication list includes a Sunday School curriculum that covers pre-school to early teens, and puzzle and activity books. We also publish personal and family devotional titles, biographies and inspirational stories that children will love.

If you are looking for quality Bible teaching for children then we have an excellent range of Bible stories and age-specific theological books.

From pre-school board books to teenage apologetics, we have it covered!

Find us at our web page:
www.christianfocus.com

CF4·K
Because you're never
too young to know Jesus